A.S. Malik

The
Uncertain Search for
Environmental Quality

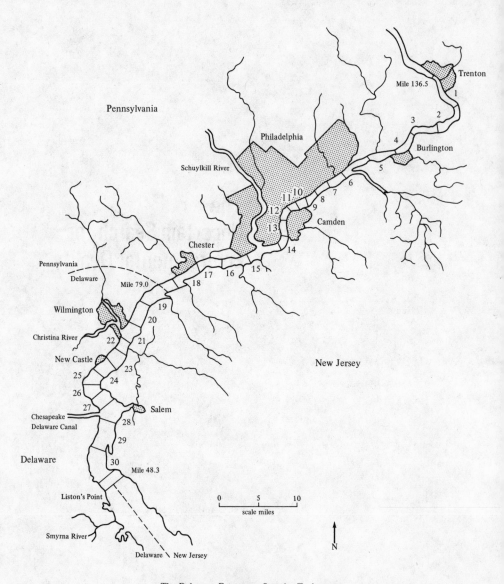

Pennsylvania

Trenton
Mile 136.5
1
2
3
4
Burlington
5
Philadelphia
Schuylkill River
6
7
8
9
10
11
12
13
14
Camden
Chester
Pennsylvania
Delaware
Mile 79.0
15
16
17
18
19
20
Wilmington
Christina River
22
21
New Castle
23
25
24
26
27
Salem
Chesapeake
Delaware Canal
28
29
Delaware
30
Mile 48.3
Liston's Point
Smyrna River
Delaware \ New Jersey

New Jersey

0   5   10
scale miles

N

The Delaware Estuary as Seen by Technocrats
(From *Delaware Estuary Comprehensive Study*)

The Uncertain Search for Environmental Quality

BRUCE A. ACKERMAN
and
SUSAN ROSE-ACKERMAN
JAMES W. SAWYER, JR.
DALE W. HENDERSON

THE FREE PRESS
A Division of Macmillan Publishing Co., Inc.
NEW YORK

Collier Macmillan Publishers
LONDON

Copyright © 1974 by The Free Press
A Division of Macmillan Publishing Co., Inc.

The Free Press
A Division of Macmillan Publishing Co., Inc.
866 Third Avenue, New York, N.Y. 10022

Collier-Macmillan Canada Ltd.

Library of Congress Catalog Card Number: 73-21305

Printed in the United States of America

printing number
1 2 3 4 5 6 7 8 9 10

Library of Congress Cataloging in Publication Data

Ackerman, Bruce A
    The uncertain search for environmental quality.

    Bibliography: p.
    1. Water--Pollution--Economic aspects--Delaware
River. 2. Environmental policy--Middle Atlantic
States. I. Title.
HC107.A123P552   333.9'162'09749   73-21305
ISBN 0-02-900200-1

To Our Parents

Biographical Notes

Bruce A. Ackerman (LL.B., Yale Law School) is Professor of Law at the Yale Law School. He was formerly Professor of Law and Public Policy Analysis at the University of Pennsylvania, and has been law clerk to Justice John Marshall Harlan, U.S. Supreme Court, and to Judge Henry J. Friendly, U.S. Court of Appeals.

Susan Rose-Ackerman (Ph.D., Yale University) is Lecturer at the Institution for Social and Policy Studies at Yale University. She was previously Assistant Professor of Public Policy and Economics at the University of Pennsylvania.

James W. Sawyer (Ph.D., University of Pennsylvania) is Research Associate, Resources for the Future, Washington, D.C. He was formerly a research engineer with E.I. duPont de Nemours & Company.

Dale W. Henderson (M. Phil., Yale University) is Chief, Trade and Financial Studies Section, Board of Governors of the Federal Reserve System. He has also been Lecturer in Economics at the University of Pennsylvania.

Contents

Preface

This book is the product of a three-and-a-half-year effort centered at the University of Pennsylvania, in which a large number of people played important roles. Acting with the assistance of a generous grant from the Council on Law-Related Studies, a group of faculty and graduate students under the direction of Bruce Ackerman made an intensive effort during the summer of 1970 to scrutinize the diverse aspects of the decision-making process which led to the adoption of a massive program to clean up the Delaware River. Officials at all levels of government were interviewed at often-lengthy sessions; officials of more than 80 of the Delaware's polluters were also engaged in face-to-face discussions, typically more than an hour long; the official scientific and economic analyses that formed the basis for decision making were considered with care. This initial effort could not have been undertaken by the authors without the enthusiastic assistance of a task force of dedicated law and graduate students: John Endicott, James Halpern, James Keeney, Barry Klickstein, Julian LeGrand, Ellsworth McMeen, Jeffrey O'Connell, and Fred Smith.

The three years following this broadly based data-collection effort have been spent thinking about and organizing the original material, and engaging in additional research as gaps in our 1970 data appeared to view. Much of this work took the form of three separate but related collaborative enterprises between Bruce Ackerman and the book's three coauthors. Thus Chapters 3, 4, and 5 are the joint product of B.A. and J.S.; Chapters 6, 15, 16, 17, and 18, the joint product of B.A. and S.R.A.; Chapters 7 and 8, the joint product of B.A. and D.H.

While the other chapters are principally the work of B.A., these, too, would have been impossible to write without the extraordinarily helpful assistance of two students: Bruce Ludwig (Chapters 12 and 13) and James Keeney (Chapter 19). Also, when the book was being put into final form in the summer of 1973, it profited greatly from the criticism and further research undertaken by Kent Bernard and James Morris. We are also grateful for the assistance provided by the editors of the *University of Pennsylvania Law Review,* in which earlier versions of Chapters 3 through

9 appeared, and for the critical commentary provided by many of our colleagues in the academic community, particularly William Nelson, Clifford Russell and Robert Thomann.

Our debt to the Council on Law-Related Studies extends beyond its generous initial grant to include the moral support provided by the Council's principal officers, David Cavers and Edward Selig. Following the summer 1970 effort, additional research funds were provided not only by the Council but also by Dean Bernard Wolfman of the Law School and Director Julius Margolis of the Fels Center of Government, both at the University of Pennsylvania, and Dean Abraham Goldstein of the Yale Law School. Without the time and assistance these grants made possible, we could not have completed this effort to study the mixed promise of the modern revolution in the art of government.

Introduction: Of Science, Politics, and Law

THREE TASKS FOR PUBLIC POLICY ANALYSIS

Since the beginning of human society, the claims of men possessing esoteric knowledge have been weighty in human affairs. The shaman resolving blood feuds on the basis of ritual incantations, the Roman consulting the auguries before battle, the medieval churchman excommunicating erring laymen in a tongue inaccessible to the ordinary man, all have their counterparts in a contemporary society which, though secular, still recognizes that some have gained insights denied the common run of men.

The esoteric language today is mathematics; the special means of inspiration, the computer; the forbidding path of truth, science. The existence of esoteric knowledge of social importance poses obvious difficulties in a society committed in principle both to the Enlightenment and to Democracy. Democratic control—of whatever sort—presupposes general intelligibility. Yet it is unlikely that the mathematical language of scientific enlightenment will be accessible even to the lawyer and businessman generalists who control the affairs of the American state, let alone to the

1

public at large. To make matters worse, our modern day shamans, caught up in specialization, do not often feel the need to discuss the general implications of their particular sciences even in their academic journals.

This split between science and democratic decision making has, of course, been perceived and condemned by many. It becomes even more troublesome when the social sciences (particularly economics) take on an exceedingly mathematical garb which purports to provide a conceptual framework that not only describes facts but prescribes substantive policy outcomes. Yet mere expressions of alarm will do nothing to bridge the gap. The conflict between latter-day Enlightenment and Democracy can, however, be ameliorated in part (but only in part) by three parallel endeavors. First, in each important area in which science permeates policy making, an effort must be made (by whoever is capable of the task) not merely to translate basic scientific concepts into the English language but also to define both the limits and the strengths of the scientific perspective. Second, serious attention must be given to the assessment of alternative institutional mechanisms which promise to facilitate the integration of scientific insight and democratic policy making. Third, the legal system must be scrutinized to determine the extent to which traditional modes of legal sanction and control can effectively implement sophisticated policies defined with the aid of modern science.

Despite the importance of these three tasks, only the most preliminary work has been attempted;[1] nothing like a general theory on either the normative or empirical level has yet emerged which satisfactorily enlightens the complex interrelationships between technocratic intelligence, political decision making, and legal enforcement in modern government. This book is an effort to prepare the way for fruitful theorizing by carefully exploring an actual decision-making process which reveals in a paradigmatic fashion

To save space, all references have been cited in abbreviated form. For a full description, see the Bibliography.

1. A large share of the valuable work available seems to have been attempted by economists (see Cooley, 1963; Hirshleifer et al., 1960; Kneese and Bower, 1968; Nelkin, 1971; Nelkin, 1972; Peck and Scherer, 1962; Smolensky and Gomery, 1973; and sources cited in Ch. 6, nn. 1, 4). As a consequence, the analysis attempts substantive critiques of particular policy areas but does little to illuminate the last two concerns expressed in the text.

Interesting political science work in this field includes Churchman, 1967; Kurth, 1971; Price, 1954; Price, 1965; Schultze, 1968. Some political scientists have taken a more general approach to the entire problem of interdisciplinary analysis and decision making. Maass, 1966 and Wildavsky, 1966 provide solid analyses of the problem of "unquantifiable" goals as well as the political costs and benefits which tend to be excluded from consideration by the presuppositions of an economist's cost–benefit structure. In this context see also Wildavsky, 1962. For an attempt at a multidisciplinary analysis, see Tribe, *Channeling Technology,* 1973.

the nature of both the challenge and the opportunity that technocratic intelligence offers to a contemporary democracy.

AN INTRODUCTION TO THE DRBC: THE FOUR PHASES OF POLICY MAKING

We shall be scrutinizing the way in which a model regional agency, hailed by many as representing one of the few triumphs of American environmental policy,[2] has attempted to define, shape, and enforce a comprehensive response to a typical policy problem generated by contemporary urban industrialism. When the members of the Delaware River Basin Commission (DRBC) met at Dover, Delaware, on March 2, 1967 to adopt a massive pollution control program for the river, the event had significance not only for environmentalists but for every student of American institutions. The decision to take regional action seemed to vindicate the American faith in the power of men to create both new modes of thought and novel organizational forms that promise to control the problems of a rapidly changing industrialized society. Indeed, at every critical stage along the way, the Commission's decision-making processes seemed to embody the very essence of enlightened American opinion concerning the proper operation of government.

First, in framing environmental policy for the river, the Commission was not obliged to content itself with an impressionistic factual account of the "pollution problem" it confronted. Instead, it could take advantage of the most sophisticated fact-finding effort ever yet attempted in the exploration of any environmental issue. After four years of systematic scientific study, an expert staff had constructed a mathematical model that simulated the impact of pollutants discharged by the industries and cities bordering the river. Thus, the Commission could understand both the nature of conditions on the river at present and the way the environmental situation would change in the future if one or another control program were instituted.

Second, the Commission not only availed itself of a sophisticated fact-finding process but also took advantage of an economic analysis of the costs and benefits associated with each of a wide range of plausible strategies for water quality improvement. As a consequence, decision makers

2. Kneese and Bower, 1968; Grad, 1963. For a sensitive introduction to the problem of constituency definition with an emphasis on the particular difficulties involved in organizing river basin pollution control authorities, see Roberts, 1971, pp. 83–113, which also contains a comprehensive review of previous work in the area.

were capable of a carefully modulated response to the facts of environmental degradation. They did not need to choose between a crash program to clean up the Delaware on the one hand and a policy of benign neglect on the other. Instead, the cost–benefit analyses permitted them to consider the wisdom of a number of intermediate strategies in the light of the harsh fact that, even in the richest society in the world, resources are far from unlimited.

Third, the Commission structure itself represented an innovative attempt to construct a regional government that proceeded from the perception that the coherent development of the Delaware River's resources would be impossible if left to the uncoordinated decisions of each of the four riparian states—New York, Pennsylvania, New Jersey, and Delaware—as well as a large number of powerful federal agencies, especially the Army Corps of Engineers. To accommodate both state and federal interests, the Delaware River Basin Compact, approved in 1961,[3] broke new ground by providing that the federal government, as well as each riparian state, would have a voting member on the Commission.[4] Moreover, unlike so many earlier interstate compacts, the signatory governments were not niggardly in granting broad—though not unlimited—powers to the Commission, which seemed to give the agency a realistic opportunity to effectuate a comprehensive plan that concerned itself with water quality as well as water supply, hydroelectric power, recreational areas, wildlife conservation, and flood protection.[5] Equally important, the voting members of the Commission were neither obscure bureaucrats nor retired politicians in search of a sinecure. On matters of the first importance, such as the ones considered here, the governors of the four states and the Secretary of the Interior cast their ballots personally after considering the arguments tendered to them by their staff and others.

The Commission is, then, one of the most sophisticated forms of "cooperative federalism" yet attempted—the epitome of the American effort to obtain the advantages of decentralized decision making while simultaneously avoiding the perils of provincialism. At the same time it

3. The compact and formal acts of consent to the compact by the signatory governments may be found at: Act of Sept. 27, 1961, Pub. L. No. 87–328, 75 Stat. 688; DEL. CODE ANN. tit. 7, §§6501–13 (Supp. 1970); N.J. STAT. ANN. §§32-11 D-1 through 32-110–115 (Supp. 1971); N.Y. CONSERV. LAW §§801–12 (McKinney, 1967); PA. STAT. ANN. tit. 32, §§815.101–815.106 (Purdon, 1967).
4. DELAWARE RIVER BASIN COMPACT §2.5.
5. Id. arts. 4–10; see Grad, 1963. See also Leach and Sugg, 1959, pp. 22–49, for examples of typical, less generously endowed, compact agencies. For a discussion of the problems of allocating power, which may be inherent in the structure of a federalist system, see Leach, 1970 and the sources cited in Ch. 12, nn. 45, 46.

represents an attractive effort to reconcile the seemingly conflicting demands of technocratic intelligence and democratic decision making. The scientific analysis of facts, costs, and benefits promised to give structure and discipline to decision making; but politicians—whose *raison d'être* is the expression of broad streams of popular opinion—retained the ultimate responsibility for approving or modifying the technocratic solution.

Fourth, the DRBC did not content itself with framing policy in the abstract but proceeded with a sophisticated effort to design a legal system of controls which promised to fulfill its environmental objectives. No more would the legal requirements imposed upon polluters be grounded on little more than rule of thumb; instead they would be carefully crafted so that those who could prevent the greatest harm at the least expense would be ordered to do so.

It should be no surprise, then, that the DRBC has been hailed as a high point in the recent American experience in institutional construction: it blended a sophisticated fact-finding apparatus, an expert assessment of the costs and benefits of a wide range of control strategies, a responsible political decision by those intimately concerned with the fate of the region, and a mature use of the legal system to effectuate the goals adopted for the region. It is rare indeed for an institution of government to conform so closely to society's ideals; here Scientific Enlightenment and Democracy, Policy and Law, all seemed harmoniously combined.

Now it should not be surprising that, as we analyze the harmonies with care, dissonances aplenty will reveal themselves. Nevertheless, the rewards of studying an institution that even remotely approximates an ideal are manifold, for the analysis will permit a more refined understanding of the limits of our ideals, as well as a clearer sense of the ways in which institutions can be designed to more realistically fulfill our expectations. Thus, as we probe each of the four phases of the DRBC's policy-making process, we shall be concerned not only to describe the fundamental problems involved in scientific fact finding, economic cost–benefit analysis, political decision making, and legal regulation, but also to probe the limits of the esoteric forms of intelligence and innovative organizational structures developed to govern the course of policy along the river. As a consequence, we shall be in a position, as each phase of the analysis is concluded, to consider structural alterations that may promise to improve the quality of institutional performance in the future.

At the same time, it will also prove possible to explore the uncertain intellectual foundations of the substance of environmental policy in the United States today. For it happens that the policy objectives selected by the path-breaking DRBC in the mid-1960's have been imposed in similar form by statute upon the nation in the mid-1970's.[6] These goals, we shall argue, are fundamentally misconceived and will cost American society many billions of dollars which could be better spent on projects of far greater environmental or social value than those currently being undertaken along the Delaware and other industrial rivers. Indeed, it is likely that major environmental undertakings in other areas of concern suffer from some of the same failures to reconcile in a satisfactory fashion the inevitable tensions between industrialized man and nature that we shall examine here. Thus, in addition to scrutinizing the limitations of contemporary institutional structures and modern forms of scientific and economic analysis, we shall simultaneously attempt a substantive critique of an increasingly important area of public policy.

In undertaking this inquiry, we have assumed the perspective of no single academic specialty. Indeed, our goal has been to indicate the ways in which a number of fields of academic learning—natural science, economics, politics, law, philosophy—can contribute to the coherent formulation of public policy; to suggest that many of the most important and interesting issues concerning the art of government involve the interrelationship of various disciplines and hence fall beyond the purview of any single one. In short, we are speaking to the intelligent generalist, whatever his discipline, who wishes to understand enough of a body of knowledge to see how it relates to others that are relevant to the sound construction of decision-making institutions and substantive programs. Consequently, we have made strenuous efforts to write in English rather than mathematics, and to consign to the footnotes points of interest only to specialists. Doubtless this approach will seem terribly unsystematic to some; nevertheless, ever since Aristotle, the development of a systematic policy science has continued to elude man's grasp. All we can do for the moment is grope among a multitude of disciplines for tools that promise a sounder means of institutional reconstruction than those we now possess.

6. See our discussion of the Water Pollution Act of 1972 in Ch. 20.

PART
I

The Technocratic Model: Of Scientific Fact Finding and Public Policy

The Technocratic Enterprise

THE FOUR PURPOSES OF THE ANALYSIS

Since we will be talking a great deal about the technocratic enterprise, it is wise to begin by presenting our understanding of the characteristics which set the technocratic intelligence apart from other modes of analysis. On the most general level, we discern two elements that define the nature of this form of intellectual enterprise. First, the technocrat attempts to analyze reality in *quantitative* rather than qualitative terms; any insight that cannot be expressed in mathematical terms is (by our definition) excluded from the technocrat's ken. Second, the quantitative analysis provided by the technocrat attempts, as much as possible, to be divorced from the analyst's personal preferences and is instead grounded in a general theory that aspires to both internal consistency and empirical verification.[1]

1. We shall resist the temptation either to engage in an elaborate consideration of alternative definitions of the technocratic mentality or to explore the relationship of our definition to the fundamental issues that it raises in the philosophy of science. For a consideration of these issues, the reader should consult the works of Ludwig Wittgenstein, which contain both the clearest statement of the philosophical founda-

So conceived, there are numerous varieties of technocratic expertise which may be of assistance in understanding the dimensions of any single policy problem. In this book, however, we shall be dealing only with those two which were applied in the analysis of the pollution problem afflicting the densely populated section of the Delaware River Valley. In the present part of the essay, we shall consider the attempt to construct a mathematical model, based on concepts in natural science, which permitted both a more precise description of the present polluted state of the river and a series of predictions indicating the way present conditions would change upon the adoption of one or another pollution control strategy. In Part II, we shall turn to consider the way in which a technocratic team, employing the concepts of economic theory, sought to quantify the costs and benefits of embarking upon each of a number of competing programs of environmental protection. While our study therefore does not consider the particular problems raised by the deployment of other modes of technocratic analysis, there is good reason to believe that the issues we shall canvass are typical of a broader range. The scientific and economic modes we shall assess here are, relatively speaking, far more advanced than other technocratic disciplines when judged by the two fundamental criteria enumerated previously; so the problems that are raised in their use are suggestive of problems that will afflict other kinds of expertise as they reach relative technocratic maturity.

In assessing the ambitious two-pronged technocratic effort along the Delaware, we have four ends in view. First, the substantive elaboration and critique of the scientific and economic concepts used in the Delaware study will permit an appraisal of the wisdom of the pollution policy currently being pursued at great expense in every urban center of the United States. Second, we invite the reader to form a judgment (however tentative) concerning the kinds of decision makers who should be given ultimate policy making authority over issues like those raised along the Delaware; that is, rather than reposing ultimate authority in a group of politicians, should the Basin Compact have entrusted the task to a group of technocrats? If decision making by either technocrats or politicians has its serious flaws, is it possible to design an alternative decision-making structure that promises a sounder development of environmental policy?[2] In order to begin to

---

tions of technocracy and the most profound repudiation of these same premises. A good place to begin is with Pears, 1970. For important recent discussions which permit a view of technocracy from several different disciplinary perspectives, see Kuhn, 1970; Lindblom, 1965; and Tribe, 1972.
2. See Ch. 14.

frame ,intelligent answers to these questions, it is essential to gain an appreciation of the strengths and weaknesses of applied natural science and applied welfare economics as they are practiced in real-life situations. Third, whether technocratic analysis is to be used either as a guide to decision or as the ultimate touchstone of policy, institutional steps must be taken to maximize the chance that these esoteric forms of intelligence will be invoked responsibly. As a consequence, it is necessary to scrutinize the institutional structure as well as the substance of the Delaware enterprise in order to determine how the quality of analysis may be improved.

Finally, in attempting to achieve these three objectives we shall be simultaneously fulfilling a fourth purpose of great importance. Like it or not, technocratic intelligence—in the forms epitomized along the Delaware —is here to stay for a very long time to come. It is incumbent upon the University community—whence the authors come—to provide the tools and techniques through which our students, who all too soon will be manipulating and appraising technocratic documents, can do so with a proper appreciation of their value. However obvious the importance of this task, it seems to us equally obvious that it is not being discharged. There are more than enough courses dealing with the manipulation of one or another technique, but far too few of them address the question of how to proceed intelligently in the light of the fact that these techniques— though often powerful—are sometimes (or often or always) inadequate. The result of this imbalance in the educational enterprise is easy to see: on the one hand, bands of technocrats are "solving" problems in ways that beg fundamental issues; on the other, bands of angry humanists—innocent of all learning in the technocratic arts—are denying the validity of solutions proffered by the experts and proposing alternative solutions which, however lovely in conception, do not stand up to careful examination. If there is a middle way between a narrow technocracy and an equally narrow obscurantism, it is for the academy to define its parameters.

THE COURSE OF TECHNOCRATIC ENTERPRISE ALONG THE DELAWARE: AN OVERVIEW

At the very beginning of our story, we encounter a problem that will complicate it to the end: the fractionalization of decision making and planning authority. When the DRBC became a functioning entity in September 1961, it found that an independent study of the water pollution problem in the Delaware had already been initiated by a technocratic group that was first lodged in the U.S. Public Health Service and was subsequently transferred to the Federal Water Pollution Control Administration in the Department of the Interior. Indeed, both the Interior study and the DRBC itself were the products of the same natural disaster that changed the direction of water policy along the river. In the mid-1950's the valley had experienced a series of disastrous floods that had focussed local and state attention on the river with an unaccustomed intensity, catalyzing the energies of a broad range of groups.

The way the floods of the 1950's generated political pressures leading to the establishment of the DRBC has been adequately detailed by others.[3] The history of the Interior Department's study, however, is less well known. Within a relatively short time after the floods, the Army Corps of Engineers was requested by the concerned states to make a comprehensive study of the Delaware watershed. Given the Corps' own institutional biases, together with the fact that floods had precipitated its investigation, the Engineers were principally concerned with devising a plan for building a series of dams for flood control. The Corps believed, however, that water quality, as well as water quantity, was within its mandate, and asked the Public Health Service (PHS) to conduct a study in this area as part of the over-all effort. Thus, when the Engineers' report was published in the late 1950's it included a chapter containing primitive data on the pollution problem in the valley.[4]

Matters might have been left in this primitive condition but for developments within the Public Health bureaucracy in Washington. Cost–benefit analysis was a relatively new idea in Washington during the waning Eisenhower years and the PHS was eager to apply the new learning to the solution of water quality problems. In light of the fact that some work had already been undertaken on the Delaware, the river basin was selected as the testing ground for the new techniques. Thus, by 1962, the Service's plans had matured to the point where it could launch its Delaware Estuary Comprehensive Study (DECS), which undertook a path-breaking scientific analysis of the Delaware's pollution problem, at a cost of $1.2 million over the next four years.[5] During the earlier years of the study, the DECS proceeded on its way with very little assistance or guidance from the DRBC,

3. Martin, et al., 1960, pp. 3–61; Zimmerman and Wendell, 1963, pp. 157, 162.
4. *U.S. Army Engineer Report,* pp. 91–189.
5. Interview with James F. Wright, Executive Director of the Delaware River Basin Commission, Dec. 1970; interview with Blair Bower, Resources for the Future, Nov. 1970; interview with Walter Lyon, Director of Bureau of Sanitary Engineering, Department of Environmental Resources, Commonwealth of Pennsylvania, Aug. 1970; interview with Professor Matthew Sobel, Yale University, Dec. 1971.

the political agency with ultimate decision-making authority. In part, DECS' independence was explained by the capriciousness of nature. No longer was the valley victimized by severe floods; instead, the early and middle 1960's was an era of ever-deepening drought along the Delaware. As drinking water became scarce, New York City and Philadelphia became enmeshed in one of their periodic clashes over their respective rights to tap the Delaware for water, and the infant DRBC's prime concern was to mediate the conflict between these cities, as well as among other concerned communities.[6] Water quality seemed of relatively small importance when compared with the consequences of inadequate water quantity.

The preoccupation of the DRBC was not the only reason for the independence of DECS. At its inception, the DECS investigators understood their task principally in academic terms. DECS' research director, Robert Thomann, was a young sanitary engineer whose doctoral thesis had proposed a new mathematical model for dealing with the physical impact of pollutants on estuaries like the Delaware.[7] It was his intention to demonstrate his model's utility in actual practice, and it was easy to recruit a youthful staff who shared this exciting goal. The DECS staff, driven by their desire to vindicate the new scientific methodology, would not have taken kindly to "guidance" by an agency like the DRBC, which at that time did not contain engineers with similar mathematical competence. Given the DRBC's preoccupation with other matters, however, no substantial conflicts along these lines occurred, and the DECS was permitted to go along its own way.

All this began to change dramatically with the passage of the Federal Water Quality Act of 1965,[8] which for the first time required the states to submit water quality standards for federal approval, with the deadline for submission set for June 30, 1967.[9] Suddenly, the DECS study was perceived from a more practical perspective. It was no longer basically a research operation that might inform decision makers in the indefinite future. Rather, it became an action-oriented project promising a suitable basis for establishing regional pollution control objectives. By this time, however, the DECS staff had developed enough momentum so that it would have been even more difficult for the DRBC—still in the midst of the water shortage crisis—to affect significantly the shape of the DECS study. Thus it was the DECS, not the DRBC staff itself, which was princi-

6. Hogarty, 1966.
7. Thomann, 1963.
8. Water Quality Act of 1965, Pub. L. No. 89–234, 79 Stat. 903; codified at 33 U.S.C.A. §466 (1970).
9. *Id.* §5 (c) (1); 33 U.S.C.A. §466(g)(c) (1970).

pally responsible for the critical task of *framing the alternatives* to be presented to the political decision makers on the DRBC. In response to the 1965 act, the expert Interior staff accelerated the pace of its work, issuing a "preliminary" report in the middle of 1966, in time for use by the DRBC in its efforts to develop water quality standards.[10] This is not to say that the DECS staff framed the alternatives in a vacuum. The staff perceptively organized a complex set of advisory committees incorporating interested industrial, governmental, and citizen groups, so that important political constituencies would define their own positions fully armed with the facts as the DECS understood them, and so that the DECS could incorporate ideas from concerned groups into its definition of alternative water quality strategies.[11] Nevertheless, it is fair to consider the DECS staff itself as having played the principal role in articulating the nature of the basic choices confronting the citizens of the Delaware Valley.

The core of the DECS preliminary report analyzed the quantifiable costs and benefits involved in attaining five hypothesized water quality programs with widely different ambitions. The least ambitious plan took as its goal the prevention of further degradation in river quality (Objective Set [OS] V); the most ambitious program contemplated the greatest possible effort consistent with the limitations of existing technology (Objective Set I); Objective Set numbers II through IV contemplated water quality improvements of descending magnitude. When presented in tabular form, the DECS computer printout provided information that promised to be of the highest utility to decision makers. Thus, under the method of allocating pollution loads most seriously considered,[12] the DECS cost–benefit analysis generated the figures in Table 1.

In a sense, all that follows in the first half of this book is a commentary on this table from the perspectives suggested by our preceding statement of purpose. We shall first consider in Part I the way in which the DECS scientific team undertook to describe "the facts" about the pollution problem and the steps that could be taken to ameliorate environmental conditions by moving from Objective Set V to more ambitious programs (Chapters 3–5). We then turn to consider in Part II the way in which the DECS team sought to quantify both the costs and benefits of each of the

10. DECS, pp. 68, 69.
11. These committees played an important role in the political process that ultimately defined the river's water quality objectives. They will be discussed in more detail in Part III.
12. This system required different polluters to treat their wastes to different degrees depending on the discharger's geographic location on the river. The system will be explained in detail in Part IV.

Table 1.   Cost–Benefit Analysis of DECS Pollution Plans[13]

Objective Set	Cost[14]	High Estimate–Low Estimate of Benefits[15]
I	$490 million	$355–155 million
II	275 ”	320–135 ”
III	155 ”	310–125 ”
IV	110 ”	280–115 ”
V	30 ”	——

five programs it had defined (Chapters 6–8). Finally, having concluded the survey of the basic scientific and economic concepts, the last two chapters in Part II consider the basic limitations of the technocratic enterprise. Thus, Chapter 9 assesses the inherent inadequacies of technocratic decision-making criteria and then proceeds to sketch the outlines of a new environmental policy that seems to us to represent an appropriate reconciliation of both technocratic and nontechnocratic insights. Chapter 10 shifts the focus from the substance of policy to consideration of institutional structures: What kinds promise best to improve the chances that esoteric forms of intelligence will enlighten, rather than obscure, public policy issues?

Our survey of the strengths and limits of technocratic decision making, moreover, provides a necessary starting point for the issues canvassed in the second half of this essay. It is only after an appraisal of the DECS Report that it is possible in Part III to assess the fashion in which the politicians and their aides came to an ultimate decision on the objectives to be pursued on the Delaware. When the state governors and the Secretary of the Interior convened in March, 1967 to chart a course for the River, they did not rubber-stamp the counsel of their technocratic advisors. An inspection of Table 1 indicates that the wisdom of an ambitious clean-

13. The benefit estimates are for recreation only and come from DECS, Table 20, p. 77. The cost estimates come from DECS, Table 16, p. 66. Capital costs are counted as occurring in the present with operating and maintenance costs discounted at 3 percent for 20 years. The benefit estimates represent the present value of a 20-year stream of benefits also discounted at 3 percent.
14. These estimates represent costs over and above the costs incurred in 1964 for pollution control.
15. The benefit estimates represent the additional recreation benefits, over and above recreation benefits afforded by the river in its 1964 condition. As a consequence no benefits are shown for OS V.

up program along the Delaware Estuary seemed very dubious from the perspective of cost–benefit analysis. Moving from Objective IV to Objective III, for example, seems to generate no more than $30 million more in benefits, while anticipated costs increase by $45 million; and Objective II requires an extra investment of $120 million to obtain a $10 million gain over Objective III. Despite this, the political officials on the DRBC rejected not only Objective IV but Objective III as well, and proceeded to adopt a slightly modified version of Objective II[16] to serve as the water quality objective for the Delaware.

The decision on the Delaware thus poses a sharp challenge to the technocratic enterprise. Before we can determine whether the political judgment was ultimately sound or unsound, we must determine the extent to which the technocratic analysis itself enlightened the search for a sound environmental policy.

16. For a discussion of the relatively minor way in which Objective II was modified, see Ch. 13, n. 9.

Defining the "Pollution Problem" Technocratically

INTRODUCTION

A layman taking a slow boat trip down the Delaware as it flows through the densely populated conurbation stretching from Trenton, New Jersey, through Philadelphia, to Wilmington, Delaware, is offered an unusual perspective on contemporary urban industrial civilization.[1] As he looks up from his boat, he sees enormous factories lined up one after another, belching smoke into the air and dumping stuff of various kinds into the river; giant tankers and other vessels steam by, perhaps the ultimate source of the occasional small oil slick that can be observed; the river is extremely cloudy, with little in the way of aquatic life visible. Despite all this, the number of pleasure boats on the river is surprisingly large, though it is very rare to see a person hardy enough to dare swimming in what is obviously a "polluted" stream.

There is, doubtless, much in this scene that would disturb a citizen concerned with the pollution problem; there is even more that does not meet the eye. Indeed, the problem with the "pollution problem" is that the

1. The authors did in fact take such a journey during the summer of 1970.

label subsumes too many discrete issues that must be understood individually before their interrelationships can be mastered in an intellectual synthesis. And in this perception lies the importance of the question with which this chapter is concerned: in its efforts to describe "the facts" in a systematic way, which aspects of the problem did the DECS staff emphasize and which did they ignore? To answer this question, we must explore the premises and character of a mathematical model that was the principal analytical tool used by the DECS to describe the factual relationships obtaining between various "pollution sources" and the river's "water quality."

WATER QUALITY AND DISSOLVED OXYGEN

To write an equation relating waste discharges to a river's water quality, it is first necessary to define the meaning of "waste" and "water quality" *in terms susceptible of quantification.* Since waste may properly be defined as anything that impairs water quality, it will be sufficient at the outset to concentrate on defining the latter term; how, then, are we to *measure* "water quality"?

DECS answered this threshold question by taking recourse to the received wisdom of the sanitary engineering profession. Traditionally, the amount of dissolved oxygen (DO) in the water has served sanitary engineers as the principal benchmark of water quality, and DECS adopted this indicator to serve as the focus of its analysis. DO had several advantages for the DECS. First, and most important for model building purposes, DO can be measured. Second, the amount of DO in the stream has an impact on several important river uses. Fish need dissolved oxygen to breathe. If DO sags below a certain level—at best ill-defined, but between three and four parts per million (ppm) of water—they will have increasing difficulty breathing. If oxygen deficiencies are substantial and sustained, the fish will die.[2] If DO sags yet further to levels approaching zero for sub-

2. Tarzwell, 1957, cited in Camp, 1963, p. 119. Camp indicates that:

> for a well-rounded warm water fish population, the dissolved oxygen must not be below 5 ppm for more than 8 hours of any 24-hour period and at no time should it be below 3 ppm. For the maintenance of a coarse fish population, the dissolved oxygen should not be below 5 ppm for more than 8 hours of any 24-hour period and at no time should it be below 2 ppm.

Similar standards may be found in *Water Quality Criteria,* p. 44, which suggests that at 3 ppm many species, especially game fish, suffer a significant retardation of normal growth and activity. For the approach taken by DECS, see Morris and Pence, undated.

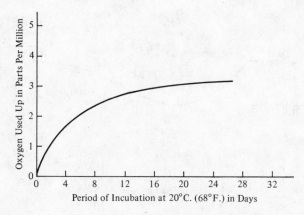

Figure 1
Oxygen Consumption vs. Period of Incubation for a
Carbonaceous Material

stantial periods of time, a group of microorganisms attack many organic wastes and degrade them in a way that throws off offensive odors, notably those associated with the rotten egg smell of hydrogen sulfide.[3] Needless to say, the presence of these odors makes the river an unpleasant place to boat or swim, and picnicking (or even travelling) nearby is not an attractive prospect.

Given these facts, it is obviously important to determine the extent to which the pollutants discharged into a river like the Delaware affect the stream's DO level, and it is precisely this problem that the DECS model sought to solve. The pollutants of greatest concern here include almost all organic compounds like those present in human feces and many industrial effluents. Perhaps the best way to understand the impact of these wastes is to imagine an experiment in which a small lump of sugar is added to a bottle of clean water. If the amount of oxygen consumed by the microorganisms in the bottle as they decompose the lump of sugar is measured, a curve similar to the one in Figure 1 is obtained as time passes.[4] In the shorthand of engineers, the curve depicted in Figure 1 indicates the Biochemical Oxygen Demand[5] (BOD) exerted by the sugar over time. As the

3. Camp, 1963, p. 64. Hydrogen sulfide is produced by microbial decomposition of organic matter in the absence of air (anaerobic decomposition).
4. For a more sophisticated treatment of organic decomposition, see Camp, 1963, pp. 219–87.
5. *Ibid.*, pp. 243–51. BOD is defined as the number of pounds of oxygen that will be consumed in the biochemical oxidation of the organic impurity present. *Ibid.*, p. 243.

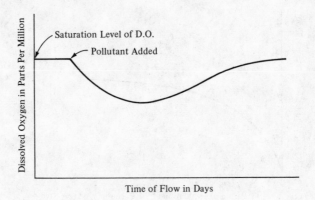

Figure 2
A Typical Oxygen Sag Curve

shape of the curve indicates, the more concentrated the pollutant, the greater the rate at which it is decomposed,[6] and the faster DO is depleted.

Now suppose that a polluter discharges a lot of waste into a river. Since the consumption of dissolved oxygen is a function of the concentration of pollutant present, it follows that the concentration of DO will initially fall off rapidly at the pollutant's point of entry. As time passes, a given sample of polluted water will move downstream and the concentration of pollutant will decrease. As the concentration of pollutant decreases, DO consumption diminishes. Another effect also takes place. As the concentration of DO decreases, oxygen diffuses into the river from the air. This process is called reaeration. As the DO deficit increases, increasingly large amounts of oxygen diffuse into the river. The combined actions of the microorganisms consuming the pollutant in the water, the water flowing downstream, and the reaeration effect, result in a DO profile as shown in Figure 2.[7] This curve is known, appropriately enough, as the oxygen sag curve. To complicate matters, the DO sag is also affected by water temperature (the warmer the water, the less oxygen it can dissolve and the

6. The correct differential equation describing the decomposition process is simply:

$$\frac{dx}{dt} = -kx$$

where k represents the "decomposition rate constant"; x, the concentration of BOD; and t, time. It should be noted that while k is a constant, the *rate* at which BOD is consumed over time $\left(\frac{dx}{dt}\right)$ is proportional to the negative of the concentration of BOD (x).

7. For a more extensive discussion, see Camp, 1963, pp. 287–313. In this introductory explanation, we are assuming away the problems posed by the fact that the Delaware is an estuary experiencing tidal action. These problems will be discussed in detail in Ch. 4, nn. 4–47 and accompanying text.

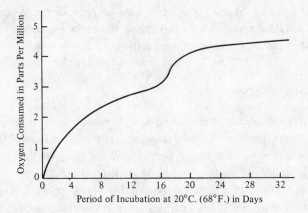

Figure 3
Oxygen Consumption vs. Period of Incubation for a
Hydrocarbon Containing Nitrogen

faster the microorganisms consume oxygen), by changes in the river's flow rate (the faster the current, the farther downstream the oxygen sag), and by the river's cross-sectional area (which affects the rate at which a waste discharge diffuses across the river).[8]

Even when all these factors are taken into account the student of the Delaware will not observe a DO curve precisely resembling the simple shape depicted above. The Delaware is endowed with a hundred or so significant dischargers, each at a different point in the river, each making its own contribution to the DO profile. Moreover, the impact on the river of many wastes is complicated by the fact that many pollutants contain elements other than the oxygen, carbon, and hydrogen, which are the constituents of sugar. Most wastes contain nitrogen as well, and in these cases the biochemical oxygen demand of the material is a two-stage affair, as is shown in Figure 3.[9] Under laboratory conditions, the nitrogen in untreated wastes begins oxidation approximately 15 days after the test begins, in contrast to carbonaceous activity, which begins at once. Thus nitrogenous demand begins at a time when approximately 90 percent of the carbonaceous activity has been exerted; this explains the hump in the curve. It should be noted, however, that about 10 percent of the carbon oxidation is yet to occur when nitrogenous decomposition begins even in the case of untreated waste. Nevertheless, sanitary engineers are accustomed to describing BOD in terms of "carbonaceous oxygen demand" (often called "First Stage Ultimate Oxygen Demand" or FSUOD) and "nitrogenous

8. The relationship between these factors and the DO profile was first systematically articulated by Streeter and Phelps in an equation reproduced in Ch. 4, n. 5.
9. For a more extended discussion, see Camp, 1963, pp. 245–51.

oxygen demand" ("Second Stage Ultimate Oxygen Demand" or SSUOD), although FSUOD and SSUOD cannot be precisely measured since carbonaceous demand has not ended when nitrogenous begins.[10]

SOURCES OF BOD

In addition to the discharges emitted by treatment plants owned by riparian cities and industries, substantial loadings are imposed upon the estuary from three other sources. Large portions of the river bottom are endowed with thick sludge deposits continually in the process of being consumed by microorganisms that require oxygen for subsistence. The oxygen demand from this source (called benthic oxygen demand) accounts for about 12 percent[11] of the total demand imposed upon the estuary. In addition, the major cities of Trenton, Camden, Philadelphia, and Wilmington all possess combined sewer systems serving as conduits for both sewage and storm water run-off from the cities' streets. This means that the sewer pipes transmit dramatically larger volumes of waste water during and after heavy storms. Municipal treatment facilities, alas, are not constructed to cope with these inundations but, rather, are built to treat the volume of sewage associated with ordinary weather conditions. Consequently, the four major cities are obliged, on an average of ten rainy days a year,[12] simply to divert raw sewage *cum* rainwater directly into the Delaware, without any treatment whatsoever. These discharges account for approximately 4 percent of the total annual load on the river.[13] Finally, about 12 percent of the total load is contributed by the Upper Delaware above Trenton, as well as the hundred or so tributaries feeding into the estuary itself.[14]

Despite the complex interaction of BOD from industry, municipal treatment plants, river sludge, storm sewer run-off, and the estuary's tributaries, a well defined DO profile, complete with oxygen sags, may be dis-

10. After the fifteenth day, when both nitrogenous and carbonaceous materials are decaying simultaneously, the carbonaceous contribution is calculated by extrapolating the curve based on the first two weeks of data collection, a period during which nitrogenous activity is almost absent. The remaining excess oxygen demand prevailing after the fifteenth day is attributed to nitrogenous activity. (Interview with G.D. Pence, Jr., Delaware Estuary Comprehensive Survey staff, in Edison, N.J., July 1970).

Moreover, it is an oversimplification to assert that nitrogenous activity does not commence until the fifteenth day. In fact the lag before the onset of nitrogenous demand is a function of other variables as well, including the degree of treatment of waste before it is dumped into the river.

11. Porges and Seltzer, 1968, p. 80. To avoid confusion, it should be noted that BOD stands for biochemical oxygen demand, *not* benthic oxygen demand.

12. Unpublished chapter of DECS Final Report, on file in Biddle Law Library, University of Pennsylvania.

13. Porges and Seltzer, 1968, p. 80.

14. *Ibid.*

cerned by a student of the estuary. It is depicted in Figure 4.[15] For purposes of this analysis the river below Trenton was divided by the DECS into 30 sections, some 10,000 feet and some 20,000 feet in length. At Trenton, just above the estuarine portion of the river, DO levels are high, and indeed approach saturation. The "sag" begins immediately below Trenton, where the combined effects of tidal action, a rapid increase in depth, a decrease in velocity, and the presence of polluting matter result in an increased rate of oxygen consumption by microorganisms. The sag at Burlington, however, is followed by a slight increase in DO, which has never been adequately explained. Up to section 7 (22 miles from Trenton), just north of Philadelphia, the total FSUOD discharge from municipal and industrial sources is relatively small, amounting to 20,000 pounds per day for all seven sections combined. At Philadelphia, however, FSUOD inputs dramatically increase, averaging 75,000 pounds per day in each section through section 22 (65 miles from Trenton), which is just beyond Wilmington, the last major city bordering the estuary. The three major treatment plants operated by Philadelphia contribute the lion's share of these wastes, discharging 450,000 pounds of FSUOD daily in 1964, which represented 45 percent of the total FSUOD discharged by cities and industries along the estuary. During the same year, Camden's two plants discharged 62,250 pounds of FSUOD; Wilmington dumped 87,000 pounds; the chemical plants located along the heavily industrialized shore dumped 210,000 pounds; oil refineries, 95,000; paper plants, 30,000.

As a result of this series of discharges, DO drops precipitously in sec-

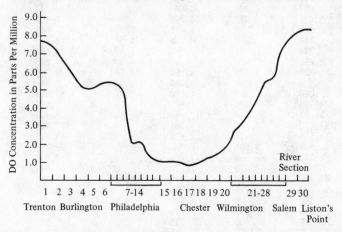

Figure 4
Profile of Average Summer Dissolved Oxygen in 1964
(From Delaware Estuary Comprehensive Study)

15. This figure is based on one provided to us by the DECS staff.

tions 7 through 11, a distance of merely six miles, from 5½ ppm to 1½ ppm and remains roughly constant for about the next 30 miles through section 19, which is a bit beyond the Pennsylvania-Delaware state line. DO begins to recover at this point since the river is increasing in size as it nears Delaware Bay, diluting the waste to a greater degree as well as permitting accelerated reaeration. With the virtual cessation of substantial industrial and municipal loadings at Wilmington,[16] six miles beyond the state line, DO levels recover rapidly. Thus, the DO level in section 25 (70 miles from Trenton) is equal to the DO level in section 7 (22 miles from Trenton); indeed, DO reaches near-saturation levels as the river meets the bay at Liston's Point.[17]

16. The only sizeable discharge beyond this point is contributed by an oil refinery owned by the Getty Oil Co., located in section 26 of the river, 70 miles from Trenton. In 1964, DECS estimated that the refinery was discharging 2500 pounds of FSUOD per day. Pence, et al., 1968, p. 393.

17. Our description of the river is based on DECS' measurements of BOD loadings and DO that obtained in 1964. For a more precise description of the BOD loads imposed in each section of the river, we provide the following chart, taken from Pence, et al., 1968, p. 393:

1964 Waste Loading in the Delaware Estuary, in Pounds Per Day of Carbonaceous Biochemical Oxygen Demand

Section (1)	Municipal (2)	Industry (3)	Tributary (4)	Storm Water Overflow (5)	Total BOD Source (6)	P, Total DO Sink (7)
1	3,570	0	2,869	1,360	7,799	22,280
2	2,100	2,750	4,107		8,957	8,622
3	3,380	1,635	982		5,997	4,140
4	2,720	2,850	1,078		6,648	2,700
5	900	1,400	2,047		4,347	4,800
6	1,075	435	5,798		7,308	5,040
7	0	0	1,875	230	2,105	890
8	520	0	4,309	1,580	6,409	2,125
9	795	35	3,095	8,570	12,496	2,250
10	128,610	7,550	3,146	4,390	143,695	2,250
11	720	1,570	3,189	16,780	22,259	5,760
12	0	0	1,105	4,480	5,585	1,350
13	62,080	13,925	1,800	7,410	85,215	3,240
14	174,520	19,670	1,566	2,080	197,836	3,960
15	3,330	39,550	17,649	18,860	79,389	14,700
16	158,070	25,650	3,761		187,481	6,750
17	14,575	42,420	8,678	1,950	67,623	11,475
18	10,185	14,535	6,003		30,723	7,200
19	1,820	64,360	1,668		67,848	16,200
20	0	0	1,071		1,071	15,750
21	87,400	8,480	6,848	8,320	111,048	6,930
22	0	116,755	294		117,049	6,000
23	1,870	0	306		2,176	13,050
24	0	370	421		791	11,000
25	0	0	855		855	9,300
26	0	2,500	1,416		3,916	12,000
27	660	0	322		992	15,000
28	1,730	0	9,078		10,808	15,000
29	0	0	5,011		5,011	0
30	0	0	5,509		5,509	0
Totals	660,630	366,440	174,719	76,010	1,277,799	229,762

Although this sketch of the relationship between waste discharges exerting BOD and the resulting DO profile has been oversimplified, it suggests the magnitude of the task the DECS undertook in attempting to explain the shape of the Delaware's DO profile. Even more important for our purposes, it permits the beginning of an answer to the question to which this chapter is addressed: To what extent did the DECS' attempt to describe "the facts" about DO emphasize certain aspects of the "pollution problem" at the expense of other dimensions of equal or greater importance?

SHORTCOMINGS OF THE DO INDEX

We have said enough to explain why a policy maker would want to know the DO levels prevailing at various locations along the stream with which he is concerned. Nevertheless, a decision maker would be extremely myopic if he were to adopt DO as the exclusive touchstone of water quality. DO has little impact upon the ability of modern treatment plants to process water for human consumption, so long as anaerobic conditions producing serious odor problems are avoided.[18] Turning next to a river's potential recreational uses, DO is a far from sufficient indicator of water quality. Although a DO near zero indicates that a river cannot be used for swimming, fishing, or boating because of the "river stink" resulting from complete oxygen depletion, a higher DO does not necessarily indicate that the river is suitable for these uses. That a river has a relatively high DO does

18. DECS recognized that increasing DO will not result in substantial monetary savings for the major water treatment plant on the estuary, at Torresdale, Pa., which provides half of Philadelphia's water.

> The major source of municipal supply that may benefit from improved quality is the Torresdale Water Treatment Plant of Philadelphia. The fact that this plant is able to produce a potable water from an estuarine source of the present quality at a relatively low cost obscures the benefits picture for water supply. It is probable that the net monetary benefits in terms of dollar savings in treatment costs at Philadelphia's Torresdale plant will be relatively small at the alternative levels of water quality enhancement. What may result, however, after pollution abatement is carried out, will be a reduction in the taste and odor problem; and therefore an increase in Philadelphia's ability to produce a more palatable drinking water. (DECS, p. 71)

No evidence is advanced to support the assertion that Philadelphia's water "may" become more palatable by improving the DO curve. Philadelphia's Water Department denies that this will occur, arguing that chlorination will still be a necessity to eliminate disease-carrying organisms, and thus whatever taste problems arise from occasional over-chlorination will still exist (from an interview with Samuel Baxter, Philadelphia Water Commissioner, Aug. 1970). Thus the claim that the plant's ability to produce high quality water "may" be enhanced seems a pious hope, rather than a well founded estimate.

not necessarily mean that the water will look clean to the typical swimmer, boater, or fisherman. At present, the Delaware is an extremely turbid river: over large sections, sunlight does not penetrate more than two feet beneath the surface.[19] Reducing BOD loads on the stream will not necessarily change this dreary reality substantially since the river's turbidity is explained in large part by tides stirring up the river bottom, dredging operations required for large-scale shipping, and the introduction of large quantities of sediment from the river's banks and tributaries. Thus, to understand the impact a cleanup of industrial and domestic waste would have on swimming and boating in the Delaware, it is not sufficient to have a DO model of the river. A model must be available that calculates the impact a cleanup will have on river turbidity.

19. DECS studies indicated that, in the mid-1960's, the average depth to which only 1 percent of sunlight penetrated the Delaware was 3 feet, ranging from 7 feet at Trenton to 2 feet in the "critical regions" in the Philadelphia area. (Letter from Prof. R. Thomann, Nov. 1971) More recent data are difficult to obtain, indicating the professional pollution control community's continuing failure to transcend its preoccupation with BOD and DO as the primary water quality parameters. During one year in the mid-1960's, for example, the U.S. Geological Survey monitored turbidity levels around Philadelphia. This practice was discontinued, however, both because of uncertainty concerning the quality of the data collected and because no individual or organization had evinced any interest in the information the USGS compiled. (Telephone communications with Richard W. Paulson, U.S. Geological Survey, Harrisburg, Pa., Sept. 1970, Apr. 1971)

We have obtained informal estimates from experts who have done substantial research on turbidity levels in the Delaware Valley. An engineer who is the turbidity expert for the region's Army Corps of Engineers has informed us that in most parts of the river it is impossible to see an object 2 feet below the surface. (Interview with Mr. Paul Hartzell, May 1971) Similarly, Professor Robert E. Ricklefs, of the University of Pennsylvania's Department of Biology informs us that along the lower Schuylkill, near the point where it joins the Delaware, the intensity of sunlight is attenuated by 10 to 30 percent per centimeter of depth. Even assuming the lower value, this means that the intensity of sunlight 1 foot below the surface would be less than 1 percent of surface level intensity. While Professor Ricklefs has not done similar research on the main stem of the Delaware, he ventures to guess that results would be comparable along large sections of the river. (Personal communications with Prof. Robert E. Ricklefs, Aug. 1970, Apr. 1971) Finally, our own visual inspections of the estuary, particularly on boat trips that extended along its entire length, lead us to concur completely with Messrs. Hartzell and Ricklefs.

Data on present levels of photosynthetic activity are also incomplete and contradictory. Dr. C. Hull, now head of the DRBC's Program Planning Branch, did extensive studies of this problem and concluded that despite high turbidity levels significant photosynthesis was occurring (Hull, 1964). The DECS study, however, concluded that the net production of oxygen by photosynthetic activity was negligible (see Thomann, 1964). Even assuming that Dr. Thomann is correct and Dr. Hull completely mistaken, the present state of the Delaware is not our fundamental concern. We are concerned about the future: when Mr. Hartzell was asked whether the DRBC's projected cleanup would make algae bloom, he stated that neither he nor anyone else he knew was in a position to say. He indicated, however, that if the DRBC were to limit not only industrial and municipal discharges but also storm sewer overflow, it could happen that turbidity might decline sufficiently to allow significant algae growth in the shallow sections of the river along the shore.

It is even unclear that swimmers and boaters would benefit if an increase in DO did in fact indicate a dramatic reduction in turbidity. At present, the cloudy Delaware is a relatively inhospitable home for algal growth precisely because the high turbidity prevents algae from photosynthesizing nutrients like phosphates and nitrates that are abundant in the water. If turbidity is reduced as a result of a BOD clean-up campaign, the algae may be in a perfect position to multiply. Increasing DO may simply mean that the valley is trading a brown river for a green one.[20] On the other hand, if turbidity is not substantially reduced as a consequence of a BOD cutback, the impact of an increase in DO beyond the river-stink level will probably not be significant.

While aesthetics is probably the chief concern of boaters, swimmers are concerned also with the presence of disease-carrying organisms and toxic chemicals, whose absence—once again—is not assured by high DO levels. In contrast, DO levels are of greater importance to fishermen, assuming they are willing to fish despite aesthetic affront. Here too, however, an adequate analysis would require an understanding of the impact of heat and toxic substances on aquatic life. If this much additional information is needed for a sophisticated understanding of the recreational uses of a river, even more is needed by a policy maker who wishes to take into account the longer range ecological consequences of the alternative pollution programs he is considering. Once again, while adequate DO levels are a necessary condition for the survival of various forms of aquatic life, they are not a sufficient condition. Nor does the DO profile provide an adequate basis for determining the impact the Delaware has in the larger ecological balance upon which man ultimately depends for his survival.

Paradoxically, it is only with respect to one activity that DO serves as a relatively adequate indicator of water quality. Industries bordering the river use vast quantities of water for cooling as well as for other industrial purposes. From their point of view, the DECS' use of DO as an indicator of water pollution is perverse for the simple reason that oxygen-rich water corrodes piping systems at a more rapid rate.[21] The more polluted the water is (as measured by DO), the *better* it is for industrial water users. As soon as one moves beyond industrial processes, however, to consider the relationship between water and life, human or otherwise, the DO pro-

20. And one that will smell when the algae begin to die. Rotting matter creates high BOD, eventually resulting in depletion of DO leading to anaerobic decomposition. For the practical consequences to the man in the street of this same phenomenon occurring on the Potomac, see Kohn, "Warning: the Green Slime Is Here," *The New York Times Magazine,* Mar. 22, 1970, p. 26.
21. DECS, p. 72.

file serves as an extremely imprecise measure of water quality: generally speaking, a high DO is a necessary but far from sufficient condition for beneficial water use.

PLAYING THE ENVIRONMENTAL NUMBERS GAME

All this means that the use of DO as an index for water quality facilitates a way of thinking about the pollution problem that is fraught with danger. Once a simple number is provided as a "proxy" for water quality, it may take on a life of its own, tempting all concerned to evaluate alternative programs solely in terms of the number, without asking more fundamental questions.[22] Thus, a policy maker guided by the DO numbers would have little difficulty locating the part of the Delaware River experiencing "the most acute pollution problem"; it would appear obvious that the region between Philadelphia and Wilmington suffering the most acute oxygen sag has the most urgent claims on public concern. For is it not perfectly clear that society should first attempt to "solve" its "most serious" pollution problems before moving on to solve the others?

But is it true that the pollution problem is most serious in those regions characterized by severe oxygen depletion? Is it really clear that raising the DO level from 1 ppm to 2 or 3 or 4 ppm on the average in the "critical sections" between Philadelphia and Wilmington would substantially improve the quality of life of the inhabitants of the Delaware Valley? Would such a triumph of index numbers permit the urban masses to swim in the river, for example? As we have suggested, there is no reason to think so. It is even possible that increasing DO will merely serve to transform the Delaware's color from a muddy brown to an even more unattractive green. And what of the nasty habit indulged in by municipalities obliged to discharge raw sewage into the river whenever there are heavy rains? If achieving a DO goal of 3 or 4 ppm permits the cities to continue this practice (as is in fact the case), will it be healthy for anyone to swim in the river for a substantial period after each rainstorm? Regardless of the health question, will people want to swim in the river after they have learned about the raw sewage?

All this aside, how easy will it be for people to swim in a cleaned-up "critical" region whose shoreline is now occupied by heavy industry? Even if access were assured at convenient places, how many would want to bathe on a beach bordered on one side by a belching chemical plant and

22. A similar difficulty may be discerned in the failure, until the 1970's, of air pollution authorities to transcend their preoccupation with hydrocarbon and nitrogen oxide emissions (see Currie, 1970, p. 1085).

on the other by a sewage treatment facility? Will swimmers enjoy their sport quite as much when they encounter the wake of the latest intercontinental oil tanker steaming by to satisfy the needs of a neighboring factory? All these problems (and others) must be resolved successfully before a decision maker intent on providing new swimming areas would consider a region characterized by intensive oxygen depletion important for his plans. Indeed, instead of developing the most polluted segment of the river for this purpose, it may be far wiser to develop one (or more) of the river's major tributaries in *all* of the ways necessary to ensure an attractive body of water in which people would enjoy swimming and other water-based recreation. To achieve this goal might cost a great deal of money, but it might well cost far less than would the triumph of an index number in the so-called critical region.

For other water uses, of course, DO has greater utility as an indicator. If fish are unable to live in the critical region, we should be concerned, and DO helps to indicate whether or not the fish will die. But even here, keeping score by the numbers is far from sufficient. We still must ask: Why is it important to reclaim the critical region for the sake of the fish? If the purpose is to sustain a complex and variegated aquatic life system, the absence of certain aquatic species from the river near Philadelphia, while important, may be far from the most critical ecological threat facing the valley. As we have suggested, raising DO levels to three or four ppm will not in and of itself transform the ecological consequences of twentieth century urban industrialism. Some fish now dying will survive in the critical region, and others will more successfully migrate through it. But to imagine that the original ecological complexes displaced by industrialism will thereby be restored is simply folly. In contrast, 40 miles downstream from Philadelphia's critical DO zone lies one of the few remaining major ocean-front areas in the Northeast yet to be significantly affected by heavy industry and concentrated population. In the marshes of the lower Delaware River and (even more important) the Delaware Bay, the complex interactions between land and water characteristic of relatively untouched areas still continue in a way whose fundamental ecological importance is only now being appreciated. Yet without sophisticated planning, the bay may be transformed by urban industrialism in an all-too-familiar way in the coming decades. Which, then, was the more significant problem facing a pollution control policy in 1967: the nonexistence of fish near Philadelphia or the preservation of the fundamental character of the bay? Paradoxically, it may be that the most "critical" ecological problem arises in an area which, like the bay, at present contains oxygen-rich water rather than in the DO sag region.

It would be premature to argue here that a sounder pollution strategy would have deemphasized the problem caused by oxygen depletion in the most polluted area in the heart of the urban core of Philadelphia and other cities, and thereby freed billions of dollars to pursue the twin goals of *preserving* ecologically significant zones (like the Delaware Bay) which remain relatively untouched by the twentieth century while *creating* new areas for mass recreation within the city by taking *all* the costly steps necessary to reclaim even a small stream from the ravages of industrialism and population density. To make out this case persuasively will require an extensive discussion of both the theory of cost–benefit analysis and its practice on the Delaware. Consequently, we defer a full defense of an alternative environmental program until Chapter 9, when our explication and critique of the substance of the present effort on the Delaware is completed.

Nevertheless, even at this early stage in the discussion, the importance of a sophisticated, scientific fact-finding process to the ultimate policy outcome can be readily discerned. For it was during the process of defining what is to count as a "fact" that the technocratic effort to chart future policy took the wrong course. While the technocratic intelligence seems to promise to the lay decision maker a comprehensive assay of the problem to be confronted, the fact of the matter is that, both because resources are finite and knowledge imperfect, only certain aspects of the problem can be approached with suitably "scientific" rigor and decisiveness. Thus one part of the problem is explored with intensity while other aspects—of equal or greater importance—are left in limbo.[23] Of course, a truly comprehensive analysis of the facts is impossible in a necessarily limited period of time. All this means, however, is that the most vigorous efforts must be made to insure that the array of "facts" now *known* is not confused with the range and kinds of "facts" which are *important* for intelligent policy making.[24] The particular failure to make clear the limitations of DO as a policy indicator or—more important—to design institutions which would adequately uncover the hidden premises of technocratic fact finding, is one of the most important sources of the general failure to design a sound pollution control program on the river. Moreover, until professionals involved, including those who design institutions, show a greater sensitivity to the profound effect of inevitably incomplete "factual" descriptions on the nature of the policy options perceived to be open, mistakes like the ones we shall explore will continue to recur with frustrating frequency.

23. For a related point, see Tribe, 1971, pp. 1361–65.
24. For an intelligent discussion of this and related points, see Lindblom, 1965, Ch. 9.

Explaining the Facts Technocratically

OVERVIEW

Given the concerns of the model builders, it should prove no surprise that the most important difference between each of the programs they proffered to the politicians on the DRBC was the DO level that was set as the policy goal: the less ambitious programs were content with relatively oxygen-poor water, while the more ambitious insisted on higher DO levels. Moreover, it should be clear from our previous discussion that policy makers would "naturally" be concerned with the DO levels obtaining in the most polluted areas between Philadelphia and the Pennsylvania-Delaware state line, for it is in this region that river stink and fish-kills pose the greatest dangers. Consequently, the cost–benefit chart[1] presented in Chapter 3 may appropriately be amended to indicate the DO levels contemplated by each

1. This chart is derived from information to be found in DECS, pp. 56–58, 66, 77. For an explanation of the cost and benefit figures appearing in the chart, see Ch. 2, nn. 13–15.

Table 2.

Objective Set	Average DO in PPM in Most Polluted Region	Cost	High Estimate–Low Estimate of Benefits
I	4.5	$490 million	$355–155 million
II	4.0	275 "	320–135 "
III	3.0	155 "	310–125 "
IV	2.5	110 "	280–115 "
V	1.0	30 "	———

of the proposed programs within the "critical" oxygen sag region below Philadelphia.[2]

Whatever the ultimate value of the DECS' concentration on the DO profile, even a casual inspection of the revised chart reveals the significance of a second major issue in an appraisal of the DECS' fact-finding performance. The chart demonstrates that a small improvement in the DO profile represents a substantial additional expenditure on pollution control. Thus, Objective I achieves a ½-ppm improvement in DO at twice the cost of Objective II, which in turn attains a 1-ppm increase at twice the cost of Objective III. This means that a relatively small error in the DO model predictions will be of great importance to decision makers. Imagine, for example, that instead of making perfect predictions, the DO model has a "standard error" of 1 ppm.[3] This means that there is about a two-thirds chance actual river conditions existing after any particular program is effectuated will be within 1 ppm of the model's prediction. Even this relatively small error would indicate that Objective II, similar to the one ultimately adopted by the DRBC, could result in DO levels as high as those of Objective I (costing twice as much) or as low as those contemplated by Objective III (costing half as much). Of course, by selecting Objective II, the agency increases the chances that a DO level of 4.0 ppm will be attained. Nevertheless, the intrusion of even a relatively small error into the DO predictions introduces a very significant new dimension into the decision maker's problem: How should he orient himself to the fact of

2. For an interpretation of the cost and benefit figures in this table, see Chs. 6 through 8.
3. For a discussion of the term "standard error," see Hoel, 1962, p. 141.

uncertainty? Should he be risk-averse or risk-prone or risk-neutral? As the error in the model's prediction increases, the last of these questions becomes increasingly important in policy formulation, dwarfing in significance the particular cost and benefit figures generated by the model.

In short, assessing the reliability of the model's predictions is a matter of the first importance if one is to determine the adequacy of scientific fact finding in the present stage of its development. The present chapter, however, not only attempts to gain a sense of the size of the "standard error" involved in the model's predictions but also considers whether the model is systematically biased so that its predictions are consistently optimistic or pessimistic. While a detailed examination of the model reveals elements both of optimism and pessimism, it appears to us that the model significantly overstates the ease with which a program of BOD removal will significantly ameliorate the DO conditions prevailing along the highly industrialized sectors of the Delaware. Unfortunately, we have been unable to undertake the extensive theoretical, empirical, and computational work necessary to form a precise estimate of the extent of the bias. All we can do here is to delineate the factors underlying our rough appraisal.

The issues we shall canvass in this chapter are perhaps the most technical ones in the entire book. We have tried to explain the workings and defects of the model in plain English, however, because the basic points raised are of fundamental importance. First, the analysis provides the only sure way to understand the difficulties of harnessing the scientific enterprise into the policy-making effort. Second, it dramatizes the extraordinary expense and difficulty of improving the DO profile on a heavily industrialized river, let alone "cleaning it up" in a way that would make it an all-purpose resource for city folk. Third, it permits the reader to begin to consider the ways in which institutions could be designed so that studies of the DECS type *educate* lay decision makers to appreciate the ways in which scientific predictions can distort perceptions as well as clarify them. Before attempting to criticize the BOD-DO model and define its utility within the larger context of policy making, however, it is best to obtain an understanding of the model's basic principles. And it is this task with which the immediately succeeding discussion is principally concerned.

THE PROBLEM WITH ESTUARIES

The principal conceptual obstacle that rivers like the Delaware (below Trenton) pose to sanitary engineers is that they are estuaries and are therefore influenced by ocean tides. This means that BOD flows not only downstream but upstream as well, complicating all calculations immensely. Thus, a systematic effort at predicting the DO profile had to await the development of the modern digital computer. Most of the elements necessary to run a computer program, however, had been developed much earlier in the study of nonestuarine rivers. In 1925, Streeter and Phelps, in a classic study of the Ohio River,[4] developed an equation quantifying the relationships among DO, BOD, and the diverse factors we have already discussed.[5]

Nevertheless, a systematic attempt to deal with the problem of tidal action was delayed until the 1960's, when the advent of the computer made the work seem worth while. In 1960, O'Connor developed the mathematical concepts that permitted the quantitative description of the manner in which a substance discharged in a tidal estuary would be distributed along its length over time.[6] Armed with O'Connor's contribution, Robert Thomann, then a graduate student, synthesized this work with that of Streeter and Phelps, and developed in his doctoral dissertation[7] the first systematic mathematical treatment of an estuary with multiple pollution sources and varying temperature and flow rate along the length of the river. Thomann then became Technical Director of the DECS and attempted to put his model to the empirical test.

Thomann's contribution is of classic simplicity.[8] The 86-mile estuary is divided into 30 sections, some 10,000 and some 20,000 feet in length.

---

4. Streeter and Phelps, 1925.
5. The original Streeter-Phelps equation is:

$$\frac{dD}{dt} = 2.3(-k_2D + k_1L) - a,$$

where D is the oxygen deficit in ppm, L is the first-stage demand in ppm, t is the time of flow in days, k_2 is the atmospheric reaeration coefficient in reciprocal days, k_1 is the deoxygenation constant in reciprocal days, and a is the oxygen production by photosynthesis in ppm per day. In the original equation a was equal to 0 (Camp, 1963, p. 295).
6. O'Connor, 1960, p. 35. As is normal in such enterprises, O'Connor was obliged to make a major simplifying assumption in order to achieve his theoretical advance. His description of tidal action assumes both that DO measured one foot below the surface is equal to the DO at the river's bottom and that DO levels are essentially uniform across the width of the river. In other words, O'Connor assumes away the river's breadth and depth. This oversimplification, while not inherent in the Thomann model, was used in its application to the Delaware Estuary.
7. Thomann, 1963.
8. Although his Ph.D. thesis remained unpublished, the model developed there and subsequent elaborations are described in a substantial literature. Some of the significant references are: Hetling, *Potomac Estuary,* 1968; Bunce and Hetling, 1967; Hetling, *Simulation,* 1968; Quirk, et al., 1970; Schaumberg, 1967; *Water Quality Model,* 1965; Hetling, *Water Quality Models,* 1968; Mamelak and Radziul, 1969; Morris and Pence,

The DO level in each section is calculated by the use of two equations—one computes the BOD load on the section, the other describes the amount of DO both entering and leaving each section. To determine the BOD load in each section the model requires data that accurately describe the amount of BOD dumped by each pollution source into the river. This information alone, however, is insufficient for the purposes at hand. Even if we knew, for example, that industrial and municipal sources discharge 50,000 pounds of BOD per day in section 3, we must know several other facts before we can predict the amount of BOD that section 3's discharge contributes to section 4. First, it is necessary to determine the rate at which the 50,000 pounds per day of BOD are being oxidized: if 10,000 pounds are oxidized in section 3, only 40,000 pounds will move on to section 4. Indeed, as we have already indicated, it is overly simple to use a single rate of oxidation (often called the "decay rate") for all BOD materials, since the rate at which nitrogenous oxidation occurs differs from that of carbonaceous oxidation. Even after we have determined the decay rates for FSUOD and SSUOD, however, our task will still not be completed. To know the impact of the pollution discharged into section 3 upon water quality in section 4, one must determine the rate at which BOD is moving from one section to the others. The rate of movement in turn is a function of two different factors: first, the faster the flow downstream the faster BOD will flow in that direction; second, if BOD is more concentrated in section 3 than section 4, there will be a natural tendency for it to diffuse into section 4. (Engineers call the latter process "dispersive transport."[9]) Thus it is necessary both to know the flow rate and to have some measure of the speed at which dispersive transport is taking place between sections. Using FSUOD and SSUOD decay rates, as well as stream flow rates and a coefficient measuring dispersive transport, the Thomann model predicts not only the BOD impact that polluters in section 3 will have on section 4 but also the BOD impact these polluters will have on each of the other sections in an analogous way.

---

unpublished; O'Connor, et al., 1968; Pence, et al., 1968; Pence, et al., 1970; Thomann, 1963; Thomann, 1968.

Despite this documentation, many substantial problems have never been canvassed in the published literature. The lack of complete documentation has made our task more difficult than it should have been. The failure to present a systematic and complete analysis of the Delaware stands in stark contrast to the 609-page report issued by a similar contemporaneous investigation of the Thames Estuary (see the *Thames Report*).

9. The rate at which pollutants move between sections via dispersive transport is affected by tidal action within the estuary, and this effect is taken into account in the construction of the model.

Similarly, using these same four factors, the model predicts the BOD load that polluters discharging into the other sections of the river will impose on section 3. By doing all this simultaneously, a set of BOD concentrations in the river can be predicted, given discharges from municipal and industrial sources. Similarly, if BOD loads from storm sewers and tributaries, as well as their oxidation rates, are known, an analogous calculation can be made, and the concentration of BOD in each section can then be determined by summing the contributions from each of the four sources —municipalities, industries, tributaries, and storm sewers.[10]

From this description, it should be reasonably clear that the following inquiries are necessary for an assessment of the accuracy of the model's first equation predicting BOD concentrations. How does the theoretical formulation deal with:

a.   FSUOD and SSUOD decay rates?

b.   storm sewer run-off and tributary loads?

c.   flow and dispersive transport?

If the model deals with any of these factors improperly, it will systematically misestimate the impact of BOD discharges on the DO profile.[11]

As we have already indicated,[12] the model's prediction of BOD concentrations in each of the 30 sections is only a preliminary step in the larger task of estimating the DO profile that can be expected from a given set of BOD loads. To move from BOD concentrations to DO profile, the DECS model must assess three factors that were irrelevant in the BOD prediction, but that are considered in the model's second equation, which concerns DO inputs and outputs in each section. First, the DECS model must calculate the saturation level of oxygen at a given temperature; second, it must calculate the rate at which oxygen will diffuse into the river as BOD creates a DO deficit in the section; third, it must take into account the fact that the sludge deposits on the bottom of each section of the river continually consume oxygen in the way we have described.

10. In the earlier discussion of BOD sources, a fifth source, benthic oxygen demand, was included. See text preceding Ch. 3, n. 11. In Thomann's model, however, this source is considered in a second equation dealing with DO levels, and so we shall discuss it at a later stage.
11. In addition to the factors mentioned in the text the model also contains a term that attempts to account for the impact on the DO curve of oxygen generated by photosynthetic activity. The DECS, however, assumed that no net oxygen demand was exerted by this force. We have already suggested, however, that this resolution of the problem is subject to serious question (see Ch. 3, n. 19).
12. See pp. 20–22.

There is little difficulty in measuring the solubility of oxygen in water, and hence the model's value for the saturation concentration of dissolved oxygen at a given temperature poses no serious problem. The same cannot be said for the other two steps by which the model moves from BOD concentration to DO prediction, and thus we shall consider in detail the treatment of (a) reaeration and (b) benthic demand.[13]

THE STEADY STATE ASSUMPTION

Using the DECS BOD-DO model, it is *in principle* possible to predict the Delaware's DO profile at any point in time. Of course, if the policy maker wishes to predict the DO profile for a particular day (say the July 4 peak vacation day), extensive data will be required by the model. Not only will it be necessary to hypothesize the flow, temperature, and BOD conditions prevailing on July 4, but it will also be necessary to assume that during the month before July 4 river conditions developed in a particular way, since the July 4 DO profile will in large measure depend on the pattern of temperature, flow rate, and BOD discharges prevailing during the previous 30 days. Moreover, an effort to predict the way in which DO will vary with time requires a relatively high expenditure on computational facilities —for example, an attempt to trace the way the Delaware's DO profile varies over the year as a result of hypothesized *weekly* changes in temperature, flow rate, and BOD inputs will require about 30 minutes' time of a highly sophisticated "third generation" IBM 360/75.[14] And, of course, before the policy maker could gain a modest insight into the probable effects over time of a given pollution control policy, a very large number of computer runs simulating a broad range of recurring river histories would be demanded.

To reduce the data base and computational resources required for a "time varying analysis" the DECS primarily attempted to predict the DO curve on the hypothesis that the *relevant river conditions remained constant over time*. This approach is so common to modelling efforts of diverse kinds that it has its own name: the "steady state" approach. Unfortunately, things are far from steady on the estuary. First, BOD loads vary substantially from day to day and throughout the year. Second, so does the flow

13. For readers who would prefer a mathematical description of the model, we have provided one in Appendix A in which the matters discussed in this section are presented in a mathematical format.
14. Interview with G.D. Pence, Jr., Delaware Estuary Comprehensive Survey Staff, in Edison, N.J., Oct. 1970.

rate. Third, DO varies over the course of the year, as the river's temperature moves from near-freezing to as high as 80°F. during the summer. As
the river gets colder, oxygen becomes increasingly soluble in water; for
example, at 40°F. fully saturated water contains 13 ppm of oxygen, while
at 80°F., it contains 8 ppm.[15] Thus, an oxygen-rich stream can oxidize
much greater quantities of BOD during the winter without endangering
aquatic life or generating noxious odors. Even if DO levels momentarily
drop to a relatively low level, the river's capacity for recovery is much
greater in the wintertime. This is because the farther away water is from
saturation, the faster oxygen diffuses into the river to redress the imbalance. Thus, if DO is 4 ppm and saturation is 16 ppm, oxygen will
diffuse three times more rapidly into the river than if the saturation level
of DO is 8 ppm,[16] as it is during the summer. Finally, the microorganisms
that consume BOD are much less active as water temperature declines. As
a consequence, discharges of BOD are oxidized more slowly in the colder
months, thereby permitting the increased rate of reaeration then prevailing
to counterbalance the oxidation process more rapidly. For this reason the
Delaware Estuary has no substantial DO depletion problem during the
winter. The oxygen sag is most acute from July through September, since
these months are characterized by high water temperatures, low oxygen
saturation levels, maximum biological activity, and minimum reaeration.

This situation permitted the DECS to attempt a "steady state" approach in analyzing important pollution problems. While it is fruitless to
indulge in "steady state" thinking to predict DO levels prevailing *over the
year,* if the model builder is willing to ignore all differences between any
particular summer day and the average day for the summer, it is plausible
to apply a "steady state" approach in an effort to predict average DO
throughout the summer. Although this technique simplified the DECS
fact-finding problem, it inevitably introduced an element of imprecision in

15. Camp, 1963, p. 292. The saturation solubility of oxygen in water is also a function of the water's salinity. According to DECS measurements, however, salinity
effects are minimal in the Delaware. (Letter from Prof. R. Thomann, Nov. 1971)
See also the *Thames Report,* 1964.
16. The appropriate differential equation may be written

$$\frac{d(C_s-C)}{dt} = -k_2(C_s-C)$$

where C_s represents the saturation concentration of DO, C represents the actual concentration of DO, and t represents time. In words, the equation states that the rate of
change of the oxygen deficit (C_s-C) with respect to time is proportional to the negative of the difference between the saturation concentration of DO and the actual
concentration of DO.

the "steady state" model.[17] As our analysis of the DECS equations proceeds, it will become clear that "steady state" thinking has important policy
implications that can be easily neglected by the fact finder anxious to reduce his own problem to manageable proportions. It is to the high credit
of the DECS, however, that it did not (like so many other studies) simply
ignore the limitations of the "steady state." In spite of the difficulties, the
staff applied Thomann's general model in an effort to explore the implications of changing river conditions in those cases in which this seemed
important to the rational formulation of policy. We shall assess the success
of these efforts to develop a more sophisticated "time varying" approach,
however, after the simpler "steady state" structure is analyzed.

SOURCES OF ERROR: THE BOD EQUATION

Treatment of Decay Rates

DRBC officials, using DECS data, report that in 1964 carbonaceous
oxygen-demanding materials dumped by industries and cities accounted
for 53 percent of the total BOD along the estuary, while nitrogenous
oxygen demand from these sources represented 22 percent of the total
load.[18] With the adoption of the new DRBC control program, however,
the relative importance of carbonaceous demand (FSUOD) and nitrogenous demand (SSUOD) will shift dramatically since, under DRBC requirements, each of the firms and cities bordering the estuary will be required
in the near future to build "secondary treatment" facilities that reduce
FSUOD by 87 to 93 percent but that reduce SSUOD to a much lesser
degree.[19] We must therefore scrutinize with special care the manner in
which the model predicts the impact SSUOD will have on DO after the
clean-up program is completed.

17. The DECS reports that the standard day-to-day deviation around the summer
average in a typical section of the river is 0.3 ppm. That is to say, if the DECS predicted the summer average DO concentration, the actual concentration would be
within 0.3 ppm of this value on approximately two days out of three and would be
within 0.6 ppm of this value on 95 percent of the days (Thomann, 1967, p. 22).
Given the methodological frailties in the DECS "verification" analysis, to be considered at pp. 56–62, we have, however, little confidence in the reliability of this
DECS estimate.
18. See Porges and Selzer, 1968, pp. 75, 80.
19. Most "primary" and "secondary" treatment plants are designed mainly for the
purpose of removing FSUOD. Measurements of the efficiency of SSUOD removal by
five different treatment plants may be found in Barth, et al., 1966, pp. 1208–18. The
Barth data indicate that treatment plants containing both primary and secondary
phases removed from 13 percent to 61 percent of SSUOD, with the average removal
being 33 percent.

As we have explained, laboratory tests indicate that no substantial nitrogenous demand is exerted by untreated waste until approximately 15 days after the substance is introduced into the water,[20] because a substantial period of time is required before nitrogen-consuming bacteria reproduce in such numbers that a significant oxygen demand ensues. To take into account the delayed response time, the DECS treated the nitrogenous component of a discharge as if it occurred at a place farther down the river than its actual point of entry.[21]

This procedure suffers from several important defects. Unlike laboratory water, the river contains large numbers of nitrogen-consuming microorganisms already present, feasting on previously discharged nitrogenous matter, at the time the BOD sample is discharged. Thus, it does not follow that the 15-day nitrogenous lag observed in the laboratory will also take place in the river.[22] Moreover, subsequent investigators have explained the nitrogen lag phenomenon on more plausible grounds, with which the DECS model altogether fails to deal. O'Connor, in a 1966 study of the DECS model,[23] argues persuasively that the microorganisms that oxidize nitrogenous waste do not thrive in conditions in which large carbonaceous loads deplete oxygen levels greatly. Consequently, when carbonaceous loadings are reduced, nitrifying bacteria—whose growth was formerly frustrated—will flourish and generate substantial oxygen demand *in precisely those areas in which the DO deficit is currently most critical.* This means that as the current DRBC program succeeds, the predictive powers of the model will progressively deteriorate, since the nitrogenous share of total load will be increasing and the distribution of this load will be altered and

20. See p. 21, Ch. 3; Barth, 1966, p. 1217.
21. The *Thames Report,* p. 212, provides a good statement of accepted doctrine concerning the delayed response of nitrogenous oxygen demand:

> This [delayed response] is believed to be because the concentration of nitrifying bacteria initially present is usually small and because the rate of growth of these organisms is slow, especially when compared with that of the heterotrophic bacteria which oxidize carbon; the rate of oxidation of nitrite to nitrate is particularly slow in the initial stages since it tends to be limited by the rate of formation of nitrite from ammonia.

22. Indeed, subsequent unpublished course materials prepared by Professor Thomann indicate that this assumption was faulty:

> In the BOD test, there is a pronounced lag between the carbonaceous oxidation and the nitrification step, the latter following by as much as ten days. The lag is less for the treated samples and is on the order of one or two days for highly treated effluents. In the stream, the two stages frequently proceed simultaneously, although there may be lags in the nitrification stage in highly polluted streams, or those with low dissolved oxygen. (Thomann, *Reactions,* undated ms., p. 24)

23. O'Connor, *Water Quality Analysis,* 1966, p. 45.

move upstream into the area between Philadelphia and the Pennsylvania-Delaware state line, the area of maximum oxygen deficit, in ways that the model was powerless to predict at the time of the DRBC decision.[24]

Not only, then, is there a source of error in the model's structure but it is one that will systematically yield overly optimistic predictions of the consequences of ambitious clean-up programs on the DO profile, especially in the most polluted river sections. We have not attempted to develop alternative modes of dealing with SSUOD in an effort to determine precisely the degree of error involved in the DECS model, since such an attempt would require very extensive theoretical and empirical investigation. Nevertheless, the importance of even a moderate error can scarcely be overestimated when it is recalled that the model is being used to delineate the costs and benefits of alternative water quality programs that may differ by hundreds of millions of dollars in cost but by only 1 ppm in their impact on the DO curve for the most polluted sections of the Delaware.[25]

In addition to the structural failures in the treatment of SSUOD decay, the DECS also utilized a questionable procedure in its attempt to measure decay rates for both FSUOD and SSUOD. The decay rate in each section was estimated from laboratory experiments on samples of Delaware River water from that section.[26] This would seem to be a sound method for estimating decay rates as of 1964 (before the cleanup) except for a caveat we shall discuss in a footnote.[27] But what of the situation after cleanup? There is no reason to believe that a decay rate for a given section in 1975, after clean-up measures are taken, will equal the decay rate in 1964. The best evidence available indicates that the more treatment wastes receive before entering the river, the slower will be the decay rate thereafter.[28]

24. *Ibid.,* pp. 51, 52.
25. Further work on this problem has been attempted subsequent to the publication of the "preliminary" DECS Report of 1966 and the DRBC decision of 1967. Our concern at this point in the essay, however, is to analyze in detail the validity of the information provided to the decision makers at the time they made their decision.
26. Interview with G.D. Pence, Jr., Delaware Estuary Comprehensive Survey staff, in Edison, N.J., July 1970.
27. The caveat centers on the DECS' assumption that the river water samples measured in the laboratory decay in the same manner as they would under river conditions. As two leading authorities point out, the assumption that the rate of consumption of organics in laboratory equipment is equal to the rate of consumption in natural waste "overlooks the fact that the biophysical as well as the biochemical environment of BOD bottles cannot possibly be like that of every kind of stream, even when the temperature of incubation of the bottles is that of the stream water" (Fair and Geyer, 1954, p. 835). Nevertheless, these authors assert that, in general, there seems to be a relatively good correlation between river and lab decay rates, as well as between laboratory and river BOD consumption rates (*ibid.,* pp. 835–36).
28. *Thames Report,* pp. 216, 226.

Thus as pollution loads on the river decrease, decay rates will probably decrease also. The effect of this will be to shift the oxygen sag downstream, though to what extent we cannot guess.

Combined Sewers and Raw Sewage

Four percent of the total BOD discharged into the river during the year is contributed by raw sewage discharged during heavy rains by the combined sewer systems of Trenton, Camden, Philadelphia, and Wilmington.[29] The relatively small annual contribution from this source, however, grossly understates its importance in policy formulation. The sewers do not discharge relatively small amounts of effluent continuously, but enormous quantities sporadically. Since the sewers overflow about ten days a year,[30] the 4 percent *annual* percentage means that the total BOD contributed by raw sewage during and after a stormy period can exceed the BOD from all other sources combined.[31] Moreover, the bulk of these untreated wastes will be emitted by Philadelphia and Camden, thereby threatening oxygen reserves at the core of the "critical area" already characterized by severe oxygen depletion. Thus, it is of prime importance to a decision maker to understand the impact raw sewage will have on DO on those occasions on which it is present in quantity. Indeed, if the model builder provided only the summer *average* DO anticipated in the critical region, in the manner conveyed by Table 2, the information could be profoundly misleading. For example, Table 2 reports that Objective II (costing $250 million) will achieve an average DO of 4 ppm during the summer, while Objective III (costing $120 million) will achieve an average DO of 3 ppm. Thus, on the surface, the more expensive program seems to promise more varied forms of aquatic life even in the heavily polluted region. If, however, the intermittent discharge of raw sewage will for sustained periods reduce DO levels to 2 ppm under Objective II and 1 ppm under Objective III, the more expensive program's promise of a more extensive aquatic life will be largely illusory, since living things must breathe all of the time, not most of the time. On the other hand, it *may* be that Objective II will assure varied aquatic life even during the intermittent inundations of raw sewage, while Objective III will not. But if there is a real difference between the two programs in this respect, it surely is not obvious. It is precisely issues of this kind that led decision makers to search for expert fact finders in the first place.

29. See p. 22, Ch. 3.
30. *Ibid.*
31. See the detailed calculation to be found in nn. 35, 36, following.

Despite its importance for the rational formulation of policy, the DECS "steady state" model was incapable of treating the storm overflow problem in a way that would clarify its dimensions; for it should be recalled [32] that the fundamental limitation of a "steady state" model lies precisely in its assumption that river conditions remain constant over time. Given this framework, the "steady state" model builders, in making their predictions, were forced to assume that the sewers were *constantly* emitting a BOD flow equal to 4 percent of the total loading. Consequently, the "summer average" DO level DECS associated with each of the proposed programs slightly understates the DO that could be anticipated during dry spells but grossly overstates the impact of pollution control during and after heavy rains. Thus "steady state" thinking could easily induce policy makers to overestimate the benefits of embarking on any of the programs under consideration: it obscures the probability that *none* of these programs would significantly alter environmental conditions *unless the sewer problem was resolved*. Once this possibility is raised, its policy implications can be seen to have critical importance. If it is necessary to eliminate the storm sewer problem in order to generate substantial environmental improvements in the "critical sections," the costs of meaningful pollution control become enormous. "Solving" the raw sewage problem would require a city like Philadelphia to rip up most of its busy streets and replace the present piping system with one that would prevent raw sewage from sweeping into the Delaware during heavy rains. To accomplish this objective, it would be necessary to segregate sanitary sewage from rain water run-off by channelling wastes into a piping system completely separate from the one used to transport rainwater. In this two-pipe system, which is common in more recently developed communities, municipal treatment plants are not overloaded with rainwater for the simple reason that the rain pipes conduct the relatively unpolluted run-off to the river directly. Since the water in the pipe carrying domestic and industrial waste does not expand during the stormy periods, it is perfectly feasible for the city plant to treat the waste on foul, as well as fair, days before discharging it into the river. While installing a two-pipe system would solve the raw sewage problem, such a solution not only would cause Philadelphia's inhabitants substantial inconvenience but would cost the public a sum in excess of a billion dollars. [33]

32. See pp. 37–39.
33. The cost of separating the combined sewer systems presently serving some 60 million Americans are enormous, with estimates seeming to cluster around the $50 billion figure (see Council on Environmental Quality, *Annual Report*, 1971, p. 145; Starr and Carlson, 1968, pp. 104, 122). While no solid estimates for Philadelphia have been developed we have encountered no knowledgeable observer who would dispute the billion-dollar price tag suggested in the text.

Are costs of this magnitude worth the benefits to be gained when, even after the sewer problem is solved, it is far from clear that the river's critical section will be a pleasant place for swimming (let alone a refuge for the sensitive man seeking communion with nature)? If, however, the cost of installing new piping systems far exceeds the benefits, what is the justification for embarking on *any* of the quality improvement programs tendered by DECS to DRBC? Is there any reason to believe that, *absent the elimination of raw sewage,* the reduction of BOD from other sources contemplated by Objectives I or II or III or IV will significantly improve the bleak environmental picture in the critical region? Lacking a thoroughgoing effort to clean up the Delaware, will half-measures, however expensive, make a real difference? When faced with the costs of a thoroughgoing effort, do we still want to clean up the critical region? These fundamental questions can be avoided only by remaining within the confines of "steady state" thinking; for once the intermittent flood of raw sewage is treated as if it were a constant trickle, the policy problems evaporate.

While the cost–benefit analysis presented in Table 2 does not transcend the "steady state" approach and hence fails to consider these basic questions, the DECS scientific staff, led by Dr. Thomann, attempted some time varying analyses which cast light on the importance of the storm run-off problem. For example, the staff's model predicted that a sudden temporary impulse of 200,000 pounds of BOD introduced into section 15 (in the middle of the river's critical region) would induce a temporary decline of .15 ppm of DO in that section during the following week.[34] The DECS staff, however, nowhere suggests that storm run-off will be limited to a mere 200,000 pounds when it occurs.[35] Rather, as we have suggested, DECS data indicate that a heavy storm may induce *an impulse far in excess of one million* pounds of FSUOD per day in the critical region.[36] Thus if

---

34. DECS, p. 41, Fig. 29. The maximum decrease in DO is predicted to occur some two or three days after the 200,000 pounds are introduced into the system. Of course, the discharge in section 15 also has a significant impact in other sections. For example, the maximum decrease in DO in section 18 is .1 ppm and occurs five days after discharge, while in section 24 (downstream from the "critical zone" of oxygen depletion) the maximum impact is about .02 ppm some two weeks after the discharge.

35. In discussing these findings in its 1966 Report, the DECS does not even refer to the problem posed by raw sewage run-off. Its calculation of a .15 ppm DO decline is premised upon the analysis of a "short duration discharge such as an accidental spill" (*ibid.*, p. 41).

36. We arrive at this conclusion by two different and complementary routes. DECS indicates that, at present, Philadelphia's three major plants discharge 450,000 pounds of FSUOD per day after the waste is treated by presently existing processes that remove approximately half of the FSUOD. Thus, when a major rainfall requires the plants to dump their wastes without treating them, it is reasonable to expect an added impulse of 450,000 pounds of FSUOD per day to be imposed on the system. More-

the 4 ppm *summer average* predicted for the critical region by the DECS "steady state" model *had been correct in all other respects,* a time varying analysis would imply that during the week after a heavy storm, DO in the Philadelphia metropolitan area could plummet to 3 ppm or even less.[37] Unfortunately, while the DECS time varying effort itself suggested the seriousness of the storm sewer problem, the implications of its analysis were not articulated in the report tendered to decision makers in 1966.

Loads Imposed by Nonestuarine Branches of the Delaware Basin

A similar defect afflicts the DECS treatment of the loads imposed on the estuary by the Upper Delaware[38] and the tributaries of the main stem.

---

over, the organic debris on the city's streets will also be swept into the river without treatment, adding an unknown but surely very substantial BOD input. Similarly, Camden's two plants, after treatment (of about 50 percent), discharged 62,250 pounds in 1964 and so can be expected to impose an extra impulse of 62,500 pounds during storms, together with a substantial addition contributed by street debris. Thus, under 1964 conditions, BOD well in excess of 500,000 pounds of FSUOD will be introduced by Philadelphia and Camden. Under the pollution control program adopted by the DRBC (a variant of Program II in Table 2), however, both cities will be required to reduce FSUOD by 85 to 90 percent instead of 50 percent. Thus, when treatment is made impossible by storm overflow, these cities will contribute each day of the storm an added impulse of one million pounds of FSUOD plus the very considerable quantity of street debris flushed into the river by the rain.

An even more depressing conclusion can be reached by considering another set of DECS data. Since it is reported that storm overflow accounts for 4 percent of the annual load on the estuary, and since it is also reported that overflow occurs approximately ten times a year (Porges and Seltzer, 1968, pp. 75, 80), simple mathematical calculation indicates that the impulse of untreated sewage for an average storm will be 2.5 to 3 million pounds of BOD. Since the bulk of these wastes will be contributed by Philadelphia and Camden, the consequences of the storm sewer problem seem even more serious than the preceding discussion suggests.

37. Since the model's equations are linear there is no difficulty in assuming, as does the text, that if 200,000 pounds of BOD depresses DO by .15 ppm, one million pounds will depress DO by exactly five times that amount.

It is also true that not all of the storm overflow will be imposed in only one of the estuary's "critical sections"; nevertheless, it is clear that the bulk will be imposed over no more than a six- or seven-mile stretch of the river, and it is equally clear (see n. 34 herein) that this distance will not substantially ameliorate the storm run-off's impact on DO.

38. It is not clear exactly what figure was used by DECS to represent the average load imposed by the Upper Delaware on the estuary at Trenton. While the published literature indicates that 22,000 pounds was used as the FSUOD loading (see table at Ch. 3, n. 17), there has clearly been an omission of a large load of approximately 86,000 pounds in the tributary inputs listed in the table, since the individual loads do not sum up to the total load. Contradicting the published work, an unpublished chapter of the final DECS Report indicates the existence of an FSUOD load at Trenton of 84,933 pounds and an SSUOD load at Trenton of 84,593 pounds. When we inquired at the DRBC concerning this substantial discrepancy we were told that the initial loadings used were corrected upward. It is unclear, however, whether any effort has been made to chart the DO consequences of this substantial adjustment of BOD inputs.

DECS reports that in 1964, 12 percent of total FSUOD was contributed by these sources.[39] Once again, however, these loads do not remain constant over time; there is a periodic cycle in which BOD inputs reach an annual peak between April and June as a result of the normal spring thaw. Thus during April 1964 the Upper Delaware contributed an average of 168,500 pounds of FSUOD each day to the estuary while during August only 40,200 pounds were discharged.[40] Nevertheless, in its mathematical model the DECS used an annual average to express this load. The significance of ignoring seasonal variations of such substantial dimensions can be appreciated when it is recognized that Philadelphia, the largest polluter along the estuary, was limited to 131,500 pounds of FSUOD under the allocation plan adopted by the DRBC.[41]

The DECS treatment of the tributaries and Upper Delaware was defective in yet another respect. Our inspection of unpublished DECS documents reveals[42] that the study assumed that in this case SSUOD was equal to FSUOD. From all that appears in the unpublished documentation—which is inadequate—no data exist to support this assumption.[43] Thus once again the DECS treatment of nitrogenous demand appears to suffer from an overly large dose of simplification.[44]

---

39. See Ch. 3, n. 14 and p. 22.

40. DECS Report No. BDZ (basic stream quality data sheets nos. 27 & 28: estimates based on unpublished data from Water Resources Div., Geological Survey, U.S. Dep't of the Interior [available in file no. 4639, Trenton, New Jersey]).

41. Philadelphia's three municipal plants contributed about 45 percent of the carbonaceous load discharged by all of the polluters bordering the estuary in 1964. Its DRBC allocation may be found in an unpublished table of waste load allocations provided by the DRBC, on file in Biddle Law Library, University of Pennsylvania.

42. These documents have been made available to us by an anonymous nongovernmental source.

43. Professor Thomann explains that the 1:1 ratio of FSUOD to SSUOD is "generally supported" by available sanitary engineering literature (Letter to the authors, Nov. 1971). However this may be, the ratio is not supported by empirical study of the relevant tributarial conditions, and it does not seem consistent with the FSUOD-SSUOD ratios that were generated by measurements on the Delaware's main stem, which suggested that SSUOD played a smaller role than is implied by the 1:1 relationship.

44. The reader will recall that the model also attempts to relate flow and dispersive transport to the distribution of BOD concentrations on the estuary. See pp. 35, 36. So far as flow is concerned, no significant conceptual or measurement problem arises. Although many problems arise in the treatment of dispersive transport, these issues may safely be ignored by the average reader, since DO predictions are insensitive even to large changes in the dispersive transport coefficient. (Telephone conversation with R.A. Norris of Quirk, Lawler, and Matusky, Consulting Eng'rs, N.Y.C., Aug. 1970; interview with N. Jaworski, Middle Atlantic Region FWQA, in Annapolis, Aug. 1970; interview with G.D. Pence, Jr., Delaware Estuary Comprehensive Survey staff, in Edison, N.J., July 1970) For a more detailed discussion, see Hetling, 1968; Paulson, 1969; Paulson, 1970.

The BOD Equation: Proof of the Pudding

Our discussion of the BOD equation suggests that its use to predict BOD concentrations along the length of the estuary will generate significant errors. While there are elements in the DECS' approach that may over-estimate the amount of BOD afflicting the estuary during the summer months,[45] the BOD analysis as a whole is unduly optimistic in its appraisal of the possibilities of cleanup. Especially in its treatment of nitrogenous demand and the raw sewage discharged by combination sewers the analysis conceals highly important factors that may well erode substantially (or entirely) the benefits anticipated from the various program options prof-fered by the DECS to the political actors on the DRBC.[46] Given the limited resources at our command, we have been unable to undertake the substantial work required before a precise estimate of the model's error could be attempted. We are aware, however, of one study in which a skilled investigator has attempted to determine the extent to which the DECS model accurately predicts BOD. When Professor O'Connor con-sidered this question in a 1966 paper, DECS provided him with all their data, thereby permitting him to determine in a reliable way the power of the model's BOD equation. When O'Connor compared the predicted and actual BOD profiles, he found extraordinary disparities between DECS estimates and the river's realities. Figure 5 graphically demonstrates the extreme discrepancies.

O'Connor's data demonstrate a consistent tendency of DECS to under-state the magnitude of BOD concentrations in the estuary, providing addi-tional evidence of the overoptimistic tendency we have adduced.[47]

---

45. We refer to the likely change in decay rate after the DRBC's treatment program is effectuated (see text accompanying n. 27 herein) and the use of an annual average to depict the impact of BOD introduced by the Upper Delaware on summer DO (see pp. 45, 46).

46. See Table 2 and text at pp. 31–33.

47. O'Connor, 1966, Fig. 11. O'Connor notes that "The correlation of BOD data is observed to be unsatisfactory." He then adds, "However, if a background level of 2.0 mg/l, a value frequently observed above known sources of pollution at Trenton, is assigned to the system, better agreement would be realized." (O'Connor, 1966, p. 48). These two short sentences constitute his complete discussion of the discrepancy in-volved and, given the importance of ascertaining the reliability of the model's BOD predictions, are extraordinarily laconic. Moreover, the suggestion that the model's predictive powers should be improved by adding an arbitrary constant of 2 ppm is advocating the use of a "fudge" factor well known in engineering circles. Such factors have two notable defects. First, they represent unexplained behavior in the system; it is more productive to recognize this harsh reality than to gloss over it. Second, fudge factors may not remain constant over time, as O'Connor assumes. Even if one were to assign the 2 ppm background level as O'Connor suggests, one would have no way of knowing whether an identical constant should be assigned after clean-up

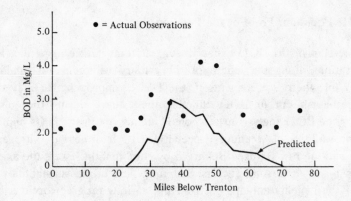

Figure 5
Comparison of Actual and Predicted BOD for August 1964
(*From* Delaware Estuary Comprehensive Study)

THE DO EQUATION

Thus far, our analysis has focused on the first of the two equations used in the DECS model, the purpose of which was to predict BOD concentrations along the estuary. On the basis of these concentrations, the model's second equation calculates expected DO concentrations. Analysis of this "DO equation" reveals two important additional sources of error.

Reaeration

In a river suffering an oxygen deficit, oxygen begins to move through the air-water interface, reducing the deficit over time until the saturation point of DO is reached. One of the major tasks of the DECS' DO equation is to describe accurately the rate at which this reaeration process takes place. Two major difficulties arise with the model's estimation of reaeration rate —one is of fundamental conceptual importance; the other involves the way in which reaeration is measured. As is often the case, the error in conception and the error in measurement are closely related.

The technical literature contains numerous proposed equations for the prediction of reaeration coefficients (constants reflecting the rate at which

activities have been completed. Thus, it is evident that the model predicts BOD behavior very badly, and the introduction of "assigned" factors, as suggested by O'Connor, would only make the problem worse. The way to handle "background BOD," if empirical data prove this concept tenable, would be to include it explicitly as a term in the model's predicting equations.

oxygen is replaced by aeration), yielding values that vary substantially from one another. DECS used values, for example, derived from a 1958 paper by O'Connor and Dobbins [48] that vary considerably from those proposed by more recent researchers. [49] We have provided the reader with a footnote illustrating these substantial differences in tabular form. [50]

The differences in measurement, however, only suggest a fundamental conceptual problem. Overwhelming evidence developed by British investigators supports the intuitive notion that wind velocity at the water's surface is a critical determinant of reaeration rate. When the wind was blowing at 20 miles per hour, oxygen entered the Thames more than five times as rapidly as when there was no wind. [51] Yet none of the estimates cited above considers wind velocity. Moreover, the O'Connor-Dobbins equation was

48. O'Connor and Dobbins, 1958. For evidence of the DECS' reliance on the O'Connor-Dobbins equation, see Pence, et al., 1968, p. 381.
49. Krenkel, unpublished ms.; Churchill, et al., 1962. See also Krenkel and Orlob, 1962.
50. As the following chart indicates, the reaeration rate is a function of channel depth and flow rate, among other factors (see *Water Quality Model*, p. 44). The

Values of Reaeration Coefficients

For a deep channel (40′)	O'Connor and Dobbins	Churchill	Krenkel and Orlob
Velocity 1′/sec	0.051	0.024	0.063
2	0.072	0.048	0.125
3	0.088	0.072	0.188
4	0.102	0.096	0.250
For a shallow channel (5′)			
Velocity 1′/sec	0.407	0.249	0.250
2	0.577	0.498	0.500
3	0.706	0.747	0.750
4	0.814	0.996	1.000

complexity of the process of estimating reaeration rates will be appreciated when it is noted that the depth of the Delaware Estuary varies from 16 to 34 feet (see Pence, et al., 1968, p. 390). Flow velocities in the Delaware, at the Delaware Memorial Bridge, moreover, vary from −3 ft/sec to +3 ft/sec as a consequence of tidal action (see DECS, p. 13). This further complicates the analysis.

Dr. Clifford Russell, of Resources for the Future, in his extremely useful written commentary on an earlier draft of this chapter, suggests that our criticism of the DECS' reliance on the O'Connor-Dobbins reaeration coefficients ignores the fact that the values for deep channels like the Delaware generally fall between the values given by the other two equations. While this is true, we do not find it overly comforting. Although the values do fall between the other two sets, there remains a very substantial disparity among the three equations which remains extremely important given the admitted sensitivity of the DECS' DO prediction to the particular reaeration coefficients selected.
51. *Thames Report,* pp. 357–58.

derived principally from a study of nontidal rivers.[52] Since "[in] an estuary the adjustment for the effects of waves is likely to be of greater importance than in fresh-water streams"[53] because of increased wind velocities and tidal action, the accuracy of the O'Connor-Dobbins equation in the context of the Delaware seems doubtful.

More is involved than the question whether the DECS equation is correct. At stake is the validity of the DECS' assumption that reaeration can be described properly by the use of an equation not containing wind velocity as an independent variable. The Thames study, which was available to DECS, demonstrates that this assumption is untenable,[54] and we are frankly at a loss to understand why the DECS never confronted the problem. Once the issue is articulated, it is apparent not only that wind velocity should be included but that no single reaeration coefficient can be expected to prevail in a given section at all times. Instead, a sophisticated approach would first attempt to determine the range of probable values associated with varying wind velocities on each section of the Delaware. Then, at a minimum, it would develop a coefficient based on the average wind speed in the section under consideration. In fact, it would be possible to develop a more sensitive approach that would explicitly make reaeration a function of wind velocity. If this were done, one could give the administrator an indication of the range in which DO would fluctuate as wind speed changed. The importance of the DECS' failure to conceptualize the reaeration problem properly, which led to the use of a questionable coefficient, is recog-

52. It should be noted, however, that some measurements taken from the San Diego Bay agreed with the predicted values rather well. An examination of the Thames Report on this problem suggests that the agreement between San Diego Bay data and the estimating equation is probably a coincidence (*Thames Report* 1964, p. 569) A recent paper makes the DECS methodology appear even more vulnerable. Juliano, 1969, p. 1165, 1176–77 reports:

> Extensive measurements and investigation of the reaeration constant and its controlling mechanisms suggests [sic] that surface reaeration in the Sacramento-San Joaquin Delta does not lend itself to mathematical definition.
> ... [T]he writer feels that reaeration is best determined by methods which take into account each system's unique environmental conditions. . . .
> Surface turbulence proved to be the most important factor controlling diffusion. Wind velocity is the most significant parameter causing surface turbulence. A specific wind velocity will result in varying degrees of surface turbulence depending on channel size and configuration, tidal phase, levee height, and wind direction. This accounts for the appearance of a more or less random variation in reaeration.
> ... The magnitude of surface reaeration is best determined by in situ measurements which consider the complex action and interactions of environmental factors effecting the reaeration constant.

53. *Thames Report,* p. 569.
54. *Loc. cit.*

nized once one takes into account the candid admission by the DECS staff, supported by the testimony of other experts who have worked with similar models, that the model's predictions are extremely sensitive to changes in the reaeration value.[55]

Benthic Demand

The final component in the DO equation deals with the benthic oxygen demand resulting from sludge deposits on the bottom of the river. The model assumes that a pollution control program that reduces BOD loads from other sources does not affect the level of benthic demand. The load was 230,000 pounds in 1964, and it is assumed that it will remain so indefinitely.[56] While this is obviously a simplification, its speculative character is revealed by both the Thames study and students of the Delaware who have worked independently of DECS. The English report reveals that sludge samples containing large numbers of a common worm ("tubificid," to be precise) exert an oxygen demand ten times that of an identical sample without worms.[57] At present, these worms exist in large numbers in the Delaware; they are plentiful enough to support the activity of local entrepreneurs who harvest the worms and sell some 600 gallons per day (272 million worms) to tropical fish stores as feed.[58] It appears likely, therefore, that a substantial portion of the benthic demand may ultimately be traced to the oxygen requirements of the worms, which are one of the organisms that can live at extremely low DO levels.

As oxygen levels increase as a result of the clean-up program, the number of worms may be expected to multiply, thereby radically increasing the benthic demand levels. As oxygen levels increase, the worms' natural predators may also multiply in the area, killing off some of the worms and creating a new ecological equilibrium at which benthic demand will assume some new value; but even this is speculative.[59] Thus, the model's

55. Telephone conversation with R. A. Norris of Quirk, Lawler, and Matusky, Consulting Eng'rs, N.Y.C., Aug. 1970; interview with N. Jaworski, Middle Atlantic Region FWQA, in Annapolis, Aug. 1970; interview with G.D. Pence, Jr., Delaware Estuary Comprehensive Survey staff, in Edison, N.J., July 1970; letter from R. Thomann, Nov. 1971.
56. See Ch. 3, n. 17.
57. *Thames Report,* pp. 205–06.
58. Cox, unpublished ms., r 91.
59. Dr. Russell, of Resources for the Future, reports to us that an ecologist serving on the RFF staff, when questioned concerning the problem posed in the text, responded that "If one is talking about increases in DO from near zero to, say, 2 or 3 ppm, it may be that the worm population would increase substantially. If, on the other hand, the expected increases are from 2 or 3 ppm to something higher, it is

simplistic assumption that the benthic load will remain immutable is suspect. We are especially concerned that neither the DECS nor the DRBC has ever seriously considered the question, despite the possibility that the worms will multiply exponentially and thereby significantly offset the impact of the BOD cutbacks made on other fronts.[60]

There is reason to believe that the DECS' failure to confront the worm problem not only has led to a faulty prediction regarding the Delaware of the future, but also has permitted a misestimate of benthic demand in the river of today. Research by one of Professor Zemaitas' doctoral students, Dr. Geraldine Cox, indicates that the DECS staff measured benthic demand in samples containing no live worms.[61] This means that the 230,000 pounds of oxygen demand attributed to benthic demand by the DECS could be a serious underestimate of present conditions.[62] The problem is made even more complex by the fact that, according to Dr. Cox, the worms are not distributed evenly throughout the river bed, making a sophisticated biological survey a necessity if one is to have an accurate view of the problem.[63]

We must conclude, then, that the DECS modelling effort was once again seriously limited by its failure to deal with the problem of change over time. In its treatment of reaeration rates, the DO equation failed to

---

very likely that the growth of a predator population will result in a significant decrease in the worm population." (Letter to the authors, Aug. 1971) We do not, of course, suggest that this is anything more than a guess, made without the intensive analysis that would justify a moderately confident prediction. Nevertheless, the guess does seem to suggest the merit of further consideration, since—as we have suggested—it is far from clear whether DO around Philadelphia will be higher or lower than 3 ppm after the present pollution program is effectuated.

60. Professor Zemaitas of Drexel University believes this likely. (Personal communications with Dr. Zamaitas in Philadelphia, Aug. 1970, Sept. 1970, and Mar. 1971)

61. Cox, unpublished ms., p. 70.

62. In a memorandum to the Industrial Subcommittee of the DECS, one of the attachments summarizing a presentation delivered to the group by Dr. Thomann reported that the oxygen uptake rates of bottom material on the Delaware Estuary measured by the DECS were about half those reported in the literature. (Memorandum from L. Falk, Industrial Representative to U.S. Public Health Service, DECS, Technical Advisory Committee, Industrial Subcommittee, Sept. 30, 1965, at Exhibit B—Minutes of Technical Advisory Committee meeting for Sept. 8, 1965)

63. Loc. cit. This would help explain the fact that in the DECS samples the worms were not even considered a problem. Indeed, it is claimed they were not present. (Interview with G.D. Pence, Jr., Delaware Estuary Comprehensive Survey staff, Dec. 1970) In his written comments on an earlier draft of this study, Professor Thomann, disagreeing with his DECS colleague, G.D. Pence, Jr., recollects that sludge worms were present in some of the sludge samples collected. (Letter to the authors from Prof. Thomann, Nov. 1971) It is not clear from Professor Thomann's commentary whether these worms were dead or alive when the oxygen demand of the samples was ascertained. However this may be, it remains clear that the DECS did not investigate the problem seriously.

recognize the importance of constantly varying wind speeds on the process being modelled; similarly, benthic demand was described as if it were an immutable fact of nature, while in reality it is a dynamic process intimately affected by a larger ecological dynamic.

BEYOND THE STEADY STATE:
THE TIME VARYING MODEL

Despite the profound policy limitations of an approach which so ignored the fact of temporal variation, the DECS decision to put first priority on generating a set of "steady state" DO predictions made a good deal of sense from the scientific perspective. Thomann's basic model was, after all, untested on an estuary; thus it was wisest to assess the model by simplifying the real world as much as possible without so departing from reality that the model's predictive powers could not be ascertained at all. Since during the summer months river flow rates and temperatures were relatively constant[64] it was desirable to use a steady state approach to predict the summer average DO profile, as a first attempt to test the reliability of the Thomann construction.

We have, however, demonstrated that, especially in its treatment of storm sewer run-off and the loadings imposed on the river by the upper Delaware beyond Trenton as well as the tributaries of the main stem, steady state methodology served to conceal important policy dimensions from the decision maker.[65] Equally important, steady state thinking proved inadequate when it was recognized that the estuary's pollution problems were not completely restricted to summer months. Each spring, adult Atlantic shad swim through the estuary on the way to and from their spawning grounds in the upper reaches of the Delaware; each fall, juvenile shad swim through the estuary and out to the sea. During these migration periods, temperature and flow conditions on the estuary fluctuate dramatically. In the beginning of April 1964 (when the shad began their move upstream)[66] the river's temperature was 49°F.[67] while the temperature in early June 1964 (when the last of the shad left the estuary for the upstream waters)[68] was 72°F.[69] Similarly, the flow at Trenton in April was 15,000

64. As we shall see, however, things are not so very steady even during the summer. See nn 81 and 92 herein.
65. See pp. 42–46.
66. Morris and Pence, unpublished ms., p. 5.
67. Pence, et al., 1968, p. 392.
68. Morris and Pence, unpublished ms., p. 5.
69. Pence, et al., 1968, p. 392.

cubic feet per second (cfs), while by June it had fallen to between 4000–5000 cfs.[70] Analogous changes occur during the fall when the young shad travel to the ocean.[71] When the survival of the shad became an important issue in the political process defining the water quality objectives for the Delaware, the model builders were invited to define more precisely the degree to which adoption of each of the five competing quality programs would protect the shad in their struggle up- and downstream.

In undertaking this task, it was apparent to the DECS that, given the wide variations in flow rate and temperature during the migration periods, it would be pointless to use a steady state approach. Instead, the staff attempted to develop a time varying model that could take into account the impact of changing conditions. In its basic conceptual structure, this model is identical to the one we have already analyzed: it deals with the lag in nitrogenous oxidation, FSUOD and SSUOD decay rates, dispersive transport, reaeration, and benthic demand in the same way as did the steady state model.[72] All our criticisms of that model's use of these basic concepts apply here with equal force.[73] Moreover, in moving to a time varying analysis, the DECS staff did not desert its steady state thinking with regard to a fundamental factor, and thereby further undermined the reliability of its conclusions. While the model builders did vary temperature and flow conditions to mirror typical patterns obtaining during the spring and fall migrations, the shad studies failed to take into account the way in which the DO profile varied with the temporal variation in BOD loadings, assuming instead that throughout the spring and fall all BOD inputs remained constant at their average annual level. This assumption was especially hazardous because the model attempted to describe transient conditions. Most important, it is quite untenable to treat storm overflow and BOD loadings from the Upper Delaware as if they were constant over time. Furthermore, our interviews with polluters reveal that a substantial number of them expect their secondary treatment plants to be less effective in the colder months than in the summer.[74] All this was ignored by the

---

70. *Ibid.*
71. In 1964, the flow rate at Trenton stayed fairly constant at about 2200 cfs throughout the fall until late December. The temperature fell rapidly from 78°F. in late August, to 63°F. in late September, to 60°F. in late October, to 50° in late November (see Morris and Pence, unpublished ms.). Apparently river conditions for shad survival are most critical in the spring months (*ibid.*).
72. Pence, et al., 1968, pp. 383–84.
73. See pp. 39–42, n. 44, and pp. 48–53.
74. The effectiveness of sewage treatment plants is strongly related to the rate of biological activity of the microorganisms that consume BOD in the treatment facility before the waste is discharged into the river. The rate of this activity drops significantly as temperature decreases, thereby reducing the percentage of BOD removed in the plant.

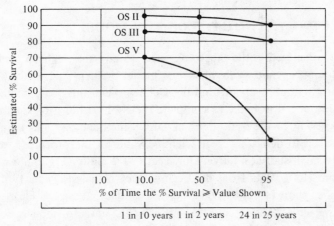

Figure 6
Estimated Upstream Shad Passage for Objectives II, III and V
(*From* Delaware Estuary Comprehensive Study)

DECS in estimating the impact each clean-up level would have on the survival of shad. Instead, using the model with all these defects, the staff provided the DRBC with a chart that attempted to delineate the shad's prospects under alternative BOD cutback regimes. The graph in Figure 6 indicates that under river conditions likely to prevail 50 percent of the time, ambitious pollution programs like those required to implement OS II and III will significantly increase the percentage of shad surviving the trip through the estuary. While the model predicts that at least 60 percent of the shad will survive under present conditions (Objective V), at least 85 percent will survive under Objective III and 95 percent under Objective II. This substantial difference becomes even greater in the 50 percent of the years during which river conditions accentuate the impact of waste discharges on the DO profile. Thus under present conditions, the model predicts, no more than 40 percent of the shad will survive their spring migration during the one worst year in every three, while only 20 percent will complete their journey in the four worst years in every century. In contrast, survival rates remain high under Objectives III and II.

We do not mean to flail a dead horse. We shall say only that we think it remarkable that at no point in the DECS' 1966 report is there any indication of the limitations on the value of these predictions.[76]

75. DECS, p. 60.
76. Nor is there any such indication in a paper on this subject written by two DECS staff members (see Morris and Pence, unpublished ms.). For a further discussion of the DECS' effort to quantify the chances of shad survival, see pp. 120–123, Ch. 8.

APPRAISING THE UTILITY OF THE MODEL

We have attempted in the preceding pages to give the reader a lively sense of the complex reality with which the model builders had to deal in their ambitious attempt to understand the Delaware and the many compromises they were obliged to make to complete their job within a reasonable time. Our discussion of the limitations of DECS methodology and data should not be taken to deny the great scientific value of the project. After all, a relatively small staff at relatively low cost ($1.2 million) within a relatively short time (four years from the beginning of actual study in 1962 to the first public report in 1966) constructed a model that was an effort at comprehensive understanding and has served as the basis for models developed for such estuaries as the Hudson,[77] the Potomac,[78] and the San Joaquin.[79] Indeed it is precisely the path-breaking character of the investigation that gives importance to our question: Given the fact that DECS represented the frontier of applied scientific fact finding in 1966, to what extent did it help or hinder the decision maker in defining policy?

Apart from indicating the sources of error in the model's construction and in its data base, we have taken special care to focus upon those features that tended to lead the DECS to be either overly optimistic or pessimistic in their assessment of the impacts alternative clean-up programs will have on the river's DO profile. Our discussion of the DECS treatment of nitrogenous oxygen demand, raw sewage emitted by storm sewers, and benthic oxygen demand leads us to conclude that, in the aggregate,[80] the DECS' analysis substantially underestimated the difficulty of improving environmental quality in the so-called critical region of the estuary. Particularly troublesome is the fact that, at least as far as benthic and nitrogenous demand is concerned, the model's predictive powers will deteriorate with a substantial change of the status quo. Thus the degree to which the model successfully explains the present DO profile does not constitute an entirely adequate indication of its utility to a policy maker who is principally concerned with the degree to which the model will successfully predict the future conditions that will result from the implementation of far-reaching pollution control measures. Nevertheless, the model's ability to

---

77. Telephone communication with R.A. Norris of Quirk, Lawler, and Matusky, Consulting Eng'rs, N.Y.C., Aug. 1970.
78. Hetling, *Potomac Estuary,* 1968; Hetling, *Water Quality Model,* 1968. Interview with N. Jaworski, Chesapeake Technical Support Laboratory, Middle Atlantic Region, FWQA, in Annapolis, July 1970.
79. Hetling, *Water Quality Model,* 1968.
80. For the countervailing factors, see n. 45.

describe present conditions provides some indication of its trustworthiness in the future, and so we shall investigate this matter in some detail.

DECS attempted to "verify" its model by comparing the actual DO profiles observed on the Delaware each week during the summers of 1964 and 1966 with the DO profile that the model predicted would occur during these two seasons.[81] At no point in the DECS' 1966 report, however, was there any precise indication of the degree to which the model's 1964 predictions were erroneous.[82] In our conversations with both state and DRBC officials, though, there seemed a broad consensus that the model's predictions had a "standard error" of .5 ppm.[83, 84] This means that the *predicted* summer average DO in each of the 30 sections would not diverge more than .5 ppm from the *actual* summer DO in about two out of three sum-

81. To calculate the average DO profile on the river during 1964 and 1966, the DECS took weekly readings of the DO level prevailing in most of the river's 30 sections. It was then possible to derive a summer average for each section simply by calculating the arithmetic mean of the weekly samples tested. Unfortunately, the DECS definition of the season changed between 1964 and 1966. In 1964, data collected during June, July, and August were used for the verification analysis; in 1966, data for July, August, and September were substituted.

We do not know for certain why the DECS definition of a summer changed over so short a time. However, as the following table shows, June 1966 was a relatively rainy month, in which the flow of the Delaware was quite high:

Flow Rate at Trenton (cfs)

	June	July	August	September
1964	4437	3102	2472	2136
1966	6215	2554	2484	2726

Source: Water Resources Division, *New Jersey,* 1964, p. 88; Water Resources Division, *Pennsylvania,* 1966, Part 1, p. 47.

Given the DECS model's use of a steady state approach, if the DECS had tested its predictions in 1966 for the months June–August, the dissimilarity between the flow in June 1966 and that in July and August of 1966 would probably have dramatically increased the error in the model's predictions. Thus the shift in definition could conceivably have its source in a desire to put the model's reliability in its best light.
82. The clearest statement concerning verification to be found in the DECS Report states that the comparisons between predicted and actual results "indicate that the model can be used with a *sufficient* degree of accuracy" (DECS, p. 40, [emphasis added]).
83. Interviews with state and DRBC officials, who wish to remain anonymous.
84. The most common measure of error used by engineers to evaluate the validity of this sort of model is the "root mean squared error," or "standard error." It is defined as the square root of the sum of the squares of the differences between the predicted and actual values divided by the number of differences. For example, suppose we are examining a phenomenon that has successive average values of 1.0, 2.0, 3.0, 4.0, and 5.0. If our model predicts successively 1.0, 1.5, 3.2, 5.0, and 6.5, the differences are 0, −0.5, 0.2, 1.0, and 1.5. The squares of the differences are 0, 0.25, 0.04, 1.0, and 2.25. The sum of the squares of the differences is 3.54. And 3.54/5 is approximately 0.71. Thus, the square root of 0.71, or about 0.84, is the root mean squared error for this example.

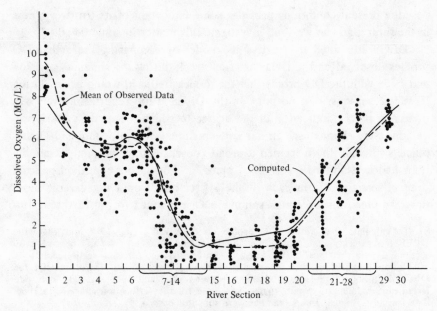

Figure 7
Predicted DO Profile Compared to Observed Data
(*From* Delaware Estuary Comprehensive Study)

mers. On the basis of unpublished information provided by the DECS staff, we have calculated the error with somewhat greater precision. These data indicate that during the summer of 1964 the staff took a weekly measurement of DO concentrations at virtually every one of the estuary's 30 sections. On the basis of these 15 to 20 weekly samples, it was possible to calculate an average DO concentration prevailing during the summer at each of the 30 sections.[85] When we compared the observed average with the predicted average, we found that the model's predictions had a standard error[86] of .46 ppm. In other words, if DECS predicted a DO level of 4.0 ppm in a section, the observed DO was between 3.5 and 4.5 about two times out of three. A graphic presentation of the data is given in Figure 7. The model's error is of the same order of magnitude if one concentrates exclusively on the accuracy with which it predicted the summer average prevailing in sections 12–19, which experience the most acute oxygen shortage. Over these sections the model's standard error was .43 ppm.

85. Personal communication with G.D. Pence, Jr., DECS staff, in Edison, N.J., Aug. 1970.
86. For a definition of this term, see n. 84.

For these critical sections, however, this value appears to overstate the model's accuracy. The key fact here is that it is physically impossible for DO to go any lower than zero ppm. Imagine, for example, that the model predicted a DO concentration of .5 ppm in section 18 and that the summer average in that section was observed to be zero ppm. This does not imply that the error is only .5 ppm. For it may be that the section is so over-loaded with BOD that even if some is removed, the section will still register a zero DO level, despite the model's prediction that section 18 "should" have a DO concentration far greater than .5 ppm. Turning to the case at hand, a glance at the 1964 data indicates that the model has systematically overestimated the DO concentrations prevailing in the critical sections, and that the DECS investigators many times observed a DO approaching zero in these areas. Thus, the model's .43 ppm error could well understate the extent to which its predictions diverge from reality.[87]

Up to the present point, we have assumed that the DO profile predicted by the model in 1964 constitutes an appropriate starting point for testing the accuracy of the model's predictions. This assumption must be discarded once the procedure DECS used to predict the 1964 DO profile is assessed. The fact is that the DECS staff distorted its verification procedure in a way that deprived the standard error of .46 ppm of any significance to a decision maker attempting to assess the model's reliability. Instead of test-ing the model's predictions by comparing them with real-world observations, the DECS staff *changed* the model's original predictions so that they would best *conform* to the observed DO data. When the DECS staff first com-pared their 1964 predictions with the actual results observed in 1964, before any "adjustments," they found a far greater disparity between pre-dicted and actual DO, whose precise dimension we cannot report because the necessary data were not provided to us by the DECS and are not available in the published literature. The substantial disparity, however, did not convince the DECS that the basic structure of the model was mis-conceived or in any way incomplete. Nor was any attempt made to remeasure those independent parameters for which measurement errors could have been substantial.[88] Rather, the DECS concerned itself exclu-

87. Moreover, even if .43 were the correct figure, it would only establish that the average weekly deviation from the predicted summer average was .43 for that sum-mer. This is a long way from establishing that the model will err by only .43 ppm in its prediction of a summer average in two years out of three. For example, if a model predicts law school class attendance in 1964 to be 50 percent and actual average weekly attendance is between 45 and 55 percent approximately two-thirds of the time, it does not follow that this degree of accuracy will hold over the decade of the 1960's, particularly when law school conditions change substantially.
88. Examples are storm sewer overflows, see pp. 42–45; benthic demand, see pp. 51–53; and tributarial loadings, see pp. 45, 46.

sively with the possibility that the coefficients that related the variables to one another had been misestimated. Indeed the concern was even narrower than this. As we have suggested,[89] the coefficients used for the decay rate of nitrogenous oxygen demand (SSUOD) and the reaeration rates were both plagued with substantial uncertainty. Nevertheless, the DECS chose simply to determine whether the model's accuracy would be improved if the reaeration coefficients in the individual sections were varied, ignoring SSUOD decay entirely.[90]

Moreover, the DECS engaged in this effort in a highly imprecise way. If precision had been desired it would have been possible to determine the degree to which the reaeration rate had actually varied in the experiments that formed the basis for the DECS' original reaeration estimates. Then, DECS could have defined accurately the range over which the reaeration coefficient could plausibly be permitted to vary. Instead of undertaking this task, however, a large number of computer runs were made in accordance with the staff's intuitive notions of the "reasonable" range of the coefficient involved in each of the estuary's 30 sections. From this quantity of computer printout, the staff chose the set of predictions that "best fit" the observations and adopted the coefficients that were a consequence of this selection.[91] Once again, however, the selection of the "best fit" was completely intuitive and without reference to standard statistical techniques.

These deficiencies in detail reflect an utter lack of sophistication in statistical analysis. There is no justification for arbitrarily selecting one of the large number of parameters—reaeration coefficient, SSUOD decay rate, benthic demand, municipal and industrial discharges, tributarial load—all of which must have a significant error attached to their measurement. For all one knows, the original reaeration coefficients chosen were the best possible set, and the entire error could be best explained by suitable variations in the other parameters. Indeed, it will not do simply to fiddle with any or all of the variables or coefficients in an effort to have the 1964 predictions closely fit the 1964 observations. There are countless combinations that would do this trick. A change in one coefficient can be offset by an equivalent and opposite change in another. To detect the correct relationship between all the coefficients in each of the 30 sections by observing the river, it would be necessary to have a very large number of observations that would permit the use of standard statistical techniques to estimate each

89. See pp. 39–42 and 48–51.
90. Personal communication with G.D. Pence, Jr., Delaware Estuary Comprehensive Survey staff, July 1970.
91. Interviews with G.D. Pence, Jr., E. Smith, and A. Morris, all members of the DECS staff, June 1970; interview with G.D. Pence, Jr., Nov. 1970.

of the coefficients with a tolerably small standard error. Even if this task were accomplished, the results obtained would be biased, since there are probably substantial errors in the measurement of independent variables that represent the numerous BOD inputs into the system. That the DECS obtained a moderately close fit of the 1964 data by unscientifically adjusting a single coefficient does not in any way suggest that the model will predict with the same degree of accuracy DO levels prevailing in another year with another flow rate and another set of BOD loads.

In its second effort at "verification," the DECS staff attempted to determine the degree to which its model could successfully predict the DO profile in 1966.[92] Unfortunately, DECS had not attempted to conduct a systematic monitoring of BOD influents from point sources, tributaries, and sludge in 1966. Consequently the staff had little choice but to use their *1964* BOD inputs to predict the *1966* DO profile. This introduced an error of unknown dimensions into the analysis: even if the model had predicted the 1966 profile perfectly, one would not know how to assess this feat unless one were certain that BOD loads had remained constant. Even more important than this, the DECS staff was unable to test the accuracy of the model along the dimension that is most important to the policy maker. By using 1964 BOD loads, DECS disabled itself from reporting how well the model could predict DO under BOD conditions somewhat different from those in 1964. Yet this is the question in which the administrator is most interested since, after all, he wants the model to assist his decision on how much he should force polluters to cut back on their BOD discharges. While a model's ability to predict accurately the impact of small BOD changes on one occasion does not necessarily mean that it will similarly predict the impact of large changes in the DO profile

92. The DECS has never explained why it did not also use 1965 data to test the model. It seems particularly important that this be done since one of the major parameters in the model is the flow rate, and flows differed markedly in 1965 from those that prevailed in either 1964 or 1966. In 1964 the average flow rate at Trenton for July and August was 2787 cubic feet per second (cfs) (Water Resources Division, *Pennsylvania,* 1964, p. 41). In 1965, it was 1678 cfs. (Water Resources Division, *Pennsylvania,* 1965, Part I, p. 42). In 1966, however, average flow was 2519 cfs, closely resembling 1964 (Water Resources Division, *Pennsylvania,* 1966, Part I, p. 47). Thus a proper verification run on 1964 and 1965 data would have been far more revealing than a verification for 1964 and 1966. Similarly, verification runs on the three years following 1966 would have been illuminating since the average flow rates at Trenton for the months of July and August were 7859 cfs in 1967, 5745 cfs in 1968, and 4821 cfs in 1969. The 4821 cfs given for 1969 is for the first 20 days of the period. After that, a deluge raised the average flow rate for the entire period to 13,320 cfs. (Water Resources Division, *Pennsylvania,* 1967, Part I, p. 47; Water Resources Division, *New Jersey,* 1968, Part I, p. 99; Water Resources Division, U.S. Department of the Interior, Geological Survey [unpublished figures on file in Biddle Law Library, University of Pennsylvania.]).

resulting from an ambitious pollution control plan, it is at least a small step in the right direction. The DECS' use of 1964 BOD data in its 1966 "verification" prevented it from taking even this first small step. Moreover, other river conditions prevailing during the summer of 1966 happened to resemble quite closely those that had obtained in 1964,[93] when the equations were fiddled with to obtain the "best possible" results. Thus, it should prove no surprise that the typical error in the model's predictions was only somewhat greater in 1966 than in 1964, with a standard error[94] of .63 ppm when all sections are reported[95] and a smaller (.47) ppm error when the comparison is limited to the model's predictions of DO concentrations prevailing in the zone of maximum oxygen depletion.

CONCLUSIONS: OF SCIENTIFIC FACT FINDING AND ITS CONTROL

Assessing the DECS Analysis of Proposed Pollution Programs

All this means that if the decision maker were to gain any sense of the model's accuracy, it would have been necessary for him to move beyond the DECS presentation and insist that the staff report the disparity it found between actual and predicted DO profiles before it began distorting its procedures to obtain the set of predictions that "best fit" the observed data. Whatever the defects in the original coefficients (and we have shown that they are substantial), at least they were not manipulated for the purpose of putting the model in the best possible light.

93. For flow rate comparisons, see note 81. Below are comparisons of temperature during the two summers:

Delaware River Water Temperature at Trenton, Degrees F.

	June	July	August	September
1964	72	78	75	72
1966	73	79	77	70

Source: Water Resources Division, *Pennsylvania,* 1964, p. 24.
Water Resources Division, *Pennsylvania,* 1966, Part 2, p. 27.

94. For a definition of the term "standard error," see n. 84.
95. The 1966 exercise is further compromised by the fact that the model's predictions were compared to the observed facts in only the central part of the estuary, between sections 6 and 19. No attempt was made to determine the extent to which the model could predict accurately the conditions prevailing between Trenton and Burlington or between Marcus Hook and the Delaware Bay. Since the 1964 verification indicated that the model's error was greatest between sections 1 and 7 (Trenton and Burlington, see Figure 7) it is likely that the error indicated in the text is an understatement.

Even if this disparity were known, however, it would not be of much significance to the policy maker wishing to chart the future course of pollution control on the Delaware. As we have seen, the model's power to predict the consequences of adopting ambitious cutback plans will be significantly worse than its ability to predict conditions like those presently prevailing on the river. Thus, given the various kinds of error afflicting the model's predictions, it would be not at all surprising if the DECS forecasts of the DO impact of pollution control programs in the critical sections were to have a standard error that was in excess of 1 ppm rather than the .46 ppm generated by the 1964 "verification" analysis.[96] Not only do the model's predictions contain a substantial error but there is reason to believe that its predictions will consistently err toward an overly optimistic assessment of the impact of the pollution control programs under consideration.[97] A reader sensitive to these factors will look with new insight at Table 3, which reproduces the chart that best encapsulates the DECS analysis:

Table 3.

Objective Set	Average DO in PPM in Most Polluted Region	Cost	High Estimate–Low Estimate of Benefits
I	4.5	$490 million	$355–155 million
II	4.0	275 "	320–135 "
III	3.0	155 "	310–125 "
IV	2.5	110 "	280–115 "
V	1.0	30 "	——

Instead of a set of predictions that nowhere indicates substantial uncertainty as to whether a given program of BOD cutbacks *will* lead to a given DO objective, would not the DECS effort have been far more useful to decision makers if the staff had appended the following caution to its presentation?

96. We can only rest this claim on intuition, in the absence of data. For a somewhat more precise, but still far from adequate, manner of assessing the model's sensitivity, see Appendix A.
97. See p. 56.

WARNING TO DECISION MAKERS: When we report that Program II will lead to an average DO of 4.0 ppm during the summer in the "critical" sections of the river, we wish to emphasize that during periods of heavy rain DO levels will be far lower for substantial periods as a result of the discharge of raw sewage from Philadelphia and Camden. It may well be that forcing cities and firms to reduce their output of FSUOD will not improve the DO profile as much as we expect, because more SSUOD will then be exerted in the critical sectors; also, it may well be that the worms inhabiting the river sludge will increase in population and consume much of the oxygen that the BOD cutback program is intended to restore to the Delaware's waters; also, despite the fact we botched our verification procedures, decision makers should recognize that the model consistently predicts a higher DO concentration for the critical sections than the observed data indicate, thereby suggesting again that our predictions have an overly optimistic bias.

Even if none of these tendencies toward overoptimism materializes, you should know that we would not be surprised if Program II, which promises a DO level of 4.0 ppm, will in fact during many summers achieve an average DO concentration of only 3.0 ppm or even less. On the other hand, it may be 5.0 ppm or even more.

Even if the program succeeds in achieving its DO goal, the result may simply be that the river will turn from a turbid brown to an unattractive green, thanks to algae bloom. We have not studied this.

Similar caveats are appropriate in considering our predictions concerning the DO consequences of the other programs.

(For more caveats and qualifications, see our detailed report.)

When confronted with this precis, the reader is doubtless tempted to conclude that the DECS exercise, when properly understood, contributed nothing of value to a more precise understanding of the problems confronting the sensitive decision maker. But this would be a mistake; for it is only as a result of our effort to trace the DECS' investigations that it has been possible to obtain a perspective on the probable consequences of the costly program of pollution control which the DRBC has adopted. Our basic complaint does not go to the wisdom of the effort at sustained understanding of river dynamics but to the way in which the DECS staff chose to *translate their insights into language comprehensible to decision makers.* After all, the "Warning" we have written could easily have been made clear by the DECS in its 1966 Report.

Rather than describe the problems it had confronted, however, the DECS chose instead to transmit its work product primarily in the form of a set of quantitative predictions. Indeed, since the DECS analysis was conspicuously devoid of cautions to decision makers about the limitations of its predictions, it invited a decision maker to avoid a confrontation with the unpleasant realization that even relatively expensive programs could not be counted on to ameliorate significantly, let alone cure, the environmental degradation characteristic of the darkest corners of our urban civilization. The report's manner of presentation itself constituted an assurance to laymen that they should be confident that the experts had found DO to be a convenient index of "water quality" and that the experts had predicted that alternative pollution control programs will raise the DO index in the "critical reaches" from 1 to 2.5, or 3 or 4, ppm. Given this setting, it is but a short step for laymen involved in the political process to limit themselves to haggling about whether the pollution control goal "should be" 2.5 or 3 or 4, never facing the more troubling issues that lie submerged below the numerical facade: Is our society willing to make the enormous expenditures required to revolutionize environmental conditions next to the industrial plants on the Delaware River? If not, are we willing to spend a quarter of a billion dollars (or more) to take half measures that may well not improve matters significantly? Even if the DO goal is fulfilled, could more pressing environmental goals have been achieved with more certainty elsewhere at much lower expenditures? Considering the immense number of demands for social justice properly advanced by blacks and other deprived minorities, is it appropriate to divert substantial social resources to ameliorate only marginally the admittedly undesirable conditions in the Delaware's "critical sections"?

While we have already intimated our own view on these questions,[98] which will be elaborated in our subsequent discussion of cost–benefit analysis, we do not suggest that there is any one "correct" answer to them. Our point here is simply that the style of the DECS' analysis did not invite the policy maker to confront these fundamental questions and that this failing is a matter of substantial concern. It is particularly unfortunate since if the DECS had taken pains to articulate the factors that made the achievement of meaningful environmental improvement uncertain, its analysis would have induced decision makers to explore the basic premises of pollution control policy in a far more probing way than in fact was attempted on the Delaware.

In short, the basic failing of the DECS Report was not so much that it failed to achieve a degree of comprehensiveness and exactitude that is never achieved outside the most fantastic science fiction; what was seriously defective was the manner in which the DECS Report understood the very idea of "achievement." The DECS succeeded insofar as it developed a set of equations defining a system that accurately described a small piece of

98. See pp. 28–30.

reality. Thus, in emphasizing its achievement, the research staff emphasized the accuracy of the numbers its model generated. While this may be fine in a scientific forum in which the findings will be scrutinized by other experts concerned with the development of truth within a single disciplinary specialty, it is nothing short of disastrous when the same attitude is transposed into the policy-making arena. Here, the researcher is successful insofar as he recognizes that, whatever his contribution to a particular discipline, it will in all likelihood fail to explain comprehensively the dynamics of an important piece of reality. It is therefore of critical importance for the expert to gain a perspective upon the kit bag of his disciplinary techniques so that he may educate nonexperts in the important factors which—because of necessary simplifications required by the always incomplete nature of scientific understanding—have been ignored in the technocratic fact-finding exercise.

Of course, to state the need for a sense of perspective is in a way to confess the difficulty of the problem revealed by an analysis of the DECS Report. A sense of perspective—seeing the way in which one's activities relate to others'—will always be in short supply, and to rely on staffers to possess rich stores of this commodity is clearly utopian. This is especially the case in a situation like the present one, in which the staff will probably maximize its short-run (or even long-run) bureaucratic prestige and power by emphasizing the "scientific" aspect of its report and the extent to which it approximated the science fiction ideal of a comprehensive and exact analysis of reality. Indeed, a confession of imperfection—like the one contained in the Warning—would be likely to discredit the staff in the eyes of politicians and other laymen who may embrace the science fiction ideal with a fervor far greater than that held by thoughtful scientists themselves.[99]

99. For a very different view of the way technocratic intelligence should be deployed, see Esposito, 1970, pp. 280–87. He argues that presentations to decision makers should not lay bare the areas which remain uncertain or unresolved. If warnings like the ones proposed here were included in reports, Esposito fears that decision makers would ignore scientific insights entirely, and also that industrial interests would then be in a position to exploit unavoidable ambiguities to advance a go-slow policy. So far as these risks are real ones, it would seem far better, however, to design institutions to control them directly, as suggested in Chapters 10 and 14, rather than suppress the inevitable shortcomings of technocratic intelligence on the dubious assumption that ignorance will generate sound policy.

Controlling Technocratic Fact Finding: Federalism and the Pursuit of Science

INTRODUCTION

In sum, we have been presenting an understandable, yet depressing, tale. An admirable scientific endeavor in river dynamics was transformed by the force of events into a decision-making tool without a comparable shift in the way the staff perceived the nature of its inquiry. As we have indicated, this failure to shift conceptual gears is partly attributable to the professional training of the DECS staff. Nevertheless we should probe further and inquire whether, in addition to professional mores, the structure of institutions shaped the character of the DECS fact-finding performance. The discussion presented in the preceding chapter provides the first focal point for our institutional inquiry: Did the decision-making structure create any special incentives to the DECS to overstate the importance of their analysis to policy makers?

In addition to the question of technocratic oversell, however, the Delaware experience raises a second institutional issue of great importance. Our study of the DECS' work should make it apparent that four years is a very short time even for an adequately funded staff of high caliber to do more than make a promising beginning to the scientific understanding of a complex phenomenon. It is only a disciplined, long-lived investigation lasting over decades that promises any great utility to decision making along the Delaware, since only such an ongoing effort can determine the consequences of past policy decisions and also delineate policy options which from time to time seem most promising. This insight motivates the second basic question to be considered in this chapter: To what extent did the institutional structure facilitate or frustrate the further development of the scientific enterprise *beyond 1966,* when the DECS staff tendered their analysis to the DRBC?

To confront this issue, we must first trace the dynamics of the fact-finding enterprise beyond 1966. After doing so, we shall embark upon a more theoretical effort to develop an answer to the two basic institutional questions suggested by the DECS' fact-finding enterprise.

BEYOND 1966: FOLLOWING THROUGH ON THE DECS WORK

When viewed from the perspective of our second question, the Delaware is the scene of a story that is still more disappointing. After the short-term pollution control decisions had been made in 1966, the scientific enterprise lost its vitality. Decision makers charting the course of the Delaware in the 1970's and 1980's will be constrained once again to activate a crash research program which, with inadequate data and analysis, will nonetheless crank out predictions of limited value to the solution of policy problems that then seem salient. Moreover, decision makers and scientists studying other rivers will not be able profitably to use the Delaware experience as it developed over time.

The Federal Failure to Follow Through

At the time it published its preliminary report for use by the DRBC in the summer of 1966, the DECS promised a much more detailed and definitive "final" document by the end of 1967. As of the publication of this volume, the report has not yet been issued, and although a number of chapters have been circulated informally, it does not appear that significant progress is now being made toward publication of the complete report in the forseeable future. Even if the document should ultimately see the light of day, its utility will be limited by the fact that the DECS staff apparently has not integrated post-1966 data into its work, for the simple reason that the staff did not generate adequate data after 1966. Fundamentally, by 1970 the DECS staff had ceased to function. Only three of its members remained with the regional office of the Federal Water Quality Administration at Edison, New Jersey, and they were devoting only a small fraction of their time to the Delaware, working instead on projects the FWQA deemed of greater immediate importance.

The Regional Failure to Follow Through

With the publication of the DECS preliminary report, then, primary responsibility for further scientific work shifted from the federal to the regional level. Advances along several fronts were possible: first, improvements in the model's structure could have been attempted; second, the relevant coefficients (like those describing the reaeration rate and the decay of SSUOD) could have been remeasured with greater sophistication; third, the BOD loadings imposed by the diverse pollution sources could have been constantly monitored to test the ability of the model to relate changing BOD loadings to the resulting DO profile. Nevertheless, while the desirability of embarking on these tasks was made clear to the DRBC by the departing DECS staffers,[1] the progress made has been inconsiderable.

While the BOD monitoring program seems the most prosaic of tasks, it is nevertheless critical to a sustained advance in the art of understanding rivers in quantitative terms. It is only by maintaining a reliable data base that innovations in the model can be tested empirically. Unfortunately, this basic task has been poorly discharged since 1966. Indeed, it is fair to say that the concerned agencies have less satisfactory data on BOD loadings at the time of this writing[2] than the DECS possessed in 1966.

To understand the source of one of the principal data problems it is necessary, once again, to take into account the customs of the sanitary engineering profession. Engineers have been wont to measure the BOD content of waste samples by determining the quantity of oxygen the waste consumes at a standard temperature of 20°C. during a five-day period. (This value is often written BOD_5.) Since carbonaceous oxygen demand

1. DECS, pp. 91–94.
2. While our comprehensive effort to gather data concerning the DECS scientific study occurred in the summer of 1970, we have tried to keep current with work done through the summer of 1973. While some work has in fact been attempted during this period, it does not require important alterations of the discussion found in the text.

is still exerted after the first five days, a constant is used that permits the engineer to extrapolate to FSUOD in a highly imprecise way;[3] SSUOD is not even measured under traditional practice. DECS, however, revolutionized measurement practices, attempting to calculate FSUOD and SSUOD more satisfactorily, and strongly recommended a continuation of its sophisticated measurement techniques.[4] Since 1965, however, the main task of measurement has passed from the DECS to the DRBC, which, in turn, negotiated contracts with the three states bordering the estuary. We have inspected the data collected by the states with some care,[5] and they indicate unequivocally a relapse into the traditional defective measurement procedures. Almost all of the data sent by the states to the DRBC are expressed in terms of traditional BOD_5.

Even more remarkable is the manner in which the states collect BOD samples from the dischargers. There are clear dangers when an inspector arrives at a plant and merely takes a sample of the untreated waste and the treated effluent at a single point in time. First, considering the extreme variability of the waste loads, a one-shot "grab sample" is not representative; second, the procedure permits polluters who are dishonest to cheat quite easily if they have cause to expect the investigator to arrive on the premises at a particular time; third, since there is a substantial error in the BOD test[6] several samples should be taken at the same time to allow an averaging of results. Instead of relying on a single grab sample, a more expensive composite sampling technique is necessary if reliable waste load estimates are to be expected. Under the composite method, several samples are taken hourly over a 24-hour period, and an average of the test results is used as a measure of BOD load.

Our inspection of the state reports makes it clear that all three states rely principally on grab samples. Moreover, when composite samples are attempted, the manner of execution undermines one's confidence in the results obtained. The 24-hour procedure is relatively expensive, since it requires an inspector to be at a single plant both day and night. Our interviews with Pennsylvania staff personnel indicate that in order to save their time and the state's money, the polluter is called in advance and told to start collecting hourly samples; the inspector arrives on the scene later, and

3. Camp, 1963, p. 243.
4. DECS, pp. 83–85.
5. Members of the study group, working under Bruce Ackerman's supervision, collected the state reports concerning industrial and municipal discharges made available by the state authorities of Delaware, New Jersey, and Pennsylvania. The data, at present, are in the project's files, in Professor Ackerman's possession.
6. Personal communication with G.D. Pence, Jr., Delaware Estuary Comprehensive Survey staff, in Edison, N.J., July 1970.

leaves before the sampling is completed.[7] Obviously, this practice under-mines the neutrality that a state sampling program is intended to obtain. Equally extraordinary is the Pennsylvania bureaucracy's acceptance of the demand made upon them by several large industrial firms that require the inspector to call the company before he arrives even to take a grab sample.[8] We do not know whether similar practices obtain in Delaware and New Jersey.

Sampling frequency presents another problem. At present both New Jersey and Delaware sample major industrial and municipal plants monthly; Pennsylvania samples major plants once every second month at best. Since sampling is expensive, a trade-off must be made between accuracy and cost: in judging whether the monitoring is too frequent, the critical factor must be the variability in the results obtained. Our inspection of the state reports indicates, unfortunately, that in both industry and municipal facili-ties the variability is significant: often samples reveal a 50-percent variation from observation to observation. Similar variances are revealed when samples from the same month of consecutive years are compared. These differences should not be surprising, given the grab samples on which they are based. What appears to be a year-to-year variation may actually be a variation in waste concentration from hour to hour. Thus the chaotic con-dition of the reports may simply reflect the inspector's arrival at nine A.M. on one visit and at five P.M. on another. Nevertheless, the record suggests that a more frequent monitoring schedule would be required at least for certain polluters before data of sufficient reliability could be gathered to justify the confident use of even an improved mathematical model.

Finally, a substantial number of the reports show obvious incompe-tence. Often reports fail to indicate the rate at which effluent is pouring through the outfall, noting only the phrase "meter broken" in the few cases in which any explanation for the failure is vouchsafed at all. This makes the report worthless, since it is impossible to determine a plant's daily BOD load without knowing both the concentration and the volume of effluent; and volume can be determined only if one knows the flow rate. Similarly, a substantial number of the reports indicate that daily volume has been "estimated" but do not describe the manner of estimation. Even worse, reports sometimes indicate that the BOD concentration of the treated effluent was found to be *greater* than the BOD of the raw waste. The anomalous readings may be the result of careless mislabelling of bottles or they may be the result of the grab sample practice if, at the time

7. Interviews with state officials who prefer to remain anonymous, summer 1970.
8. *Ibid.*

of sampling, the raw waste entering the treatment plant exerted less BOD than the partially treated, but initially more heavily polluted, wastes leaving the plant. In any event, it is deplorable that, when the laboratory BOD analysis is received, such data are placed in the file without any indication of their intrinsic implausibility or any attempt to rectify the apparent mistakes.

The DRBC staff is aware of these failings and has thus far unsuccessfully tried to induce the state pollution control bureaucracies that collect the BOD data to adopt more elaborate and expensive procedures. When DRBC staff members meet with their state counterparts at regular meetings of the Water Quality Advisory Committee, frequent pleas are made to supply data that will permit the accurate calculation of FSUOD.[9] Even here, however, we have found no indication that the DRBC has put any substantial pressure on the states to provide data on nitrogenous demand. This vacuum is significant now and will become increasingly important over time. We have already noted that the DECS model is deficient in its treatment of nitrogenous demand; yet data are not being collected that could serve as the basis for reliable theoretical work on the problem. Moreover, as traditional secondary treatment facilities of the sort being constructed under the DRBC cleanup primarily eliminate carbonaceous demand and only incidentally remove nitrogenous, SSUOD's share of the total will increase dramatically after the anticipated cleanup. In short, the DRBC is not now receiving the data on municipal and industrial treatment plants that either permit it to have a sophisticated understanding of the Delaware of today[10] or enable it to make a more accurate prediction of the impact its program will have on the Delaware of the future.

Turning to the DRBC's efforts to measure other BOD inputs, the results are similarly disappointing. No significant work has been attempted on the measurement of benthic demand or on the analysis of BOD entering the estuary from the river's tributaries.[11] In contrast, the agency has been taking important steps to expand its scientific knowledge of conditions prevailing in the relatively unpolluted waters of the Delaware above Trenton. Members of the staff are at present collecting data that will permit the application of a Thomann-type model to this region, and the

9. DRBC Hearings, minutes of meetings of March 18, 1969, Oct. 2, 1969, and April 16, 1970.
10. This is particularly unfortunate since river conditions during these years differed substantially from those prevailing in 1964 and 1966 (see Ch. 4, note 92); thus a "verification" run on newer data would have provided extremely revealing information regarding the model's utility.
11. While a chapter of the unpublished DECS Final Report is devoted to the benthic problem, it contains no suggestion that its analysis is based on data gathered after 1966.

information gathered in this study should illuminate the impact the Upper Delaware has upon the estuary below Trenton, thereby improving the quality of the data used by the DECS model in this single respect.

Just as the data-collection effort has proceeded at a crawl, so too has new theoretical work sponsored by the DRBC. No explorations of reaeration rates have been attempted by the agency, despite the inadequacy of the DECS' treatment and their importance to the model's predictions. Nor has there been a significant effort to understand turbidity or the dynamics of benthic demand any better. On the other hand, a substantial amount of theoretical work has been attempted to define better the impact nitrogenous demand will have on the estuary after the anticipated cleanup has been attempted. It is difficult, however, to determine the validity of such theoretical work without the assistance of detailed data on nitrogenous loadings, which the DRBC has failed to collect.

Given the failure of the agency to move substantially beyond the DECS' work, it should not be surprising that little has been done to determine the extent to which the DECS model successfully predicts the DO profiles prevailing along the estuary since DECS' final verification analysis of 1966. To run even a moderately satisfactory analysis it would be necessary to obtain reliable data on BOD loadings that are more recent than those DECS obtained in 1964. Since this essential work has not been attempted, meaningful verification efforts are impossible. Thus, while members of the DRBC staff attempted verification on the basis of fragmentary 1968 BOD data,[12] we have reason to believe that the DRBC staff itself considers this endeavor to be of no real significance.[13]

THINKING AGENCIES, ACTING AGENCIES, AND THE DYNAMICS OF COOPERATIVE FEDERALISM

Having traced the course of fact finding beyond 1966, we are now in a position to confront the two basic institutional issues raised in the introduction to this chapter:

1. Why did the DECS oversell the utility of its 1966 Report?
2. Why did the technocratic enterprise fall apart after 1966?

Although these two questions appear quite different on the surface, it seems to us that their answers have much in common. A successful re-

12. MacEwen and Tortoriello, 1970, p. 99.
13. Interview with a member of the DRBC staff, Oct. 1970 (anonymous).

sponse to either question requires an understanding of the significance of the institutional division of responsibility between the DECS, a creature of the federal agency charged with water pollution control, and the DRBC, a regional agency formed by the concerned states and the federal government. To divide the "thinkers" (DECS) from the "doers" (DRBC) in this way is to ask for several kinds of trouble. The "thinking agency" has little incentive to stay with the problem over the long haul. Instead, it may well maximize its bureaucratic prestige by publishing a preliminary report which loudly claims to be "relevant" to the decision makers' problems, prematurely leaving the area in search of new problems that are capable of "innovative" solutions. A pure "thinking" agency may be expected not only to plan episodically, but also to justify its existence by overselling the accuracy and importance of its preliminary reports by underemphasizing the uncertainties underlying its predictions.

In overselling its innovative enterprises, the thinking agency is aided by the action agency for several reasons. First, the action agency does not possess large numbers of personnel equipped with the necessary analytical skills both to understand the model and to take steps to improve the model's structure and data base. Since agency funds are always limited, there is a natural tendency for the available money to be allocated to uses the existing action officials understand—to the prejudice of those they do not. Second, the action agency, after it adopts one of the competing pollution programs delineated by the thinkers, will have a natural tendency to seek to prove that the plan it has selected is the one the thinkers' report supports most persuasively. In short, even if the report in fact played a relatively unimportant role in the minds of the decision makers, the action agency will seek to legitimate its decision by proclaiming that it is rooted in the expert analysis provided by the thinkers, who have themselves sought to proclaim its importance for the reasons outlined above.[14] After this

14. A tendency evident in the DRBC experience. The DECS study played an important role in official statements legitimating the DRBC's decision:

A U.S. Public Health Service Report issued in 1966 found the river's overburdened estuary—the 86-mile stretch from below Wilmington to Trenton—to be "a polluted waterway which depresses esthetic values, reduces recreational, sport and commercial fishing, and inhibits municipal and industrial water use."
This important if uncomplimentary document, *probably more than anything*, represented the turning point for the polluted, oxygen-shy lower Delaware. Its findings of degraded conditions and extensive options for improving them (and surprisingly even for not improving them) startled the three-state area and spurred it into a solemn clean-up commitment. (*DRBC Annual Report*, 1969, p. 6 [emphasis added]). See also *DRBC Annual Report*, 1967, pp. 6–8.

public episode, any further attempts by the action agency to launch a systematic effort to move beyond (or even update) the DECS model become something of an embarrassment. If it is necessary to improve the DECS model, does not this suggest that something was seriously wrong with the original analysis already publicly proclaimed to legitimate the original decision? Third, after the basic pollution control program has been selected, the action agency's bureaucracy can be expected to concentrate its energies on enforcing the decision rather than engaging in the more basic research that will ultimately be needed for future planning efforts on the Delaware and elsewhere. After all, the action agency has yet to make its bureaucratic reputation, and, over the short term, rewards will be governed by successfully implementing the program already adopted rather than conducting experiments and collecting the data necessary for future planning along the estuary. All this, of course, does not mean that an action agency is not correct in placing first priority on implementing the pollution control program selected by decision makers. We simply argue that powerful bureaucratic forces will induce such an agency to ignore the necessity of following through the planning work initiated by others.[15]

Having discerned the significance of the division of responsibility between DECS and DRBC, it is necessary to inquire more deeply into the reasons that brought separation about. From the legal viewpoint, nothing was foreordained about the division of the planning and decision-making roles. The DRBC's charter provides ample authority for sponsoring planning efforts of this magnitude.[16] As we have seen, the development of an institutionally separate DECS effort had much to do with two accidents of history: the interest of the Public Health Service in novel forms of cost–benefit analysis, and the infant DRBC's concern with the pressing issues emerging from the deepening drought along the river.[17] Nevertheless, the same institutional bifurcation might have resulted even if the DRBC had not been diverted by the water shortage from pollution control research. The administrative pattern revealed along the Delaware is a fundamental aspect of the "cooperative federalism," which, in increasing complex forms, is playing a central role within the contemporary polity: a federal task force providing "technical" assistance to local decision makers, who "implement" decisions with substantial federal oversight.[18] And it is doubtful

15. For a discussion concerning the relationship between policy formation and research objectives which has certain parallels with our analysis, see Jacoby, 1973.
16. Delaware River Basin Compact, art. 13 (1961).
17. See p. 13, Ch. 2.
18. A systematic legally-oriented analysis of the premises underlying the numerous patterns along which federal-state relationships have been structured has yet to be

that the DRBC could have transcended this pattern. The agency, after all, had no legal authority to veto the federal study, or to require that its own personnel undertake the work;[19] nor would it have made sense to institute a parallel effort of its own that would only replicate much of the same work at additional cost. Only if the federal authorities had delegated the project to the regional body could the bifurcation have been avoided. But this result was most unlikely: first, the Public Health Service would have been reluctant to abandon a project likely to redound to its bureaucratic prestige; second, given the prevailing philosophy of "cooperative federalism," which legitimates federal technical assistance, it is most unlikely that anyone within the federal bureaucracy would have thought it incongruous for a federal task force to investigate a regional problem instead of the regional agency established for that purpose.

Nonetheless, this structural division was of substantial significance for the future of regional government along the Delaware. A regional authority must develop its staff's planning capacities if it is to become anything more than a loose confederation in which representatives of the federal and state bureaucracies compromise their differences without any substantial effort to view the Delaware River's problems from a regional perspective. And the failure to develop planning resources feeds upon itself: it was in large part because the DRBC was not obliged to undertake a DECS-type study with its own personnel that it was poorly equipped to follow through on the task when the federal innovators left the scene.

Since the regional agency lacked an active research component, it was only natural that the essential task of data collection was delegated to the respective states, whose agencies have responded in such an unsatisfactory manner. Once again, it is too easy to explain the states' poor data collection practices by invoking the well-worn notion that state bureaucrats are more incompetent than their counterparts at other levels of government. However this may be, a more compelling explanation exists for the case at hand. Since the states' officials are not responsible for maintaining the

---

written, although the importance of the problem has been perceived by political scientists (Maass, 1959), historians (Elazar, 1962, and Elazar, 1964), economists (Break, 1967 and Musgrave, 1955), as well as legal academics (Michelman and Sandalow, 1970, pp. 970–1212). See also sources cited in Ch. 12, n. 46.

19. Indeed, §1.5 of the Compact reads:

It is the purpose of the signatory parties to preserve and utilize the functions, powers and duties of existing offices and agencies of government to the extent not inconsistent with this compact, and the commision is authorized and directed to utilize and employ such offices and agencies for the purpose of this compact to the fullest extent it finds feasible and advantageous.

model's accuracy, they have little incentive to collect data useful to run the model, if that effort requires them to change their cheap and easy grab-sampling technique for BOD_5. In short, one of the important reasons that the data are not being collected properly is that the states are responsible for data *collection* while the DRBC is responsible for data *manipulation*. Since state officials are not dependent on the DRBC staff for their promotion or job security, DRBC personnel have no sanction to impose when the relevant data do not arrive. Moreover, since the DRBC staff does not even work in close geographic proximity with most of their state counterparts, even informal sanctions are relatively ineffective.[20] The DRBC staff's primary recourse is an occasional plea for better data at the regular meetings of DRBC personnel with their state counterparts.

The relationships between federal, regional, and state authorities we have charted should serve as a caution that the vague slogan of "cooperative federalism," which has an honored place in both Democratic and Republican rhetoric, is in need of much more precise analysis than it has yet been given.[21] At least in decisions requiring a significant scientific input of a continuing nature, it will not suffice to place bits and pieces of the scientific enterprise in different bureaucratic structures at different levels of government.[22] The course of events along the Delaware eloquently warns against placing the federal "thinkers" in one bureaucratic box, then shifting the responsibility for scientific follow-through to the regional "decision-making" agency, simultaneously consigning the task of data gathering to yet another set of state agencies. In such a structure each component is prone to lose sight of the function it should be performing to enhance the rationality of the pollution control scheme that is the ultimate product of all the sound and fury.

UNANSWERED QUESTIONS

It is one thing to perceive the unfortunate consequences of fractionalizing the fact-finding function that may proceed under the beguiling label of "cooperative federalism." It is quite another thing to design a fact-finding structure that promises greater success in resolving the two basic issues

20. The Commission's staff works in Trenton, close to their New Jersey counterparts, but far from Albany, Harrisburg, and Dover.
21. For the conventional wisdom concerning the institutional division between "thinking" and "acting" agencies wrought by "cooperative federalism," see Maga, 1967.
22. For a similar point, see Engelbert, 1957.

with which this chapter has been concerned. It would be premature, however, to make even a tentative attempt to design superior fact-finding institutions at this early stage in our investigation. For our discussion of the second aspect of the technocratic enterprise, in which the DECS attempted to assess the costs and benefits of each of its five proposed water quality programs, will further enrich an analysis of the factors that must be taken into account in the proper design of technocratic structures. Consequently, it is only when our survey of the substance of the DECS' economic analysis has been concluded that we will turn, in Chapter 10, to a consideration of some tentative principles of institutional construction which may promise a more satisfactory operation of the technocratic enterprise in the future.

The Technocratic Enterprise: Of Economic Reasoning and Public Policy

Counting the Costs
Technocratically

INTRODUCTION

A "scientific" description of the present and possible future states of the Delaware River—no matter how comprehensive and accurate—cannot do more than serve as a necessary preliminary to the ultimate policy-making problem: What *ought* the river to look like in coming years? As we move from the descriptive to the normative inquiry, however, it is not necessary (though it may be desirable) to transcend the quantitative orientation characteristic of the technocratic approach. Instead, the committed technocrat may contend that all that is required is a shift from the concepts of natural science to those of economic science.

Using contemporary welfare economics as a conceptual base, professional economists over the past generation have sought to develop the techniques of cost–benefit analysis to permit the resolution of complex public policy issues in more familiar market terms.[1] Just as—under perfect

1. Water resource development has been one of the principal fields in which economists have attempted to apply "cost–benefit" techniques. See, e.g., Bain, et. al., 1966;

competition—the firm that sets production at the point where its marginal cost is equal to marginal revenue is acting in the public interest, in that it facilitates the efficient allocation of resources, so too a pollution control agency should select water quality goals at which the marginal cost of abatement equals the marginal benefit to society. In doing this, the agency will be furthering the public interest in efficient resource allocation. Thus technocracy seems to offer, through cost–benefit analysis, not merely a way of *describing* reality with numerical precision but a mode of *prescribing* the policy solution which represents the most efficient use of society's finite resources.

Now, it should be apparent that there are many deep problems involved in the use of cost–benefit analysis as a policy tool: Is efficiency (even broadly conceived) the only value at stake in framing environmental policy? Before recommending a policy on cost–benefit grounds, must the analyst insist that those who are hurt by the project be compensated by those who gain? In calculating costs and benefits, should the analyst give extra weight in his calculations to costs (or benefits) which accrue to the poor or some favored social group?[2]

In the course of our analysis, we shall address some of these ultimate questions as they arise; most notably, Chapter 9 will consider at length the extent to which economic efficiency, even broadly conceived, can be considered the sole value served by environmental protection.[3] Nevertheless, the chapters immediately following have an objective which—though not so profound—is equally important. While basic theoretical problems in cost–benefit analysis have generated a substantial, if inconclusive, literature, the way in which cost–benefit analysis is actually practiced deserves far

---

Kneese and Bower, 1968; Kneese and Smith, 1966; Krutilla, 1967; Krutilla and Eckstein, 1958; Maass, et. al., 1962. See also Dorfman and Jacoby, 1973 (which arrived too late for use in this study).

2. These issues are raised, if not resolved, in Harberger, 1971; Krutilla, 1967; Mishan, 1971, and Musgrave, 1969. Issues of equal importance involve the propriety of partial equilibrium cost–benefit analysis in a world afflicted by market imperfections (see Lipsey and Lancaster, 1956; Davis and Whinston, 1967; Fishlow and David, 1961; McManus, 1958–59; Turvey, 1969, Prest and Turvey, 1965, and Mishan, 1965). Finally, the proper approach to determining the social rate of discount is a controversial matter (see Ch. 8, n. 22). For an early and excellent critique of the foundations of cost–benefit analysis, see Little, 1957; for a more recent study, see Mishan, 1971.

3. We shall see, however, that other fundamental conceptual problems of cost–benefit analysis mentioned in the text and in n. 2 are not important enough in the present case to justify exhaustive treatment. Consequently, we shall take note of their existence where appropriate and content ourselves with explaining why they do not decisively alter the basic character of the analysis.

more careful attention than it has been given.[4] If the University is to train students who will later use the cost–benefit tool in a sensitive manner, it is not enough to advert summarily to the inevitable imperfections of cost–benefit analysis in the "real world"; one must instead treat the problems of practice seriously so that students can know the nature of the problems concealed by a set of summary cost–benefit ratios, and the ways in which their adequacy may be ascertained. These questions are of importance even to those who—like us—do not believe that all the answers to society's urgent problems lie in a perfected Technocracy. So long as it is conceded that a disciplined evaluation of costs and benefits is desirable before the rendering of a policy judgment, the powerful conceptual tools preferred by the economist are of obvious, if not ultimate, value.

Moreover, a study of the way the cost–benefit enterprise functioned along the estuary permits an important insight into the fundamental question left unresolved in our consideration of the DECS' scientific fact-finding effort. We saw there that the task of translating the significance of the BOD-DO analysis into a form most useful to policy making was one which could easily elude the typical technocratic fact finder. It may be, however, that the chasm between natural science and policy making can be intermediated by the applied social scientist. Perhaps in conducting a cost–benefit analysis, an expert staff, guided by the conceptual structure of applied welfare economics, would itself come to the recognition that the scientific statement of the facts had disguised salient policy dimensions of the problem at hand. Thus, one aspect of the technocratic approach could serve as a potent critique of the other, generating a whole greater than the sum of its parts.

Unfortunately, this was not to happen on the Delaware. Instead of questioning the definition of the pollution problem and statement of the facts developed by the BOD-DO model, the DECS cost–benefit analysis proceeded to analyze only those aspects of the issue which the fact-finding effort made most salient. Thus, the oversimplifications of the fact-finding process were simply projected onto a larger canvas and given greater authority by the economic study.

This chapter begins an assessment of the practical utility of applied economic reasoning by focussing on the aspect of the cost–benefit discipline whose usefulness seems most self-evident and implementation least prob-

---

4. This is not to say that such analysis has never been attempted. Among the recent works in this area are Barsby, 1972; Dorfman, 1965; Haveman, 1972; Haveman and Margolis, 1970; Margolis, 1969, pp. 372–83; Merewitz and Sosnick, 1971, especially Ch. 11, pp. 239–72; Rivlin, 1971.

lematic. While many deny that economic analysis can contribute very much to the evaluation of the benefits generated by environmental control, so many of which appear to be impossible to quantify, a similar reluctance is not widespread when it comes to the assessment of program costs. Here, we have to do with humdrum things not beyond the economist's ken, however limited it may be: a factory installs a new treatment facility, a town is obliged to invest heavily in a new sewer piping system. The resources devoted to such expenditures could otherwise be devoted to the satisfaction of other private and social values; hence a mature appraisal of the value of pollution control must take into account its cost measured in terms of the opportunities lost to fulfill other, competing objectives. It is this task which an economic analysis of program costs seeks to perform.[5] It seems wise, then, first to explore the problems that arise in implementing the technocratic program in a field in which its ultimate utility seems generally conceded before considering, in Chapters 7 through 9, the larger issues involved in assessing the technocratic effort to measure the benefits of environmental protection. For we shall see that, even in this relatively uncontroversial area, the problems of controlling the technocratic intelligence are formidable.

NARROWING THE RANGE OF INQUIRY

The nature of the scientific model on which the DECS cost analysis was based significantly affected the way the economic problem was understood. As a result of the model's emphasis on DO, the economic analysis, naturally enough, concentrated on estimating the costs of removing oxygen-demanding wastes and only incidentally considered other pollutants.[6] Even

5. In evaluating in dollar terms the resources that are diverted from other possible uses to pollution control, we are assuming that the existing economic structure does not contain such dramatic imperfections that the prices generated give profoundly misleading indications of the opportunity costs involved. In the economist's jargon, we are assuming that "second best" factors are not so preponderant as to undermine the viability of partial equilibrium cost–benefit analysis. This assumption is generally made in work of this kind and it appears neither more nor less valid here than elsewhere. For discussions of its theoretical merit, see the works cited in n. 2.
6. After calculating the cost of reaching the dissolved oxygen objectives, the DECS staff checked the results to determine whether its water quality standards for acidity and bacteria were met. If not, the costs of meeting these standards were added (DECS, p. 63 and Table 16, p. 66). These additional costs were relatively small. For example, of the $275 million cost of reaching Objective Set II, $20 million represents the additional cost of acidity and bacteria removal. Costs of removing particular poisons were not explicitly calculated. In fact, a footnote to DECS Table 16 states that the standards for other parameters of water quality (except chlorides) were

when the nature of the pollution problem had been so drastically simplified, however, the DECS found it necessary to focus its concern even more narrowly in order to make headway in what it considered to be the most important aspects of the problem of cost estimation. We do not mean to suggest in any way that the decision to narrow the field of inquiry was an unwise one. It was necessary for the DECS to simplify its task at the beginning of its investigations. But the consequence of many of the simplifying assumptions proved to be distortions of reality which substantially limited the range and validity of the cost estimates provided to the DRBC at the time of its initial decision in 1967.

The "Fourty Four" Polluters

As we have seen,[7] the hundred polluters discharging directly into the estuary constitute only the most visible part of the estuary's pollution problem. The "critical region's" oxygen supply is depleted further by the blanket of sludge on the River's bottom, as well as the wastes entering the estuary both from the Upper Delaware above Trenton and the major tributaries flowing into the main stem at various points. In order to make their task manageable, however, the DECS staff concentrated their energies on the 44 most important point-source polluters discharging directly into the estuary. This decision was justified on the ground that these 44 sources contributed more than 95 percent of all wastes emitted by point sources discharging directly into the main stem. In fact, however, when other sources of waste are taken into account, these 44 polluters contribute only 65 percent of the total load imposed on the estuary. Most important, the nonestuarine branches of the river contributed 12 percent of the total load in 1964. Since a number of the major tributaries are the scenes of rapid industrial and residential growth, the waste load from these sources will increase substantially over time.[8] Nevertheless, by focussing concern solely

---

assumed to be met by DO, pH, and bacterial control measures. Furthermore, the DECS does not present the results of looking at the program in reverse by first estimating the cost of meeting pH and bacterial objectives and *then* recording the additional cost of meeting DO objectives. As we shall see, this would have been a most useful exercise for policy makers.

7. See Ch. 3, p. 22 and n. 17.

8. See Ch. 4, pp. 45, 46. While the old central cities along the main stem of the river (Philadelphia, Trenton, Wilmington, Chester, Bristol, Marcus Hook, Morrisville, Camden, Bordentown, and Burlington) suffered a population loss of over 4 percent between 1960 and 1970, the remainder of the Trenton and Philadelphia Standard Metropolitan Statistical Areas (SMSA's) and the Delaware and New Jersey sections of the Wilmington SMSA gained 22 percent in population, the bulk of this growth occurring in the drainage basins of tributaries to the Delaware (*Census of Population,* 1972, parts 9, 32, 40). Similarly, population projections for the Delaware Valley

on polluters on the main stem, this increasingly important cost factor was ignored in the estimates.

Time

Even after restricting the focus of their inquiry to a single—if important— group of dischargers and an extremely limited class of pollutants, the DECS was obliged to resolve yet another complex issue before it could proceed. We refer to the problem posed by the existence of time, which manifested itself in two equally important ways. First, as we have seen, the cost of attaining a given water quality objective fluctuates widely over the course of a year.[9] Most important, on the ten rainiest days of the year, waste discharged into the river will more than double,[10] thanks to the combined sewers of Trenton, Camden, Philadelphia, and Wilmington. This means that if a pollution program is to permit a broad range of aquatic life to maintain itself in previously heavily polluted sections of the river, the costs of dealing with stormy weather should be one of the most important components of the analysis. Second, besides varying within a single time period, compliance costs will increase over a longer time horizon as population and industrial growth in the valley require each polluter to eliminate greater percentages of its raw load if water quality is not to deteriorate. Unfortunately, however, the staff treated both of these issues in a highly simplified way.

The first issue—raised most dramatically by the storm sewer problem— provides compelling evidence of the way in which a scientific statement of "the facts" can distort subsequent stages of the policy analysis. As we have seen,[11] the DECS' primary fact-finding tool was a steady state model that ignored all transient phenomena, treating all discharges and river conditions as if they remained constant over time. Thus, instead of confronting the consequences of the sewers' massive intermittent discharges on water

---

predict the older urban areas will suffer a 2.2 percent loss in population between 1960 and 1985; that older suburbs, including older towns other than Philadelphia, Camden, and Trenton, will increase by 39 percent and the remainder of the region by 108 percent (*1985 Regional Projection; Final Population Projections,* 1972; *1985 Estimates,* 1966; *New Jersey Population Projections,* 1971). For a description of the definitions of "older urban areas" and "older suburbs" see *Impact of Highway Construction,* 1972, p. A-1. "Value-added" in manufacturing establishments located outside the old center cities on the main stem equals value-added within these old cities, and the proportion generated by the suburbs is growing. It was 48 percent of the total in 1963 and 50 percent in 1967 (*Census of Manufacturers,* 1967).

9. See Ch. 4, pp. 37, 38.
10. *Ibid.,* pp. 42–45.
11. *Ibid.,* pp. 37–39.

quality, the DECS' scientific model treated storms sewers *as if they constantly discharged a relative trickle into the river day in and day out*. Since on an *annual average* basis, storm sewers account for only 4 percent of the total BOD loadings, the DECS' steady state model could not express the basic importance of this source in the over-all pollution control scheme.

Given the fact that the scientific model provided the framework in which the economic analysis was to be performed, it became a relatively simple matter for the cost estimates to fail to come to grips with the vexing sewer issue. After all, sewers accounted for only 4 percent of the "average" daily load—so the model assured the staff. Consequently, it seemed sensible to avoid any well focussed discussion of the costs of correcting this problem in all the DECS' published writings,[12] despite the fact that it will cost at least one billion dollars to control Philadelphia's storm sewer problem (and even this large sum may be conservative).[13] In other words, coping with this "4 percent of the average daily load" will be more expensive than dealing with the normal wastes generated by the estuary's polluters, even if these discharges were reduced as drastically as contemplated by the most stringent clean-up objective of the five advanced to the DRBC for consideration.[14]

While the combined sewer issue seems to have been submerged by the steady state approach, the DECS did perceive the existence of the problem posed by the growth of pollution loads over time. Unfortunately, however, its treatment of this issue was primitive. In seeking to estimate the costs of compliance for a 20-year period between 1965 and 1985,[15] the staff assumed that none of the 22 firms in the sample would leave the valley and—even more important—that no major new industrial dischargers

12. To be more precise, the DECS staff did recognize the importance of storm water overflow and performed a special study to determine the frequency of such impulses and their impact on water quality (DECS, pp. 24–25, Fig. 13). Moreover, the DECS Report notes that sewer discharges pose a special problem and list control of storm water discharges as one of the methods by which water quality might be improved (*Loc. cit.*) Nothing more is said, however, and in the actual cost–benefit analysis, the variability of storm sewer overflow is not considered.

13. See n. 33, Ch. 4.

14. Industrial loads are also extremely variable, depending on the products being manufactured and the level of operations. DECS, p. 22, notes this variability but the staff did not incorporate the information into their analysis. Certainly, one possible way to improve river conditions during critical periods would be to requre industrial polluters to dump less on such days than on others. As the volume of waste is under the control of the plant management and does not depend on the vagaries of the weather, such an approach could be quite useful.

15. The validity of using a 20-year time horizon is critically examined in Ch. 8 as is the DECS use of a 3-percent discount rate to calculate the present value of costs and benefits accruing over time.

would locate on the banks of the river.[16] This second assumption seems particularly untenable when it is recognized that substantial quantities of shoreline in the highly industrialized Philadelphia-Camden metropolitan area are still available for development on the New Jersey side of the river, and that a new bridge is under construction which will link this land directly to markets in Pennsylvania and the West.[17]

While it is obvious that any treatment of these new industries must contain elements of uncertainty, to ignore completely what almost surely will occur because its details cannot be known is to pursue hard data at the cost of generating sensible estimates. Instead, DECS should have produced a *series* of cost estimates envisioning a number of plausible scenarios for the development of vacant land in the urbanized zone over the next generation. Such an approach would, of course, require a number of informed guesses as to the nature of industries moving to the river, their probable locations, the amount of waste they would generate, and the costs of treatment at the time the industry entered the region. Nevertheless, it would give the decision maker a sense of the probable range in which the cost of compliance would fall. This seems far better than providing the policy maker with a single number that ignores the possibility of entry entirely.

Turning to the way the DECS dealt with its 44 polluters, the staff's treatment of temporal change again appears simplistic. In attempting to obtain cost data from the dischargers themselves, the DECS reports that the staff asked each of the 44 polluters to "reflect load increases for about a 10-year period (1965 to 1975) by estimating the cost of treatment to maintain certain levels of discharge through that time period."[18] Although the staff expected the polluters to report substantial growth, only nine of

---

16. DECS, p. 62.
17. The compact providing for the Chester-Bridgeport Bridge was finally approved in August 1966, when the DECS was still at work on its report. The bridge is scheduled for completion in 1974. (Interview with Delaware River Port Authority personnel, August 1972.)
18. DECS, p. 62; confirmed by David Marks, former member of the DECS staff, in a telephone interview in April 1972. However, Schaumberg, 1967, pp. 50, 51, reports that the question asked was actually:

> How much would it cost you to reduce BOD discharges by the year 1975? Give present discharges and the cost to reduce BOD discharges (nearly) to zero. If possible give one or two levels of BOD reduction and the corresponding costs of achieving these reductions. Be sure to consider process change as an alternative to waste treatment in your estimation of costs.

This passage is ambiguous about how growth in loads should be considered and it is not surprising that, as Mr. Marks and a fellow DECS staffer report, numerous meetings with the polluters were necessary in order to explain what data were actually desired. (Interview with M. Sobel, April 1972.)

the 44 dischargers responded that they were anticipating any increase in waste production between 1965 and 1975.[19] Since all nine growing dischargers were small municipalities,[20] the DECS questionnaires generated the rather surprising conclusion that the cost of controlling future growth was a mere $20 million.[21] The DECS explained this small figure by claiming that any increase in raw loads which might be expected to occur would be "accounted for by reduction of waste through plant modification, and by revenue obtained through product recovery."[22]

There is, however, a far more plausible explanation for the failure of the questionnaires to reveal substantial waste load growth. In industry the typical addressees of such questionnaires are plant managers, who are unlikely to have an accurate view of expansion plans being made at the head office, and hence may respond conservatively by assuming no growth at all in the future. Moreover, it is doubtful that even head office personnel— if their views are obtained—have very clear plans over a 10- or 15-year time horizon.[23]

While questionnaires have their place, they cannot provide the sole source for a sensible estimate of the costs of compliance over time. At the very least the questionnaires must be checked for consistency with estimates of over-all regional growth devised either by the staff itself or by other agencies concerned with regional development. The DECS had access to such regional estimates, and in fact, discussed them in its 1966 Report, without, however, recognizing the importance of this information in assessing the validity of its own growth estimates. The regional growth analysis portrayed a booming Delaware Valley in which population would grow by 30 percent between 1964 and 1975 and industry would develop at a far more rapid rate. Translating these aggregate estimates into wasteload projections, the staff prophesied that by 1975 municipal loads would be 230

19. Ethan Smith, in a letter to Professor Susan Rose-Ackerman, June 1971. While the text of DECS, p. 31, indicates that estimates of load increases were made for all 44 dischargers, staffer Smith reports, however, that this was not actually done for 13 major municipal sources.
20. *Ibid.*
21. The actual figure given in the DECS for Objective Set V, which is said to contemplate the maintenance of 1964 conditions, is $30 million. However, the study states that $10 million of this sum represents the cost of raising five sources to primary treatment (DECS, p. 66), a cost that should not correctly be included in the cost of maintaining 1964 conditions since it would, in fact, improve conditions.
22. DECS, p. 30.
23. We have in the text described the problems in assessing growth in industrial wasteloads through the interview technique. Our interviews suggest, however, that the 22 municipalities in the sample were not asked to provide cost estimates. Instead, DECS used estimates of the municipalities' loadings to generate cost estimates. (Interview with M. Sobel, April 1972.)

percent and industrial wastes 187 percent of their 1964 levels.[24] If the staff had compared these aggregate estimates with the data accumulated by questionnaire, it would at once have perceived the dramatic inconsistency. If any credence had been given to the over-all *regional* estimates, it would have been clear that it would cost far more than $20 million to control future growth. In saying this, we do not mean to suggest that the regional growth figures are any more correct than the questionnaire data.[25] The divergence, however, suggests the magnitude of the problem and the degree to which the DECS' failure to confront the problem flawed its analysis. Of course, if the DECS *had* confronted the problem squarely, it would not have been possible to resolve it in any simple way. Inevitably, instead of presenting decision makers with a single number that purported to indicate the cost of a given control program, the staff would have been obliged to suggest that compliance costs would vary considerably under plausible growth scenarios.[26]

Manipulating the Data

Having derived each polluter's cost curve from questionnaire data, the DECS problems in data manipulation were not at an end. First, in order to use a linear program that calculated the cost of reaching each of the

24. DECS, p. 29. DECS projected raw waste loads generated by point-source polluters along the Delaware Estuary in 1975. These estimates show that industrial raw loads are expected to grow from 700,000 lbs/day of carbonaceous oxygen demand to 1,200,000 lbs/day in 1975 (DECS, pp. 29–30). These estimates were obtained, DECS explains, by considering the major Standard Industrial Classifications represented along the estuary; estimating production in dollars for those discharging directly into the estuary; projecting this over time, and estimating raw load by using factors that related units of pollution to dollars of production in each time period. Technical change was accounted for in a rough way by changes in the factors relating pollution to dollars of output. Municipal loads are expected to grow from 1.2 billion lbs/day in 1964 to 2.8 billion in 1975.

25. The actual increase in population in the Delaware Valley between 1960 and 1970 was 12 percent (*Census of Population,* 1972, Vol. I, Parts 9, 32 and 40). In fact, projections of the Delaware Valley Regional Planning Commission and the states of Delaware and New Jersey indicate that population in the region is expected to grow only by an additional 5 percent between 1970 and 1975 (*1985 Regional Projections; Final Population Projections,* 1972; *Preliminary Population Projections,* 1971). Total employment also grew by only 12 percent over the same period—a figure that appears inconsistent with a growth of 187 percent in industrial waste loads between 1964 and 1975 (*Employment and Earnings,* 1971).

26. The problem is not as intractable as it might at first appear, however, since a few large dischargers account for the bulk of the waste discharged into the river, and obtaining growth estimates for these large polluters alone would result in a good estimate of over-all growth. Of the total load of 1,025,000 lbs/day of FSUOD discharged by point-source polluters in 1964, 424,000 lbs (41 percent) came from Philadelphia's three plants. Camden, Wilmington, and the Dupont plant at Chambers, N.J., account for another 231,000. Thus these four polluters (actually six sources,

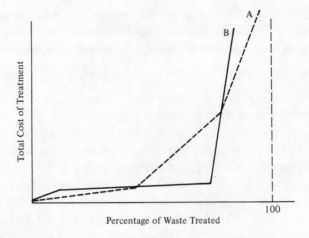

Figure 8
Hypothetical Pollution Control Cost Function for a
Discharger with a Given Raw Load

proposed water quality objectives, the staff was constrained to choose only a finite set of points representing the costs of reaching certain levels of waste removal for each polluter. The cost of waste removal at any intermediate point was assumed to lie on the straight line connecting the chosen points (line A in Figure 8). Such an approximation may lead to serious over- or underestimates of costs if the solution to the linear program occurs at a level of treatment where the linear approximation differs substantially from the actual cost of cleanup (portrayed by line B in Figure 8). Although in the early phase of its work the DECS experimented with different, discrete treatment cost points in order to select those that best approximated continuous cost estimates in the neighborhood of the solution,[27] this practice seems to have been abandoned in later work when industry provided some hard data concerning the costs of attaining one, two, or three levels of treatment.[28]

The restrictions imposed by linear programming are reflected again in the DECS' treatment of capital expenses. If a firm now treating at 65 per-

because Philadelphia has three plants) accounted for 64 percent of the 1964 discharge. The addition of the next 12 largest dischargers (ten industries and two municipalities) raises the percentage covered to 88. (Calculated from DRBC data on 1964 discharges.)

27. Interview with M. Sobel, April 1972.

28. Evidence for this statement consists of the three sets of cost data provided by the DECS staff to various researchers over the years. For a discussion of these data, see Appendix B.

cent reported to DECS that it would require a capital investment of $500,000 to raise its treatment level to 85 percent, DECS assumed that the investment required for 80 percent treatment was three-fourths of $500,000 or $375,000, (i.e. $K(x) = \$500,000 \left(\dfrac{x - 65}{85 - 65} \right)$ where $x =$ percent removal, $K =$ capital investment). Thus, the DECS assumed that capital expenditures were never "lumpy." Unfortunately, however, it sometimes may cost as much to build a plant which removes 80 percent of BOD as it does to build one which removes 85 percent. The only difference between the two plants will appear in the somewhat lower operating costs experienced by the 80 percent plant. When this is true, the DECS procedure will underestimate the cost of compliance, since it will predict a capital cost of $375,000, while the actual cost will be $500,000. On the other hand, the DECS procedure may sometimes lead to an overestimate of costs. Suppose that a polluter reported to DECS that it would incur $500,000 in capital costs to remove 85 percent of its BOD but one million dollars to remove 95 percent. Following its approach the DECS assumed that the firm's cost of removing 90 percent of BOD was $750,000. In fact, however, no new capital investment may be required to move from 85 to 90 percent treatment, since the 85 percent plant, operated in a more costly fashion, will achieve the 90 percent objective. While the DECS approach may thus result either in an overestimate or an underestimate of compliance costs, our own manipulation of the DECS data reveals that if we assumed that the "lumpiness effect" consistently operated to inflate capital expenses, the total cost of attaining the DRBC's objective would increase by 15 percent or $40 million.[29] Although this assumption is, of course, an extreme one, it serves to demonstrate the extent to which even a minor simplification may mask significant problems when the data base is as weak as the one on which DECS operated.

To make matters worse it is not at all clear that substantial improvements in the quality of data would be easy to achieve. One alternative is to develop comprehensive information about the costs of pollution control in different industries. While general cost information of modest accuracy already exists for municipal sewage treatment,[30] estimating such data for

29. This increase represents an upper bound, since the estimate was obtained by assuming that if the load removed at one data point were exceeded by only one pound, then the total capital cost of the load removed at the next data point would be incurred. Once the cost data were assigned to particular polluters, as described in Appendix B, such an estimate was relatively simple to obtain under the clean-up scheme chosen by the DRBC.
30. *Economics of Clean Water*, 1970. For engineering specifications, see White, 1970 and Goodman, 1971.

industry is a far more difficult problem. A firm's entire production process must be understood in order to discover the possibilities of waste-saving process change as an alternative to separate treatment at the end of the process. Although path-breaking efforts have been attempted,[31] we are far from the day when analysts will possess studies for many different industries relating plant age and product mix to waste water characteristics and waste reduction costs. The issue is further complicated by the fact that the current interest in pollution control should lead to a shift of engineering and scientific talent into this field with a consequent increase in the rate of technical change. Thus, the uncertainties haunting the DECS data will be typical of all but the most ambitious and expensive efforts within the foreseeable future.

BEYOND 1966: DEALING WITH COST OVERRUNS

Far from presenting a comprehensive accounting of the costs of cleaning up the environment, the DECS analysis provided a necessarily tentative view of the tip of an iceberg. Just as with the BOD-DO model, the fundamental DECS error resided not so much in its failure to reach the unattainable ideal of perfect accuracy and comprehensiveness, but in its failure to explore the policy implications resulting from the oversimplifications necessarily involved in its ambitious effort at systematic analysis. As a result, decision makers were presented with a series of numbers without any effort to explain the factors which the estimates had ignored.

Similarly, the fate of the technocratic effort to refine cost estimates after the original DRBC decision in 1966 was almost as unhappy as the analogous effort to develop the BOD-DO analysis further. Neither the DECS nor the DRBC has made a substantial investment in extraeconomic sophistication. Nevertheless, despite the lack of institutional support, the remaining members of the DECS staff generated enough additional research on compliance costs to raise profound doubts as to the wisdom of the DRBC program. Moreover, the institutional response by the DRBC and other concerned agencies to these troubling data will permit additional

31. See Löf and Kneese, 1968; Russell, 1973. For a summary of the difficulties posed by lack of information in determining costs of waste cutbacks within a given industry, see Vol. II, Part II, pp. 91–94 of *Cost of Clean Water,* 1968.

Under the 1972 federal statute, the Environmental Protection Agency is required to undertake this difficult task as a preliminary to setting discharge standards (33 U.S.C.A. §1314(b)(1)(B), Supp. 1973). It seems plain, however, that given the present state of understanding, the EPA's work will of necessity be speculative and imprecise.

insights into the way the technocratic enterprise should be structured to counteract the twin tendencies to oversell the value of preliminary work and to halt analysis prematurely just at the point where real sophistication begins.

Official Revisions of the Cost Data

As we have seen, the future of the technocratic enterprise along the Delaware rested in large measure with the three remaining DECS staffers who remained at the regional office of the Federal Water Quality Administration. Although the FWQA required them to spend the bulk of their time on other projects, these career civil servants made conscientious efforts to improve the initial cost estimates as best they could without the aid of substantial additional resources.

First, cost data were obtained on 47 small polluters to supplement the original analysis of the 44 most important estuarine dischargers. As these small polluters contributed no more than 5 percent of the point-source load on the estuary,[32] the new data increased the total expected costs of reaching the DRBC water quality goal by only 10 percent.[33] More important, the staff reconsidered the 1966 report's estimate that an investment of only $20 million would be required to deal adequately with anticipated growth in wasteloads between 1965 and 1985. Finding the initial estimates far too low, they jacked up the price of dealing with growth to $140 million.[34] Although we can well understand why the early estimate was found to be so seriously mistaken, it remains far from clear how this new number was obtained. When queried by the authors on this matter, the staffers explained that:

. . . the later estimate of $140 million included [the] nine sources [originally considered by the 1966 report] plus numerous other municipal sources which in our opinion must experience additional costs to abate increasing loads as population growth continues, even if they are to discharge no greater load than in 1964.[35]

So far as it appears from this response, no effort was made to address more satisfactorily the problem of growth in industrial loads from existing sources. Nor does it appear that any effort was made to cure another

32. These cost functions were calculated by combining population data and information on existing facilities with engineering cost estimates to obtain separate estimates for each small town. (Interview with Smith and Morris, summer 1970.)
33. Letter from E. Smith to Professor Susan Rose-Ackerman.
34. Smith and Morris, 1969, p. 1640.
35. Letter from E. Smith to Professor Susan Rose-Ackerman.

serious deficiency in the earlier report by considering the cost implications of additional waste loads imposed on the mainstream by dramatically increasing population and industrial concentrations located along the Delaware tributaries.[36]

We are doubtful, however, that the reappraisal of costs attempted by the remaining DECS researchers was as narrow as their written response to the authors suggests. While the DECS obtained its cost data from individual polluters under a pledge of confidentiality, it has nevertheless proved possible for us to identify each discharger's cost data through a complex series of inferences from public documents detailed in Appendix B. As a result of this analysis, we have concluded that the cost estimates of no more than 14 municipalities and four industries have changed between 1966 and 1970. Moreover, it is difficult to understand how these relatively small changes could possibly have accounted for such a large increase in costs of dealing with growth. It appears more likely that the new $140 million figure includes, in addition to the growth in particular municipal sources cited in the letter, some rough over-all estimate of the costs of treating regional growth not assigned to particular polluters.[37]

All the imprecisions and gaps in these more recent cost estimates may be traced ultimately to a single source: neither the Federal Water Quality Administration (FWQA)[38] nor the DRBC had any real interest in a continuing effort to ascertain the costs of complying with the ambitious pro-

36. See n. 8.
37. A very rough estimate could have been obtained by estimating the total increase in load from regional projections of population and industrial growth and then using a standard sanitary engineering text to estimate the cost of building a secondary treatment plant capable of handling such a load. A more conceptually correct method would first have assigned the increased load to the various river sections on the basis of regional projections and information about the availability of vacant land and, second, have predicted the 1975 DO profile on the assumption that none of the new load would be treated. The cost of growth could then be calculated by estimating the cost of raising the predicted profile to the actual 1964 level using as estimates the marginal cost data already available. Costs of higher levels of cleanliness would then be calculated upward from the percentage of waste removal required to maintain 1964 conditions. The most serious problem with this method is that in practice the marginal costs of different levels of percentage removal will change as raw loads change.
     A third possibility is perhaps the most sensible. Since the bulk of the growth will occur along the tributaries, the detailed population and employment projection of the Delaware Valley Regional Planning Commission could be used to predict growth in each creek valley; one could then estimate the cost of building regional treatment plants at the mouth of each creek to handle this load.
38. With the increasing importance of environmental regulation on the federal level, the responsibility for water pollution control shifted from the Department of Health, Education and Welfare to the Federal Water Pollution Control Administration in the Department of the Interior in 1966 and then to the Water Quality Office of the Environmental Protection Agency (1970). For purposes of convenience, except where it would be misleading, we shall refer to the federal water control agency as the FWQA, since that was its name during much of the period under discussion.

gram selected for the Delaware River. Without resources provided by either of these agencies, three busy men working only intermittently on the problem could do little more than in fact was accomplished. Far more important than the imperfections of the new cost estimates was the way they were used by the relevant decision-making agencies, especially the DRBC. In brief, the DRBC staff ignored the implications of the sharp increase in the cost estimates; indeed our interviews with the relevant policy makers suggest that this early warning signal was never presented to the representatives of the states and the federal government who meet each month on the Commission.[39]

The remnant of the DECS staff was not, however, willing simply to ignore the problem posed by mushrooming compliance costs. In 1969, the FWQA prepared for public release a summary of the DECS' latest findings, which contained a set of cost estimates even higher than the initial revisions. In this summary, entitled *Where Man and Water Meet,* the cost of dealing with anticipated regional growth jumps once more—from $140 million to $218 million[40]—and total compliance costs were estimated at $503 million (in 1964 dollars), $233 million more than the sum proffered to the DRBC when the governors and Interior Secretary made their initial decision. Upon circulating this memo for comment to the states and the DRBC, the FWQA learned that the new higher cost estimates were bitterly resented by officials in these agencies precisely because they cast grave doubt on the wisdom of the program they were responsible for administering. In response to this protest, FWQA suppressed the document's publication and no further exploration of this problem, so far as we know,[41] has been attempted by the agencies involved.[42]

39. Interviews with delegates from the four states represented on the DRBC as well as the federal government: Harold Jacobs (Del.), Matt Adams (N.J.), Maurice Goodard (Pa.), R. Stewart Kilborne (N.Y.), Vernon Northup and Paul Van Wegen (U.S.). All interviewed during the summer of 1972 except Mr. Goddard, who was interviewed in September 1970.
40. Ethan Smith states in a letter to Professor Susan Rose-Ackerman that the "$78 million is the increase in cost estimated by DECS due to the fact that the DRBC program now calls for nearly 90 percent removal whereas the DECS program called for 85 percent (uniform) removal. The 90 percent requirement is caused by the establishment of a reserve for new sources by DRBC."
41. It should be noted that two of the DECS staffers did publish their updated cost estimates in a professional journal (Smith and Morris, 1969). Their article, however, serves mainly to justify the DRBC program; it does not make clear the limitations of the original DECS analysis nor does it urge the reappraisal of policy in the light of the new estimates. In short, the article reflects an understandable reluctance on the part of subordinate officials to criticize openly the programs that had the explicit support of their superiors.
42. Furthermore, the final version of DECS' Report has never appeared. Several chapters exist in draft form, but the sections on the dollar values of costs and benefits have apparently never been circulated for comment.

Independent Cost Estimates

As a part of the present study, however, we sought to gain some sense of the probable costs of compliance by attempting to interview, in the summer of 1970, all of the polluters whose discharges are currently being regulated by the DRBC. In these interviews we did not attempt to take the growth problem explicitly into account, but simply inquired how much the polluter would have to invest to meet the clean-up requirements set for his discharge. Since dischargers typically plan ahead and build their treatment facilities large enough to handle anticipated growth in waste loads, however, their responses to some indeterminate extent do reflect expected growth.[43] Whenever it was possible, we attempted to check the verbal estimates presented in our interviews with estimates contained in the written reports filed for the polluters by consultants who have been hired to plan the treatment projects. Whenever a discharger refused to give us an interview, we used the same figures DECS uses in its most recent estimates.

When examining our data, based principally on interviews, we found that firms and municipalities were more confident of the capital costs of building treatment facilities and making process changes than they were in estimating the costs of operating the treatment plants which, at the time of the interviews, had not yet been constructed. Consequently, in making our rough estimates, we concentrated on capital costs and process changes. Our data indicate that these costs, when measured in 1970 dollars, totalled some $350 million.[44] In order to make our estimate comparable to the

43. Naturally, it will also reflect growth that has occurred between 1964 and 1970.
44. This estimate was obtained by combining interview data and data from consultants' reports. When no independent estimates were available, DECS estimates were used. The DECS figures, which constituted only a small proportion of the total in the new estimate, were multiplied by a factor of 1.3 to represent the increase in construction cost between 1964 and 1970 (see Smith, et. al., 1709–07/70, Fig. 6). The estimate breaks down as follows:

Dischargers	In millions of 1970 dollars
Philadelphia	$100
Gloucester City Regional	40
Camden City Regional	38
Camden County Regional	25
Wilmington	17
Other cities reporting costs	16
Firms reporting costs, not included in Deepwater Plant	30
Firms included in Deepwater Plant	65
Dischargers not reporting costs	7
	$338 million

In addition to the results of interviews, the estimates relied on information from *Deepwater Study,* prepared for the DRBC, June 1970; Reuter Associates, *Camden Study,* 1967; Reuter Associates, *Gloucester Study,* 1967.
The estimate for the *Deepwater Study* represents the cost of constructing a large

DECS' we assumed—as did the official study—that the discounted present value of operating and maintenance costs would be approximately equal to investment in capital and process changes.[45] Thus our impressionistic survey suggests that compliance will cost $700 million in the foreseeable future. In short, when inflation is taken into account,[46] our estimates correspond moderately well to the last set of figures generated by the DECS, which were suppressed in *Where Man and Water Meet*.

Of course, in corroborating these latest figures, we have done no more than gain a somewhat better understanding of the tip of the iceberg. Aside from the crude way we have dealt with the growing waste loads of the dischargers along the main stem, our figures do not take into account the costs borne by new entrants, or those borne along many of the booming tributaries, or those which will result if the DRBC finds itself obliged to order more stringent BOD cutbacks in order to meet its objectives,[47] or those involved in solving the combined sewer problem. When all these factors are taken into account, the magnitude of the agency's commitment to improving the DO profile marginally in the most polluted area of the river can be appreciated, if not reduced to a single easy number.

CONCLUSIONS: THE RELATIONSHIP BETWEEN SCIENTIFIC FACT FINDING AND ECONOMIC ANALYSIS

As we suggested at the beginning of this chapter, it is possible to look to economic analysis as a source of a potent critique of the fact-finding branch of the technocratic enterprise: Will not the analyst, in his effort at a comprehensive cost accounting, notice that certain crucial aspects of reality have been given insufficient attention in the technocratic statement of "the facts"? If this question can be answered affirmatively, the problem of devising institutional mechanisms to control technocratic intelligence,

---

facility which was intended to service a substantial number of industrial dischargers in New Jersey. Since this regional plant will not be built (see Ch. 19, pp. 301–309), the actual costs of separate compliance can be expected to be higher. The *Deepwater Study* lists $79 million as the total cost of on-site treatment (Table XIII-3). Using this figure instead of $65 million yields a total of $352 million.

45. For purposes of comparison we thus assumed the same 3 percent discount rate and 20-year life assumed by DECS. These DECS assumptions, however, can be criticized on several grounds (see Ch. 8).

46. The Gross National Product deflator rose by almost 25 percent between 1964 and 1970, but the E.M. Boeth index of the cost of constructing commercial and factory buildings in 20 cities, including Philadelphia, rose by more than 40 percent in the same period.

47. See Ch. 20 for a discussion of the more stringent cutbacks that will be required under the new federal Pollution Control Act of 1972.

which perplexed us in Chapter 5, loses some of its importance; even without subtle structural devices, one aspect of the technocratic intelligence could then be expected to control the worst abuses of the other.

Unfortunately, however, the DECS experience suggests the wisdom of structuring institutions on the assumption that a fruitful interchange between the two components of the technocratic enterprise will not take place. Instead of reappraising the "scientific" description of reality, the DECS cost estimates accepted the BOD-DO model's version of the facts uncritically. Thus the staff did not move beyond the steady state model to perceive the obvious importance of the storm sewer problem, nor did it significantly transcend the scientific fixation with BOD and DO to measure the costs of removing a wide range of additional pollutants.

While this blind acceptance of "the facts" is regrettable, it is nevertheless an altogether predictable response to the demands of practical policy making and so should not be considered merely an aberration from the norm. Since the report must be proffered before the time for decision has passed, the cost–benefit team is understandably reluctant to conclude that the scientific fact-gathering effort—however commendable as an enterprise —has not generated information about the issues most relevant to economic analysis. Unless this warning can be given at a very early stage in the technocratic enterprise, there will simply not be enough time to redesign the fact-finding operation in fundamental ways. Moreover, aside from the embarrassment of raising basic issues when there is nothing much that can be done to resolve them technocratically, a second related factor must be taken into account. This chapter indicates that even a tentative effort to estimate some of the costs of pollution control in a systematic manner is a difficult task in itself, requiring a substantial investment of time and energy. It is thus perfectly understandable once again that the technocratic team would wish to get on with work which is obviously required— like an estimate of the costs to be born by the 44 "most important" dischargers—without anxiously considering elements of the problem which are less salient, under the prevailing technocratic definition of the problem. Thus, the economic analyst's natural desire to understand at least certain aspects of the problem before him in a technically competent fashion is at war with the larger policy-making need to scrutinize the basic premises of the entire technocratic analysis tendered after such great effort.[48]

48. In short, the conceptual framework suggested by the DECS' experience is the one suggested by March and Simon, 1958, and Lindblom, 1965, which emphasizes the necessity, in structuring institutions, of recognizing that none of the participants has sufficient time or inclination to rethink all of the first premises of the organizational effort. Instead, even a technocratic team that attempts a comprehensive analysis in fact places quite narrow boundaries on its analysis.

In addition to emphasizing the necessity of institutional controls on technocratic intelligence, the story of the DECS' cost analysis also suggests that the task of design is even more complex than our earlier discussion in Chapter 5 indicated. There, we were content to emphasize the difficulties involved simply in assuring the balanced evaluation of technocratic documents at the time of initial decision and the sustaining of long-term research after the first decision has been made. This chapter indicates, however, that even if these problems were resolved, further steps would be demanded to assure that subsequent analyses will be taken into account at the policy-making level. Otherwise, even enterprising staffers may be discouraged from pointed exposition of their findings because of their subordinate positions in the agency structure.[49] Even when staffers do attempt to raise the cost question, the agencies concerned may simply dig their heads into the sand. Internal reports can be ignored or suppressed, as in the case of *Where Man and Water Meet*.

Once again, however, we shall postpone sustained consideration of ways to control the tendency to repress unpleasant information until our survey of the DECS' effort at economic analysis is completed. For an assessment of the technocratic effort to measure the benefits of pollution control will add new dimensions to our understanding of the challenge of designing institutions that can cope with contemporary forms of esoteric analysis.

49. When these subordinates do make their findings public, it is done in a way which conceals their policy implications (see, n. 41).

Counting the Benefits: The Economist's Approach

INTRODUCTION

We now turn to that aspect of the technocratic enterprise which has engendered the greatest suspicion among large numbers of people, both in government and in the environmental movement, who take a skeptical view of the effort to bring greater "rationality" to decision making through systematic analysis. While recognizing that certain benefits could not be readily translated into dollar terms,[1] the DECS nevertheless attempted to assist policy makers by placing dollar values on the principal recreational and commercial uses that a cleaner Delaware would make possible. The difficulty of this enterprise, however, prompted the DECS staff to enlist the aid of the Institute of Environmental Studies of the University of Pennsylvania. Thus, while the DECS staff modified some aspects of the work undertaken by the Institute, it is this leading academic organization

1. DECS, pp. 71, 74, 80. The unquantifiable benefits mentioned include preservation of fish and wildlife and improved drinking water and aesthetics.

that was primarily responsible for the DECS' method of computing benefits.[2]

Since more than 95 percent of the clean-up benefits were found by the DECS to reside in the river's recreational potential, we shall concentrate on the value of these uses.[3] The dollar values DECS placed on enhanced swimming, fishing and boating possibilities are shown in Table 4. The columns labeled "Net Benefits" show the benefits that would be enjoyed for each improvement program *in addition* to the benefits associated with maintaining current conditions (Objective V). A quick glance at the chart should at once place the conscientious decision maker on his guard. The figures reveal a puzzling pattern; they suggest that a *modest* program of

2. The DECS itself estimated the money value of benefits it believed would accrue to municipal and industrial users and to commercial fishermen. For estimates of benefits generated by enhanced recreational opportunities, the DECS relied heavily on the IES Study. This study, conducted by Anthony R. Tomazinis and Iskandar Gabbour, was carried out for DECS under a contract with the Public Health Service of the Department of Health, Education and Welfare. For convenience in exposition we shall refer to the recreation benefits estimates as "DECS estimates," since the DECS did make use of the IES results, thereby implicitly endorsing them.

When the DECS Report was published in 1966, the final IES Study had not been completed. The recreation benefits estimates in the DECS Report are based on a preliminary version of the IES estimates. Since completion of the final version of the IES Study the DECS staff have used these estimates in their further analyses of recreation benefits. See, for example, Smith and Morris, 1969, p. 1635.

3. The DECS' estimates for each catagory of net quantifiable benefits for each improvement program over and above the benefits associated with maintaining 1964 conditions are given in the following table.

Present Value of All Net Quantifiable Benefits
In Millions of 1964 Dollars

Objective	Type of Estimate	Recreation	Commercial Fishing	Industrial	Total
I	Maximum	355	12	−15	350
	Minimum	155	9		160
II	Maximum	320	12	−13	320
	Minimum	135	9		140
III	Maximum	310	7	−10	310
	Minimum	125	5		130
IV	Maximum	280	5	−7	280
	Minimum	115	3		120

Sources: All estimates come from the DECS Report: recreation benefits from Table 20, p. 77; commercial fishing benefits from Table 21, p. 80; industrial benefits from Figure 43, p. 74; and total benefits from p. 81.

The negative numbers in the industrial column reflect the DECS staff's discovery that cleaner water would actually impose extra costs on industrial users "primarily due to increased corrosion rates at higher oxygen levels" (DECS, p. 72). The DECS staff does not explain why the sums of the subcategories do not equal the total benefit figure for any of the programs.

Table 4. [4] **Estimated Recreational Benefits (in Millions of Dollars, at Present Value)**

	Net Benefits		Net Marginal Benefits	
Objective	Max.	Min.	Max.	Min.
I	355	155		
			35	20
II	320	135		
			10	10
III	310	125		
			30	10
IV	280	115		

river quality improvement will generate relatively *large* benefits ($115 million if one is a pessimist, $280 million if an optimist), while far more ambitious programs will generate only relatively small additional benefits to the citizens of the valley. Thus, the exceedingly expensive Objective I will produce benefits valued at only $40 million (or $75 million to an optimist) greater than the far less costly Objective IV.

Such a dramatic decline in the returns from additional expenditure on pollution control is not, of course, impossible in reality. Nevertheless, the prediction should be enough to invite the decision maker to probe further:

4. This table is taken from DECS, p. 77. The differences between the maximum and minimum benefit estimates are detailed in DECS, p. 76. The maximum benefit estimates assume that no swimming occurs at present, that boats contain an average of four people (four activity-days per boat) and that 25 percent of the users value their recreational experience at $5.00 per activity-day, with the remainder valuing the experience at $1.25. The minimum estimates asume that swimming occurs at present in the lower estuary, that each boat averages 3.5 people, and that 25 percent of the users value their experience at $3.00 per activity-day, with 75 percent valuing an activity-day at $0.75. The IES Study, pp. 44–56, also reports maximum and minimum net benefit estimates. These are based on assumptions different from those underlying estimates in the DECS Report. In particular, in the IES Study both maximum and minimum estimates assume that swimming could take place in the lower estuary under 1964 conditions and that boats used on the estuary carry an average of four people. Also, the assumptions regarding the valuation of activity-days are different and somewhat more complicated. We learned through correspondence with Ethan Smith of the DECS staff that the staff has adopted the IES assumptions for use in its subsequent analyses of recreation benefits.

DECS discusses the benefits data as if only swimming, boating, and fishing benefits were included. However, the discrepencies between the IES estimates and the DECS figures indicate that the DECS data may include the dollar value of picnicking benefits as well. For a fuller discussion of picnicking in light of these discrepencies, see Appendix C.

Is DECS wrong in belittling the extra benefits to be gained from far more expensive programs? Alternatively, could DECS be wrong in placing a high valuation on the improvements resulting from moving beyond the relatively inexpensive Objective V? In this and succeeding chapters, we shall demonstrate that DECS committed the second error and grossly *overstated* the dollar value of benefits to be gained from cleaning up the river both under Objective IV and under more ambitious proposals. Since the methodology that generated these overestimates is in general use,[5] we shall take care to expose its basic conceptual flaws as well as the serious errors in execution that marred the DECS effort.

The basic point of our criticism is simply that the benefit analysis pursued along the Delaware (and elsewhere) bears little relationship to the analysis suggested by relatively straightforward economic reasoning. As a result, the DECS obscured, rather than clarified, the nature of the policy choices to be made by the DRBC. In stating these criticisms, we do *not* suggest that coherent economic analysis permits the decision maker to reach a single correct answer to the benefits problem. Indeed, after our exposition of the economist's approach is completed, we shall elaborate upon its fundamental limitations.[6] Our point here is more modest; as classical forms of economic reasoning *can* illuminate *certain* dimensions of the pollution problem, an approach that ignores the economist's insights is at least as defective as one that looks to the dismal science as the exclusive repository of public policy.

A CONCEPTUAL FRAMEWORK

Before considering the particular difficulties involved in setting values on the benefits of pollution control, let us consider the more general problem. Suppose that the results of a government-financed research effort led to the introduction of a new product, say automatic washing machines, which produced cheaper and better washes than the prior technology, say hand

5. The basic conceptual framework of the IES Study, on which the DECS estimates are based, is the same as the one employed by the Bureau of Outdoor Recreation of the U.S. Department of the Interior in many of its studies. For a discussion of some variants of the basic framework and a list of the studies to which they were applied, see *Chesapeake Bay Study,* vol. III, pp. 99–117. A relatively recent application of this framework is in *Feasibility Report,* 1968, p. 49. For a study performed by researchers outside the Bureau of Outdoor Recreation, but which uses the same basic framework, see Edwards and Kelcey, Inc., 1970, and the associated technical reports, especially Technical Reports 7, 8, and 9. A succinct summary of the basic steps used in applying the framework is given by Grubb and Goodwin, 1968, p. 6.
6. See Chapter 9.

washing. Imagine that an economist was asked to measure the benefits generated by the research effort so that they could be compared with its costs. How would he go about this task?

On first consideration, the novice might be tempted simply to calculate the total amount spent for the machines and declare that figure to be the total benefit generated by the new product. But this would fundamentally misconceive the role of the market price in a competitive economy. If the washing machine market is in equilibrium at $100, the number of machines demanded by consumers is just equal to the number producers find it profitable to supply. At a slightly higher price (say $101), some "marginal" consumers will balk at the offer of a washer and choose another set of competing goods instead. For these marginal purchasers, buying a washing machine at $100 *provides them with virtually no more satisfaction than they would have if washing machines were not offered on the market at all.* Thus, if we wish to estimate the benefits generated by the new technology we must consider exclusively the situation of those "intramarginal" consumers (often the great majority) who would still purchase washing machines even if the price were significantly higher than $100.

Suppose, for example, we interviewed an intramarginal consumer named Jones and learned that he would have purchased his machine even if the price had been $150.[7] Since the market only requires Jones to pay $100, Jones could be required to sacrifice $50 and still be no worse off than he was before washing machines became available.[8] If we do not

7. We assume that Jones will tell the truth. It is easy to see why he might not. If Jones knew that he would have to pay the amount he quotes, he might understate his willingness to pay. On the other hand, if he thought his reply might affect the decision of a public authority to subsidize washing machine production, he might overstate the maximum price he would pay. For further discussion of the problems of relying on interviews with consumers, see text accompanying n. 11.

8. This "sacrifice test" is better known to economists as the "compensation test," and the sacrifice measure of benefits is called the "compensating variation." Unfortunately, the attempt to place a dollar value on the improvement in consumers' positions brought about by a change in their opportunities is confronted with a fundamental ambiguity, except under very special circumstances. While the conceptual experiment we have called the sacrifice test seems to be a reasonable one, another equally reasonable experiment can be devised. We might ask consumers how much of a *bribe* they would demand before they would consider themselves as well off without washing machines as they are with their original money income and the availability of washing machines at $100. Economists have dubbed the results of this "bribe test" the "equilibrating variation." The sacrifices (compensating variations) consumers would make in order to buy washing machines for $100 are equal to the bribes (equilibrating variations) they would accept in return for foregoing this opportunity only under the quite stringent assumption that purchases of the good under consideration do not change when all prices are held constant and money income is increased. For a proof of this assertion see Patinkin, 1963, p. 94.

Although some authorities have argued that it will be clear from the situation under consideration whether the sacrifice test or the bribe test is appropriate (Patin-

exact this $50 sacrifice from Jones, the introduction of the new good has in effect put $50 in extra income into Jones' pocket. It is this "consumer's surplus" of $50, not the $100 market price, that the economist counts as the benefit to Jones of his obtaining a washing machine. The total benefit accruing from the new product is obtained by summing the amount of money beyond the market price that each intramarginal consumer would sacrifice[9] before forsaking his washing machine.[10]

---

kin, 1963, p. 95) there seem to be no purely logical grounds for choosing between the two. This fundamental ambiguity in the measurement of the benefits to consumers from changes in their opportunities has practical implications. The benefits from a proposed change must be compared to the costs of achieving the change. If both the sacrifice test and the bribe test yield benefits estimates which are larger or smaller than the costs of the change, there is no problem; but if one measure of benefits exceeds costs and the other falls short of them, the decision maker is faced with a dilemma which seems insoluble in principle. Our analysis will suggest, however, that this potentially troublesome ambiguity does not cause a problem in evaluating the proposed pollution control schemes for the Delaware Estuary, since the costs of the DRBC program quite clearly outweigh the benefits, however defined.

9. The figure obtained by the application of the sacrifice test to the information supplied by Jones and his fellow intramarginal consumers is a completely accurate measure of the benefits to society of the government research on washing machine technology only under a set of quite stringent assumptions. First, it must be assumed that all goods and factor markets are perfectly competitive and that there are no taxes or subsidies associated with the consumption or production of any good or the use of any factor. Second, there must be no external effects in either consumption or production; that is, the satisfaction derived by each consumer from a given bundle of goods must be independent of how much other consumers purchase, and the level of output of each good associated with a given factor input must be independent of the level of output of all other goods. Third, it must be true that the prices of all goods except washing machines and the prices of all factors of production remain unchanged when some factors of production are switched from the production of all other goods to the production of washing machines. The assumption of constant prices allows a useful first approximation when the production of the good being considered (washing machines) makes relatively limited demands on the resources available to the economy and when its production does not require specialized factors of production with few alternative uses. Fourth, it must be assumed that washing machines can be produced at a constant cost of $100 per machine throughout the relevant range. Finally, decision makers must be convinced that a dollar's worth of sacrifice means the same thing to society no matter which consumer makes it.

For a discussion of the problems encountered when these restrictions are relaxed and for a pessimistic conclusion regarding the usefulness of the sacrifice test, see Little, 1957, pp. 174–84. For a discussion of how to deal with some of these problems, and a defense of the usefulness of the sacrifice test, see Harberger, 1971, p. 785. Some economists argue that the restrictive assumptions and information inputs required for a completely correct application of the sacrifice test under more general circumstances are so many and so complex that they cannot even be closely approximated in a practical application. But at the same time, even many purists would agree that when the costs of a project *far* exceed its benefits, or vice versa, cost–benefit analysis remains a valuable tool, even though both cost and benefit estimates have been obtained by application of the sacrifice test to a situation which does not meet many of the restrictions which are required in principle. We shall argue that the Delaware represents just such a case.

10. Jones and his fellow consumers will probably purchase one washing machine each. Applying the sacrifice test to the more usual case, in which the number of units of a

While we are not interested in washing machines, assessing pollution control benefits leads us to ask the same basic questions. Since pollution control provides improved opportunities for recreation, we must ask in this case: *How much money would recreationists sacrifice before they were indifferent to the choice between their improved set of opportunities and the old set previously available to them?* Once again, this question *cannot* be answered simply by ascertaining how much money people will in fact spend in order to take advantage of the better swimming, fishing, and boating opportunities made available by different levels of Delaware cleanup. Our first concern remains with the consumer surplus obtained by the intramarginal recreationist who avails himself of the improved opportunities.

If the effect of pollution control is really to make available a "new" good, our discussion of washing machines provides us with a sense of direction but it does not provide much help with the difficult task of trying to gain a sense of the magnitude of the consumers' surplus generated by pollution control. In applying the "sacrifice test," we imagined that satisfactory answers could be obtained by interviewing intramarginal consumers. But there are serious difficulties with this technique. Not only would the procedure be costly but the answers received could well be extremely unreliable indicators of the sacrifice consumers would in fact make: people are unused to speculating seriously about their potential responses to hypothetical events such as the availability of swimming in the Delaware. Similarly, while statistical analyses could in principle be developed which might give better information than consumer surveys, neither the state of the art nor the existing data base for the Delaware Valley is adequate for such an effort.[11] In sum, an economist attempting to be helpful to decision makers by placing a money value on "new" goods cannot take refuge in an expert manipulation of complex data, but must rely instead on a more informal approach which is nevertheless consistent with the basic principles we have discussed.

In order to understand how the analyst can gain a rough estimate of the increase in consumer surplus without the use of the elaborate fact-finding apparatus just described, it is again helpful to explore the implications of a simple example. Rather than research generating a new product

---

good purchased by each consumer continues to increase as the price of the good falls when all other prices and money incomes are held constant, involves no new principles. However, the use of market data to determine the amount consumers are willing to sacrifice requires somewhat greater care in this case (see n. 13).

11. A second cost–benefit study of pollution control on the Delaware Estuary (Davidson, et al., 1966, pp. 175–211) used more sophisticated statistical techniques than did the DECS and the IES Study for estimating recreational demand. However, this study did not attempt to apply the sacrifice test to measure benefits.

(like washing machines), consider this time the problem posed when a technological improvement simply makes it cheaper to supply an already existing good. Imagine, for instance, that paperback books formerly available for $2.50 are now reduced in price to $2.00. How can the economist estimate in a common sense way the amount consumers will sacrifice before they are no worse off than in the old situation in which paperbacks cost $2.50?

To make the problem simple, imagine further that the economist is told that at the old price, two million books were bought annually while at the new lower price 2.4 million books are purchased.[12] Given this fact, it is a simple matter to derive a lower limit on the dollar amount consumers would be willing to sacrifice. For we know from history that two million books were purchased at $2.50; thus, the purchasers of these books will save 50¢ a book under the new regime, and could be required to sacrifice one million dollars without considering themselves any worse off.

To see that one million dollars is indeed a lower limit on the benefit estimate, it is necessary to turn our attention to the extra 400,000 books which by hypothesis are purchased at the lower two-dollar price. It is reasonable to suppose that some consumer surplus will accrue to the purchasers of these volumes, although the precise magnitude of this quantity is a good deal more difficult to determine. It is possible, however, to obtain a first approximation. To do this, we must take into account the fact that these books would not (by hypothesis) have been purchased at $2.50. This means that if we required the consumers of these volumes to sacrifice a total of $200,000 (50¢ × 400,000 books), they would consider themselves *worse* off than they had been under the old regime. Thus, the consumer surplus associated with the purchase of the extra 400,000 paperbacks must be between $200,000 and zero.

In order to be more exact than this, it would be necessary to know the number of books that would be purchased at each price between $2.50 and $2.00. Even in the absence of this information, however, it is possible for the analyst to say something meaningful and relatively precise about the size of the benefit consumers as a class will obtain without resort to any elaborate apparatus. The money benefit of the decline in price to paperback purchasers is between $1 million and $1.2 million per year.[13]

12. We assume that the assumptions in note 9 are met.
13. The discussion in the text could be elaborated to yield a more precise measure of consumers' surplus if we knew the number of books each consumer would purchase at each price between $2.50 and $2.00 if his real income were held constant at the level preceding the price change. For a discussion of this more precise concept— the "real income compensated demand curve"—see Patinkin, 1963.

Having explored the economics of one form of recreation, reading paperbacks, we can consider whether anything has been learned about other forms of recreation, like swimming, boating, and fishing in the Delaware River. If investment in pollution control can be viewed simply as a means of reducing the cost consumers must incur in order to engage in already existing recreational activities, then our paperback example suggests a simple methodology. Thus, if pollution control permits consumers to travel to a nearby swimming beach at a cost of $2.00 instead of to an otherwise identical beach further away for $2.50, calculating the consumers' surplus resulting from the pollution program should be just as easy in principle as in the paperback book example. If, however, pollution control generates services perceived to be substantially different in quality so that they may more appropriately be regarded as "new goods," it will be necessary to employ heavier doses of subjective judgment and intuition in estimating the amount of money consumers will be willing to sacrifice and still be no worse off. For here the paradigm is the case of the washing machines rather than the paperbacks.

The appropriate paradigm for an economic analysis of the benefits of pollution control cannot, of course, be determined a priori. Environmental improvement may generate "new" products or may simply reduce the cost of obtaining "old" ones or both. Nevertheless, our theoretical examination has prepared us to apply the paradigms sensitively in the analysis of concrete cases, to which we shall now turn.

APPLYING THE FRAMEWORK TO THE POLLUTION PROBLEM IN THE DELAWARE

Swimming in the Delaware?

Consider the swimming opportunities available at present to a resident of center-city Philadelphia. Close to home, he may pay an admission fee and swim in the pool of his choice, either public or private.[14] At a greater distance, he has four options: (1) he may drive between an hour and an

14. The IES Study, Phase I, p. 26, reports that there were 826 public and private pools in the five Pennsylvania counties (Bucks, Chester, Delaware, Montgomery, and Philadelphia) in and around Philadelphia in 1965. This estimate is based on the number of pool permits on record in the files of the Pennsylvania Department of Health, Regional Office VII, in Philadelphia. The private pools included in the estimate are those at Y.M.C.A.'s, country clubs, motels, and similar semipublic locations. Backyard pools are not included.

hour and a half[15] and sample the delights of Atlantic City, or some less crowded beach at a somewhat greater distance on the Jersey shore; (2) he may visit one of the mountain lakes between two and a half and three and a quarter hours away in the Pocono Mountains;[16] (3) he may drive southwest for two and a quarter hours to the relatively deserted shores of the Delaware Bay which lie at the mouth of the Delaware River;[17] (4) he may drive for an hour or two to the relatively small number of public swimming facilities along the Delaware River above Trenton.[18] How will adopting one of the competing clean-up programs broaden these options?

The answer is extremely disappointing. Even if one accepts completely the DECS predictions as to the physical consequences of abating pollution on the Delaware, swimming and other water-contact recreation will be impossible under *any* of the proposed programs (including the most expensive Objective I) in the industrialized area stretching from just inside the northeast city limit of Philadelphia to just below Wilmington (sections 7–22 in map at frontispiece).[19] Moreover, we have provided many reasons to believe that the DECS water quality estimates are overly optimistic.[20] Thus it is extremely doubtful that swimming would be possible, even under Objective I, anywhere in the estuary except perhaps in the relatively unpopulated area below Wilmington near the Delaware Bay. In any event Objective I was never seriously considered, and the potential for swimming between Trenton and Philadelphia under less ambitious clean-up projects is even more conjectural. While DECS continues to predict swimming in this region under either Objectives II or III,[21] this prediction seems a fond hope rather than a probable outcome, given Trenton's sewer problem and

15. We estimate that the travel times to Atlantic City, Cape May, and Toms River are 65 minutes, 85 minutes, and 90 minutes respectively. This calculation was made by measuring the distance to these locations along established routes and assuming an average speed of 60 miles per hour for expressways and 30 miles per hour for all other roads. Our estimates are probably best interpreted as referring to an average week day. The experience of two of the authors, Bruce and Susan Ackerman, indicates that on peak summer weekends the trip to Atlantic City takes between one and two hours.
16. Using the method described in n. 15 herein, we estimate that the driving time to Mount Pocono is 155 minutes and to Lake Wallenpaupack 195 minutes.
17. The approach in n. 15 yields an estimate of 135 minutes' driving time to Woodland Beach, located on the Delaware Bay five miles below the boundary between the bay and the estuary.
18. Using the approach of n. 15, we estimate that it takes 125 minutes to drive to the Delaware Water Gap.
19. DECS, p. 55.
20. See Ch. 4, pp. 39–56.
21. DECS, p. 55, shows river sections 1–4 to be suitable for water-contact recreation under Objectives II and III. This river segment begins opposite the middle of Trenton and ends opposite the middle of Burlington.

the significant run-off from diffuse sources in a heavily populated area. Otherwise, DECS more realistically predicts that water-contact recreation will be likely only at the bottom of the estuary under Objectives II, III *or* IV.[22]

It should be clear, however, that making swimming possible in the lower estuary near the Delaware Bay broadens only slightly the range of choice open to the resident of center-city Philadelphia. But we can be more precise than that. In order to assess the amount a typical citizen of Philadelphia would sacrifice to swim in the lower estuary near the Delaware Bay, we must determine whether the problem is amenable to the relatively easy approach suggested by our discussion of paperback books or whether it involves the difficulties suggested by our study of washing machines. The critical difference between the two paradigms, it should be recalled, is whether the good evaluated is so different in quality from those previously available that it must be considered a "new" good for purposes of benefit analysis. In considering the issue of relative quality, we should first inquire whether any existing water resource provides a swimming experience similar to that offered by the lower estuary.

The Delaware Bay is an obvious candidate. Indeed, the place where the estuary ends and the bay begins is not apparent to the would-be swimmer, but instead is defined scientifically on the basis of salt concentration. It is possible, of course, that even though the natural character of the two areas is identical, the man-made environments are substantially different. Most important, if the bay's swimming areas were crowded and it was impossible or ecologically undesirable to expand these facilities, making the lower estuary available would generate benefits for those intramarginal users of the bay area who very much dislike crowding.[23] Moreover, more consumers might choose bay-estuary swimming if crowding were noticeably reduced. The bay's swimming potential, however, is far from exhausted, given its vast shoreline and the low population density of the surrounding area.[24] Clearly the effect of pollution control on the Delaware is simply to bring an *already existing* type of swimming opportunity somewhat closer

22. DECS, p. 55, shows river sections 27–30 to be suitable for water contact recreation under Objectives II, III, and IV. Section 27 begins about ten miles below Wilmington, and section 30 ends at the beginning of the Delaware Bay.
23. For a recent effort to analyze the crowding phenomenon, together with a useful bibliography, see Haveman, 1973.
24. A telephone conversation with Richard Howell of the Delaware Division of Public Health in September 1972 confirmed that the Delaware beaches with acceptable water quality on the Delaware Bay are relatively underutilized. On the New Jersey side of the bay there are virtually no developed recreational facilities because the region is remote from population centers and relatively inaccessible.

to the center-city Philadelphian. For purposes of swimming, then, cleaning up the Delaware River is equivalent to building a better highway to the Delaware Bay with a consequent reduction in travel time and expense. It is properly comprehended under the paperback book paradigm as a cheaper form of a good already on the market. Proceeding with our analysis of that simple hypothetical, we note first that those already travelling to the bay for swimming would sacrifice a sum equal to their saving in travel costs[25] times the number of trips they were already making. For those new trips induced by the bay-estuary area's new proximity, the analysis is somewhat less conclusive. Nevertheless, it should be clear that each new traveller, like each new purchaser of books in the paradigm case, will obtain less intramarginal surplus than any of the old Delaware Bay swimmers who now use the new facilities, because they formerly did not value bay-estuary swimming sufficiently to make the trip to the bay areas. Thus, the total money benefit resulting from the new trips will be obtained by multiplying a number which is less than the travel cost saving (but greater than zero) by the number of new trips taken.[26]

25. Travel cost includes the price of a mass transit ticket or the gas, oil, and depreciation costs of travelling by automobile plus a valuation of the traveller's time. If the trip is a long one, meal and lodging costs above those that would be incurred if the swimmer stayed at home should also be included. Several studies have employed estimates of travel cost; among them are Grubb and Goodwin, 1968, and Knetsch and Davis, 1966, pp. 138–142. These two studies assume that travel cost is related simply to distance travelled—an assumption that may not be justified if some roads are more congested than others—and do not attempt to value the time spent travelling. For a more recent attempt to deal with the problem of valuing travel time, see Gronau, 1970. A good summary of similar attempts may be found in Nelson, 1968, pp. 78–119. The most satisfactory general analysis can be found in Knetsch and Clawson, 1966.
26. The benefits to swimmers from pollution control can be represented by trapezoid ABCDE in the diagram below. The rectangle ABDE represents the benefits accruing to those who already engage in bay-estuary swimming.

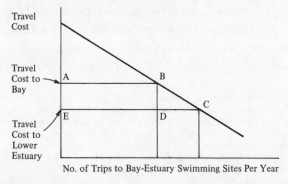

No. of Trips to Bay-Estuary Swimming Sites Per Year

The triangle BCD represents benefits generated by "new" trips. The trapezoid ABCDE is a completely accurate measure of benefits only under the restrictions outlined in nn. 9 and 13, of this chapter.

There is room for dispute as to the precise number of new trips that will be taken and the exact money saving per trip which results from making bay-estuary swimming available closer to population centers, but there can be no doubt that the total benefits resulting from the economist's calculation will be exceedingly small. At present, the Delaware Bay attracts a relatively small share of the millions of swimming days annually enjoyed by Philadelphians in pools, on the Jersey shore, the Upper Delaware and the Poconos. There is no reason to expect that improving the bay-estuary's competitive position by making it a bit closer to the metropolis will change matters significantly.

Boating on the Delaware

DECS estimates that on a pleasant weekend day as many as ten or fifteen thousand pleasure boats ply the waters of the estuary in its present "polluted" condition.[27] In other words, it would be wrong to assume (as we did in the case of swimming) that the estuary is at present an untapped boating resource. The question remains, however, whether any of the pollution programs considered would so raise the *quality* of the boating experience that (1) present users of the estuary would set an appreciably higher value on the boating experience there, or (2) the boatsmen now using either the Jersey shore or the Delaware Bay would in significant number shift to the estuary,[28] or (3) many others would abandon their former nonboating pursuits to become Delaware boatsmen.

If these are the questions, the answers are rather straightforward. There is no reason to believe that *any* of the pollution control programs will significantly improve the quality of the boating experience on the Delaware. "Pollution" may reduce the pleasure of boating if it causes such substantial oxygen depletion that the water emits a palpable stench,[29] contains elements corrosive to hulls, or impairs the appearance of the river by increasing the water's turbidity.[30] As to the first threat, the presence of a large

27. DECS Final Report, Chapter 3B, p. 10, states that "[approximately] 15,000 boats use the estuary." This figure was reached "by estimating . . . from boat registration data and from estimates from state shore patrols." The IES Study, Phase I, pp. 30–32, using an undisclosed method, estimated that 10,000 boats were in use on the estuary "on the Pennsylvania side" in 1965 and that 3,125 boats used the estuary "on the New Jersey side."
28. Of course, if a substantial change in quality were to occur, boaters who now use lakes in the Poconos, Chesapeake Bay, or the Susquehanna River might switch to the estuary.
29. See Ch. 3, pp. 18, 19, and 25.
30. "Pollution" may also take the form of oil slicks, which are both a nuisance and a danger to boaters. Although they may well be a more important problem for

number of boating parties indicates, and the testimony of DRBC officials confirms,[31] that there is no significant odor problem on the estuary at present and that any program which seeks to *improve* oxygen levels cannot be substantially justified on the ground that it is necessary to eliminate this nonexistent nuisance. As to the second risk, there is little evidence that the extra corrosion due to pollution generates costs of any considerable magnitude.[32] The third problem, dealing with visual aesthetics, is more complex. Although the Delaware is at present an extremely turbid river, none of the proposed programs is likely to transform the situation substantially, since the river's cloudiness is caused largely by tides stirring up the river bottom, dredging operations required for large-scale shipping, and the introduction of sediment from the river's banks and tributaries.[33] Even if turbidity is somewhat reduced, this "quality improvement" may not be an unmixed blessing to the boatsmen. We have seen that "solving" the turbidity problem may create a more serious algae problem: boaters may be greeted by green scum which upon the algae's death will be transformed into a stinking mass of decomposing matter.[34]

Assuming, however, that turbidity will be reduced without a counterbalancing aesthetic disadvantage, it would be easy to overestimate the impact of this improvement on the total boating experience. The river is the scene of far more arresting activities: major industrial complexes dominate the shoreline, large tankers steam by, and a host of other activities on river and shore remind the boatsman that he is coexisting with the life of the port which serves the fourth largest urban complex in the United States. This visual experience has its attractions; but to imagine that a slight change in water color will so transform this experience as to attract a different class of boaters, searching for a more natural setting, is nonsense. These recreationists will go where they have always gone—to the Jersey

boaters than any of the others mentioned in the text, oil slicks were not a major concern of the DECS. DECS forecasts that there would be some reduction in the amount of oil and grease in the estuary from industrial and municipal sources as a by-product of treatment procedures designed primarily to raise the DO level. Oil slicks due to spills at refineries pose a somewhat different problem. The DECS did not include the expense of cleaning up these spills in their cost estimates for any of the pollution control programs. The DRBC, however, has begun to insist that major spills be cleaned up. The costs and benefits of the DRBC's policing of oil spills have not been systematically investigated.

31. Interviews with DRBC, Pennsylvania and New Jersey personnel who prefer to remain anonymous, 1970.
32. Nowhere in DECS, DECS Final Report, Ch. 3B, or in the IES Study is the corrosion of hulls mentioned as a deterrent to boating activity.
33. Chapter 3, pp. 25, 26.
34. Chapter 3, p. 27.

shore, the lower estuary and bay, and even farther to the Chesapeake and the Poconos. Thus the benefits, as the economist sees them, from pollution control will be no greater for boating than they were for swimming.

Fishing in the Delaware

We come, finally, to those activities whose perceived quality and price may be affected appreciably by a pollution control program of the kind proposed for the Delaware. The minimum oxygen level required for fish survival is at best ill defined and differs according to the breed of fish considered, but if DO levels remain generally at 5 parts per million (ppm) and rarely if ever fall below 3 ppm, a broad variety of aquatic life may be expected. Purporting to apply this standard, DECS used its mathematical model to predict which sections would sustain "high-usage fishing" under each of the proposed clean-up programs.[35] Similarly, it marked sections which would satisfy a somewhat less demanding DO test as suitable for "medium-usage fishing."[36] Areas available for high- and medium-usage

35. The IES Study, Phase II, p. 20, n. 10, states that a section is considered to be suitable for high-usage fishing if it is one for which there is a 90 to 95 percent chance that anadromous fish can survive passage through it.

The standard is translated into DO levels by the DECS staff in Morris and Pence, pp. 6–9, who report that shad survive in water with DO levels of 3.0 ppm but die in water with DO levels of 2.5 ppm or less. Using experts' advice, the DECS staff concludes that shad could survive for several minutes if the DO level fell below 3.0 ppm. They then argue that if there is to be a 95 percent chance of shad survival in a section, the *mean* DO level must be high enough so that variations in the DO level will not lead to observed DO levels below 3.0 ppm more than 5 percent of the time.

The DECS staff assumes that daily DO levels in each section have the familiar bell-shaped normal distribution. Under this assumption there is a 95 percent chance that the observed DO level in any section will lie within a range of two standard deviations on either side of the mean DO level for that section. The DECS staff reports that the average standard deviation of the daily DO level for *all* sections in the Delaware is aproximately 1.0 ppm. They reason that if the mean DO level in a section on a given day is 5.0 ppm, one can expect the observed DO level to lie between 3.0 ppm and 7.0 ppm for 95 percent of the time and to lie below 3.0 ppm for 2.5 percent of the time. This reasoning leads DECS to conclude that if the mean DO level in a section is 5.0 ppm on a given day, there is a 95 percent chance that a shad could pass through the section on that day. (Strictly computed, the chance of survival would be 97.5 percent.) Thus, under the DECS approach, every section for which predicted average DO is 5 ppm or more should be deemed suitable for high-usage fishing. (However, see the text pp. 118, 119 and accompanying n. 46.)

36. None of the DECS reports we have obtained states specifically what standard DECS used to determine whether a section was suitable for medium-usage fishing. We have argued in note 35 that the fragmentary evidence available suggests that a section was considered suitable for high-usage fishing if the predicted summer average DO level was 5 ppm or greater. If this inference is correct, then sections with summer average DO levels of between 5 ppm and some lower bound were considered suitable for medium-usage fishing. This lower bound appears to be 3.5 ppm. DECS, pp. 55–58, shows that under Objective IV, sections 23–27 have a predicted summer

Table 5. [37]

Objective	Sections Suitable for High-Usage Fishing	Sections Suitable for Medium-Usage Fishing
I	1–10, 18–30	11–17
II	1–7, 28–30	8–27
III	1–7, 28–30	8–9, 22–27
IV	1–3, 28–30	4–9, 22–27
V	1–3, 28–30	4–9, 22–27

fishing at the time of the survey (1964) were also recorded, permitting the DECS to chart the fishing range available under each of the five objectives.

In sketching the way an economist would assess the impact of a DO improvement program on fishermen, we will focus on the availability of high-usage fishing resources in the upper estuary between Philadelphia and Trenton,[38] which the DECS subdivided into sections 1–7. Under Objectives IV and V, high-usage fishing is available only near Trenton in sections 1–3, consisting of 28 shore miles; under II and III, high-usage fishing is also available in sections 4–7, enlarging the area by 32.4 shore miles.[39]

average DO level of 3.5 ppm, and these sections are designated as suitable for medium-usage fishing. Under Objective III, sections 18–21 have a predicted summer average DO level of 3 ppm, and these sections are not designated as suitable for medium-usage fishing (see n. 46 *infra*).

Sections deemed suitable for neither high- nor medium-usage fishing were designated as suitable for low-usage fishing.

37. The data for this table were derived from DECS, pp. 55–58. The section numbers in the table are identical to those shown on the frontispiece map.

38. We have limited our concern to assessing the benefits in the upper estuary since, as Table 5 indicates, the benefits of high-usage fishing (however small) are far more significant there than in the southern section, where, under all but the most expensive program, no area expansion whatsoever is contemplated for this use.

39. These measurements include the shore length of the islands in sections 2 and 4. Without the islands the shore length for sections 1–3 is 24.4 miles and for sections 4–7, 28.7 miles. These measurements were obtained by following the shoreline with a "map reader" on Map No. 295 of the U.S. Department of Commerce, Environmental Science Administration, Coast and Geodetic Survey. The boundaries of the sections were fixed by reference to the DECS, p. 34.

In performing our own map measurements we discovered that the IES had seriously mismeasured the shoreline of the estuary. For example, the study asserts (Phase II, Table 7, p. 22) that the total shoreline in sections 1–7 and sections 28–30 is 254,700 feet. As a simple check, one can measure the length of the navigation channel in these sections and double it to obtain a rough estimate of the length of the shoreline, arriving, in this case, at 385,950 feet. More exact measurement according to the method previously mentioned yields a figure of 430,300 feet, excluding islands, and 480,760 feet including islands. We have not been able to discover the source of the IES error.

Once again, we ask whether the *quality* of the fishing experience which Objectives II and III promise in sections 1–7 is comparable to the experience provided in sections 1–3 by Objectives IV or V. As the physical characteristics of the river throughout sections 1–7 are roughly the same, we again focus on the man-made elements of the environment, particularly the crowding phenomenon. If a crowding problem does exist in sections 1–3, some benefits will accrue to those intramarginal fishermen who value solitude, since the population of fishermen will become somewhat more diffuse when sections 4–7 are opened up as high-usage areas.[40] While data are inadequate for a firm judgment, the information we do possess suggests that crowding is not such a problem that a significant number of fishermen would be willing to make a substantial sacrifice for more seclusion.[41] The only systematic census of estuary fishermen that has come to our attention is one attempted by the DECS in the mid-1960's which found that "7,960 fishermen use[d] the estuary per day."[42] If eight thousand fishermen use the entire estuary, it seems highly unlikely that more than three thousand use sections 1–3; the substantial shoreline available in these sections renders it implausible that a substantial fraction of even this small number of fishermen would sacrifice a considerable sum for greater seclusion, especially if it is conceded that the fishermen who value solitude the most will not fish in the river anyway but will seek their peace in more natural settings farther from the metropolis.

Thus, as in the case of swimming, the paperback book paradigm seems controlling; the principal benefit obtained by adding sections 4–7 as high-usage areas can be measured by the savings in transportation time and expense accruing to fishermen in Philadelphia who will find good fishing closer at hand. In addition, increasing the proximity of good fishing will induce some citizens to substitute high-usage estuary fishing for other activities. These "new" fishermen will receive a smaller benefit per trip than that obtained by the "old," as they were unwilling to pay the old travel cost in order to engage in high quality estuary fishing. It is, of course,

40. Fishermen would also be attracted from other sites and other pursuits to fish in the estuary if crowding were reduced. These fishermen would be willing to sacrifice somewhat less for the improvement in quality than those who were already using the estuary, since they did not consider it worth their while to engage in estuary fishing before the change.
41. DECS, p. 51, states that the area between Trenton and Florence, N.J., which corresponds roughly to DECS sections 1–3, is not heavily utilized.
42. DECS Final Report, Ch. 3B, p. 12. The method used in this census is not described in the DECS Final Report, and we were unable to find out about it from the DECS staff. It is not clear whether the census refers to a weekday or to a weekend day, whether or not an average of several samples was taken, or how the fishermen were distributed among the various sections of the estuary.

impossible to guess precisely how many "new" fishermen would arrive on the scene as a result of reducing the auto travel time between downtown Philadelphia and the fishing area from a minimum of 36 minutes to a minimum of 24 minutes.[43] In light of this modest change and the relatively small number of fishermen now using sections 1–3, it seems reasonable to believe, however, that the number of new fishermen attracted to sections 4–7 will be small.[44]

Up to this point, our analysis compels the conclusion that increasing the area of rich aquatic life will generate only extremely modest benefits for the estuary's recreational fishermen. This conclusion must, however, be modified in an even more pessimistic direction once the frailties of the DECS procedure are considered. First, if, as DECS claimed,[45] the high-usage fishing area is defined as including all river sections for which the summer average DO level is 5 ppm and whose likely fluctuations will depress DO to no less than 3 ppm, the DECS has erred substantially in selecting the sections that satisfy the standard under the proposed programs. When we applied this standard to the DECS DO predictions,[46] our results diverged as shown in Table 6.

43. These estimates were obtained by using the method described in n. 15. Thirty-six minutes is the average weekday travel time to Tullytown, which is located at the boundary of section 3 nearest Philadelphia, while 24 minutes is the time to the Tacony-Palmyra Bridge, which marks the boundary of section 7 nearest Philadelphia.
44. Moreover, the benefits generated by the increased availability of medium-usage fishing seem insubstantial. As Table 5 indicates, neither Objective III nor IV generate any increase in the area available for medium-usage fishing. While Objectives I and II do lead to large increases in the area available for medium-usage fishing, the estuary is virtually inaccessible on the Pennsylvania side from section 8 to section 15 because of the waterside development of the city of Philadelphia and its suburbs, and on the New Jersey side from section 9 to section 14 because of the shoreline development of the city of Camden and its suburbs. On the Pennsylvania-Delaware side, most of sections 17 through 21 are inaccessible because of the cities of Chester and Wilmington and the oil unloading facilities at Marcus Hook. Except for section 16 and parts of sections 17 and 21, the New Jersey side is accessible along most of this shoreline. Furthermore, the most attractive forms of game fish need DO levels higher than those required to meet the medium-usage fishing standard (see nn. 35–36). Finally, one should consider the prospect that medium-usage fishing may not fully materialize in these areas. Sections 8–22 are the ones in which periodic severe oxygen problems due to storm water run-off are a serious threat to the survival of fish. Although it would be very difficult to give a precise dollar estimate of the increase in benefits due to medium-usage fishing as a result of the increase in water quality projected for sections 10–21 under Objectives I and II, it seems for these reasons that the benefits are not large.
45. See p. 115.
46. For the DECS DO predictions, see DECS, pp. 56–58. We find that sections 4–7 meet the 5 ppm standard under Objectives IV and V, while the DECS staff contends that these sections become suitable only under Objective III. Our case for Objective V rests on the DECS DO predictions. The DECS predictions show a *lower* summer average DO level for sections 1–7 under Objective IV than under Objective V (1964 conditions). Since Objective IV involves more treatment, we consider this result to be

Table 6. Estimates of Areas (by Section Nos.) Available for High-Usage Fishing under Each Objective

Objective	DECS Estimate	Authors' Estimate
I	1–10, 18–30	1–10, 18–30
II	1–7, 28–30	1–7, 20–30
III	1–7, 28–30	1–7, 28–30
IV	1–3, 28–30	1–7, 28–30
V	1–3, 28–30	1–7, 28–30

If our designations are correct, no benefits at all will accrue as a result of moving from Objective V to Objective III. Some benefits, however, will be generated as a result of a movement to Objective II, since high-usage fishing will, it is claimed, be possible in seven additional sections below Wilmington, although these benefits will be small considering the area's proximity to the lower estuary and the bay. Moreover, given the systematically optimistic nature of the predictions generated by the BOD-DO model,[47] it is best to recognize that attaining even this meager benefit is by no means certain.

---

unlikely, so we assume that conditions in sections 1–7 would be at least as good under Objective IV as they are under Objective V. We find that sections 20–27 meet the 5 ppm standard under Objective II, whereas the DECS staff holds that these sections become suitable only under Objective I. Here again we rely on the DECS DO predictions.

In addition, some revisions of the sections regarded as suitable for medium-usage fishing by DECS are required. The revisions are summarized in the following table.

Estimates of Areas (by Section Nos.) Available for Medium-Usage
Fishing under each Objective

Objective	DECS Estimate	Authors' Estimate
I	11–17	11–17
II	8–27	8–19
III	8–9, 22–27	8–9, 22–27
IV	4–9, 22–27	8–9, 22–27
V	4–9, 22–27	8–9, 22–27

Sections 8, 9 and 22 are included under Objectives IV and III because they appear to be suitable under Objective V, and although the DECS predicts that DO levels will deteriorate in these sections under programs which involve more treatment, we consider this outcome to be unlikely.

47. See Ch. 4.

The Shad Problem

Up to the present point, we have spoken as if the only significant effect of DO improvement on fishing is its impact on recreational opportunities in the estuary itself. This is, however, to take too narrow a view. The estuary serves as a vital conduit for anadromous fish (most notably the Atlantic shad) who begin their lives in the headwaters of the river, spend much of their adulthood in the ocean, and return through the estuary to up-river spawning grounds to complete the reproductive cycle. Shad fishing in the Delaware River above Trenton is an important attraction for sportsmen[48] in New York, Pennsylvania, and New Jersey.[49]

In order to understand what effect raising the DO level in the estuary might have on the shad fishery one must know a little more about the life pattern of the shad.[50] An adult Delaware shad heads up the river from the ocean some time during an eight-week period beginning in late March or early April and ending in middle or late May.[51] If he or she is an early migrator, chances for a safe passage up the estuary to the headwaters are good; the combination of early spring high flow and relatively low water temperature makes it likely that the dissolved oxygen level in even the most polluted regions of the estuary will exceed 3 ppm,[52] the level below

48. There is also a small commercial shad fishery in the Delaware. The importance attached to the shad by those involved with the pollution control decision in the estuary evoked this summary statement and warning from the DECS staff:

> ... During the development of the alternative water quality programs for the estuary, the passage of anadromous fish, specifically the shad *Alosa sapidissima,* became a matter of great interest to those having to decide on which water quality management program to select. The concern evidenced for this annual visitor to the estuary came from many quarters. The reasons for the concern were almost as numerous as the interests involved. Basically the interest was not economic—the annual value of the shad fishery is small (i.e., $20,000 commercial and $50,000 recreational benefits). The main argument seemed to be that if the river inhibits the shad migration, it is unacceptable to the general public.

Morris and Pence, p. 1. The $20,000 figure is a DECS staff estimate of the market value of the yearly commercial catch. We have been unable to learn the source of the $50,000 figure.

49. Almost all sport fishing for shad takes place at sites above Trenton, according to Joseph P. Miller, coordinator of the Delaware River Anadromous Fishery Project (DRAFP). During the same telephone conversation (in May 1972), Mr. Miller also stated that sport fishing does not have a substantial impact on the size of the Delaware's shad population.

50. The description of the life pattern of the shad in the Delaware which follows is based on the *DRAFP Annual Report, 1972,* and a telephone conversation with Joseph P. Miller (see n. 49).

51. The beginning of the shad run depends primarily on water temperature. For a more detailed discussion, see Morris and Pence, pp. 4–6; *DRAFP Annual Report, 1972,* pp. 12–34 and the literature cited in these two sources.

52. Morris and Pence, p. 6.

which few shad can survive for any length of time.[53] The problem for the early migrator arises once the eggs have been laid and fertilized. Adult shad do not normally eat in the river during the spawning run; they attempt to return to the ocean to feed. But by the time many of the spawned-out shad have arrived again at the estuary, reduced flow and rising temperatures, combined with about the same discharge of waste materials as before, have reduced DO in some sections to lethal levels. Barred by this pollution block from the ocean, their natural feeding place, the spent shad die of starvation.[54] Not many early migrators travel twice up to the headwaters of the Delaware.

The lot of the late migrator is a happier one. By the time he begins his trip, DO in some sections is low enough to prevent his passage through the estuary. Consequently, he heads up a lower tributary to spawn or makes his way through the Delaware and Chesapeake Canal to the Chesapeake Bay and from there to the Susquehanna River in response to his reproductive urge.[55] Since his return route to the ocean is probably still open, a second or third spawning trip is likely.

While the offspring of the late migrators probably have little trouble making the normal fall trip to the ocean, where they will mature, juveniles born of early migrators face the same pollution block encountered by their unfortunate parents. Because juveniles feed in the river, their need to return to the ocean is not so urgent, but they must reach the ocean to mature, and so must wait until temperatures are low enough to insure that DO is above minimum survival levels. Apparently juveniles enjoy reasonable success in reaching the ocean.[56]

To gain a sense of the extent to which pollution control will benefit the shad, the DECS, as we have seen, used its time varying model to predict the probability of shad survival during their spring migration. While the model predicted a substantial improvement in shad prospects as a result of adopting Objective II or III, compared to Objective V,[57] these predictions must be viewed with caution for three reasons. First, the DECS' survival data do not in fact measure what they purport to quan-

---

53. See n. 35.
54. *DRAFP Annual Report, 1972*, p. 56.
55. *Ibid.*, pp. 26–30.
56. *Ibid.*, p. 60.
57. See Ch. 4, pp. 53–55. It should be recalled, however, that the difference between Objectives II and III so far as the shad were concerned was quite small. Thus, the DECS model indicated that under river conditions likely to prevail during half the shad runs, 95 percent of the shad will "survive" under Objective II while 85 percent will "survive" under Objective III. Under the conditions prevailing in the worst year of every 25, 90 percent of the shad will survive under Objective II and 80 percent will survive under Objective III.

tify.[58] As we have shown, late migrators do not, in fact, die in the Delaware, but live in the Susquehanna and elsewhere. Moreover, the shad that do die have already completed at least one reproductive cycle, while many of the youthful shad spawned in the Delaware simply wait until the pollution block lifts before completing their journey to the ocean. Second, we have shown that the DECS' projections contain substantial elements of overoptimism, and that the DECS' time varying predictions are particularly unreliable.[59]

Third, the DECS' predictions must be viewed against the Army Corps of Engineers' plans for the construction of a large dam at Tocks Island in the Upper Delaware as part of the DRBC's flood control program. The Tocks Island Dam, as the DECS itself notes in an unrelated section of its report, "will probably be a hindrance to the normal migration of shad to and from the principal spawning areas above the Dam site . . . and it is the general opinion of biologists that shad spawning success will be considerably reduced in the Delaware River."[60] The DRBC's recent pronouncements are somewhat more sanguine, but they must be balanced against conservationists' claims that Atlantic shad are simply too weak to climb the proposed dam's fish ladder and hence will die. The uncertainty surrounding the dam is compounded by the success of conservationists thus far in delaying its construction despite the DRBC's continuing support of the project.

Until the dam's fate is determined and its impact is better understood, it would seem reasonable to defer any large expenditure justified primarily on shad-protection grounds. This wait-and-see strategy finds support in the plain fact that a sizeable shad population is currently sustaining itself under present conditions.[61] Although a further deterioration of DO levels in the estuary over time could mean that no shad would reach the Upper Delaware, maintaining present conditions (as contemplated by Objective V) is a viable short-run alternative until the long-range prospects can be

58. The DECS "survival" data relate only to the percentage of shad which could pass through the estuary on the way up the river to spawn (see DECS, p. 61, and Morris and Pence, p. 4, both of which use "passage" and "survival" interchangeably), but our discussion on p. 121 and in the accompanying note shows that migrating shad blocked from passage may well "survive."

59. See Ch. 4, pp. 53–55.

60. DECS, p. 79.

61. According to the *DRAFP Annual Report, 1972*, p. 41, techniques used so far have not succeeded in generating enough data for a reliable statistical estimate of the number of American shad spawning in the upper reaches of the Delaware River. Estimates of the size of the shad population must, therefore, be quite impressionistic. The New Jersey Bureau of Sport Fisheries and Wildlife, *DRAFP Annual Report, 1970*, p. 17, for example, states that "there appeared to be a fair run of adult spawning shad . . ." in the early spring of 1969.

more intelligently assessed. Rather than counsel such a strategy, however, the DECS study ignored the dam problem and proceeded to offer decision makers a misleading set of shad "survival" probabilities for each pollution program.

Conclusion

The DECS rests its case for pollution control almost entirely on the benefits to be derived by swimmers, boaters, and fishermen from enhanced recreational opportunities.[62] Yet, *from an economist's perspective,* these benefits seem trivial in comparison to the costs we have estimated the DRBC's program will impose. Although we shall later consider whether a persuasive noneconomic case for pollution control can be made on grounds not considered by conventional cost–benefit analysis, it is important at this point to consider the fundamental reasons why the DECS estimated recreational benefits to be many times the order of magnitude we have suggested. For an exploration of the basic conceptual errors in the DECS approach, common to many similar efforts,[63] reveals how a quantitative method divorced from a solid foundation in elementary economic theory can be worse than useless, resulting in a set of numbers that obscure the fundamental issues at stake.

62. See n. 4.
63. See n. 5.

The DECS Approach to Benefit Estimation

INTRODUCTION

The hallmark of the simple economic approach we have considered thus far is its emphasis on the consumer's perspective. From this perspective, the central fact is that the Delaware Valley consumer already has a wide range of water-based recreational alternatives open to him; it is this fact that makes cleaning up the Delaware of relatively small importance. Obviously, if other recreational facilities were less bountiful in the valley, consumers would be willing to sacrifice more for improved fishing and swimming opportunities even in sections of the estuary relatively far from population centers. It is this consistent effort to view pollution control as a way of adding to an *already existing set* of consumer activities which sets the economist's approach apart from that pursued by the DECS and many other similar studies.

THE DECS DEFINITION OF THE "STUDY AREA"

Instead of taking a consumer's perspective, the DECS suffered from a characteristic form of planner's myopia. After all, the planner has been charged with the task of investigating the effects of pollution control *on the estuary;* what could be more natural than to isolate the estuary in the analysis and give it more prominence than it deserves from the consumer's perspective? For example, the analyst's first task is to fix the boundaries of the "study area" to be considered in detail. Under the economist's approach, any consumer who considers himself substantially affected by enhancing water quality in the Delaware should be included in the "relevant population" of consumers. By the same principle, the study area should include not only the estuary but all those sites considered important recreational alternatives by a substantial part of the relevant population.[1] The DECS, however, limited its "study area" to the population and the alternative recreational sites located in the highly urbanized 11 counties nearest the estuary.[2] Under this arrangement, the fact that residents of Trenton, Camden, Philadelphia, and Wilmington might prefer to go to the Jersey Shore or the Poconos or the Delaware Bay could be ignored on the question-begging ground that these recreational sites, by far the most popular ones, were outside the study area.[3] Thus it seemed as if the residents of the 11 urbanized counties who ventured outside this area were being required to undertake an onerous journey to another country to fulfill their desires for a good swim, while in fact they were only taking the familiar one-day excursion on the specially-built expressway to Atlantic

1. Of course judgment must be used in giving empirical content to the general concepts of the "relevant population" and the "important recreational alternatives considered by a substantial portion of the population." It is usually not practical to include every user or potential user in the relevant population or to account for people who will never visit the site being evaluated but who may benefit from its existence because the sites they do visit will become less crowded. For a study which confronts these problems sensibly, see Grubb and Goodwin, 1968.

2. The "study area" which served as the basis for the DECS benefits estimates is described in the IES Study, Phase I, p. 1. The counties included are: New Castle in Delaware; Burlington, Camden, Gloucester, Hunterdon, Mercer, and Salem in New Jersey; and Bucks, Chester, Delaware, Montgomery, and Philadelphia in Pennsylvania.

3. The DECS approach also failed to take into account some people who would seriously consider the improved estuary and/or sites made less crowded as places for recreation. However, given the distribution of population in the Delaware Valley and surrounding area, the DECS "study area" probably contains a large fraction of the relevant population, so the deflation of benefits produced by considering only the population of the 11 counties nearest the estuary seems relatively small.

City.[4] In contrast, the DECS assumed that residents of the 11 counties could move costlessly throughout the study area. Because there are few alternative water resources in the 11 counties beyond some swimming pools, the artificial circumscription of the study area ensured a DECS prediction that sections of the estuary made available for recreation by pollution control would be heavily utilized. Since the population of the 11 counties exceeds four million, one might be led by the DECS approach to conjure up the prospect of teeming masses of city dwellers converging on each square foot of the reclaimed estuary, seeking their place in the sun.

THE CONCEPT OF "CAPACITY"

If it had been clearly perceived, such an implausible result would have called into question the basic premises of the DECS approach. Unfortunately the introduction of another concept prevented a retreat to common sense informed by basic economic theory. The concept that obscured the DECS logic was a peculiar notion of "capacity,"[5] much used by planners of public projects. When understood in one limited sense, capacity has a clear, if trivial, conceptual content. For example, a given stretch of river front is "filled to capacity" by fishermen when it is so crowded that it is *physically impossible* for another fisherman to muscle his way to the water's edge. This notion of ultimate physical constraint was not, however, the key to the DECS' concept of capacity. Rather, the DECS used the idea to mask a confused set of economic and ethical premises. For example, the capacity of the estuary for fishing was calculated on the assumption that each fisherman in some sense required ten feet of shoreline in order to operate successfully.[6] Since it is physically possible for fishermen to be spaced more closely than this, the fishing capacity calculation must be based on some other ground. The capacity notion might depend on a normative judgment about how much shoreline ought, *in the analyst's*

4. Using the methodology described in Ch. 7, n. 15, we estimate that the travel time from center-city Philadelphia to Atlantic City along the limited access Atlantic Expressway on an average weekday is 65 minutes. The same methodology suggests that a Philadelphia resident would have to drive for 95 minutes, for example, to reach Augustine Beach, a potential swimming site on the lower estuary.
5. The concept of capacity is discussed briefly in DECS, p. 75. As Ch. 7, n. 2 explained, the DECS recreation benefits estimates were based on the IES Study, which refers to the concept of capacity at several points in its analysis. Examples are Phase II, pp. 12, 17, 18 and 22. See also DECS Final Report, Chs. 3, 4, and 5, and Figs. 13, 44, and 45.
6. IES Study, p. 22.

view, to be allocated to each fisherman. However, it seems quite improper for a technocratic analyst to use the capacity concept to disguise his implicit value biases from those political actors who are charged with making the ultimate value decision.[7]

We suspect that, if pressed, the analyst would defend the capacity concept in a quite different way. Instead of invoking his own personal norms, he would appeal to an economics-based argument which, though it possesses some surface appeal, is fundamentally misconceived. In defense of its capacity concept, DECS might have reasoned that it is only when fishermen become too closely packed along the estuary that they will venture beyond the study area to seek a satisfactory experience. While this argument contains an element of truth, the capacity concept distorts the role of crowding in a completely unacceptable way. It implies that, as far as the estuary is concerned, crowding has *no* effect on fishermen's preferences before the magic ten-foot standard is reached, but that if the standard is exceeded, *no* fishermen would consider the site attractive. This is highly implausible. More important, it ignores the fact that recreationists may well choose to fish at locations outside the study area even though the estuary is not crowded at all, for the simple reason that fishing is more enjoyable elsewhere.

THE DEMAND FOR RECREATION IN THE STUDY AREA

Having determined the size of the new recreational "capacity" that would be generated by pollution control expenditures, the DECS turned to consider whether consumer demand would fill this increased "capacity." Even at this stage in the analysis, it would have been possible to transcend the limitations of the DECS conceptual structure by a set of carefully designed demand estimates based on a comparison of the desirability of the estuary with other, more popular, recreational areas. No matter how great the estuary's "capacity," its recreational value would be appreciably diminished if it were ignored by the overwhelming majority of would-be swimmers, boatsmen and fishermen.

The DECS demand estimates, however, were designed in a way that obscured the bleak prospects such an inquiry might have disclosed. To determine the number of days the residents of the 11-county area wished to spend boating, fishing and swimming, the DECS took recourse, as have many other analysts before and since, to a basic study performed by a

7. This follows from our definition of the technocratic enterprise in Ch. 2.

special Outdoor Recreation Resources Review Commission (ORRRC) sponsored by the Bureau of Outdoor Recreation in the Department of the Interior.[8]

The ORRRC study is based on a set of questions asked of a sample of people over 12 years of age throughout the United States in 1960. The questionnaires asked the respondents to report whether or not they participated at all in a given recreational activity during the survey period and, if they participated, how many times. Each respondent was also asked to supply certain demographic data about himself: his age, income, sex, race, educational level, occupation, and residence.[9] The ORRRC investigators used this information to determine the rate at which various groups participate in each of several types of recreational activity. Speaking more technically, an ORRRC "participation rate" is the number of days per year that the average person over age 12 in a well defined subgroup of the population can be expected to engage in a particular activity.[10] Once the participation rate for a given population subgroup has been found, obtaining the DECS measure of the total demand for a given recreational activity is simply an exercise in multiplication. If, for example, there are 10,000 white males between the ages of 20 and 30 earning between $10,000 and $20,000, etc., and ORRRC has found that the participation rate for fishing for this group is three days per year, then the number of days the group can be expected to fish in a year is simply 30,000 days.[11]

The aspect of this exercise most important for our purposes is its failure to take adequately into account the recreational opportunities facing

8. *Outdoor Recreation Resources,* 1962.
9. *Ibid.,* Report No. 19, pp. 377–387.
10. In *Outdoor Recreation Resources,* Report No. 26, the ORRRC participation rates are determined directly, using a relatively complicated procedure based on the results of *Outdoor Recreation Resources,* Report No. 20. More recent studies have relied on data from *Outdoor Recreation Resources,* Report No. 19, and the *1965 Survey* to estimate participation rates, using a two-step procedure. Under this system, the investigator first estimates percent participation, the proportion of each well-defined subgroup which will take part in the given activity at least once in a given year. He then determines what might be called an activity rate, the number of days that the average participant in each well-defined subgroup will engage in the given activity during the year. The product of the percentage participation figure and the activity rate gives the participation rate. For a summary discussion of these studies and a comprehensive bibliography see Cicchetti, 1972, pp. 90–107.
11. *Outdoor Recreation Resources,* Report No. 26, forecasts the participation rate of the total population over 12 years of age in a given geographical area, for a given year, by multiplying the participation rate for each well-defined subgroup of the population by the proportion of that subgroup in the population in the year in question, and adding the results. The participation figures so generated are reported on pp. 17–19, and reprinted in IES Study, p. 81. To obtain total demand for a given activity in a given year by the total population over age 12 in a particular geographical area, the weighted participation rate described above is multiplied by the total population figure. This procedure is used to generate the total demand figures in IES Study, Phase II, p. 5.

each of the respondents in the sample. In estimating participation rates, ORRRC divided the entire country into four regions; its estimates therefore represent the response of a consumer facing the *average* opportunities prevailing in each region. As the DECS made use of ORRRC figures for the Northeast, an element of error will enter if the opportunities actually open to residents of the 11-county region are not representative of the Northeast. Far more important for our purposes, however, is the error that will result from an arbitrary restriction of the area in which the demand will be satisfied—which is precisely the technique that DECS employed in drawing the boundaries of its study area to exclude the Jersey Shore, the Upper Delaware, the Poconos and the Delaware Bay. After restricting its "study area" in this way, the DECS should not have relied on ORRRC demand estimates, which assumed the opportunities available within the study area are representative of those prevailing in the entire Northeast. Only by mistakenly using the ORRRC participation rates in conjunction with a drastically truncated inventory of recreational opportunities could the DECS have arrived at its conclusion that, in general, new estuarine opportunities will be "fully" utilized.[12]

The power of a misconceived methodology to blind the analyst is thrown into high relief when the facts available to the DECS are considered. According to the DECS, the sections of the estuary available in 1966 for high-usage fishing before *any* water quality enhancement was undertaken have the "capacity" to accommodate 390,000 activity-days of fishing each fishing season.[13] Yet DECS notes elsewhere that in fact fisher-

12. IES Study, Phase II, Table 4, p. 16; Table 6, p. 21, and Table 8, p. 24.
13. IES Study, Phase II, Table 7, p. 22. The DECS staff seems to have adopted the IES Study figure in their later work (DECS Final Report, Ch. 3B, Fig. 13, p. 45). However, DECS, p. 48, gives 1,620,000 activity-days per year as the figure for the *present capacity of the estuary* for fishing. In the IES Study, Phase II, n. 12, p. 22, this figure is reported to be the fishing capacity of *nonestuary inland water in their 11-county study area.*

In addition it should be noted that the IES Study capacity calculations (for all the proposed clean-up programs as well as for existing conditions) contain a fundamental technical error. The IES capacity formula, IES Study, p. 22 and DECS Final Report, Ch. 3B, Table 4, p. 20, is:

$$C_i = .66\,L_i \times M \times T \times P$$

where .66 = Proportion of total shoreline in region of "high-usage fishing" assumed to be accessible
   C_i = Capacity under Objective i (in activity-days per year)
   L_i = Total shore length designated for "high-usage fishing" under Objective i (in feet)
   M = Average spacing of anglers (one person per ten feet)
   T = Turnover rate (two anglers per space per day)
   P = Average number of activity-days per fisherman (20 activity-days per person per year)

The product of .66 L_i, M, and T yields the number of anglers who could

men spend only 130,000 days along the estuary annually.[14] The implications of this brute fact are simply ignored, for according to DECS, every ten feet of riverfront should contain a fisherman at all times during the fishing season. Although this inconsistency should constitute a source of embarrassment to the DECS, it poses no particular difficulty for the economist's approach. All it suggests is that fishermen in heavily populated areas, when faced with the choice of travelling substantial distances either to estuarine high-usage fishing sites or to ocean, lake, or stream sites outside the study area, choose overwhelmingly the nonestuarine options. Nevertheless, the DECS not only fails to confront the fact that existing capacity remains largely unused, but predicts that the vastly expanded capacity generated by even the most ambitious control plan, Objective I, will be fully utilized.[15]

ATTACHING MONEY VALUES

We have now come to the moment of truth in any benefit analysis—the point at which the benefits of the project are translated into dollars. Under the economist's approach,[16] the rationale for money evaluation is straightforward. The analyst simply seeks to estimate the amount consumers would be willing to sacrifice rather than do without the new facilities.

---

hypothetically be accommodated along the estuary per day. The number of anglers who can be accommodated in one day should be multiplied by the number of activity-days per angler per day, presumably one, and then by an estimate of *the length of the fishing season in days* to obtain a meaningful measure of capacity. A conceptually consistent formula is:

$$C_i = .66 \, L_i \times M \times T \times K \times S$$

where

K = Activity-days per angler per day (presumably one)
S = Length of the fishing season in days

The use of P in the formula employed by the IES Study and DECS Final Report yields a nonsense result.

14. This figure, DECS, p. 48, is not explained in any of the documents we have been able to obtain. In the DECS Final Report, p. 12, the figure was reduced to 51,750 activity-days per year. The 51,750 figure was obtained by multiplying 7,960 fishermen, an estimate of the number using the estuary per day (Ch. 7, n. 39), by 6.5 activity-days per year per fisherman, a DECS' estimate of the number of days per year the average fisherman spends fishing.

This calculation is fundamentally misconceived. In order to obtain a sensible usage figure, 7,960 should be multiplied by an estimate of the length of the fishing season, not by an estimate of the number of days the average angler spends fishing.

15. According to the IES Study, Phase II, Table 8, p. 24, demand for fishing exceeded the nonestuary "capacity" within the study area by more than enough to insure full usage of estuary capacity in 1965.

16. See Ch. 7, pp. 104–109.

Given the DECS methodology, however, it was impossible for the analyst either to pose the sacrifice question in coherent form or to devise a means for supplying even a rough answer. In order to think in terms of the sacrifice test, it is necessary to have (a) a clear idea of the recreational options open to consumers before any pollution expenditure; (b) a careful account of the kinds of change pollution control will generate; and (c) an estimate of the extent to which consumers will modify their conduct in the light of their new options. As we have seen, at each basic stage in the DECS analysis concepts were developed that obscured the simple logic of this approach. The DECS definition of the "study area," its notion of "capacity," and its effort to derive "demand" estimates not closely tied to a clear conception of available opportunities both before and after pollution control, all made it impossible to ask: How much money is it reasonable to expect the residents of the Delaware Valley to sacrifice in exchange for the changes in their environmental situation wrought by each of the proposed programs?

As the DECS was unable to articulate the relevant question, it is not surprising that its translation of benefits into money terms was fundamentally arbitrary. Even if it were otherwise flawless, the DECS analysis indicates merely that the new "capacity" generated by pollution control would be utilized. Yet this, in itself, is insufficient; in the absence of water quality improvement, the "new" recreationists on the reclaimed portions of the Delaware would have been doing something else. What a benefit analysis must determine, in one way or another, is the extent to which these recreationists consider themselves better off as a result of their *change* in activity. Precluded by its own methodology from appealing to economically informed common sense, the DECS was instead obliged to resort to Authority. Since the methodological quandary we have portrayed is characteristic of many benefit studies, Authority has supplied a set of dollar figures enshrined in Supplement No. 1 to Senate Document 97.[17] This Supplement, published in 1964, reports the consensus of experts in the field of recreational benefit evaluation on the dollar value to be associated with each of a wide range of recreational activities. It should be plain that this Platonic approach is of no value, for it attempts to establish the intrinsic worth of a day of fishing in one place independently of the other opportunities available to a region's fishermen. It should be banished from

17. *Evaluation Standards*, 1964, p. 4. A "general" outdoor recreation day is said to be "worth" between $.50 and $1.50, while a "specialized" outdoor recreation day is worth between $2.00 and $6.00. The activities that are supposed to fall into each of the two categories are set out in detail at p. 3 of the Supplement.

all subsequent efforts at an economic analysis of the problems posed by environmental degradation.[18]

INTRODUCING THE TIME DIMENSION

There remains one aspect of the DECS approach to be considered. Up to the present point, we have not confronted the problem posed by the fact that the benefits generated by pollution control accrue over time. In order to take this fact into account, the DECS followed a common, straight-forward approach. First, it assumed that only benefits accruing within a 20-year period from the date the analysis was undertaken were relevant in assessing the desirability of the competing control programs;[19] the relevant time horizon became 1965–1985. Second, it attempted to establish the money value of the recreational benefits that would accrue in a base year, using the method we have criticized above. In this case, the base year was 1976, the approximate midpoint of the selected time horizon. Third, it assumed that the dollar value of the benefits accruing in 1976 would also be realized in each of the other 19 years considered relevant.[20] Fourth, it used

18. The concept of the "intrinsic worth" of an activity-day of recreation has not yet been banished from the analysis of recreation benefits. Recently in *Proposed Principles,* 1972, p. 24,157, a group of experts in the evaluation of water-related projects, while taking notice (p. 24,153) of the relevance of consumers' willingness to pay in placing money values on a project (incorrectly, it would seem, judging from the diagram and discussion on pp. 24,153–54), still recommended unit values for recreation days. A "general" recreation day is now supposed to be worth between \$.75 and \$2.25, while a "specialized" day should currently be valued at between \$3.00 and \$9.00. According to these experts, unit values must still be used because recreation evaluation methodology is not well enough developed to yield a better measure of benefits. It would seem to us *far* better, however, to refrain from using numbers at all than to abuse quantification in this way. For criticism of other aspects of the Water Resources Council's proposals, see Cicchetti et al., *Benefits,* 1972, p. 18.

19. DECS, p. 76. At certain points, the DECS documents suggest that a different time period was used. For example, DECS states that "the maximum and minimum values of the range of recreational benefits to 1975–80 were computed" (DECS, p. 76). This seems to imply that the time horizon considered was at most 15 years (1965–1980). The DECS goes on to report however that "In accordance with the other economic calculations in this report the 1975–1980 recreation benefits in terms of 1964 dollars are reported as Present Values [sic] calculated with an interest rate of 3 percent and a time horizon of 20 years" (*loc. cit.*). Correspondence with Ethan Smith of the DECS staff (Ch. 6, n. 19) indicates, moreover, that "the important thing here is that the annual monetary values are discounted to compute the present values at 3 percent, 20 years." And there can be no doubt that the 20-year time horizon is implied in the DECS calculations.

20. Correspondence with Ethan Smith (Ch. 6, n. 19) confirmed both that 1976 was used as the base year and that DECS assumed, at least implicitly, that the monetary benefits that would accrue in 1976 would also accrue in each of the other 19 years. It can also be shown that this assumption is necessary to reconcile the annual figures for 1976 given in the IES Study, Phase II, Table 22, p. 54, with the present value figures presented in the DECS, Table 20, p. 77. See Appendix C.

a discount rate of 3 percent to calculate the present value of the 20-year benefit stream.[21]

There are several issues raised by this procedure. The first involves the definition of the time horizon, which seems too short for two reasons. We have been told by DECS personnel that a substantial part of the pollution control equipment has an economic life expectancy somewhat longer than 20 years. This consideration alone suggests desirability of a longer time horizon, say 25 years. More important, however, is the fact that the installation of hundreds of millions of dollars of pollution control equipment distributed along the 86-mile estuary is a time consuming affair. Even taking an optimistic view of the regulatory process, the DECS should have anticipated a lag of five or more years before the entire control system was in effective operation. Thus it would appear that a 30-year time horizon would have been more appropriate than the 20-year period selected.[22]

Second, the DECS assumption that the benefits prevailing in 1976 would be available in each of the 19 years between 1965 and 1985 is suspect. At best, these benefits would be available only after the five-year regulatory lag we have mentioned, during which the system would not yet be in operation. Indeed, this is one of the reasons we have argued for a 30-year time horizon, since given the five- or six-year "regulatory lag," benefits accrue for only 14 or 15 years of the time horizon DECS used. Thus, it would appear that the DECS' neglect of regulatory lag is counterbalanced at least partially by its improper truncation of the time horizon. Sometimes two errors may be better than one.

The DECS neglect of the implications of the regulatory lag appears somewhat more troublesome when considered in light of another aspect of its procedure: the use of a discount rate of 3 percent to calculate the present value of the anticipated benefit stream. Although few benefits will be generated until virtually the entire system is in operation after five years or more, a substantial part of the capital costs of pollution control will be incurred during the first five years as one after another of the estuary's dischargers is induced to comply with the DRBC's regulations by making large capital expenditures. Thus, instead of the DECS' assumption of instantaneous compliance, coupled with the realization of maximum

21. DECS, p. 76.
22. If, as is likely, investments are made at different times, the useful lives of these investments will end at different times. If pollution control equipment really lasts only about 20 years and a 30-year time horizon is chosen, new investment toward the end of the time period will be required by the firms that comply early. The costs of these added investments must be considered, as well as the fact that equipment installed near the end of the period will have many years of useful life after the 30-year period.

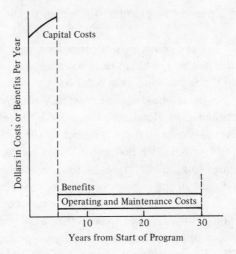

Figure 9

benefits in the first year of the time period, a more realistic view is portrayed graphically in Figure 9. Since it is of the essence of any discounting methodology that earlier years count for more than later years, the pattern of benefits and costs which takes the regulatory lag into account is less favorable to pollution control than is the DECS hypothesis, which unrealistically neglects the lag.

We come finally to the DECS choice of 3 percent as the appropriate rate to use in calculating the present value of costs and benefits. In the light of the ongoing controversy over whether the appropriate discount rate for public projects should be equal to one of the rates of return prevailing in the private sector or to a figure somewhat lower or higher than prevailing market rates,[23] it would seem prudent for the cost–benefit analyst to generate calculations using a range of discount rates. This would properly focus the attention of the political process on the importance of an informed debate about, and principled resolution of, this basic issue. Of course, the higher the rate used, the lower the level of pollution control that will seem desirable, because a large proportion of control costs accrue

23. A good summary of the arguments of those who support the use of one of the rates of return prevailing in the private economy is contained in Hirshleifer and Shapiro, 1970, pp. 291–313. The view that policy makers should use a rate different from, and perhaps lower than, private rates of return is presented in Marglin, 1967, pp. 93–99. For other provocative contributions see Baumol, 1970, pp. 273–90; Harberger, 1968, p. 43.

early in the time period, whereas the benefits are spread more evenly through the years.

Although the fate of a large number of public projects depends critically upon the resolution of the issues surrounding the selection of an appropriate rate of discount, it is a common mistake to assume that this controversy vitiates the usefulness of the cost–benefit tool. The case before us provides a powerful counterexample. A sensible cost–benefit analysis would inevitably have concluded that even if the discount rate chosen were zero, no program which contemplated spending hundreds of millions of dollars on DO improvement could be justified on the basis of the negligible benefits provided to boaters and swimmers and the quite modest benefits generated for the region's fishermen.[24]

24. As we have explained (Ch. 7, n. 2), the DECS recognized its own lack of expertise in the field of benefit analysis and so contracted the task out to a leading academic body in the region, the Institute for Environmental Studies of the University of Pennsylvania. When the Institute's study group completed its project and provided the DECS with numbers, its contract had been successfully completed. Neither the DECS nor the Department of the Interior has funded any further analysis of the benefits generated by the clean-up program in the six years since the IES completed its work—another example of the failure to take adequate institutional steps to assure continuing reappraisal of a complex and ongoing problem (see Chs. 5 and 10).

Beyond Cost-Benefit Analysis: Defining a New Environmental Policy

INTRODUCTION

Even if it is conceded that the economist cannot make a case for massive investment in a program that will raise DO levels only marginally on the Delaware, it does not follow that a proper policy can be based on this single insight. Indeed, it is a truism that many benefits generated by environmental protection are "unquantifiable" and hence beyond the economist's ken. Only by going beyond the level of platitude to examine the precise senses in which economic analysis provides an inadequate guide to policy, however, can we fairly assess the value of the current effort on the Delaware and sketch an alternative environmental program grounded in a sounder sense of both technocratic and nontechnocratic factors.

DEFINING THE UNQUANTIFIABLE: ECOLOGICAL CATASTROPHE

Benefit analysis of the kind we have attempted has sought to place a value on relatively common things—a day's boating or fishing or swimming—

and thus seems far removed from the predictions of impending ecological doom heard with increasing frequency over the past decade. Nonetheless, in the strict sense the value of avoiding world doom is not unquantifiable. Indeed, it seems safe to assume that the present inhabitants of Earth would pay almost everything in their possession to avoid imminent disaster.

Thus the only thing difficult about quantifying the costs of human destruction is in assessing the chances that adopting Objective II rather than Objective V for the Delaware River will measurably affect the probability of continued human survival. Even here, the question is susceptible of an easy answer *if one assumes that pollution loads on other river systems do not increase over time.* Once this assumption is made, we have found no reputable scientist who believes that the absence of various forms of aquatic life in the "critical regions" around Philadelphia has a significant impact on the prospects for continued human survival. This, coupled with the simple fact that the Delaware's DO problem does not impair the ability of modern treatment plants to provide potable water at a low cost, destroys any basis for the notion that even the choice of Objective I over Objective V will have a significant impact on the prospects of continued human life.

The problem arises only if our critical *ceteris paribus* assumption is relaxed and a world is imagined in which all (or at least a large number of) river systems resemble the oxygen-depleted part of the estuary. It is only then that a serious ecological risk to man may be discerned, although our knowledge in this regard is so imperfect that the number of oxygen-depleted segments that can be tolerated without any significant risk of cataclysm is indeed unquantifiable at present. Nevertheless, it does not follow from this insight that the DRBC program can be placed on a solid, if unquantifiable, intellectual foundation.

First, even after three quarters of a billion dollars is spent to raise the Delaware's DO profile marginally, the critical region of the river will still not be an important source of diverse acquatic life. Significant gains might be realized, however, if a substantial portion of that three quarters of a billion dollars were transferred from the Delaware to areas which have suffered little damage from urban industrialism, or even to the Susquehanna or Potomac river systems, which at their worst offer more promising sites for the preservation and expansion of the natural ecological complexes that have long since been banished from the banks of Philadelphia and Camden.

Second, the DO threat should not be considered apart from other ecological risks with which our society is confronted. Given our society's present tolerance of the discharge of substantial quantities of poisons, heavy metals, and unknown chemicals into its streams, it seems capricious to single out the DO threat as justifying such enormous expenditures. If a fraction of the money spent on the removal of oxygen-demanding wastes were instead devoted to understanding and stringently controlling the impact of these other types of pollution on the Delaware River, the results could well prove far more important for human health and survival.

Third, even if DO depletion should be given more importance on ecological catastrophe grounds than seems justified at present, it will be possible at some point in the future to reconsider the matter while incurring little cost during the interim period, since it is a relatively inexpensive matter to maintain the environmental status quo.[1] Moreover, the fact that oxygen-demanding wastes will continue to be discharged in substantial quantities for the next decade or longer will not make it appreciably more difficult to improve DO whenever the decision is taken, for oxygen-demanding wastes are biodegradable and do not generate long-lived effects. Indeed, the costs of waste removal a decade or two hence should be lower than at present, because for the first time in history considerable money is now being spent on research and development of new forms of treatment technology.

In conclusion, as soon as it is recognized that we can tolerate the existence of *some* river segments with a relatively low DO, it would be only prudent to permit rivers that are *most expensive to improve* to remain in a degraded condition. Even if we posit that the worldwide DO problem is serious enough to justify the expensive improvement of DO profiles in the northeastern quadrant of the United States in order to prevent ecological catastrophe, it seems clear that DO should be improved along rivers like the Potomac and the Susquehanna, where DO improvements can be generated at lower cost,[2] rather than along rivers like the Delaware and Hudson, which have borne the brunt of twentieth century technology.

DEFINING THE UNQUANTIFIABLE: MAN AND NATURE IN INDUSTRIALIZED SOCIETY

Even if it is conceded that the DRBC's program cannot be justified by invoking a plausible, though unquantifiable, threat to human health or existence, there remains another dimension of the problem which may be considered unquantifiable in a different sense. This factor requires a con-

1. See Ch. 6.
2. For a sensitive discussion of the DO problem in the Potomac, see Davis, 1968.

sideration of rather abstract issues going to the question of what place the human species ought to play in the natural order.

The Rights of Non-Human Species

When the economist attempts to quantify the benefits of an environmental improvement in dollar terms, he is merely considering the amount of money human beings will sacrifice for the improvement. To consider the case at hand, the DECS attempted to calculate the benefit *accruing to fishermen* as a result of an increased population of fish in the estuary. One looks in vain to the economist to provide a value for the benefit *accruing to fish,* which have no money to sacrifice. Thus, the adequacy of the economist's approach may be attacked on the ground that the present distribution of economic power between man and other life forms is unjust. This claim is obviously grounded in an ethical-religious conception of the proper relationship between man and nature; but so is the claim of the sceptic who responds that man is the measure of all things, and the fate of other forms should be determined by man's convenience. The validity of neither claim is self-evident.

Although a systematic discussion of these matters is beyond the scope of this book,[3] some progress can be made in understanding the issues if we first consider two extreme positions. Imagine, first, that the critic of man-centered cost–benefit analysis were to claim that the life of even one shad is priceless and hence that the DRBC's effort to improve the DO profile is well worth the three quarters of a billion dollars it will cost.[4] While this argument may be made sincerely, it rests on premises not generally accepted in our society. For example, it appears to require a universal commitment to vegetarianism, because it is inconsistent to demand that society refrain from the unintentional killing of fish through the discharge of oxygen-demanding wastes while tolerating the intentional murder of fish for purposes of food.

Consequently, to make his position more widely acceptable to contemporary mores, the critic must adopt a fall-back position not quite so extreme: conceding that men may destroy animals for some purposes, he could argue that nevertheless they ought not destroy them simply to permit human beings the benefits of industrialized society. In a society that toler-

3. While the absence of serious work on this question has been noted by contemporary philosophers (see Rawls, 1971, p. 512), only a few preliminary efforts have in fact been attempted. (See Morris, 1964, p. 185; Stone, 1972, p. 450, and Tribe, 1973, pp. 641–57.)
4. For proponents of this and related arguments, see Godlovitch, et al., 1972 and Leavitt, 1968.

ates 50,000 human deaths each year for the sake of automobile transportation, however, the critic would still fail to win a significant number of adherents to his view.

Because an absolute prohibition on the foreseeable destruction of animals for the purpose of technological advance is inconsistent with the premises of contemporary life, the critic of man-centered cost–benefit analysis must revise his position once again and offer a more modest formulation if he is to have a realistic opportunity to persuade his fellow citizens. Although not all the unfortunate consequences of twentieth century industrialism can be abolished, it does not follow that the conflict of interest between industrialized man and beasts should always be resolved to suit man's convenience. The critic may still propose that men recognize the claim of nonhuman beings *by assuring that a broad range of animal and plant life exists in a substantial geographic range under conditions these life forms find congenial, even though this goal is inconsistent with the results of man-centered cost–benefit analysis.*

Even if most people assented to the notion that the human race has an obligation to assure that a broad range of animal and plant life survives, it seems implausible that they would stretch this obligation to cover the DRBC's program to improve DO along the Delaware. Since the Delaware's critical region, even after the cleanup, will not maintain a truly diverse and vibrant range of aquatic life, it would seem wiser to invest substantial resources in the protection and enhancement of rivers that could promise far greater returns in this regard. At the same time, existing water quality levels in the Delaware seem perfectly sufficient to maintain a sustaining population of Atlantic shad. Shad runs in the less polluted estuaries on the Eastern Seaboard make one doubly sure that there is no serious risk of extinction. Finally, as the polluted segment of the estuary flows through a densely urban region, the interests in high water quality of the resident land-based animal life, so important in other contexts, need not be given great weight.

Of course, if more than enough funds were available to preserve and protect all large wilderness areas and relatively untouched river systems against the threat of encroaching industrialism, the problems posed by DO depletion in the Delaware might be given serious consideration. But nonhuman needs can only be satisfied at the cost of not satisfying pressing human wants. There would come a point, probably long before the Delaware problem was reached, at which further diversions of resources to nonhuman beings would not be acceptable even in a society that subscribed strongly to the obligation we have posited.

The Human Interest in the Integrity of Nature

The final criticism we shall consider is related to, but different from, the one we have just assessed. Instead of declaring that nonhuman life has a value *in its own right,* the critic may suggest that *humans* will obtain psychic satisfaction simply by knowing that the integrity of nonhuman life forms is being respected. He would insist that although a citizen may never himself engage in outdoor activities, he may well be willing to sacrifice a substantial amount of money simply to give himself the satisfaction of knowing that nature is preserved. This, of course, is an extreme case of "naturalism." The less extreme but more common case is represented by a person who does physically use a resource but is willing to sacrifice some amount of money to improve it *regardless of whether he will ever use the resource again.* If this amount is substantial, it must be considered an important factor in favor of cleaning up the river, one which our earlier economic analysis failed to assess.

Moreover, a rigorous estimate of the amount of money that "naturalists" are willing to sacrifice to avoid personal pain at the thought of nature ravaged could easily elude the economist researcher. The only way of estimating the money value of this consideration is to interview a sample of the population. In this case, those interviewed would have a powerful incentive to exaggerate the extent of the cost to their psyches—unless, of course, they were actually obliged to sacrifice funds to save nonhuman life forms. If, however, an actual donation to a conservation fund were required, each individual would then have a substantial incentive to pay an amount far less than his full psychic cost, knowing that the size of his individual contribution could have little effect on the total amount collected from the whole population of naturalists.

These problems, which are familiar ones in the evaluation of "public goods"[5] (to use the economists' jargon), clarify another distinct sense in which benefits can be said to be unquantifiable. Nevertheless, it is once again premature to conclude that the isolation of this unquantifiable factor will lead to the vindication of a program, like the one on the Delaware, which cannot otherwise be justified. The concern of the "naturalist" must be considered precisely. It is not enough to know, for example, that our society contains many "naturalists" and that they would be willing to sacrifice billions and billions to preserve nature, considered globally. Instead, we must ascertain the *extra amount* they are willing to spend on a particular resource (the critical region of the Delaware) in satisfying their

5. See Olsen, 1965.

naturalist interest. As soon as this is understood, an appeal to the "unquantifiable" benefits accruing to "naturalists" seems quite problematic.

It is true, of course, that many would feel poorer after learning that a site of exceptional value—like the Grand Canyon—had substantially deteriorated even though they never intended to visit the place. It seems far less plausible to assume, however, that many would be similarly affected if they learned of the deterioration of the critical region of the Delaware River, from which Nature in the classical sense has long since vanished, especially if a conservation effort of the sort we have suggested were being made to assure the existence of a vibrant nonhuman population in more appropriate geographic locales.

Even apart from the problems ordinarily inherent in the valuation of public goods, there is no way to verify this claim empirically. The fact remains that many thinking people attracted by naturalism have not yet been able to sort out their commitments in the relatively short time since environmentalism has risen to prominence. Our own values being what they are, however, we are unwilling to impute to the bulk of the population the extreme form of naturalism required to justify an attack on the Delaware's DO profile when so much remains to be done to satisfy human aspirations grounded in a compelling sense of human justice.

CONCLUSION: A NEW ENVIRONMENTAL POLICY

It is easy to imagine that when society decides to spend almost three quarters of a billion dollars to clean up a 40-mile stretch of river, something significant will come of it. The mind rebels at the thought that such vast sums are spent in vain. Yet in 1978, or 1980 or 1984, when the DRBC announces that it has "succeeded" in achieving its DO objectives on the river, the Delaware will be just as cloudy as it ever was; it will be just as difficult to obtain access to the river; boating will be neither better nor worse than it was; the drinking water will taste the same as it always did. *Perhaps* good fishing will be a few minutes closer, and during some years more shad will "survive" their journey up and down the river. Is this what all the talk about improving "the quality of life" amounts to? The question will be asked not only in the Delaware Valley but in every major industrialized area in the nation. For Congress, as we shall see, has adopted the equivalent of the DRBC's objective (Program II) to serve as national policy for the coming decade.[6] While the consequences of an

6. For a discussion of the extent to which existing federal policy mirrors the DRBC's goals, see Ch. 20.

improvement in DO levels will vary from case to case, there is no reason to expect that the Delaware will not be a typical example.

As the meager results of this multibillion dollar aspect of the environmental revolution become apparent, the public may lose much of its interest in the environment and search for another ideal as yet untarnished by serious commitment. But simply because the fundamental premise of current policy is mistaken, it does not follow that there is not much of value in environmentalism. Indeed, if one reviews the reasons why the critical region of the Delaware was the wrong place to lavish environmental concern, a sounder policy can be discerned by contrast. Investing enormous sums in an effort to improve the Delaware's DO profile was wrong because:

1. It did nothing to control the discharge of poisons that may threaten the *health* of those who depend on the water for drinking.

2. It did little to improve the *recreational opportunities* open to residents of the region.

3. It did little to improve the environment of *nonhuman forms of life* compared to the probable results of the expenditure of a similar sum of money on the preservation and development of areas relatively untouched by urban industrialism.

4. It did little to minimize the long-term *ecological risk* to mankind's continued existence compared to the probable results of the expenditure of similar sums on other pollutants and in other river basins.[7]

This summary indictment of the Delaware's program has been framed, of course, to suggest the goals of an alternative environmental program that would yield greater benefits than that under consideration. Pursuit of the objectives we have enumerated would require decision makers to develop a clear distinction between goals appropriate to the management of heavily industrialized sectors and those suitable for control of water resources still relatively untouched by twentieth century life.[8] It is in the latter areas that the unquantifiable concerns ignored by cost–benefit analysis should be given an important place in policy. Substantial sums should be expended first to preserve and then to expand the opportunities for nonhuman life forms to thrive in a congenial environment. In so doing,

7. See Ch. 20 for an elaboration of these themes.
8. Our distinction between "urban" and "nonurban" environmental policy relies on the traditional welfare economist's case for "separate facilities solutions" (see Mishan, 1967 and Dales, 1968).

policy makers will of course simultaneously be taking steps to limit significantly the risk of long-range ecological damage to mankind and preserve important recreational resources for outdoorsmen.[9]

The task of managing heavily industrialized river segments should be undertaken in a different spirit. It should be recognized that our society is unwilling to spend the billions and billions required to transform a place like the Delaware's critical zone into an area in which Nature pure and pristine shall reign once again. Decisions to improve separate aspects of the environment in such areas should be governed by the astute use of cost–benefit analysis.

Although, if we are correct, improving the DO profile on the main stem of the estuary is not warranted by such analysis, there may be circumstances in which attempting a massive cleanup of an urban waterway would be justified in economic terms. Some likely locations may even be found in the Delaware Valley itself. The Schuylkill River, for example, is one of the major tributaries of the Delaware, and flows through the center of the city of Philadelphia as well as a large suburban area. To make matters more promising, access to the river is assured even in the heart of the city, as the river flows through one of the largest urban parks in the United States. Although, at the present time, the river is the scene of substantial boating activity, making it a safe place for swimming would be an expensive proposition. It would require, among other things, the diversion of storm sewer run-off from the Schuylkill to the main stem of the Delaware, the stringent control of oil slicks and similar nuisances, and the imposition of extremely high treatment requirements on the discharge of organic waste within a 25-mile distance upriver from the swimming zone. Nevertheless, the total expense would probably be less than that generated by the DO program currently being undertaken on the far more heavily industrialized main stem of the river. Moreover, the successful completion of the Schuylkill Plan would at least permit hundreds of thousands of citizens —many from the black ghetto—to have a far pleasanter summer than is currently provided.

In speaking of the possibilities of swimming in the Schuylkill, we do not mean to suggest that the merits of a program such as envisioned in

9. In saying this, we do not mean to minimize the potential conflicts that may arise when a decision maker seeks to reserve a natural area for the purpose *both* of preserving wildlife and of providing mass-recreation. The presence of human beings in large numbers, even when they are "recreating," may endanger ecological balances and the ability of nonhuman forms to thrive. In such cases, a fundamentally unquantifiable judgment must be made to balance the competing interests at stake. For a discussion of the legal means by which recreationists can be controlled, see Kuster, 1973.

the Schuylkill Plan can be established without careful study. It is not self-evident that the half billion dollars (or even more) that cleaning up the Schuylkill requires would not be better spent on providing better schools for Philadelphians or, indeed, on providing other sorts of consumer goods through the private sector. We only wish to use the Schuylkill as an example of the kind of program that would be seriously considered if current policy were predicated on a sophisticated conception of a plausible relationship between man and nature in contemporary society. Indeed, it seems to us quite extraordinary that most policy makers asked about the Schuylkill Plan dismissed it as "impractical" (although its technical feasibility was not seriously questioned), while all thought it eminently "practical" to expend vast resources to achieve a Pyrrhic victory over the DO sag on the Delaware's main stem.

As far as the Delaware's main stem is concerned, attention should be focussed on the discharge of exotic chemicals and heavy metals which may pose a real risk to human health when present in drinking water or in sea food. Paradoxically, the real concern about the Delaware is not that the shad faces extinction but that a shad will survive only to be caught and served on the family table. For fish, by virtue both of their metabolism and their position on the food chain, may contain substantial concentrations of harmful substances present only in minute quantities in the water.[10] Although the precise magnitude of this risk to human health is unclear at present, a cost–benefit analyst would be justified in erring on the side of caution and recommending stringent controls on the esoteric discharges in question.[11] Curiously, while the DRBC has labored long on the DO issue, its concern with what should be its first priority on the estuary has been intermittent and primitive at best.[12] Indeed, this modest concern seems quite typical of the nation as a whole,[13] where even the technology required to detect, let alone control, the presence of various metals and exotic chemicals is not in widespread use.[14]

10. See, for example, *Environment Hearings,* 1970; Berglund and Berlin, 1969, and *Hazards of Mercury,* 1971.
11. For an intelligent discussion of preserving options and allocating the burden of uncertainty, see *Technology: Processes of Assessment and Choice,* 1969, pp. 32–39.
12. Conversations with DRBC officials who prefer to remain anonymous, summer 1970.
13. For a discussion of the primitive legal tools relied upon to control acquatic life which may contain hazardous substances, see Anonymous Student Author, "Health of Naturally Hazardous Foods," 1972.
14. For the relatively undeveloped state of surveillance and emerging legal problems, see Brown and Duncan, 1970; Haskins, 1970, and Murphy, 1973. Section 307 of the Federal Water Pollution Control Act Amendments of 1972, 33 U.S.C.A. §1317 (Supp. 1973), provides for the establishment of effluent controls on toxic substances;

such controls are not to be determined with an eye to the costs they impose (*H.R. Rep.* No. 92–911, 92d Cong., 2d Sess. 113 (1972), and may include absolute prohibition. However, the Administrator of the Environmental Protection Agency has discretion both in selecting the toxic substances to be regulated under §1317 and in setting the level of control (33 U.S.C.A. §1317[a][1] [Supp. 1973]). As of June 1973, no definite limitations had been imposed on such hazardous materials as algicides, pesticides, DDT, various forms of mercury, and the ions of cadmium and cyanide (see 38 Federal Register 9763, 9785 [1973] and 38 Federal Register 15868 [1973]). Section 308 of the amendments (*id.* §1318) provides for monitoring to enforce standards but does not require that a systematic program be undertaken. And at present no steps are being undertaken to embark on a thoroughgoing nationwide monitoring effort (see Ch. 20, n. 19).

Controlling Technocracy: Principles for Institutional Reconstruction

INTRODUCTION

In addition to providing a basis for a substantive critique of the premises of environmental policy, our study dramatizes the inadequacies of episodic crash planning efforts, even when they involve a team of skilled analysts. Indeed, if the limitations of the four-year DECS study were substantial, it is sobering to imagine the limited value of the numerous cost–benefit analyses generated in a matter of months or weeks which inundate the desks of government officials. It is, of course, utopian to hope for the abolition of crash programs. Policy must be formulated in the here and now; decision makers understandably want technical information and expert analysis at a time when they can use it.

Nevertheless, if technocratic analysis is to be more than a modern form of magic manipulated to enhance the legitimacy of decision, steps must be taken to design institutions that will minimize the abuse of this form of intelligence. Proceeding from our case study, this chapter will canvass, in a necessarily tentative spirit, two fundamental institutional problems raised by the Delaware experience. First, we shall consider the ways in which technocratic institutions can be structured to assure a continuous critical appraisal of regulatory premises and performance. Second, we shall assess the traditional ways in which the adequacy of individual technocratic studies has been reviewed in the past, and proceed to propose a set of institutional mechanisms that seem to us to promise more sophisticated appraisals in the future. In undertaking these tasks, we shall emphasize that no single mechanism can be relied upon to resolve all of technocracy's ills. A search for a simple panacea is misguided, because the potential failures of the technocratic enterprise are various and cannot be traced to a single institutional flaw. Indeed, as we shall see, sometimes a promising institutional cure for one technocratic disease only serves to exacerbate another form of malfunction.

ASSURING CONTINUOUS AND CRITICAL TECHNOCRATIC APPRAISAL

Our case study amply demonstrates the consequences of failing to address institutional issues with the attention they deserve. We have seen that the institutional structure which evolved in the valley neither facilitated a sustained technocratic effort over time nor effectively raised warning flags when the first signs of trouble arose. Instead, Chapter 5 demonstrates that the analytical enterprise lost its momentum after the first major decision was rendered in 1966. And Chapter 6 demonstrates that even when the remnant of the DECS staff discovered that program costs had been grossly underestimated, this warning signal did not trigger a program reappraisal but instead an impulse to suppress the threatening information.

However serious these malfunctions, a study of institutional alternatives reveals that they are not easily resolved. Indeed, steps taken to assure *continuity* of research will often create incentives for a research effort that is insufficiently *critical*, being concerned rather to establish the wisdom of existing policy.

To see this, begin by considering the kinds of institutional structure that facilitate the continuity of research. In explaining the failure to follow through on problems in the Delaware Valley, we argued that the bifurcation between a "thinking agency" (like the DECS) and an "acting agency" (like the DRBC) was of fundamental importance. After making its innovative preliminary report, the thinking agency had little incentive to undertake the hard work of refining its initial dramatic analyses: to maximize prestige, its best course was to move on to a new problem not yet systematically studied. Similarly, the acting agency, anxious to gain its own bureaucratic reputation, and without a well established research staff, will naturally defer any substantial investment in further research in favor of a single-minded effort to enforce the program selected by the ultimate decision makers.

This diagnosis of the Delaware difficulty naturally suggests an institutional approach to the problem of assuring research continuity. Instead of adopting a bifurcated structure, one might argue that an integrated agency that included both thinking and acting components would best fulfill technocratic requirements. Here researchers would be well entrenched in the agency bureaucracy and sufficiently familiar with the informal patterns of power in the administrative structure to make their influence felt. Moreover, the prestige accruing to the agency as a result of the publication of its first DECS-type report should strengthen the researchers' hands when they pressed for continuing scientific inquiry.

Unfortunately, while an integrated structure increases the chance for continuity, it diminishes even further the chance that research will critically expose fundamental problems with existing agency policies. In an integrated agency, officials committed to existing program objectives might well be in a position to employ draconian sanctions against researchers who have generated threatening analyses. Indeed, it is quite likely that in anticipation of adverse reactions from other parts of the agency, research objectives would be structured so that potentially embarrassing lines of inquiry were not pursued at all. In contrast, under a bifurcated structure, the "acting" agency personnel cannot strike out so potently against the researchers ensconced in relative safety within the separate "thinking" agency. At worst, a critical report may be suppressed at the insistence of the acting agency; researchers' jobs will only rarely be threatened.

We seem, then, to be confronted with a dilemma. On the one hand, bifurcation reduces the probability of an ongoing research effort. On the other hand, integration increases the probability that research will proceed along lines that do not raise questions that threaten existing policy in any fundamental way. It may be possible, of course, to design a system that adequately insulates an integrated agency's research staff from pressures to pursue only nonthreatening lines of inquiry. Unfortunately, however, neither our case study nor the existing theories of bureaucratic behavior suggest any simple way this can be done.[1]

1. For interesting recent efforts which may ultimately have an impact on the resolution of this problem, see Downs, 1967; Niskanen, 1971; Tullock, 1965.

Given this poverty of theory, the best we can do is curb the worst tendencies of both integrated and bifurcated structures through rather crude legislation. Thus, under bifurcation, a statute requiring the thinking agency to issue a new report once every five years might check the tendency to move on to other areas of inquiry.[2] Such a rule, however, might encounter considerable opposition both from the thinking agency, reluctant to sacrifice its autonomy, and the acting agency, opposed to the presence of independent and potentially hostile supervision. Indeed, the thinking agency could well respond to the statutory command by seeking to avoid harsh conflict with the acting agency and directing its research in relatively unthreatening directions.[3] A similar statutory approach could be taken to control an integrated agency structure. While a rule requiring the publication of technocratic reappraisal reports at regular intervals may sometimes permit the research staff to raise issues that should lead to a fundamental reappraisal, too much cannot be expected in this regard, for the reasons we have suggested.

Thus, at the present stage of our knowledge, no institutional design can promise a satisfactory solution. Nevertheless, in most cases, it seems likely that the balance of advantage will lie with the integrated agency structure. It is, we hope, not merely professorial prejudice that leads us to believe that even poorly directed research is better than no research at all. Even if it does not raise fundamental issues, competent technocratic studies will at least permit the agency some sophisticated sense of the impact of its program, and will often prove useful in implementing existing policies. Moreover, a continuous technocratic effort will provide the basis for a more probing, policy-oriented critique if for some reason it is attempted either by the agency itself or by outside forces.

ASSURING THE QUALITY OF TECHNOCRATIC REPORTS

The difficulty of designing an agency in which technocratic research will be both sustained and well directed makes it even more important to design structures that will permit a full appraisal of both the strengths and weaknesses of any particular technocratic report when it is used as the basis for a policy decision. Since administrative law evidences a good deal of concern with this question, we shall first assess the adequacy of contemporary legal controls which seek to assure the quality of technocratic analysis.

2. For an analogous but much farther-reaching proposal, see Lowi, 1962, pp. 309–10.
3. See, in general, the perceptive discussion in Downs, 1967, pp. 184–95.

After indicating the serious weaknesses of these techniques, we then consider several possible control structures before sketching an institutional approach which—while not free of difficulty—seems worthy of serious consideration.

The Traditional Legal Response: Rule Making, Hearing, and Judicial Review

The traditional legal effort to assure the quality of technocratic analysis is a two-phase affair.[4] First, before rendering its decision, the agency must afford interested parties a right to a hearing where they may present their version of the facts and law. Second, if an affected part is dissatisfied with the agency decision, he may appeal for relief to the courts.[5]

In assessing the adequacy of these quality control mechanisms, it is important to recognize that at both stages of the standard administrative process a party challenging the validity of a DECS-type report is in a relatively unfavorable position. First, under the typical agency procedure, when an agency is attempting to promulgate regulations of general application and future effect, it is constrained only by the modest procedural requirements imposed for "rule-making" proceedings.[6] Thus intervening parties do not have the right to cross-examine the experts who prepared the analyses tendered by the agency staff or other intervenors. Nor do they even have the right to present their evidence at an oral hearing, where they could at least respond to decision makers' concerns by answering questions. Instead, at the rule-making "hearing" intervenors' testimony is typically limited to a written communication containing whatever evidence and analysis the party or parties consider relevant.[7] Thus, the challenger is

4. For a general discussion, see Davis, 1972, Chs. 7, 23, 24.
5. For an enlightening discussion of the general principles guiding review of agency decisions, see Jaffe, 1965.
6. We consider here typical minimal procedural restraints in rule-making proceedings: see 5 U.S.C.A. §553 (1967), cf. §554 (agency adjudications). Other agencies, such as the Atomic Energy Commission, have imposed greater procedural restraints on their own rule-making proceedings than those required by the Administrative Procedure Act, allowing for cross-examination and rebuttal (see 10 C.F.R. §80.40 et seq. [1973]). In addition, there has been a recent tendency by some courts, notably the U.S. Court of Appeals for the District of Columbia, to impose somewhat more elaborate procedural requirements either in the name of the Constitution's due process clause or some even vaguer principles involving the proper relationship between agencies and courts. See, e.g., American Airlines v. CAB, 359 F2d 624, 631–32, *cert. denied* 385 U.S. 843 (1966); Walter Holm & Co. v. Hardin, 449 F2d 1009 (1971); International Harvester Company v. Ruckelshaus, 478 F2d 615, 650 (1973) (Bazilon, J., concurring). See generally, Boyer, 1972.
7. See 5 U.S.C.A. §553(e) (1967). But see, Portland Cement Association v. Ruckelshaus, 486 F2d 375 (D.C. Cir. 1973).

deprived of the tools needed to develop his critique of a complex technocratic document in a forceful fashion.

Similarly, if a party wishes to appeal the validity of the technocratic bases of an agency decision, he must assume an unenviable position before a reviewing court. In order to reverse the agency decision he must establish that the new rule has "no rational basis" in the record.[8] While this formula is capable of a certain degree of flexibility in application, it represents a very minimal test, which virtually any technocratic report—whatever its real quality—will satisfy. In order to conclude that an impressive-looking analysis provides "no rational basis" for a rule, appellate judges must have some solid knowledge of economics, statistics, and computer manipulation. Since they are without these skills, judges can do little except rubber-stamp their approval. It appears, then, that the typical administrative process does not seriously attempt, at either stage, a meaningful critique of technocratic intelligence.

This conclusion is not significantly altered even when the recent enactment of special administrative procedures on environmental matters is taken into account. The National Environmental Policy Act of 1969 (NEPA) places a Congressional imprimatur upon the sensitive use of cost–benefit analysis and other forms of technocratic intelligence, requiring federal agencies to prepare an "environmental impact statement" before any important decision is rendered.[9] Moreover, the courts have properly intervened when the environmental impact statement was either nonexistent or inadequate in its attention to factors enumerated in NEPA.[10] The extent to which the judiciary will move beyond this to scrutinize the substantive merits of the agency's analysis remains, however, an open question.[11] Even if this issue is ultimately resolved in favor of a relatively activist judicial response, however, the hard fact that judges simply do not have technical competence to make sense out of a DECS-type study still remains. Thus, though judges may be willing to make some hesitant forays into the technocratic preserve, it is easy to anticipate a judicious retreat when they are invited to appraise the validity of a seemingly sophisticated

8. See Davis, 1972, Ch. 30.
9. See 42 U.S.C.A. §§4332 (A) and (B) (Supp. 1973).
10. 42 U.S.C.A. §4332 (2)(c)(i)–(v) (Supp. 1973).
11. Compare, for example, McPhail vs. U.S. Corps of Engineers, 4 BNA Env. Rep. Cas. 1908 (E.D. Mich. Sept. 12, 1972) (refusing to look beyond conclusory statements of favorable cost–benefit ratios contained in a Corps of Engineers statement) with Sierra Club vs. Froehlke, 5 BNA Env. Rep. Cas. 1033 (S.D. Tex. Feb. 16, 1973) (holding that a careful judicial examination of the soundness of a Corps of Engineers cost–benefit study was warranted under NEPA and refusing to accept the Corps' proffered analysis until "substantial in-depth revision of . . . the impact statement" had been undertaken).

DECS-type analysis which argues that an agency decision squares with NEPA.

All this is not to deny that the traditional system of administrative control may occasionally play a valuable role even in decisions involving heavy technocratic components. Nevertheless, its manifest imperfections suggest the wisdom of considering alternative methods of control to supplement, if not to displace, the traditional system.

Inherent Limitations of Traditional Administrative Procedure

It is not enough to recognize that received legal doctrine imposes an ineffective set of controls on the use of technocratic intelligence. One must go on to an even more important consideration: the *inherent* limitations of traditional forms of agency hearing and judicial review. Even a more elaborate hearing system and more searching appellate scrutiny would be afflicted by three major defects. First, launching a credible critique of a DECS-type report is an exceedingly time-consuming and expensive affair. This means that only the best organized and richest interests will be capable of a sustained effort in a large number of proceedings, so that, despite the existence of a handful of "public interest" law firms, large diffuse groups will be systematically underrepresented. Moreover, groups powerful enough to intervene systematically will often use expanded hearing rights simply to delay needed substantive reform. Second, both the hearing process and judicial review are dominated by lawyers whose training does not in general equip them to probe the premises of technocratic argument. It is true, of course, that lawyers have expertise in questioning witnesses and culling relevant information from large masses of data. Nevertheless, they are untrained in the techniques of mathematical proof, statistical inference, and computer manipulation which are central to technocratic analysis. To make matters worse, these modes of argument cannot be "picked up" in the same casual way in which lawyers have gained a superficial familiarity with the expertise of other fields. Thus, although lawyers will try to ask the "right questions" of experts in preparing a coordinated attack on an agency staff analysis, they will increasingly fail to present a well focussed critique. Third, both an agency and a court must discriminate among the cacophony of voices at a hearing in order to determine which arguments have merit and which are merely partisan efforts to deflect much-needed reform. In this complex effort at winnowing out "the truth," the agency will typically rely on the very staff responsible for the original analysis. This fact makes it far less likely that valid criticisms will be given appropriate weight.[12] Even less enviable is the position of the appellate judge. It is not simply that the present generation of judges is innocent of the technocratic arts. It does not even make sense to train them when the bulk of their work does not require these skills, even assuming that they would be willing to undertake an extensive course of study.

These three structural inadequacies add up to one fundamental point: outside the agency's own staff, there exists no group with the resources and competence necessary to mount a sophisticated critique of agency analyses on a regular basis. This insight, in turn, suggests several possible approaches to institutional reform which attempt in various ways to create a body capable of a searching critique.

Before assessing the relative adequacy of these approaches, however, it is necessary to consider with greater precision the criteria by which a critique of a technocratic report should be judged. To do this, we must move beyond the traditional categories of administrative law which seek to locate all agency judgments on a continuum according to the extent to which they represent "findings of fact" or "conclusions of law."[13] Instead, our study of the DECS Report indicates that the "facts" found by a technocratic team should be scrutinized with four different questions in mind:

1. What is the empirical basis for the agency's findings and predictions? To what extent have its models been verified? (We will call this the "empirical" question, and have discussed it in Chapters 4 and 6.)

2. To what extent does the technocratic discussion of certain variables divert attention from other factors of equal or greater importance? (We call this the "diversion" question, and have discussed it in Chapter 3.)

3. Is the technocratic analysis firmly grounded in sound scientific theory? (This, the "scientific competence" question, has been discussed in Chapters 7 and 8.)

4. What questions is technocratic analysis—however well carried out— inherently incapable of considering? (This, the "inherent limitations" question, has been discussed in Chapter 9.)

12. Consider, for example, the pointed criticism of the AEC, which argues that because the agency staff is responsible for both research and development of nuclear power on the one hand and for consideration of associated risks to public health and safety on the other, it is apt to discount safety arguments it does not wish to hear. See Green, 1968 and Anonymous Student Author, "Regulation of Nuclear Power," 1970.
13. For a sensitive treatment, see Jaffe, 1965, Chs. 14 and 15.

Doubtless, the four questions suggested by our case study do not completely exhaust the relevant parameters of inquiry; nevertheless they will suffice in a necessarily preliminary canvass of forms of nonjudicial control.

Interagency Consultation

The first approach we shall consider has already been institutionalized in the formulation of environmental policy. NEPA requires that after an agency formulates its own analysis of the environmental implications of any major action it is considering, it must circulate its environmental impact statement "and obtain the comments of any Federal agency which has jurisdiction by law or special expertise with respect to any environmental impact involved."[14] Although this provision has been given scant attention by outsiders[15] the practice of interagency consultation seems widespread and has the important advantage of generating expert analysis at a relatively low cost.

Unfortunately, it has obvious difficulties as well. Each agency is naturally most interested in the projects for which it has primary responsibility and so will be reluctant to divert substantial resources to comment on the projects of others. This attitude of benign neglect will be transcended only when the agency perceives that another's project is threatening its own programs. In this case, an agency's comments will be primarily those of an advocate. Such advocacy will often be extremely valuable, highlighting sporadically the "diversion" and "inherent limitation" issues we have previously isolated. Nevertheless, this process will necessarily proceed in a hit-or-miss fashion; there seems, moreover, less reason to expect a sustained critique of "empirical" and "scientific competence" issues, given a likely reluctance by one agency to label their bureaucratic brothers incompetent.

Private Consulting Firms

A second institutional device has different defects. Instead of turning to other government institutions for comment, it is possible to imagine an agency going to the private market to hire one or more consulting firms to scrutinize the technocratic analyses generated by its staff. While this prac-

14. 42 U.S.C.A. §4332(2)(c) (Supp. 1973).
15. See the rudimentary discussion of review responsibilities in CEQ Guidelines ¶ 7, 36, Fed. Reg. 7725 (1973), which has been supplemented by a somewhat more elaborate statement—for the first time outlining, though in rather vague terms, the responsibility of reviewing agencies to assess the substantive merits of proposals—in the more recent proposed CEQ Guidelines ¶ 9, 38 Fed. Reg. 10, 859–60 (1973).

tice is often used in private industry, its disadvantages are substantial in a governmental context. Instead of providing an arm's-length critique, consulting firms will have an incentive to tell the dominant elements in the agency what they wish to hear. This incentive will be particularly powerful where the failures in DECS-type work will become apparent only after ten or twenty years, when hoped-for benefits do not materialize. For it is quite likely that even when a project fails, after some years, to live up to expectations, the connection between project failure and faulty analysis will never be made at all; the erring firm (if it still exists) may thereby evade all the costs of its failure to scrutinize the original technocratic report critically.

Insofar as consulting firms withstand the temptation to whitewash, moreover, they may be expected to concentrate their critique on issues that have clearly defined right and wrong technocratic answers. While well grounded criticisms of "empirical" and "scientific competence" issues may be resented, their relevance must be conceded by even the most hard-headed technocratic staff. In contrast, if a consulting firm attempts to address "diversion" and "inherent limitation" questions, they run the serious risk of being perceived as unprofessional dilettantes engaging in destructive criticism. This is a reputation that will be avoided by all but the most prestigious consultants.

The Need for a New Institution: The Review Board

While other agencies and private consulting firms have their uses, their limitations suggest the need for considering whether more substantial institutional reforms are required to meet the challenge of technocratic intelligence. If the four kinds of technocratic critique are to be discharged on a regular basis, the reviewing function cannot be peripheral to the agency's major business, as it is under the "interagency consultation" regime. Similarly, the reviewing body cannot, like a consulting firm, depend for its future rewards on the technocratic agency's pleasure with its critique.

Instead, the institution we have in mind should be a rather distant relative of the typical judicial mechanism. Like a court, the Review Board would be insulated from the control of the agencies whose work product it will be charged to assess. Unlike the typical court, however, many of its members would not be lawyers and all would be thoroughly trained in the techniques fundamental to technocratic analysis.[16] Moreover the Review

16. In point of fact, many commissions today are characterized by memberships with great diversity of background (see Bernstein, 1958).

Board, again unlike a court, should not conceive its task as one of adjudicating concrete disputes between private citizens or between individuals and governmental units. Instead, its fundamental concern should be to assure the quality of technocratic analysis proffered to decision makers on issues of importance.

When the Board received a technocratic analysis for review, it would question the staff that prepared the report, then issue a written evaluation. The Board's objective in each case should be to assess the analysis *in plain English* from the four different perspectives suggested here, much as we have attempted to do in this book. It should be emphasized that the Board would *not* conceive as its task to redo the study, whatever its weaknesses, nor should it seek to make a final judgment on the merits; its perspective should be basically that of a sympathetic critic of technocratic methods, concerned that a powerful and esoteric form of systematic intelligence not be abused.

Because the Board is not intended to displace the policy-making agency, we see no reason to require it to hold plenary review hearings in which all interested persons will be permitted to participate. All concerned parties will still have the right to intervene in the policy-making agency's hearing, where the Review Board's evaluation will be submitted simply as additional evidence to guide the agency's decision.[17] Instead of holding plenary hearings, the Board's procedures should be structured to facilitate a relatively rapid response. Even with expeditious procedures, a substantial number of reports will probably go unreviewed, because the time requirements of decision makers will be such that the delay involved will be considered intolerable.[18] But if our present case study itself is typical of the speed with which planning decisions for large capital-intensive projects are made, there will remain enough grist for the Review Board's mill. The DECS staff's report was made public in July 1966; the DRBC did not render its judgment until March, 1967. During the eight-month interim period, a suitably staffed Review Board would have had more than enough time to complete a useful analysis.

Even if the Review Board's sole power were the publication of written

17. It is possible, of course, that if the Review Board's expertise gains wide respect over time, courts will begin to rely significantly on the Board's opinions when they undertake the task of judicial review. Indeed, a similar symbiotic relationship is developing under NEPA with courts referring to analyses generated in the process of interagency consultation, which we have reviewed in the text.
18. If an agency certifies that a decision is so pressing that it cannot be delayed for a review by the Board, it may be wise to grant the Board power to decide to conduct a review after the decision has been rendered, thus preventing agencies from evading criticism by acting hastily.

advisory opinions, the impact of such opinions on the use of technocratic analysis should not be underestimated: as experience with the General Accounting Office indicates, the power of publicity can be very substantial indeed. In addition to its power to direct the concern of the agency and other participants to crucial value choices, the mere existence of the Review Board will improve the quality of analysis generated by the agency itself. Agencies seeking to avoid public embarrassment will have a new incentive to employ competent analysts. Moreover, the analysts themselves will be under far more pressure to develop a report which does not merely serve as a rationalization for decisions already made on other grounds.

Similarly, the Board's opinions will have a salutary impact on the institution of judicial review. Not only will judges be in a position to assess more intelligently whether an agency's decision has a rational basis in the record but—even more important—their more knowledgeable grasp of the technocratic document will permit improved performance of their central judicial function: determining whether the agency is reasonably fulfilling the purposes set out for it by a statute expressing the priorities of the political branches. Indeed, as we have suggested, without institutional innovation the traditional structure of administrative review will increasingly prove unequal to the challenge of technocratic decision making.

Finally, the Board's opinions will serve as a focus of commentary from the academic profession, especially for the nonlegal disciplines not accustomed to examining critically the use of their concepts in the policy making process. Not only will this interchange redound to the advantage of both decision makers and academics, it will also be of the greatest importance in training a new generation of policy analysts to achieve a higher level of competence and a broader conception of their mission.

Needless to say, the Review Board structure has disadvantages as well as advantages. Even if it does not attempt to redo agency reports, its staff will nevertheless be large and expensive; even more seriously, the Board might well hire some of the best personnel who would otherwise be doing the best studies. Moreover, Review Board members might include some political hacks or incompetents. Even with the best personnel, the Board's opinions may often be unwise, or prove ultimately to have deflected the course of systematic inquiry in an unfortunate direction.

To maintain perspective, however, it should be recognized that almost all these objections apply with equal or greater force to the institution of appellate judicial review. Indeed, the potential costs involved in creating appellate tribunals are far greater than those involved in the Review Board, for the judiciary's powers far exceed those with which we have endowed the Board. Nevertheless, our society has judged—rightly, we think—that it is important to have centralized judicial institutions confronting fundamental legal issues with as much self-consciousness as possible.

Similarly, at the present point in our society's development, we believe it desirable to design an institution which can confront self-consciously fundamental problems raised by the use of technocratic intelligence. It is true, of course, that in developing criteria for review of technocratic reports, the Review Board will be dependent on the existing academic disciplines that provide intellectual foundations for modern policy making. If these academic disciplines were so poorly developed that no such standards existed, the Board's task would be an impossible one. As we have tried to demonstrate in preceding chapters, however, modern technocracy is not so intellectually bankrupt that a call for a Review Board is a cry for a group of Platonic guardians capable of charting, unaided, a course between technocracy and obscurantism. So far as the "empirical" and "scientific competence" questions are concerned, there can be little doubt that coherent principles of evaluation exist. Similarly, many "diversion" issues can be spotted by intelligent Board reviewers sufficiently skilled in mathematical argument, for they will not be overly impressed by efforts to capture one or two aspects of reality in rigorous mathematical form. It is true, however, that the fourth demand imposed on the Board, which requires that it articulate the inherent limitations of the technocratic method, is one the Reviewers inevitably will prove incapable of performing to the satisfaction of all. Nevertheless, the agency's opinions could play an important role in the larger debate that is required if our society is to seek even a tentative synthesis between technocratic and unquantifiable values.

Finally, in structuring a Review Board, great care must be taken to avoid its capture by a single pressure group that would transform it into a vehicle serving a single substantive interest. Thus it would seem wisest to endow the Board with wide jurisdiction. This would not only make it more difficult for the Board to be captured by any one of the many groups interested in its opinions, it would also have a salutary impact upon the Reviewers themselves: like judges, the Reviewers would be forced to recognize that their opinions must be grounded in principles transcending any particular interest conflict, that an opinion on an environmental issue today may have implications for the analysis of a housing issue tomorrow. All this is not to deny that Reviewers, like judges, will find themselves disagreeing with one another; as long as they are confronting the right questions, however, such disagreements will throw light on complex public questions, to the considerable benefit of policy-making agencies, the courts, and the larger society.

Despite the greatest care, the chances are considerable that the Review Board would fail to fulfill its functions in even a modestly successful fashion, and this prospect should be held in mind. Nevertheless, the costs of failure would be relatively small, at least when balanced against the potential gains. An incompetent Board's opinions would fail to obtain the respect of agencies and courts that is required for its effective operation. While the creation of yet another institutional nullity is not a happy prospect, even a reasonable prospect of a moderately successful Board seems to us worth the effort.

The Review Board we have proposed may be innovative, but the need for a coordinated and sustained critique of technocratic intelligence has long been felt,[19] and embryonic institutional forms exist today which discharge some of the functions of the proposed Board. Most important, the Office of Management and Budget performs some of these critical functions, although the methodological issues are submerged in judgments on the merits, in a necessarily politically charged environment, on the basis of analyses not open for general discussion.[20] In addition, in the area of environmental regulation, the Council on Environmental Quality (CEQ), created by NEPA,[21] not only has the responsibility to frame guidelines governing agency formulation of environmental impact statements[22] but also invests a significant portion of its small but expert staff's time in reviewing the analyses generated by the policy-making agencies.[23] Unfortu-

19. See, for example, Freedman, 1968 and 1 Adm. Conf. of U.S. 122, Recommendation #6. See also Davis, 1972, pp. 147–48.
20. See also the Technology Assessment Act of 1972, 2 U.S.C.A. §471 (Supp. 1973). In contrast to the structure proposed here, the Board's membership is principally composed of Congressmen who are not merely instructed to review the work done by the agencies but also are invited to supervise primary research themselves (see 2 U.S.C.A. §§472–474 [Supp. 1973]). Statutory commands of such breadth impose impossible workloads, especially upon a part-time board of full-time politicians (see Ch. 13).

The highly politicized nature of the Office is made even clearer when the relationship between the Board and its Advisory Council of leading experts in technology assessment is considered. The Advisory Council may review a report only at the behest of the Board or the Office's Director "in consultation with the Board" or the Chairman of any Congressional committee (2 U.S.C.A. §472(d)1–3 [Supp. 1973]). Moreover, after the Board acts, it may request an Advisory Council review, although at this point its impact will generally be minimal. In short, while the Act gives Congress a much-needed source of expertise, it does little to assure the systematic performance of the Review Board's functions.
21. 42 U.S.C.A. §§4341–4347 (1973).
22. Executive Order No. 11514 §3(h), March 5, 1970.
23. CEQ itself has stated that with a staff of fewer than 60 it cannot "make a thorough study, even for advisory purposes, of every [environmental impact] state-

nately, however, it lacks the quasi-judicial independence necessary to fulfill a Review Board's functions. Our casual acquaintance with the CEQ suggests that instead of being the source of a critique of prevailing methodologies, it devotes much of its energy to mediating disputes between competing interest groups and agencies. This, of course, is what is to be expected from an agency in the Office of the President.[24] The Council's performance so far suggests, however, that the marriage of high level political coordination and sustained critique of technocratic intelilgence is doomed to be an unhappy one. Thus, it may be that the best way to begin an experiment with the Review Board idea is to create two separate institutions to discharge the different functions currently being delegated by the CEQ. On the one hand, an Environmental Review Board would be structured to achieve the coordinated critique which motivated Congress to create the CEQ in the first place.[25] On the other hand, the President's Environmental Advisor should be restricted to the task of achieving interagency political coordination.

---

ment filed with it." Instead it seeks to concentrate on "very significant projects whose environmental effects warrant careful Council review" (Council on Environmental Quality, *Annual Report, 1972*).

24. 42 U.S.C.A. §4342 (1970).

25. It should be recalled, however, that the narrower the jurisdiction of the Review Board, the greater the chance of its capture by a single substantive interest unconcerned with the basic methodological concerns which should provide the Board's *raison d'être*. Thus, restricting the Board's field to "environmental" issues—however wide the embrace of this label—may undermine substantially the Review Board's performance. Given the novelty of the Review Board proposal, however, it seems justified to suggest an experimental application, despite the risk that a Board with narrow jurisdiction will not act as effectively as one with a broader base.

PART
III

Beyond Technocracy: The Political Model and Its Alternatives

An Overview
of the Political Process
and Its Problems

INTRODUCTION

Thus far, we have entirely failed to locate the DECS Report in the larger political process of which it was a part. We have not asked how the large number of political actors who participated in the Delaware decision in fact perceived and evaluated the DECS effort in model building and economic analysis. Instead we have considered the DECS Report "on its merits" in an effort to understand both its limitations and its strengths. This process has in turn permitted a thoroughgoing reassessment of existing water pollution policies and a tentative attempt to design institutional mechanisms to improve the quality of the technocratic analyses proffered to decision makers.

While isolating the DECS Report from its political context has permitted the analysis of important substantive and institutional issues, it nevertheless deprived us of another range of insights: those concerning the interrelationship of technocratic intelligence and political decision making. As we suggested earlier,[1] the DRBC structure represented an innova-

1. See Ch. 1.

tive and seemingly attractive attempt to integrate the values of enlightenment and democracy. On the one hand, the technocrats were invited to
generate a comprehensive analysis of the environmental problem; on the
other, this analysis would not be given decisive weight in the ultimate
decision. Instead, after the Report was exposed to scrutiny in public hearings and by the staffs of each of the governors and the Secretary of the
Interior, the decision was to be made by high-level political actors who
could rely not only on technocratic criteria but on their own understanding
of the broader concerns of popular opinion. To make this effort to reconcile Enlightenment and Democracy even more interesting, we have seen
that when the Governors and Secretary Udall met at Dover to select a
policy for the estuary, they effectively repudiated technocratic analysis by
choosing a slightly modified version of Objective II, instead of one of the
far less expensive objectives the DECS Report suggested as appropriate.[2]
Thus the decision itself invites us to consider in detail the way the DECS'
technocratic analyses were perceived and evaluated by the political actors,
and to make an effort to learn more general lessons concerning the way the
flow of information can best .be structured to enhance the rationality of
decisions. Did the politicians refuse to follow DECS because, *after considering the document,* they concluded that the interests of the region
would be served best by a more vigorous (and expensive) program? Did
they instead reject the Report because they did not believe in the value of
cost–benefit analyses? Or did they simply ignore the Report without confronting its implications at all? Clearly, one's assessment of the desirability
of the complex technocratic-political decision-making process instituted
along the Delaware will depend in part on the reasons DRBC members
acted independently of their DECS advisors. To obtain information on this
point, we undertook to interview all persons who played a significant role
in the political decision. While it proved impossible to speak with every
one of them, we were able to conduct face-to-face interviews, typically
lasting between one and three hours each, with more than 120 participants—ranging from ultimate decision makers, like Secretary Udall and
Governors Shafer and Hughes, and the key figures in the bureaucracies of
the federal government and each of the states concerned, to representatives
of municipal, industrial and conservationist interests who played a role in
the decision.[3] Our description and analysis depend principally upon these
interviews, which were obtained under a pledge of confidentiality. We are
aware that the use of confidential interviews imposes a special responsi-

2. See Ch. 2.
3. For a listing of people interviewed, see Appendix B.

bility to report the facts dispassionately and we have attempted to discharge this responsibility as best we could.

THE BASIC THESIS: THE FATE
OF COOPERATIVE FEDERALISM

It should be no surprise that men like Secretary Udall or Governor Rockefeller had neither the time nor training to undertake a laborious assessment of the insights and weaknesses concealed under the DECS Report's bland, technocratic prose. Nevertheless, this fact cannot end further discussion of the way the prime political actors viewed the DECS Report. Although it was impossible for them personally to undertake a critical assessment, it was quite possible for each of the Governors and the Interior Secretary either (a) to accept the Report uncritically and vote for the relatively unambitious clean-up program it recommended or (b) to direct members of his staff to examine the DECS product carefully to determine whether an approach different from the one recommended was superior. In the following discussion, we shall show that virtually none of the prime political actors adopted either of these alternatives. Instead, they largely ignored the issues posed by the DECS Report and cast their ballots on the basis of factors which did not take the peculiar problems of the Delaware Estuary into account.

If this were the sole conclusion of our analysis, perhaps it would not warrant the extended attention we are giving to it. It is common knowledge that—on some occasions, at least—politicians choose to ignore the expert analysis proffered so eagerly to them. Nevertheless, it seems to us that our discussion, coupled with related research by others,[4] permits us to read more than this into the politicians' failure to take any steps to acquaint themselves with the problem as described by DECS.

While we postpone a full analysis until we have described the actual dynamics of the decision our central argument can be stated easily enough, and will assist the reader to evaluate the facts for himself. Our study shows that when five *state* and *national* politicians are asked to serve intermittently in a *regional* agency, they will not make any effort to understand the distinctively regional implications of the issues before them. Instead of trying to familiarize themselves, even roughly, with the problems they confront, each of the five politicians will ask himself which of the programs will best further his interest in the *state* or *national* forum that is his

4. See sources cited in Ch. 12, nn. 45, 46.

primary concern. To make matters worse, because all of the decision makers spend virtually all their time and energy handling state or federal problems, they will look for advice primarily from the *state* or *national* aides on whom they ordinarily rely and only secondarily from those bureaucrats (like the DECS and DRBC staffs) who have attempted to view the distinctive regional implications of the issues. These primary advisors, in turn, will have a natural tendency to suggest that the issues presented to the regional agency be resolved in a way that conforms to decisions made in the state or national arena, despite the fact that the regional problem is revealed as quite different from any that arise in state or national fora. In short, a regional river basin agency composed of state and national politicians will suffer from intense centrifugal forces that make it difficult for decision makers even to consider any document which addresses the region's problem from a regional perspective. It is possible, of course, to control these centrifugal forces somewhat by developing a complete regional political system in which, for instance, DRBC members would be elected by the valley's seven million residents with the assistance of regional political parties, and, after their election, respond to regionally organized interest groups and organs of public opinion. The creation of such a full-fledged political system, however, is an extremely costly exercise and would clearly be unwarranted simply to decide water management policy. In the absence of such an effort at political construction, policy would in general be made far more intelligently if regional agencies were designed so as to avoid, as much as possible, case-by-case political decision making, and instead were structured to permit the responsible use of technocratic criteria in the implementation of substantive statutory standards framed in general terms.

AN OVERVIEW OF THE ANALYSIS

We have, in stark and summary form, enumerated the principal theses that arise from our study of the political processes involved in the DRBC's decision. It is now necessary to consider the extent to which the political process affecting the Delaware decision supports the general thrust of our argument and permits us to give the basic argument additional nuance and texture. To make the issues clearer, we have organized our presentation into three chapters, with complementary concerns. In Chapter 12 we explore the fascinating efforts by relatively low-level officials in both the federal and state bureaucracies to fashion a political consensus within the region. We begin at this point because these low-visibility attempts were of fundamental importance to the final decision formally made by the Secretary and the four Governors acting as a regional agency. Chapter 13 examines the decision-making problem from the perspective of the five ultimate political decision makers and reveals the peculiar weaknesses of regional political processes. Finally, Chapter 14 considers the extent to which the weaknesses of the technocratic-political process may be avoided by designing institutions along new lines, and advances a blueprint for an institutional structure that promises to articulate a sounder set of policies than those that have prevailed both in the Delaware Valley and the nation at large.

The Bureaucratic Politics
of Decision Making:
Of Low-Level Visibility
and Its Importance

INTRODUCTION

While an assessment of the impact of lower level bureaucratic officials on ultimate decision makers is always a hazardous business, it is particularly difficult in the study of a regional agency like the DRBC. Generally speaking, when the student of the bureaucratic process seeks to analyze a state or national decision, the beginning—if not the end—of wisdom is to consider the formal organizational structure of the agency in question. While it is true that one official or another will exercise powers not formally vested in his office, nevertheless the legal structure of authority will serve as a starting point for assessing the informal structure of authority. In contrast, given the weakness of the regional level of government, it would be a serious mistake even to begin an analysis of bureaucratic power with the assumption that the small staff hired by the interstate agency charged with ultimate decision making responsibility will serve as the primary locus of bureaucratic power. The interstate agency inhabits a universe containing larger and better established state and national bureaucracies unaccustomed to deferring to the new "regional" entity. Moreover, the precise legal relationships between the regional agency and bureaucracies on the state and national levels are often poorly defined. Thus, the student of the bureaucratic process must cast his net widely, prepared for a free-for-all struggle among state, regional, and federal officials who are guided even less than ordinarily by legal structures designed to promote orderly and coherent decisions.

In our interviews, then, we made a special effort to make contact with officials in state and federal agencies with substantial interests in the Delaware issue. This effort permitted us to unearth two very different bureaucratic attempts to influence the ultimate decision. The first pattern of influence had its source in the group of *federal technocrats* in the DECS, who made an imaginative effort to fashion a political consensus among the important regional interest groups around the pollution program favored by the majority of DECS staffers. The second pattern emanated from the *state officials* responsible for state-wide pollution policy. These administrators generally had an imperfect understanding of the technocratic analyses of the DECS staff, and were far less concerned with relating their decision to the new quantitative disciplines represented in the analyses. In the end, it was this second group, the state officials, who had by far the more profound influence on the ultimate outcome. After describing the two competing influences, we shall consider some of the reasons why the outcome of the conflict between the two forces could have been readily anticipated.

DECS AND WUAC

A discussion of the larger political context must begin once again with the DECS. The staff, at a very early stage in its work, perceived a need to develop channels of communication with interests in the valley concerned in one way or another with the estuary's water quality. Consequently, the staff invited a broad range of firms, municipalities, conservationists, and "public interest" groups to serve on a Water Use Advisory Committee (WUAC) to meet at regular intervals with the DECS staff.[1] In the early

1. Because the staff's knowledge of the Delaware Valley was limited, it enlisted the aid of Frank Dressler, a resident of the area and head of the Water Resources Association for the Delaware River Basin, a large nonprofit organization which involved a variety of local interests. (The nature of the WRA/DRB will be discussed in greater detail on pp. 177–179.) Naturally enough, Dressler suggested using the membership of the WRA to serve as the Water Use Advisory Committee (WUAC). DECS, however, decided to invite non-WRA members to serve as well, and Dressler cooperated by proffering the names that came to mind. No more systematic search was undertaken. (Interviews with Everett MacLeman and Frank Dressler; see Appendix D.)

stages of the DECS study, the WUAC performed two important functions. First, its meetings gave the staff an opportunity to educate representatives of the concerned public in the technocratic concepts of water quality management. This would permit, it was thought, the relevant interest groups to act with greater insight when it came time to determine the water quality goals to be pursued along the estuary. Second, the WUAC could serve as a useful sounding board for DECS ideas, permitting the technocratic staff an insight into the dimensions of the problem that were of most interest to the wider public. As the time approached for publication of the DECS Report in 1966, however, the WUAC came to be used for a third purpose. No longer was it simply an educator of the public about DECS' methodology (and of DECS about public opinion); it began to be used by the DECS staff as a political organ within which the conflicting interests of the various water users could be reconciled so that an interest group consensus could form around one or another of the five programs advanced in the DECS document. Thus, when the DECS Report[2] was published, it contained not only the technocratic analysis considered previously but a statement of the position adopted by each of the four major interest groups sitting on the WUAC. The Report announced that while the conservationist groups believed that the relatively ambitious Objective II should be selected, the representatives of industry, municipalities, and nonconservationist "public interest" groups all agreed that Objective III (or minor variations thereof) was to be preferred.

Behind this summary statement, however, lies a fascinating study in the politics of interest group adjustment. It is unclear to us who first conceived the idea that the WUAC itself should make a policy recommendation; it is clear, however, that as the Report reached its final stages of preparation, leading members of the DECS staff called a series of meetings whose express purpose was to obtain a consensus on a recommendation which would then be announced publicly. These meetings, however, were not open to all the members of the WUAC; instead, only four representatives of the "public" attended. These four were selected in a way that seemed obvious at the time. Previously, the WUAC had been divided into four subcommittees—one composed of representatives of polluting firms, one of municipalities, one of conservationist groups, and one containing all public interest groups without an explicitly proconservation cast.[3] Each

2. As mentioned previously, no DECS "Final Report" has been issued. We are referring here and elsewhere to the "Preliminary Report" issued in July, 1966.
3. For a listing of those who served on the subcommittees, see Appendix E.

of these subcommittees then proceeded to elect a chairman from its number.[4] Given this subcommittee structure, it was natural for the DECS staff to invite the chairman of each subcommittee to participate in bargaining sessions which sought to hammer out an acceptable compromise.

During the month of March, 1966[5] the chairmen held two lengthy "consensus sessions"; in addition, each chairman discussed the competing water quality objectives proposed by DECS with members of his respective subcommittee. At the first chairmen's meeting, the DECS' hope for consensus seemed slim indeed. Both the representative of the polluting firms and representative of the polluting municipalities announced that they would support no plan more ambitious than Objective IV; the representative of the conservationist groups professed himself satisfied with nothing less than Objective I; only the representative of the public interest groups backed a variation of Objective III.[6] In order to understand the subsequent shifts in position in the direction of consensus, it is necessary to consider the different roles played by each of the four direct participants in the WUAC bargaining sessions.

THE PERSPECTIVE OF THE POLLUTERS: CARMEN GUARINO AND WILLIAM HALLADAY

Carmen Guarino, the representative of the polluting municipalities, was himself a high ranking official in the city of Philadelphia's Water Department, which had general control over the city's municipal sewage treatment facilities. Nevertheless, despite his relatively responsible position, Guarino had little independent bargaining authority, but was expected to advance the views of his chief, Samuel Baxter. Guarino's deference to Baxter was not only a product of the latter's superior official position but also of Baxter's forceful personality and significant accomplishments. Commissioner Baxter had a national reputation as a sanitary engineer and had demonstrated considerable political sagacity in maintaining himself in

4. The chairmen of the four subcommittees were: (1) *Recreation, Conservation, Fish and Wildlife:* Edmund H. Harvey, president, Delaware Wildlife Federation; (2) *General Public:* Frank W. Dressler, exec. director, Water Resources Assoc./Delaware River Basin; Paul Felton (replaced Mr. Dressler, 12/65); (3) *Industry:* William B. Halladay, supervisor of pollution control, The Atlantic Refining Co.; (4) *Local Governments and Planning Agencies:* Carmen F. Guarino, chief of sewerage operations, City of Philadelphia.
5. The crucial sessions of the chairmen took place on March 17 and 28, 1966. In total, the WUAC held approximately 14 meetings (*WUAC Minutes*).
6. *WUAC Minutes* of March 17, 1966 meeting.

the Commissioner's office for more than 15 years.[7] He had, moreover, strong personal views as to the desirability of an ambitious program for cleaning up the polluted estuary in the Philadelphia environs. In Baxter's view, a massive clean-up campaign would yield very little in the way of real environmental improvement.[8] Moreover, the Commissioner attempted, in his frequent public statements, to raise many of the issues we have canvassed in this study. Although he was unable to generate sufficient staff analyses to make his points decisively,[9] Baxter was quite unwilling to retreat from his firm convictions as to the pointlessness of large expenditures.[10]

Even if the Commissioner had been personally more uncertain on the merits, however, powerful institutional forces would have pushed him toward the position he took. Since the city of Philadelphia itself was the largest polluter in the region, a large proportion of the clean-up expense would fall on its shoulders. The costs of compliance were brought home to Baxter in the most direct way as a result of the legal structure governing his department. Under the applicable ordinances, the department was obliged to finance the costs of its pollution control operations by the imposition of sewer charges.[11] Thus, a dramatic increase in treatment costs would require the department to raise fees in a highly visible way. Moreover, in order to finance the project's capital costs, Baxter would be obliged to campaign actively for a bond issue in a citywide referendum required for the purpose.[12]

---

7. In fact, Secretary of the Interior Udall called Philadelphia's water supply and sewage disposal systems the "finest in the country" (*The Philadelphia Inquirer*, Aug. 13, 1965, p. 1, col. 7).

Baxter has served as president, director, and Pennsylvania Fellow of the American Society of Civil Engineers; president of the American Public Works Association; president and director of the American Water Works Association. He was also appointed by Governor Scranton as his advisor on the DRBC.

During his career as Water Commissioner, Baxter was offered leading positions in the Chicago and New York City Water Departments. In both cases, however, Democratic Mayor Tate of Philadelphia managed to persuade his Republican Commissioner to remain in the city.

8. Interview with Samuel Baxter; see Appendix D.

9. The City's Water Department, however, did attempt a series of scientific analyses which sought to undermine the credibility of the DECS effort (see Mamelak and Radziul, 1969).

10. See *The Philadelphia Inquirer*, May 14, 1965, p. 9, col. 2; Oct. 21, 1966, p. 30, col. 2; Jan. 27, 1967, p. 4, col. 2; April 13, 1967, p. 21, col. 5.

11. *Philadelphia, Pa., Code of General Ordinances*, §§13-201(2)(a), 13-201(2)(b).

12. PA. STAT. ANN., tit. 53 §56561 (Purdon, as amended 1965). Indeed, even without the expense of the DRBC program, in November 1966 Baxter was forced to announce increases of 22 percent in water rates and 31 percent in sewer charges, to be effective January 1, 1967 (*The Philadelphia Inquirer*, November 22, 1966, p. 8, col. 1).

Thus both personal and institutional factors impelled Baxter—and his subordinate, Guarino—to press for a relatively unambitious clean-up program. Moreover, as Guarino got in touch with officials of other municipalities serving on the WUAC subcommittee, he found these lesser cities and towns similarly reluctant to embark on expensive clean-up measures to secure benefits that did not seem to be valued by any significant body of their constituents.[13] Consequently, Guarino's position seemed simple and well defined. A heroic effort would have been required of Guarino to attempt to convert his chief and the other municipal leaders to accept a relatively ambitious program—like III or II—which promised to increase greatly the expense of compliance.

William Halladay, Coordinator of Air and Water Conservation at the Atlantic Richfield Corporation, faced a somewhat different reality in his capacity as chairman of the WUAC subcommittee composed of the estuary's industrial polluters. As his title suggests, Halladay was a senior official of a major enterprise with worldwide pollution problems. Since he was charged with a significant role in developing firm-wide pollution policy, he could take a wider view of the Delaware decision, which seemed to provide a vehicle for demonstrating that industry could play a responsible role in defining a "reasonable" environmental policy. Thus if, as a result of WUAC deliberations, a consensus could be achieved in which industry was not singled out as a villain in the public press, this result would be highly satisfactory to the management of a major oil company which appreciated the fact that environmental issues would be of considerable importance over the long run.

It should be obvious, however, that neither Atlantic Richfield nor any of the other major industrial dischargers was willing to see the WUAC experiment in interest group conciliation succeed at any price. This fact became apparent at a meeting called by Halladay to permit the group to decide on the strategy he should pursue at the "consensus-building" sessions of the subcommittee chairmen. The industrial executives were almost unanimously of the view that the DECS Report had not made out a persuasive case for a dramatic effort to improve estuarine water quality.[14] Responding to the cost–benefit analyses contained in the Report, it seemed clear to them that a program in the best interest of the region should be no more ambitious than that suggested by DECS Objective IV. Of course, these views could readily be expected from a group that was going to bear

13. Interview with Carmen Guarino; see Appendix D.
14. Interviews with Loren Forman, Dr. Nicholas Lardieri, William Halladay and W. H. Roach; see Appendix D.

a substantial cost burden as a result of the adoption of any of the proposed programs. Nevertheless, an explanation of the industrial subcommittee's position on pure self-interest grounds would be too simple. After all, if short-run self-interest were the key, the firms could well have rallied behind Objective V, the cheapest one proposed. Nevertheless, despite some poorly based doubts as to the value of the DECS benefit analysis, the mystiqu e of cost–benefit methodology, as well as the desire to appear "responsible," was sufficient to induce the industrial subcommittee to select IV as their most favored strategy.

While Mr. Halladay shared his colleagues' preference for IV, he foresaw serious difficulties if his fellow industrialists sought to bind him to single-minded advocacy of this Objective at the forthcoming consensus-building sessions. For it was plain that if firms and municipal polluters both insisted on relatively low treatment requirements while representatives of "public interest" and conservationist groups insisted on exceedingly high treatment, the WUAC would fail to reach anything resembling a consensus, and Halladay would fail in his effort to demonstrate that industry could play a responsible role in defining governmental pollution control policy. As a consequence, the Atlantic Richfield official argued strongly that his colleagues should permit him some room for maneuver. While, of course, Halladay would initially press for IV, he asked his brethren to allow him to agree to III if this step would permit all parties to arrive at a common front. After Halladay's plea for a bargaining chip, his colleagues agreed to his proposal, which later proved to be of considerable significance in the ultimate outcome.

Considering the importance of this decision, it seems desirable to speculate on the reasons why Halladay sought to induce his colleagues to permit him some bargaining leeway. Halladay's action seems a product of four quite different factors. First, doubtless Halladay's personality was one that predisposed him to value consensus and to play statesmanlike roles. Second, it is also clear that anything done in WUAC which improved industry's "public image" was something particularly in the interest of a firm like Halladay's. Third, Halladay's effort to push his brethren to a conditional acceptance of Program III may be understood from the perspective suggested by the sociological theory of coöptation.[15] In his role as a subcommittee chairman, Halladay—more than his fellows—was invited to make a greater emotional investment in the success of the DECS enterprise, and to view himself as an intermediary between the interests

15. For a lucid discussion of this concept see Selznick, 1949, especially pp. 13–17, 217–26, 233–37, 259–61.

of his group and those of other concerned parties rather than simply as an advocate of his own group's special interests. Fourth, Halladay also seems to have been motivated in part by his commitment to an ideology of "interest group pluralism," which holds that a decision is legitimated substantially when it is reached as a result of the give and take compromises of organized groups which perceive that the interests of all are affected. Thus, in Halladay's view, a successful resolution of the meeting of WUAC subcommittee chairmen would vindicate long-cherished beliefs as to the way American government ought in principle to operate.

We have stressed the complex character of the forces guiding Halladay's conduct because we do not wish to imply that the process we are about to describe will necessarily be replicated in all similar institutional contexts. It may be true, of course, that the demands of personality, firm self-interest, sociological coöptation, and political ideology may often be correlated with one another, as they seem to be in Halladay's case. It is easy, however, to imagine situations in which an industrial "representative" in the political arena will understand his role in far different terms.

The Representatives of the Nonpolluting Public:
Paul Felton and Edmund Harvey

It should be expected that the representatives of the nonpolluting public perceived the problem in terms quite different from those of their colleagues Guarino and Halladay. Nevertheless, here, too, it is necessary to discriminate between the position taken by the chairman representing conservationist and sportsmen groups and the position of the chairman representing those "public interest" groups which did not have an explicit conservationist purpose.

The representative of the public interest groups during most of the DECS effort was William Dressler, Executive Director of the Water Resources Association of the Delaware River Basin, (although his successor as head of the WRA/DRB, Paul Felton, had assumed chairmanship of the "General Public" subcommittee at the time of the "consensus building" sessions). Though the WRA/DRB has a wide range of organizations as members, its principal support comes from many of the valley's industrial enterprises.[16] Given this fact, the WRA/DRB's small staff—while not

16. In 1965, only 140 out of the 500 voting members were from nonprofit organizations, the remainder being representatives of industry (statement by Frank Dressler of the WRA/DRB before the Air and Water Pollution Subcommittee of the Committee on Public Works of the U.S. Senate at Philadelphia on June 3, 1965 [unpublished]). An examination of a 1966 list of the directors and officers of the WRA/DRB

exactly a mirror of the businessman's point of view—nevertheless takes this view seriously into account. Moreover, while Dressler and Felton undertook to engage in substantial consultations with the other groups represented on the public interest subcommittee, the fact that these groups were not primarily concerned with the water quality problem[17] permitted the chairman substantial room for leadership. As a result of his consultations, Felton led the group to a position which gave substantial—but not decisive—weight to the cost–benefit analysis tendered by DECS. Members of the General Public subcommittee read the technocratic analysis to suggest that Objective III would—all things considered—be the best water quality goal for the estuary. Although, according to DECS, Objective III required expenditure of $45 million dollars to gain advantages worth only $30 million above those promised by Objective IV, Dressler and Felton believed that substantial "unquantifiable" benefits would accrue as a result of a cleanup to Objective III specifications. In one particular, though, most of the members found III wanting. The DECS model suggested that, under III, successful shad passage through the estuary would sometimes be endangered, and the subcommittee believed that the expenditure of some $20 to $30 million beyond that required by III could be justified if it could somewhat ameliorate the shad's prospects.[18] A move to Objective II, however, was rejected because it represented an unjustified "major financial jump" above Objective III.[19]

Edmund Harvey, Chairman of the Subcommittee for Recreation, Conservation, and Fish and Wildlife groups, faced quite a different environment. Once he had been selected by his fellow committee members to serve as chairman, he found that organizations represented on the committee did not actively participate in its deliberations. Indeed, throughout the entire decision-making course, the relative passivity of organized conser-

---

indicates that approximately 30 of the 50 positions were filled by business interests. The remaining 20 officers and directors came from law firms, academic institutions, newspapers, and public interest and conservationists groups. (Memorandum from Paul M. Felton, Executive Director of the WRA/DRB, to the WUAC General Public Subcommittee on February 17, 1966; memorandum on file in Professor Ackerman's office, Yale Law School)

17. Moreover, some groups, e.g., the League of Women Voters, who were active and concerned had little expertise in the field of water quality management (interviews with Frank Dressler and Paul Felton; see Appendix D).

18. Although the shad's prospects under OS III were not all that bad, comparatively speaking. In fact, there was only a ten percentage point difference in shad survival expectations between the two programs. See Figure 6, Ch. 4, and the discussion in Ch. 7 on the meaning of the shad survival data.

19. Statement by the General Public subcommittee of WUAC, DECS, Appendix II, p. 4.

vation groups was striking, especially when compared to their intense activity when dealing with other environmental issues in the Delaware Valley, such as the ongoing controversy surrounding the Tocks Island Dam.

Harvey, who represented the State of Delaware's branch of the National Wildlife Federation, took an independent role in view of the quiescence of his committee. While, like most conservationists, he was suspicious of cost–benefit methodology, Harvey nevertheless did not consider himself an "extreme utopian" on environmental issues. A man of independent wealth, Harvey had devoted much of his adult life to conservationist causes and, in doing so, developed a sense of the importance of compromise in devising a workable environmental program.[20] Thus, while he initially expressed a preference for Objective I, both personal factors and the passivity of his committee suggested he was free to take a more flexible stance if this would generate a consensus.

The Perspective of the DECS Staff

In addition to the four interest group representatives, we must consider a fifth set of actors who were important in affecting the WUAC outcome: the senior staffers of the DECS itself. Having set about to obtain a consensus, the DECS staffers' role was not limited to calling the chairmen to a series of intensive meetings during March 1966. The staff affirmatively sought to convince the participants of the importance of finding a common ground. Moreover, the DECS staff would have been profoundly disappointed if the subcommittee chairmen had hammered out a position which bore no relationship to the analysis presented in the DECS Report. Since the Report suggested that only Objectives IV, III, and (perhaps) II were within the realm of reason, the staff steered the bulk of the discussion toward these policy options. It also appears that Everett MacLeman, DECS Project Director, who chaired the meetings, had a strong preference for Objective III on the theory that when "unquantifiable" benefits were taken into account a somewhat more ambitious program could be justified than the "economic" calculus itself suggested, and MacLeman conveyed this position to the assembled subcommittee chairmen.[21]

20. Interviews with Edmund Harvey and Everett MacLeman; see Appendix D.
21. This preference was shared by other members of the DECS staff (interviews with Everett MacLeman and Edward Geismar, Appendix D). For example, Robert Thomann, the technical director of the DECS, gave his personal recommendation for OS III at the time the DECS findings were released (*The Philadelphia Inquirer*, July 21, 1966, p. 1, col. 3).

Group Interaction: The Chairmen Meet

Having sketched the nature of the forces acting upon each of the five actors, it is possible to make some sense of the dynamics of their inter-action at the WUAC's "consensus building" sessions. As we have sug-gested, while the representatives of both cities and firms entered the meet-ings advocating Objective IV, the forces conditioning their conduct were quite different. Since little movement for compromise could be expected from Guarino, Halladay began quietly to search for common ground with Harvey, representing the environmentalists, who had earlier made known his preference for Objective I.

In seeking to persuade Harvey to adopt a more flexible stance, it was clearly impossible for Halladay or the DECS staff to expect the conserva-tionist to give great credence to the cost–benefit ratios presented in the DECS Report. As we have suggested, Harvey did not consider that eco-nomic evaluations of the benefits of pollutions control deserved any great weight in decision making. Thus if Harvey was to be moved, another form of argument was necessary. It was here that the appeal to technological feasibility was introduced into the deliberations. The DECS Report argued that Objective I, which Harvey initially favored, required for its successful achievement "tertiary treatment" facilities of a kind not yet in widespread operation in the United States. Thus, the Report offered a way for Harvey to remain faithful to the general conservationist position and yet temper his single-minded support of Objective I. All that was required was for him to accept Objective II as the best *short-term* strategy for the Delaware, while still professing support for Objective I as an appropriate *long-range* goal to be adopted whenever the "tertiary treatment" technology proved operational. If the conservationists adopted this view and industry accepted Objective III, the basis for consensus would have been established, and the WUAC process of interest group resolution would in large measure have vindicated itself in the eyes of the participants. Thus, Harvey, given his personal desire to devise a "reasonable compromise," was tempted con-siderably by the "technological impossibility" argument, since it seemed to provide a legitimate way of reconciling his role as representative of his constituency with his role as a member of the small group of subcommittee chairmen striving for consensus.

Despite the fact that adopting the "technological impossibility" argu-ment would please the DECS staff and Halladay, Harvey nevertheless experienced some difficulty in modifying his position to accept Objective II as a proper interim goal. For the fact of the matter was that, from the point of view of a committed conservationist, the argument from "technological impossibility" was not exceedingly compelling. First, even in 1966, forms of advanced tertiary treatment had been developed on an experimental basis and put into everyday operation in plants scattered around the country. Second, since any program adopted in 1966 could reasonably be expected to come into operation only in 1970 or later, the risk that tertiary treatment would fail to be fully operational at the relevant time seemed relatively slight. Third, even if the risks of technological malfunction were more serious than they then seemed, a dedicated conservationist might nevertheless plausibly hold that the best way to determine the viability of tertiary treatment was to order polluters to adopt one or another of the new forms of treatment, unless they could prove that operational technology was not yet available. Thus, when Harvey changed his position and accepted Objective II, some members of his subcommittee —most notably the representative of the Audubon Society—publicly condemned him for his concession.[22] Once again, we do not wish to suggest that compromise was foreordained. It was a combination of Harvey's independent position, his personality, and his subcommittee's quiescence that created an environment particularly suitable for flexibility.

Denouement

Once Halladay had found Harvey willing to move in the direction of consensus, he believed himself justified in playing the negotiating chip he had obtained from his brethren on the Industrial Subcommittee. Thus at a second meeting, in which DECS Director MacLeman impressed the participants with the importance of reaching common ground, Halladay announced his acceptance of III while Harvey declared that II was an acceptable interim goal for the river.

This trend toward consensus presented a difficult problem in public relations for Carmen Guarino, representative of the riparian municipalities. As long as industry had held out for Objective IV, Guarino (and his chief, Baxter) had no interest in compromising their strongly held beliefs and interests. However, once they had been deserted by their industrial colleagues, the city of Philadelphia (and its less important allies) found itself in an exposed position. Insisting on Objective IV would require Baxter and others to spend a great deal of time and political capital explaining why they remained "intransigeant" while industry was acting "responsibly."[23]

22. Interview with Edmund Harvey; see Appendix D.
23. Interviews with Samuel Baxter, Carmen Guarino, and Edward Geismar; see Appendix D.

Of course, if the DECS Report had accurately portrayed the dim prospects of significant environmental improvement, perhaps Baxter and the others would have been willing to stand by their original views. As it was, however, the prospect of maintaining an isolated position which much of the interested public was certain to perceive as stubborn, mindless, and antienvironmentalist was simply too unattractive to justify in pragmatic political terms. Consequently, after consultations with Baxter and the appropriate figures in the lesser cities, Guarino announced his subcommittee's willingness to accept Objective III.

After this point, the meetings produced no additional concessions. Nevertheless, the DECS staffers had reason to be pleased. A surprising degree of support for Objective III had been generated; three of the four chairmen supported this strategy, which, as suggested previously, also had the support of the majority of the DECS staff itself. The DECS' political achievement seemed almost as impressive as its technocratic effort, considering the numerous possibilities for impasse. Moreover, the political result attained seemed to accord rather well with the scientific and economic analyses, thereby apparently vindicating the mixed technocratic-political model of regional decision making.

BUREAUCRATIC ACTION ON THE STATE LEVEL

As they immersed themselves in the dynamics of the WUAC and ultimately hammered out a compromise, the DECS staff and the four chairmen came to view the WUAC as the principal forum for the expression of the region's political will. This illusion, however, was rapidly shattered by events occurring at the state level. While the WUAC represented an attempt to mesh political and technocratic factors in a final compromise, state decision making took place in a context far more isolated from the influence of model builders and economic analysts.

The Pennsylvania Sanitary Water Board

The next agency to consider the Delaware issue was Pennsylvania's Sanitary Water Board (PSWB). This multi-member commission[24] had the right

24. The Board was composed of Secretary of Health Dr. Thomas Georges (chairman); Secretary of Forests and Waters Maurice K. Goddard; Secretary of Mines and Mineral Industries Dr. H.B. Chormburg; Executive Director of the Fish Commission Robert J. Bielo; Secretary of Commerce Clifford Jones; and three public members appointed by the Governor: James Pierce, a mining engineer; Jack Sheffler,

to promulgate legally binding water quality standards for all polluters within the Commonwealth's jurisdiction, including Pennsylvania cities and firms discharging waste into the Delaware. Even before the DRBC had acted to hold hearings and decide on a strategy for the entire estuary, the PSWB rendered its own independent decision on the standards to be imposed on dischargers located in Pennsylvania.

The reader may well be surprised at the state agency's willingness to involve itself with the issue. After all, it was apparent to everyone that Pennsylvania could not make coherent policy without coordinating its actions with those of New Jersey, at the very least. Indeed, was not this interdependence precisely the reason for the DRBC's existence? Moreover, it was plain that the DRBC was, in fact, going to consider the water quality issue, with a full panoply of hearings and plenary sessions. Why, then, should the PSWB go over the same ground with such alacrity?

While these questions would immediately be asked by an observer viewing the decision-making process as a whole, PSWB members perceived the problem posed by the Delaware from a more parochial point of view. For them, the fundamental reality was the mandate of the Federal Water Quality Act of 1965 requiring all states to promulgate water quality standards by June 30, 1967.[25] The PSWB had accordingly embarked on a statewide series of hearings in which standards were set for all the streams within the Commonwealth.[26] Thus for the PSWB it seemed only a matter of course to consider the Delaware as a part of its statewide planning effort.

---

a sportsman; and Stewart Huston, an industrialist. The only member of the Board appointed by the newly elected Governor Shafer was Dr. Georges. Our discussion of the Board is based substantially on our interviews and conversations with all of its members save Jones and Huston (deceased) (see Appendix D). The Board was dissolved by the Act of December 3, 1970, P.L. 834, No. 275 §20, PA. STAT. ANN. tit. 71 §510-1(22) (Purdon, 1973 Supp.). Its powers and duties were assumed by the newly created Department of Environmental Resources with internal structural changes not relevant here.

25. The importance of this piece of federal legislation in transforming the DECS effort into a policy-making enterprise was discussed in Ch. 2, p. 13.

26. The second of seven hearings to establish water quality criteria for Pennsylvania interstate streams was held in Philadelphia on Oct. 20, 1966, and centered on the objectives presented in the DECS Report. As usual, industry and the city of Philadelphia supported the adoption of OS III; watershed associations, conservationists, and public organizations supported OS II, with an occasional vote for OS I.

Of the 23 persons testifying, 15 recommended OS III, six recommended OS II, and two recommended OS I. Three of the letters received supported OS II, and four supported OS III. Most important, the staff of the Department of Health backed OS II ("Summary of the Comments on Relevant Testimony Presented at Philadelphia Water Qaulity Hearings," undated).

In the Board's consideration of the Commonwealth's segment of the estuary, the DECS Report did not occupy a very prominent place. Instead of adopting a regional focus, the Board tended to view the Delaware's problem as if it existed wholly within a framework of state planning and policy. Throughout the state, the Board had adopted a general rule or guideline requiring all dischargers to construct conventional "secondary treatment" facilities, which typically remove 80–90 percent of FSUOD from the polluter's waste. This general policy had been developed without the benefit of complex mathematical models and cost–benefit analyses devised for each of the Commonwealth's river systems. Instead, secondary treatment was mandated because the PSWB believed it to be the highest level of treatment that was clearly operational. Thus, the board did not feel any pressing need to scrutinize the DECS' cost–benefit analysis in devising policy for its segment of the estuary,[27] but simply selected a standard consistent with its over-all secondary treatment goal. However, since secondary treatment was equivalent to DECS' Objective II, the Board translated its preference into "DECS-talk" and announced its intention to incorporate Objective II into Commonwealth regulations.

The Board's decision to act before the DRBC rendered its own judgment is also partially explained by the attitudes of a leading figure in the evolution of Pennsylvania's water pollution policies. Walter Lyon is the long-time chief of the Sanitary Engineering Division of the State's Department of Health. Although he is not a formal member of the PSWB, he plays a central role in its deliberations. At the Board's executive sessions, Lyon, as chief of the bureau charged with enforcing state policy, briefs the Board on the issues in the case before it and makes explicit recommendations concerning the strategy to be adopted. Typically, his recommendations are adopted by the Board.[28] In recommending prompt action by the PSWB on the estuary's quality standards, Lyon's view of regional agencies—like the DRBC—played an important role. The bureau chief believes that regional agencies are ineffective institutions for the regulation of pollution problems because they are insulated from well established political processes and so tend to act irresponsibly, sporadically, and without great effect. In contrast, Lyon argues, state bureaucracies are in constant contact with the political forces dominant in the legislative and executive branches and hence are far more responsive to the perceived needs of the citizenry.[29] Whatever the merits of Lyon's views, it is of course under-

27. Conversations with members of the PSWB; see Appendix D.
28. Conversations with members of the PSWB; see Appendix D.
29. Interview with Walter Lyon; see Appendix D.

standable that an intelligent and moderately aggressive state official in Lyon's institutional position should maintain them and, more important, act on them.[30] Thus, in Lyon's eyes, the issuance of the DECS Report provided an excellent opportunity to prove the validity of his preference for state, as opposed to regional, action. By mobilizing the PSWB and leading it to decisive action before the DRBC had considered the matter, Lyons would be proving his point about state control in an especially dramatic form.

Moreover, Lyon had doubts concerning the reliability of the DECS' innovative water quality forecasting. From his engineering experience he realized that abatement plans often fail to meet desired water quality objectives. "It is therefore important," he stated, "that we set a high goal in order to assure ourselves of a small margin of safety and success in order to protect the public's interest."[31] For Lyon, the appropriate policy response was therefore straightforward: he forcefully recommended OS II to the Board,[32] and, for reasons already examined, the PSWB experienced no difficulty in jumping the gun on the DRBC.

New Jersey

While developments within the New Jersey bureaucracy were more informal and tentative than they were in Pennsylvania, they tended toward the same outcome. Commissioner of Health Roscoe P. Kandle was in the early stages of developing a secondary treatment policy to apply throughout the state, but this policy remained informal pending full hearings and preparation of administrative regulations. Like his Pennsylvania counterparts, Kandle did not rely on the DECS Report in making his judgment on the Delaware's future, but instead viewed the situation from the perspective offered by the evolving state wide "secondary treatment" policy. Like the PSWB, Kandle translated his policy into DECS-talk and announced his intention of recommending Objective II to Governor Hughes before the DRBC hearings took place.[33]

30. This phenomenon—a state official acting on personal political convictions running counter to a regional plan or organization—is hardly unique (see Leach, 1970, pp. 165–80 and sources in n. 46).
31. Statement by Walter Lyon, Director of the Division of Sanitary Engineering of the Pennsylvania Department of Health, at the DRBC Hearings, p. 285; and interview with Walter Lyon, see Appendix D.
32. The Department of Health staff recommendation can be found in writing in its "Report to the PSWB."
33. Telephone conversation with Dr. Roscoe P. Kandle; also interviews with Richard Hughes, Alfred Fletcher, James Wright, and Matthew Adams; see Appendix D.

Nevertheless, the New Jersey bureaucracy did not take nearly as independent a position as did the PSWB. It postponed any formal decision until the DRBC had concluded its own hearings [34] and rendered a regional decision. Kandle and his staff took this tentative approach because it was clear to them that—given Philadelphia's dominant position as the estuary's largest polluter—it was unreasonable to settle on a rigid policy until Pennsylvania was committed irrevocably to one position or another.

Delaware

In Delaware's more intimate political system, Governor Charles Terry requested the Chemical Industry Council (*sic*) to form an Ad Hoc Scientific Advisory Committee to develop a position on the DECS Report. This industry group, relying on the DECS cost–benefit analysis, recommended Objective III for Delaware.[35] Similarly, the state's Water and Air Resources Commission, after holding hearings,[36] recommended OS III to the Governor, invoking the DECS' cost–benefit analysis to justify its position.[37]

New York

Although no part of the estuary runs through New York, the state retained a vote on the issue under the Delaware River Basin Compact and the state bureaucracy developed a position because it believed "water quality in the entire . . . River [to be] of direct concern . . . because it is vitally related to the maintenance of migratory species of fish, principally shad and

34. These hearings were actually designated as combined hearings for the DRBC and the state of New Jersey. (statement by Matthew Adams, New Jersey alternate to the DRBC at the DRBC Hearings).
35. Statement by Harry B. Nason, chairman of the Chemical Industry Council, with attached letter to Governor Terry of Delaware from H.A. Beekhuis, chairman of the Chemical Industry Council, at the DRBC Hearings, pp. 509–12.
36. The Delaware Water and Air Resources Commission held public hearings on the "Establishment of Water Quality Standards for the Delaware River and Bay" at Dover on Nov. 30, 1966. The hearings centered on the state Commission's proposed water quality standards, which approximated the DECS Program III. Like the hearings held by the PSWB and the DRBC, most of the formal statements recommended OS III. Of the 22 statements given, 11 endorsed OS III, eight endorsed OS II, two called for the highest practical standards, and one gave no specific recommendation.
37. Statement by A. J. Maitland, Commissioner of the Delaware Water and Air Resources Commission and chairman of the Water Pollution Control Committee, with attached transcript of the Delaware Hearings, pp. 130–48. In short, given the overwhelming impact of the upstream water uses and the relatively clean condition of the Delaware's lower stretches, Delaware did not feel it should bear the expense of the higher water quality standards (interviews with Harold Jacobs and John Barbiaz, Sr.; Appendix D).

eels."[38] The relevant New York agency, the Water Resources Commission, is an interdepartmental agency composed of seven department heads and four advisory members.[39] In recommending Objective II to the Governor, a state commission, once again, indicated that it had not relied heavily on either the DECS model or the cost–benefit analysis. The New York agency instead supported OS II because it best conformed to then-prevailing Commission policy requiring secondary treatment on a statewide basis.[40]

Denouement

A month before the Governors and Interior Secretary met at Dover to cast their ballots, representatives of the bureaucracies of each of the four states and the FWPCA met at Trenton to announce their positions at a meeting of the DRBC's Water Quality Advisory Committee. All of the states except Delaware strongly endorsed Objective II for the reasons we have suggested.[41] Only Delaware, relying on the DECS' Report, held out for OS III.

The federal representative was silent at the meeting.[42] It was clear,

38. Statement by Mr. Burdick of the New York State Water Resources Commission in DRBC Hearings, p. 121.
39. The Commission was subsequently dissolved by New York L. 1972, c. 664, §5, eff. Sept. 1, 1972, which also created the Department of Environmental Conservation. The powers and duties of the old Commission are now exercised by the new department. See N.Y. ENVIRONMENTAL CONSERVATION LAW §15–0301 (McKinney, 1972).
40. In fact, New York, unlike the other states, did not participate by sending representatives to any of the committees in the DECS project (interview with Dr. Mason Lawrence; see Appendix D).
41. This was not the first time such a committee had expressed its preference for OS II. In April, 1966, WUAC's recommendation for OS III was presented to the Policy Advisory Committee (PAC) of DECS. This committee consisted of representatives from the state bureaus, DRBC, and FWPCA. While the PAC never officially voted on the recommendation, it met several times to discuss it. Criticism at these meetings of the DECS benefits analysis by Herbert Howlett, chief engineer of the DRBC, and Walter Lyon of Pennsylvania indicated at this early date that the DECS report and the WUAC recommendation would not be welcomed in all quarters. See DECS Policy Advisory Committee, Minutes of meeting of April 19, 1966 (on file in Professor Ackerman's office, University of Pennsylvania Law School); Herbert A. Howlett, Chief Engineer, DRBC, "Confidential Draft Statement" attached to June 17, 1966 letter to Edward Geismar (on file in Professor Ackerman's office). Even though the FWPCA refused to make any vote official (see letter to Walter Lyon from Earl Anderson, Regional Program Director, Region II, FWPCA, June 22, 1966, on file in Professor Ackerman's office), the consensus which did develop for OS II was important, since state and DRBC bureaus learned of each other's preferences and so acted in their own arenas with more confidence than they would have otherwise (interviews with Edward Geismar and Alfred Fletcher; see Appendix D).
42. As mentioned earlier most of the DECS staffers favored Objective III for the estuary. Moreover, given their four years of intensive study, some staffers thought it

however, that the carefully wrought DECS effort to create a political compromise based on OS III had been rudely shattered.

CONCLUSIONS

We have previously emphasized the disadvantages of an institutional structure which insulated a group of technocratic "thinkers" in the national government from the state and regional agencies, which retained the real decision-making power.[43] It should now be apparent that this bifurcated structure not only endangers the integrity of the ongoing scientific enterprise but also reduces the probability that the analyses generated by the "thinkers" will actually be considered seriously by decision makers. From the point of view of the state officials, the DECS represented a challenge to their accustomed mode of decision making, in which neither advanced technocratic analysis nor a regional perspective played a large part. Moreover, the state officials did not have any important incentive to modify their accustomed policies in the light of the mine of information and analysis proffered to them. After all, the credit for the precedent-setting DECS study would redound principally to the DECS staffers themselves and secondarily to the DRBC. Finally, the federal agency researchers—as a result of their relative institutional isolation—had a most imperfect understanding of the informal patterns of influence prevailing on the state level. Consequently they devoted a large share of their energies to the

---

only natural to present their position on water quality standards as a formal recommendation. Yet on several possible occasions the staff failed to do so. The WUAC, for example, was informed by DECS project director Geismar that its statement at the DRBC hearings was to be made independently of federal DECS members. Any reference to the FWPCA or DECS, he ordered, would have to be made solely in terms of their technical assistance (see, DECS Water Use Advisory Committee, Minutes of meeting of September 23, 1966, on file in Professor Ackerman's office, University of Pennsylvania Law School). Although a high-ranking official of the Public Health Service—the original bureaucratic parent of DECS—did testify at the DRBC hearings, his testimony was also independent of DECS, which was then under the Department of Interior (see Sylvan C. Martin, statement at the DRBC Hearings, pp. 63–71). This failure by the staff to voice their views publicly was in part the result of pressure from the higher reaches of the Department of Interior. Commissioner James Quigley, head of the Department of Interior's Federal Water Pollution Control Administration, was reliably reported to be concerned that should the staff make, or join with the states in making, any recommendation concerning the water quality objectives developed by the comprehensive study, this would constitute an improper interference with the role of the states under the Water Quality Act of 1965. Mr. Quigley also feared that the formal staff recommendation would embarrass Secretary Udall if he should subsequently vote for Objective II (as proved to be the case). (Earl Anderson, letter of June 22, 1966 to Walter Lyon, on file in Professor Ackerman's office, Yale Law School)
43. See Ch. 5, pp. 73–77, and Ch. 10, pp. 148–150.

ambitious task of developing a political consensus independently of the other institutions. While it is perfectly understandable that a group of isolated technocrats would try this end run around existing agencies, it is equally understandable that such an effort at consensus formation would be easily fractured once the concerned officials on the state level were aroused.

Our study of the patterns of bureaucratic influence, however, not only suggests the dangers involved in placing the research function in a separate (federal) bureaucratic box; it also demonstrates that, unless careful steps are taken in designing the legal structure of a regional agency, its decision-making processes can easily be sabotaged on the state level. Since the Delaware River Basin Commission Compact did not deny the relevant state agencies the legal power to legislate for the segments of the river under their respective jurisdictions,[44] the stage had been set for a bureaucratic power play of the kind set in motion by Walter Lyon, which led the critically important Commonwealth of Pennsylvania to commit itself to a pollution policy quite independent of the course set by the DRBC.[45]

Our discussion, then, leads to a familiar conclusion. Once again, we have come upon a fundamental tension between the demands of sound technocratic decision making and the nature of American federalism. The technocratic-political decision, whatever its ultimate value, requires tight integration among fact finders, analysts, and politicians. In contrast, federalism is instinct with the demand that power be fractionalized among competing groups and levels of government, and the suspicion that a coherent, tightly organized governing structure will by virtue of that single fact possess too much power and so act irresponsibly. Unfortunately, the federalist effort to eliminate the possibility of the abuse of power can often make it impossible to use power intelligently as well.[46]

44. Indeed, the Delaware River Basin Compact expressly provides that the regional agency is to rely on state bureaus as much as possible (see §1.5), and moreover expressly reserves to each state the right to require higher levels of treatment than those demanded by the DRBC (see §5.5).

45. For evidence that this problem of preemptive state action may be a general one in state-federal relationships, see McKinley, 1955; Weidner, 1969.

46. Although the particular problems arising out of an effort to integrate technocratic intelligence into the federal system have not been canvassed previously, the difficulty of systematic planning in a federal system has been a theme in much writing by political scientists. Some feel that this inability to use power in a coherent manner is an inherent trait of federalist structures (see Leach, 1970; Levine, 1969; May, 1970; Weidner, 1969). Others assert a weaker thesis—that our current federalism is a dysfunctional system for allocating power—and do not reach the question of whether the problem inheres in the federalist structure itself. See Burton, 1970; Carroll, 1969; Englebert, 1957; Leach and Sugg, 1959; Ridgeway, 1971; Sayre and Kaufman, 1960; Wright, 1968.

The DRBC "Decides": Of Governors, Secretaries, and the "Regional Perspective"

INTRODUCTION

Having isolated the low-visibility forces within the state and federal bureaucracies which sought to influence the DRBC decision, we turn to the regional agency itself in an effort to determine the extent to which the ultimate decision makers had incentives to use the analyses generated by the DECS. Our discussion here is presented in three stages. First, we shall assess the importance of the formal public hearings conducted by the regional agency; second, we shall describe the positions adopted by the DRBC staff; third, and most important, we shall describe the environment of each of the five political decision makers in an effort to discern the factors which seemed most salient for the purposes at hand. Following our analysis of the decision-making process, we shall assess the viability of the mixed technocratic-political decision-making process illustrated by our case study.

THE DRBC HEARINGS

The least important aspect of the decision-making process was the hearings held by the DRBC at Trenton on January 26, 1967. Widely ranging interests were represented: political figures, industrial spokesmen, and members of conservationist and public interest groups all testified.[1] The hearings were of the town meeting type: each spokesman said his piece with no provision for cross-examination either by members of the Commission or by those representing different viewpoints. In general, the quality of the often rhetorical presentations was mediocre. Moreover, the positions presented contained little in the way of surprises: industry and municipal representatives spoke on behalf of III; some public interest groups, conservationists, and United States Senators and Congressmen on behalf of II, with an occasional individual supporting I. Our interviews with the leading policy makers suggest that the hearings played a minor role in their deliberations. If the hearings had any role at all, it was to emphasize the symbolic importance to many public interest groups of improving shad passage through the estuary and hence supported the tendency generated primarily on the state level to adopt Objective II, on the ground that it benefited the shad to a slightly greater degree than the less expensive programs.

THE DRBC STAFF

The Executive Director of the DRBC, James Wright, strongly supported Objective II as the water quality standard for the estuary. A complex set of factors motivated this decision. First, Wright wished to vindicate the existence of his innovative federal-state agency by embarking upon an

1. Forty-two persons presented formal testimony at the public hearings; 55 others sent in statements for the record. In the first category, 17 represented business and industry, ten were from conservation and other public groups, eight spoke for government bureaucracies, four came from academic institutions, and three were from elected positions. Twenty-four of those who sent letters represented conservationists and other "public interests," 11 were elected officials from different levels of government, ten represented business and industry, eight were government officials, one was an academic, and one an unknown. Of those testifying in person, 22 supported III, 11 endorsed II, two recommended the highest practical standards, only one suggested I, and six gave no specific endorsements. Of those submitting statements, nine supported III, 18 voted for II, 12 urged the highest practical standards, 14 gave no specific recommendation, and two were ambiguous. A more refined breakdown of positions may be obtained from the authors upon request.

aggressive clean-up program.[2] Second, he was unimpressed with the DECS'
effort at quantifying the benefits of pollution control and consequently
showed little inclination to select Objective III on the basis of the economists' cost–benefit criterion. Wright's disregard of the DECS' methodology
can be explained both by institutional and ideological considerations. Institutionally, the DECS staff was a part of the federal bureaucracy and
shaped its analytical effort rather independently of DRBC control, and so
Wright did not have a strong institutional obligation to support the DECS
study.[3] On an ideological level, it seemed clear to Wright that the principal
benefits of a cleanup were unquantifiable, thereby making rigorous benefits
analysis inappropriate.[4] When the director specified the benefits of cleanup,
however, he listed the familiar factors we have considered in our earlier
discussion of cost–benefit factors on the river: shad survival,[5] aesthetic
considerations,[6] and recreation benefits. Third, Mr. Wright pointed out that
the higher standard provided a "margin of safety," given the fact that
enforcement would—at least during early stages of the program—fall

2. The past failure of the Interstate Commission on the Delaware River (INCODEL)
was often cited as a justification for this attitude. The ineffectiveness of this agency
is well documented in Martin, et al., 1960. With the creation of the DRBC, however,
the Delaware had, as Wright proudly noted, "a substantial head start over all other
interstate river basins in the nation that are enmeshed in the same serious pollution
situation" (Wright, "Evaluation of Estuary Report," July 27, 1966, p. 1). Seeing the
innovative and unique character of this form of regional administration, Wright
recognized that a decision on water quality standards reached by the DRBC would
"influence national attitudes towards interstate river basin agencies" (James F.
Wright, Statement at the DRBC Hearings, p. 17).
3. Indeed, some of our sources have noted some tension between the two staffs. For
example, the federal representative on the DRBC, Vernon Northrup, was asked by
the DRBC staff on several occasions to pressure the DECS staff for information
which had not been forthcoming (interview with Vernon Northrup; see Appendix D).
4. Wright, like others who believed the river should be cleaned up to the highest
level technology permitted, was not searching for arguments for not cleaning up the
estuary. In his view, cost–benefit analysis posed such an argument. Consequently, he
suggested that "pollution control measures in this basin would not be nearly as well
developed as they now are had our counterparts of 25 years ago restricted their decisions to those works that could be supported by quantitative monetary benefits."
Thus, Wright recommended that a decision not be "restricted to those benefits that
can be measured only in money." Furthermore, the Director was confident that
environmentalism represented the wave of the future: "What will the pollution level
tolerance be 20 years hence?" he inquired rhetorically. That New York overwhelmingly approved the billion-dollar Pure Water bond issue was proof, in his mind, that
the public was impatient with the go-slow approaches (Wright, "Evaluation of
Estuary Report," July 27, 1966, pp. 10–12).
5. James F. Wright, Statement at DRBC Hearings, pp. 28, 30; DRBC staff, confidential administrative paper, Feb. 11, 1967, p. 11.
6. As noted in n. 4, Wright believed aesthetic benefits were unquantifiable and
therefore additional to those measured by a benefit analysis. In the Director's words:
"a clean stream, similar to a beautiful park, reflects the conscience of a community
and is an attribute far beyond monetary benefits that may be assigned" (Wright,
"Evaluation of Estuary Report," July 27, 1966, p. 11).

short of any goal set for the river.[7] Finally, Wright emphasized the significance of reconciling the DRBC program with the steps we have recounted
on the state level, and went on to minimize the importance of cost to
municipalities by pointing to the federal subsidy, which could in theory
equal 55 percent of total construction costs.[8]

POLITICAL ACTORS

A General Overview

Thus, when the Delaware problem was tendered to the ultimate political
decision makers on the DRBC, its salient features appeared quite different
from those portrayed in the DECS Report. While the Governors and
Secretary were asked to choose between DECS Objectives II and III,[9] the
DECS cost–benefit analysis played only a subordinate role in the perceived
decision-making context.[10] Instead of an effort to evaluate the benefits of
pollution control in quantitative terms, which would then be weighed
against costs, both state and DRBC bureaucrats emphasized so-called
unquantifiable interests, especially the future survival of the shad. Despite
the fact that Objective II did little more for the shad than Objective III,[11]
while the costs of II were far greater, the shad were constantly used to
justify the more ambitious program. Similarly, the DECS' political effort
to create a regional compromise around Objective III in the Water Users
Advisory Committee had been displaced by decisions made at the state

7. James F. Wright's statement at the DRBC Hearings, p. 28; DRBC staff, confidential administrative paper, Feb. 11, 1967, p. 12, on file in Professor Ackerman's
office, University of Pennsylvania Law School). This argument assumes that during
the substantial period of partial compliance the residents of the valley will obtain a
substantial portion (if not all) of the benefits of cleanup. Our discussion of the
benefits generated by Objective II in Chapters 7 and 8 suggests that partial compliance with the DRBC program will yield almost none of the advantages anticipated
from complete (or almost complete) compliance.
8. Wright, statement at DRBC Hearing, p. 31. For a discussion of the federal subsidy
programs and the extent to which the promise of 55 percent was fulfilled, see Ch. 19,
nn. 47, 48.
9. While we shall continue to speak of DECS Objective II, in reality the DRBC
staff had substituted a modified plan they labelled II B, explaining, "Basically Objective Set II B does, for all practical purposes, what Objective Set II does at a somewhat lower cost—$270 million compared to $245 million..." (DRBC staff, confidential administrative paper, Feb. 11, 1967, p. 12).
10. Interviews with DRBC representatives Mat Adams (New Jersey), Maurice
Goddard (Pennsylvania), Harold Jacobs (Delaware), Mason Lawrence (New York),
Vernon Northrup (the federal government), Governors Hughes (New Jersey) and
Shafer (Pennsylvania), and Secretary Udall (the federal government); see Appendix D.
11. Shad survival was discussed in Ch. 4, pp. 53–55, and Ch. 7, pp. 120–123.

bureaucratic level for reasons which failed to take into account the distinctive character of the regional problem. In addition to these pressures, the federal political process generated pressures that made it even more difficult for the Governors and Interior Secretary to view the problem from a regional perspective.

Secretary Udall

Secretary Udall's position provided a central reference point in the decision-making calculus of the four state Governors for two reasons. The first goes to the legal status of the DRBC's decision. Under the Water Quality Act of 1965, the DRBC was required to submit its water quality objectives to the Secretary for his approval before they could become legally effective.[12] Udall, then, was not only one of five voting members of the Commission but also sat as the sole and final judge of the Commission's proposed goals.[13] Second, Udall's presence injected considerations

12. Pub. L. No. 89-234, 79 Stat. 903 §5(c)(1) (codified at 33 U.S.C. §466[g][c] [1970]).
13. Throughout the 1960's, the fact of ultimate federal authority was invoked frequently by a wide variety of participants. On several occasions FWPCA Commissioner Quigley and Secretary of the Interior Udall reminded the DRBC of the possibility of federal intervention if the commission failed to act or to adopt high enough standards. In 1963 at a Congressional hearing, Quigley stated that the Delaware River "has to be cleaned up." Otherwise, he threatened, the federal government would step in (*The Philadelphia Inquirer,* Aug. 10, 1963, p. 13, col. 1). Responding to this threat, Governor Hughes of New Jersey warned against excessive federal control: "We see no sound reason for a federal agency setting stream or effluent standards even for interstate waters as long as the responsible state and interstate agencies propose progressive, constructive programs" (*loc. cit.,* col. 3). Even stronger was Quigley's statement at a Delaware River Basin Water Resources Conference in 1964 calling for abatement steps before 1967: "The mere fact that our department is engaged in the comprehensive survey does not mean that an enforcement action could not be called under the Federal Water Pollution Control Law" (*The Philadelphia Inquirer,* Oct. 20, 1964, p. 9, col. 4). While Quigley refused to endorse any specific objective at the July 1966 water quality conference, he did tell the gathering that the "moment of truth" was approaching for the DRBC. "If the DRBC fails to do it [adopt and enforce a water quality control program], what's left?" he asked. The answer, of course, was the federal government. Adams, the New Jersey representative to the DRBC, reassured Quigley that the DRBC was going to come up with "something that the federal government will accept." "If it doesn't," echoed General Lack, the representative from Delaware, "Mr. Quigley is going to get after us." (DRBC Minutes, pp. 14–20, July 27, 1966 meeting.)
　　In addition to Quigley's remarks, Secretary Udall at the DRBC's 1967 meeting again reminded the Governors that the standards adopted had to be reviewed by the Department of the Interior. He warned that they should not assume a "rubber stamp approval" (statement by Secretary Stewart Udall in the DRBC, Minutes of the Meeting of March 2, 1967, p. 4). This statement hinted at a similar but stronger warning which many of our interviewees claimed was uttered at the private executive session, in which only the Governors, Secretary, and supporting staff were present. After the decision was reached, two of the Governors noted that they had voted for the more stringent Objective Set in part to foreclose the possibility of federal intervention (see, n. 27, this chapter, and Ch. 14).

of national politics explicitly into the decisional dynamics. With the federal Democratic administration so clearly represented in the decision, Governors Rockefeller, Shafer, and Hughes could not be blind to the national partisan political implications of the regional action. If, for example, Governors Shafer and Rockefeller voted for III while Secretary Udall voted for II, it was easy to foresee the press reporting that two leading Republicans had come out for "dirtier" water than did the Democrats in Washington. Given the increasing importance of water pollution as a national political issue, this was a prospect not to be taken lightly.[14]

When Udall confronted the task of decision, he was obliged to reconcile several countervailing forces. On the national level, the Secretary since his appointment had cultivated a national image as an active supporter of aggressive environmental protection, and had launched a campaign to transfer the water pollution program from the Department of Health, Education and Welfare to Interior. In Udall's view, the pollution program in HEW as it was administered by the Public Health Service was too oriented to pollution research and insufficiently geared to the difficult task of inducing active state efforts at control.[15] With the passage of the Water Quality Act of 1965, which gave the federal government new supervisory powers, President Johnson was convinced that the activist Interior Department was a more suitable home for the program, and transferred authority over the federal water pollution effort (including DECS) to Udall in March 1966.

As the new head of the federal establishment, Udall felt himself obliged to prove to the President and conservationist groups that their faith in him was justified. Consequently, as he turned to make one of his early major decisions on the Delaware Estuary, the choice between II and III seemed an easy one. It was only by voting for the stricter program that Udall could prove his good faith to his constituency on the national level. In his interview, Udall emphasized the fact that the Delaware Valley is one of the richest areas in the nation; if Interior would not take a strict stand here, how could it hope to induce less wealthy areas to proceed vigorously with pollution control?[16] Moreover, the national political stakes riding on the Delaware decision were perceived to be quite high. Liberal Republicans like Rockefeller and Shafer simply could not be permitted to take the

14. Interviews with Stewart Udall, James Quigley, and Vernon Northrup, and correspondence with Henry P. Caulfield; see Appendix D. For more objective data indicating the increased importance of environmental issues between 1965 and 1968, see Davies, 1970, pp. 78–83.
15. The pressure by conservationists for aggressive leadership is described in Zwick and Benstock, 1971, pp. 269–72.
16. Indeed, it was for this reason that Udall publicly stated that action on the DRBC's program involved "the most crucial" decision to be taken in any of the 50 states (*The Philadelphia Inquirer,* March 3, 1967, p. 11, col. 2).

"clean water" issue away from the national Democratic administration in general or Udall in particular.

Given this powerful set of factors working in the Secretary's environment in Washington, D.C., the DECS' suggestion of Objective III might have carried little weight even in the best of circumstances. The bureaucratic position of the DECS staff, however, was exceptionally weak at the time it rendered its Report. DECS, after all, was a project sponsored and manned by HEW personnel who had only recently found a new home in Interior. Udall, then, did not feel the same responsibility for the project as, for example, John Gardner might have if the program had remained in HEW. Similarly, the DECS staff was far less aggressive in pushing for III than they might have been in more familiar bureaucratic surroundings, especially given Interior's view that HEW had done far too little to impose high water quality standards. Indeed, communication was so poor that Udall was not even aware of the fact that, by voting for II, he was disregarding the consensus position so laboriously developed by the DECS in the WUAC.[17]

Governor Rockefeller: The Costless Decision

New York's Governor had even fewer incentives to consider seriously the Delaware's problem from the regional perspective portrayed by DECS. Indeed, since none of the Governor's constituents would bear any of the costs of cleaning up the estuary, Rockefeller's political "cost–benefit equation" varied dramatically from that portrayed in the technocratic study.[18] While Rockefeller would incur no political costs by voting for high standards, he would obtain political benefits on both the state and national levels. On the state level, New York's Governor had in November 1965 campaigned devotedly and successfully for a billion-dollar pollution control bond issue,[19] and hence had gone on record as a strong advocate of environmental control. In the absence of significant political countervailing factors, it was only natural that the Governor remain consistent with his general position. Similarly, the fact that his own Water Resources Commission was pursuing a statewide "secondary treatment" strategy and

17. The analysis in this section is derived principally from a series of interviews with a range of federal, regional, and state officials, including Stewart Udall, James Quigley, Vernon Northrup (see Appendix D).
18. See Wildavsky, 1966, on applying cost–benefit theory to political decisions.
19. The billion-dollar Pure Water Bond Act was passed in November, 1965 by a four-to-one referendum vote. The major element of the program financed by this bond issue was the construction of municipal waste treatment facilities (see *Pure Waters Program Report,* 1969).

had recommended the same approach for the estuary was far more significant than the different conclusion reached by the DECS.[20] Finally, representatives of the New York counties bordering the upper branches of the Delaware campaigned for higher standards in the belief that the increased supply of shad would redound to the economic benefit of these recreational areas.[21]

On the national level, the decision to vote for high standards was equally obvious. Considering the Governor's national political aspirations, a vote for III would permit the national Democrats to claim the "clean water" leadership position. Moreover, the Governor saw the DRBC as a vehicle for asserting state initiative in the face of a national Democratic attempt to monopolize the pollution program.[22] In short, Rockefeller's vote for II, in disregard of the DECS' regional technocratic report, is easily explicable in terms of his response to state and national constituencies.

Governor Shafer of Pennsylvania

The Governor of Pennsylvania found himself in a very different position from that of his colleague from New York. A very large part of the pollution control costs would be incurred within his jurisdiction. The city of Philadelphia alone accounted for 40 percent of the FSUOD discharged into the river and its costs of complying with II would exceed $100 million dollars; the costs of compliance anticipated for Philadelphia's growing suburbs in Delaware County could be counted in the tens of millions; similarly the heavy industrial complex lining the Delaware shore would be required to invest large sums to comply with Objective II, with a large share accruing to the politically sophisticated oil industry, which owned major refineries in the area. While a vigorous pollution policy could be expected to assure the opposition of powerful political interests, OS II promised relatively small benefits for Pennsylvania. Since the program's benefits would accrue principally in areas both below and above the "critical regions" around Philadelphia, only a relatively small number of

20. As indicated in Ch. 12, n. 40, New York was not consulted by the DECS staff as the project ran its course (interview with Mason Lawrence; see Appendix D).
21. Officials and sportsmen's groups from the towns of Delhi and Fremont; the counties of Delaware, Orange, Otsego, Sullivan, and Westchester, and the New York State Fish and Wildlife Management Board testified to this point at the DRBC hearing. While it is unclear whether or not Governor Rockefeller was aware of these statements, they were known to the Water Resources Commission (interview with Mason Lawrence; see Appendix D).
22. Explaining his vote, Rockefeller said, "I want to preserve the leadership and responsibility of the states" (The Philadelphia Inquirer, March 3, 1967, p. 11, col. 2).

Pennsylvanians, who lived on the fringes of the Philadelphia metropolitan area, would benefit from the program, even as the DECS described it.

Despite all this, Governor Shafer voted against III and in favor of II, which promised to cost his constituents far more. Shafer's disregard of the DECS report seems to be a product of his reliance on the advice he received from Maurice Goddard, his cabinet officer in charge of environmental matters, who in turn relied on the decisions already taken by the PSWB, led by Walter Lyon.[23] It should be recalled that the PSWB decision for II was taken without a careful study of the implications of the DECS Report, but instead was perceived as an application of the "secondary treatment" policy pursued by the PSWB on a statewide basis. The fact that his subordinates had not analyzed the DECS report was not, however, made clear to Shafer. Indeed, since the Governor had assumed office only two months earlier, in January 1967, he was especially reluctant to overturn the considered views of subordinates who seemed to him far more familiar with the particular problem.

While Shafer was not terribly knowledgeable concerning the peculiar problems of the Delaware Estuary, his more general commitments were compatible with the recommendation of the PSWB and Maurice Goddard. In the previous administration (in which Shafer served as Lieutenant Governor) Governor Scranton had initiated a proposal for a half-billion dollar pollution control bond issue, which Governor Shafer strongly endorsed as part of his new administration's commitment to environmental protection.[24] As a consequence, Shafer was inclined to accept his staff's recommendation uncritically. Indeed, even when the recommendation was attacked by powerful political forces, Shafer remained confident that Goddard and the PSWB had studied the problem carefully and so should be supported.[25] While the city of Philadelphia, led by Commissioner Baxter, strenuously argued against Objective II, its impact would doubtless have been greater if the Republican Governor had been of the same political party as the Philadelphia administration. Similarly, while the affected industrial groups attempted to lobby for Objective III, the campaign was

23. As noted in Ch. 12, n. 24, Maurice Goddard, the Governor's representative on the DRBC, was also a member of the PSWB.
24. The $500-million Land and Water Conservation Fund was passed by the Pennsylvania Legislature in Jan. 1967. (It was later endorsed by referendum.) The bill earmarked $100 million for sewer and treatment plant construction (see Shafer, "Chairman's Address," in DRBC minutes, March 2, 1967, p. 2).
25. Moreover, Shafer, like Rockefeller, was concerned with preserving state initiative. He therefore supported the more stringent program, in part because he believed that "if we, as states do not assume this responsibility the federal government will" (*The Philadelphia Inquirer*, March 3, 1967, p. 11, col. 2).

poorly organized and belated.[26] In retrospect, it was clear that the critical force determining Pennsylvania's vote was not the DECS Report or the DRBC staff or the views of the Governor or the industrial or urban interests adversely affected, but Walter Lyon's ability to lead an obscure Pennsylvania state agency to a premature policy judgment, made without serious consideration of the product of four years' labor undertaken by the DECS staff.[27]

Moreover, Pennsylvania's vote in this dispute was of central importance. Since Udall and Rockefeller had little incentive to consider the particular merits of the case before them, it was up to Governor Shafer, as the representative of the largest state directly affected, to raise the issues addressed in the DECS Report. Nevertheless, those upon whom Shafer relied for advice insulated him almost completely from the federal study group. Indeed, when interviewed, Governor Shafer was not even aware of the fact that his state advisors' views were not shared by the DECS staff.[28] There can be no more dramatic evidence of the extent to which the separation of functions wrought by "cooperative federalism" can impair communication between technocrats and politicians in a regional context.[29]

Governor Hughes of New Jersey

With Rockefeller, Shafer, and Udall we have not only accounted for a majority of the five Commissioners but have also, so far as we can determine, isolated the most important actors in the decision-making process. Nevertheless, it is important to recognize that even if Governor Shafer had voted differently, there is a substantial likelihood that the decision would have come out the same way. Governor Hughes, in his interview, recalls telephone conversations with Udall and Rockefeller in which the three men reached a tentative agreement that even if Shafer voted for Objective III,

26. The Greater Philadelphia Chamber of Commerce's lobbying only took the form of a letter campaign to which Shafer never responded (interview with Charles Day; see Appendix D). More important, industry's top management was not involved in any lobbying effort. For example, the Greater Philadelphia Movement—an influential organization of business elite—was made aware of the issue only several days before the Governor's vote (interview with Loren V. Forman; see Appendix D).
27. The analysis in this section is based on a series of interviews with state, local, and industrial officials, including Messrs. Shafer and Goddard; see Appendix D.
28. Governor Shafer was interviewed for this study in 1972, six years after the events recounted here. Consequently, it is quite possible that the Governor simply failed to remember the conflicting analyses proffered by the federal and state staffs. Nevertheless, given the Governor's ability to recollect many other details, it seems quite likely that his stated belief that expert opinion unanimously supported Program II accurately reflects his understanding in 1966.
29. For a parallel inquiry, see Carroll, 1969.

they nevertheless would cast their ballots for the more ambitious program. Although the Mayor of Camden strongly opposed OS II,[30] Hughes, like Shafer, relied heavily on the judgment of New Jersey officials involved in developing intrastate policy. Moreover, Hughes was exceedingly reluctant to break with Udall, a fellow Democrat whom he personally admired. Once again, there was no direct channel of communication through which the DECS staff could forcefully detail the costs and benefits of the competing strategies. While the Governor recalled being present at a single briefing session presided over by the DRBC staff, the impact of the federal and regional officials was subordinate, in the Governor's judgment, to the views expressed by his own officials, which, as we have suggested, were formed quite independently of the DECS effort.

Governor Terry of Delaware

Unfortunately, at the time of our study both Governor Terry and his representative on the DRBC, General Lack, had died, and so our analysis must be even more tentative than that attempted in our previous discussion. From what we have gleaned from our interviews, the Governor was the only participant at the final DRBC decision-making session who forcefully invoked the DECS cost–benefit analysis to justify a lower standard. Thus, the state which stood to obtain the greatest benefits from the DRBC's ambitious program placed itself on record as opposed to the more expensive control program. After listening to Governor Terry's arguments, the other Commissioners adopted Objective II over his sole dissent.

ANALYSIS: REGIONAL GOVERNMENT WITH STATE AND NATIONAL POLITICIANS?

At the beginning of this part of the book we suggested that state and national politicians, when acting in a regional setting, will nonetheless act to pursue their state and national political interests and rely principally upon the advice of aides who normally assist them in the bulk of their work on a nonregional level of government. It appears that the Delaware experience provides substantial support for this thesis, although there is one factor which makes the evidence less strong than it could have been. We refer, of course, to the fact that while one regional bureaucracy—the DECS staff—advocated the wisdom of only moderate pollution control

30. Interview with Alfred R. Pierce; see Appendix D.

expenditures, a second regional bureaucracy—the DRBC staff led by Executive Director Wright—strongly supported Objective II. Thus, it cannot be unequivocally asserted that the politicians on the DRBC, in voting for Objective II, responded only to their parochial state or national interests, ignoring the counsel of those who sought to view the problem from a regional perspective. Nevertheless, our interview data suggest to us that even if the Executive Director Wright had followed DECS in recommending Objective III, the result most probably would have been the same. None of the three leading political actors on the Commission whom we were able to interview mentioned the recommendation of the DRBC staff as one of the most significant factors leading to a decision, while the political and administrative considerations we have detailed were repeatedly emphasized.[31] Similarly, in our numerous interviews with the lesser participants, the role of the DRBC staff was only very infrequently mentioned as a factor which, in the judgment of the respondent, had any effect on the decision, and none of our sources suggested that it was a factor of the first importance. Indeed, we ourselves are uncertain of the extent to which DRBC Director Wright's advocacy of II was more a result than a cause of the consensus developing among state and national bureaucrats and politicians around Objective II. While there can be no doubt that Wright was predisposed towards Objective II both on the merits and because he wished to have his agency be an aggressive leader in the pollution field, we have reason to believe that others on the staff were more prone to follow the DECS and recommend Objective III. Thus, it is not even clear to us that the DRBC Director would have recommended Objective II so unequivocally if the outcome had not been so clearly foreordained by the state and national factors we have enumerated.

We have spent enough time on might-have-beens, however. After all, a general theory cannot in any event be proved conclusively by scrutinizing a single case, or even two or three. All that we can hope to present here is some empirical support for the intrinsically plausible notion that powerful forces divert state and national politicians from the regional implications of decisions, despite the fact that these politicians sit on a "regional" agency. The centrifugal tendencies we have discerned, moreover, take on added significance when viewed in the light of other research which tends to support our major thesis.[32] The evidence that has been presented here

31. We are referring here to our interviews with Secretary Udall, Governors Hughes and Shafer, and four of the five individuals who served as representatives to the DRBC from the states and the federal government.
32. Some valuable work has already been done: see Leach and Sugg, 1959; Ridgeway, 1971; Weidner, 1969, and the sources cited in Ch. 12, n. 46.

should caution policy makers to search for alternate regional structures, which do not depend on politicians whose careers, in turn, depend on their success at other levels of government.[33]

ANALYSIS: REGIONAL GOVERNMENT WITH REGIONAL POLITICIANS?

In arguing against direct participation by state and national politicians in a regional setting, we do not mean to suggest that it would be better to attempt to create a cadre of distinctively *regional* politicians to formulate the river basin's pollution policies. Indeed, the Delaware story contains abundant cautions for those who would suggest designing a decision-making mechanism along these lines. We refer to the DECS' effort to use the WUAC as a forum in which the region's important political interest groups could express their political will on the pollution control issue. It is true, of course, that when contrasted to the high ranking political leaders on the DRBC, the WUAC subcommittee chairmen seem—in some important respects—better suited to serve as decision makers on the issue. At the very least, Messrs Guarino, Halladay, Felton, and Harvey spent a substantial amount of time learning about the issues; moreover, during the period in which the consensus building sessions took place, each of the chairmen made an effort to test the sentiment of the members of his interest group subcommittee. Thus, in some primitive sense, the WUAC chairmen did serve as regional representatives for important constituencies in the continuing conflict of group interests which surrounds the pollution problem.

On the other hand, the DECS' effort to construct an ad hoc political process for the resolution of a *single* issue suffered from several major weaknesses. First, because the WUAC was such a transient institution with such limited concerns, it was virtually unknown to the larger public. Consequently, unlike the politicians on the DRBC, the amateur politicians on the WUAC were not obliged to justify their actions to the press or other organs of public opinion. Second, in part because of its obscurity, only those special interest groups who were highly organized actively participated in DECS processes. Thus, William Halladay had no difficulty conducting numerous subcommittee meetings in which his industrial colleagues actively participated; similarly, Carmen Guarino found it easy to consult

33. For a different style of analysis of regional government which reaches the same conclusions, see Haefele, 1971.

with fellow officials in other municipalities over the telephone when the need presented itself. In contrast, Felton and Harvey had a great deal of difficulty in obtaining substantial exchanges of opinion from the conservationist and "public interest" subcommittees, who never fully understood the nature of the DECS effort. Third, given the absence of well established regional institutions, the DECS decision to treat Felton and Harvey as representatives of the "general public" and "conservationist" constituencies inevitably suffered from a good deal of arbitrariness. These two subcommittee chairmen were selected at the initial meetings of the two subcommittees in late 1964, when the nature of the issues to be confronted in 1966 were only dimly perceived; moreover, once selected, Harvey and Felton did not communicate with their constituents with anything like the intensity of Halladay and Guarino. Given the DECS' obscurity, none but the most directly concerned groups (like the polluting firms and cities) could be expected to participate actively.

In making these points, we do not mean to suggest that the DECS staff could reasonably have been expected to construct a more broadly based and active body than in fact was created. Indeed, it is precisely because the DECS did such a good job that the WUAC helps expose the *intrinsic* limitations of an effort to construct regional political institutions on an ad hoc basis. While the weaknesses we have catalogued did not fatally undercut the value of using the WUAC as a means of enlightening and shaping public opinion in the valley, they would have been fatal if a WUAC-type body had been constructed to serve in not an *advisory* but a *decision-making* capacity. Given the obscurity of the agency and the difficulties of organizing "public interest" groups to play an active role in an unfamiliar institutional forum, it would have been relatively easy for highly organized groups—like the cities and firms—to capture the dominant share of power in the decision.

The possibility of domination of the agency by the polluters themselves is dramatized even in the present case study, which only involved the construction of an advisory committee. When DECS Director MacLeman sought to invite "public interest" and "conservationist" groups to serve on the WUAC, he naturally turned to the Executive Director of the Water Resources Association of the Delaware River Basin for assistance. The WRA/DRB, however, is a group which looks for substantial financial support from polluting firms and has a very large business contingent on its board of directors. It happens that in the present case, the WRA's executive director did not attempt to exclude from the list of "public interest" groups forwarded to DECS those which would be unsympathetic to business interests. Nevertheless, can we be sure that he would have been able to withstand business pressures if instead of selecting an *advisory* committee he had been assisting in the creation of a *decision-making* committee? Moreover, it will be recalled that the groups on the "general public" subcommittee selected the WRA/DRB Director to serve as chairman, thereby assuring that the representative of the "Public" would be sympathetic to (though not completely dominated by) the businessman's point of view.

The difficulties experienced by the DECS in creating a viable regional political mechanism could, of course, be avoided if a full-fledged regional government were constructed in the Delaware Valley, complete with regular elections, political parties, and interest groups as well as organs of public opinion. In such a case, there would be no need for the DECS to construct a "political system" by coöpting a small number of self-styled representatives of the "Public" to make a decision on behalf of the Valley's inhabitants. While the construction of a functioning regional government would solve the DECS-WUAC problem, however, we do not believe that it can be seriously advanced as a solution to the problem of institutional design for the Delaware. First, it is not at all clear to us that the nation is capable of supporting an active regional political system without experiencing a serious deterioration in the quality of local, state, and national politics. Considering the mediocre level of participants and public debate in our three existing political systems, it does not seem wise to dilute political talent yet further by introducing a fourth system. Second, even if creating a fourth level of government were desirable, it is unlikely that the new regional polity should be geographically defined in terms of the Delaware river system. The citizens of New York's Catskill region are linked to the residents of Wilmington by the Delaware River, but they share little else which would justify placing the two areas under the same regional government. To put the matter more generally, the boundaries of a regional government should be determined by considering a broad spectrum of important problems—land use, transportation, education, employment, air pollution, recreation—and drawing the boundary lines which would permit the new government to deal effectively with as many problems as possible. When this is done, it would seem that the most viable system of regional government would be one that divided the country into "metropolitan areas," thereby permitting the coherent management of the large number of problems which naturally arise in reconciling the conflicting interests of urban core and suburban fringe. Unfortunately river systems generally do not serve to isolate metropolitan areas from one another and so would generally serve as poor boundary markers for regional entities. Consequently, even if regional government were to become a reality, it would not resolve the water pollution control problem in a satisfactory way.[34]

Our conclusions, then, are disheartening to those who wish to design a regional river basin agency with political figures serving as policy makers. An agency composed of state and national politicians is too prone to ignore the distinctive quality of regional problems; a river basin agency that seeks to develop a set of regional political institutions will tend to be dominated by the best organized groups (i.e., the polluting firms and cities) unless a full-fledged regional political system is developed with regular elections, political parties, and mature organs of public opinion. Yet, such far reaching changes in our governmental structure are unlikely to occur. Finally, even if vital regional political structures were developed, they would be organized on a geographic principle which would not solve the problem of river basin management.

To ignore these unpleasant facts and persist in the construction of a regional agency guided by politicians is to create a structure in which each of the actors has only the vaguest sense of his relationship to the other participants. Thus most of the valley's political interests were not fully aware of the importance of the PSWB; even less were they in a position to affect the Board's decision, which was also made in ignorance of the analyses generated by the DECS. Similarly Governors Hughes and Shafer, as well as Secretary Udall, made their decisions without even knowing about the efforts of the WUAC to reach a regional consensus on the water quality approach to be pursued. The parties seem to pass each other in the night, without any effort to reason with, or bargain with, one another.

CONCLUSION: BEYOND THE POLITICAL MODEL

The preceding discussion emphasized the difficulty of inducing state and national politicians to view a regional problem from a regional perspective and the practical impossibility of devising a satisfactory method of selecting politicians to guide the affairs of a regional water resources agency. In advancing our argument, we placed great stress on the peculiar difficulties of employing regional political processes in the American political system. There is, however, another perspective from which the use of the political process to resolve the Delaware pollution decision may be criticized. Even apart from the peculiar problems of regional politics, the DRBC called

34. For an enlightening discussion of the problems of constituency definition, see Dahl, 1970.

upon the Governors and Secretary to perform a function for which high level political officials are not generally well suited. In order to decide intelligently on the course to be pursued along the river, it is not enough for the politicians to frame a general policy in general terms, leaving to others the task of determining the details of its application. In addition, the Governors and Secretary were called upon to scrutinize the facts of a concrete problem and judge the best policy to be pursued on a case-by-case basis. But is it wise to call on high level political officials to make judgments of this kind?

It should be apparent that an answer cannot be framed in absolute terms. There are some situations in which high office holders *should* be expected to develop policy in a detailed way, responding to their sense of the facts of the situation. On the one hand, a problem may be so important—like the Vietnam War—that the public has a right to demand that even the highest office holders treat it with the careful attention to nuance which only a detailed factual study can provide. On the other hand, the problem may not be susceptible of resolution by reference to a set of broader principles and policies and so high level politicians may not safely confide its resolution on a case-by-case basis to others without abdicating all real power to affect the final outcome. Nevertheless, the number of case-by-case determinations that can be safely confided to high ranking politicians must necessarily be small, given the very limited amount of time at their disposal. It seems then that a decision-making structure like the DRBC, which requires high level political officials to make decisions in concrete cases, should be examined with great care before it is seriously proposed. One should ask: Will the politicians be so overloaded with other problems that they will be unable to give even a modest degree of attention to the facts in the case before them? The Delaware experience provides ample evidence of the consequences of a failure to confront the "overload" problem. Our interviews with the leading politicians on the DRBC and their close political assistants provide an outstanding example of decision by cliché. To all of the leading decision makers, it was "obvious" that "pollution" was a "bad thing" and that the Delaware was a badly polluted stream. It followed from this simplistic perception that the thing to do was to "clean up the river as much as possible" unless the polluters raised such a fuss that it was politically unwise to do so. Since, for the structural reasons we have considered in the previous chapter, the polluters had almost no chance to affect the votes of Secretary Udall and Governor Rockefeller and only a small chance of affecting Governor Hughes', the DRBC decision was foreordained: a majority (at least)

would do the "right thing" and "clean up pollution as much as possible."
Since "the experts" informed the Governors that Objective II was the
highest goal then possible, the politicians voted for II.

It should be clear, however, that the difficult problems presented by
the Delaware are not susceptible of resolution by a group of busy politicians, armed with clichés, making policy on an ad hoc basis without even
attempting to address the general implications of their decision. Instead of
embarking on this course, the Delaware experience suggests the vital
importance of clearly establishing a set of environmental priorities and
designing a set of institutions which have a better chance of effectuating
these priorities. It is to this task that we turn in Chapter 14.

CHAPTER
14

Institutional Alternatives

INTRODUCTION

It is not enough to wring one's hands in despair over the manifold failings of the technocratic-political process which led to the decision to "clean up" the Delaware. A satisfactory critique of the existing pattern of decision making must go further and indicate, albeit in a tentative fashion, the lines of institutional design that seem to promise a more satisfactory approach to the solution of environmental problems.

We shall attempt such a formulation in this chapter, taking a rather straightforward "functional" approach. In Chapter 9, we advanced suggestions for a set of environmental policy goals which, in our judgment, promised to ameliorate the tensions between man and nature generated by our urban industrial civilization. Using these principles of substantive policy as a guideline, we shall now consider, in general terms, the nature of the institutions that can be expected best to articulate and apply these policies in a sophisticated fashion. Unfortunately, given the constraints imposed by our case study, it has been impossible to embark on the lengthy series of legal and empirical examinations required before a truly satisfactory assessment of these alternative mechanisms can be attempted. This chapter, therefore, is offered simply as a starting point for the research of others, and as a point of reference for those currently attempting to draft legislation to deal with environmental control.

CONTROL OF POISONS

The most important problem in the Delaware River is not DO but the discharge of exotic chemicals and metallic compounds which may well be dangerous to human beings when they are present, even in small quantities, either in drinking water or in food.[1] Given our ignorance of the impact of these wastes on human health, it seems foolish to confide power over their control to an agency that makes its decisions on the basis of an elaborate cost–benefit analysis of the economist's sort. We simply do not know enough to engage in an intelligent assessment of the level of discharge at which the marginal cost of treatment exceeds the marginal benefit to human health. Given the real (if unquantifiable) possibility of serious harm, however, a risk-avoidance strategy appears warranted in which a Poison Control Board should be given a strong statutory mandate to outlaw or stringently limit the discharge of any substance which there is reason to believe may significantly injure human health.

Such severe regulations will impose substantial costs on limited groups of polluters who have traditionally discharged exotic substances. In order to cushion the financial blow, it seems wise to permit the Board to subsidize at least in part the development and construction of treatment facilities in the industries hardest hit. This proposal is not made so much out of solicitude for industry as out of concern that otherwise the Board would face impossible political difficulties. In the absence of a subsidy scheme, the Board would be under great political pressure to construe its statutory mandate in a modest fashion. It is true, of course, that the effective administration of a subsidy raises substantial problems of its own; however, subject to further empirical studies, it is our belief that an aggressive program of poison control will prove politically impossible unless the Control Board is armed with a carrot as well as a stick.

The Control Board will require a large scientific staff charged with the task of examining the potential impact of a broad range of exotic dis-

1. See Ch. 9.

charges. Procedures should be established for the systematic publication of the scientific staff's findings, and members of the general public, as well as the Board's own counsel, should be permitted to bring an action before the agency to ban or stringently limit discharge. As to the nature of the Board itself, it would seem that it should conform roughly to the model of the classic independent New Deal quasi-judicial agency. What is required is a group of men and women appointed with relatively long tenure and thus relatively insulated from the political battle, who have the time and temperament to consider the merits of each individual case, conscious of the importance of the policy they are charged to implement. Since the issues raised will often be technical, some of the members should have strong scientific backgrounds. Since adversary hearings will be the rule, however, a number of legally trained members should sit on the Board as well. Judicial review of the traditional kind would also seem desirable.

While it is not impossible to imagine Poison Control Boards operating moderately effectively on the state and regional levels, it would seem that the major effort should be concentrated on the national level. First, a national staff could be large enough both to engage in the broadly based research effort required and to coordinate the research concurrently going on at universities and other scientific centers. Second, many discharges of esoteric materials may affect the inhabitants of distant regions, especially when the substances are ingested by fish subsequently harvested for market. Local governments cannot be expected to respond adequately to the important interests of these distant consumers. Third, if one believes it desirable that the Poison Control Board err on the side of caution in the regulation of potentially hazardous discharges, it would seem wise to avoid a situation in which regions or states are tempted to relax their poison regulations to attract firms to their area.[2]

MASS RECREATION IN URBAN AREAS

The development of enhanced recreational opportunities should be subjected to a very different decision-making system. Rather than a quasi-judicial administrative agency of the New Deal type, what is required is an agency more closely resembling the modern corporation. Before embarking on an ambitious water pollution control project aimed at generating new recreational opportunities, a Recreation Authority should be required to undertake a sophisticated cost–benefit analysis to help it decide

2. See Peltzman and Tideman, 1972.

whether the creation of these opportunities is worth the cost. In making this analysis, the Authority must of course take into account the costs of taking *all* the steps required to assure that the promised recreational services are in fact delivered. Thus, it will be insufficient for the Authority to concern itself simply with a single water quality parameter like DO. Indeed, such an Authority would be required not only to estimate the cost of assuring water of adequate quality but also the cost of guaranteeing adequate park land for access to the water resource and adequate transportation to these parks. Doubtless on many occasions the sensible use of cost–benefit analysis will suggest that a proposed project is not worth carrying out. This is only to be expected, since the investment of enormous sums is not a matter to be taken lightly. Indeed, in many urban areas in the country, the Authority may well find that resources will most profitably be devoted to protecting and improving *existing* recreational opportunities rather than to creating new ones: in assuring that Coney Island remains swimmable rather than creating a new Jones Beach.

Let us imagine, however, that the Authority concludes that a project— say, the Schuylkill River Plan described in Chapter 9—is worth the cost. It should then possess the legal authority to act effectively to take the interrelated steps necessary to complete the project. For example, waste discharges by industries and suburbs bordering the Schuylkill must be stringently limited or eliminated completely if hundreds of thousands of Philadelphians are to swim safely in the river a few miles downstream. Similarly, large sums must be spent to assure that Philadelphia's storm sewers no longer empty into the Schuylkill, but only the Delaware. Once again, if the Recreation Authority is to have a reasonable prospect of inducing municipalities and industries to undertake extraordinary expenditures, it is quite unrealistic to arm it with only punitive sanctions. If "solving" the storm overflow problem for the Schuylkill will cost the city of Philadelphia hundreds of millions, and if restricting or eliminating industrial discharges into the river will be exceedingly costly to existing suburban firms and will deter others from locating in these developing areas; enormous resistance should be expected from interests prejudiced by the plan unless they are assured adequate compensation. Moreover, many of the aggrieved parties may plausibly argue that the Schuylkill plan imposes unjust burdens. After all, it is not clear why the economic development of certain suburbs bordering on the Schuylkill should be sacrificed disproportionately for a swimming facility which will be used mainly by inner city residents. Thus in order to obtain a relatively speedy development of major projects, as well as to avoid injustice, the Recreation Authority should be given the power to compensate interests called on to sacrifice disproportionately for the project.[3]

As soon as the need for substantial disbursement of funds is clear, it should be obvious that the Recreation Authority's decisions to embark on major new projects will be subjected to substantial political oversight. After the agency generates its own cost–benefit analysis, and after the analysis is considered critically by a Review Board, the Recreation Authority will be obliged to obtain a substantial appropriation from the legislature before beginning the project in earnest. Doubtless the legislature could refrain from reviewing the merits of each and every project. Nevertheless, the legislature's control of the purse strings will serve as a potent check on a technocratic agency that uses cost–benefit analysis as a screen to obscure arbitrary conduct. Indeed, it may be suggested that such legislative control will be too effective—that the Authority will seek to manipulate cost–benefit analysis so that projects proposed will appeal to the most potent political forces, regardless of their "true" cost–benefit ratios. Certainly, the conduct of the Army Corps of Engineers in a related area should give one pause in this regard.[4] Nevertheless, the proponent of the Recreational Authority need not contend that his institutional design is free of serious defects in order to urge its adoption. Instead, he need only suggest that such an Authority will tend to generate significantly better results in the aggregate than does the present program, epitomized by the effort to improve the DO profile on the Delaware and the other major industrial rivers. When viewed from this perspective, even a quasi-politicized technocratic Authority would seem to have considerable virtue. At the very least, the Authority, its work scrutinized by a Review Board, would be required to ask the right questions of itself, even though it would not always come up with the best answer. Instead of striking out blindly against the "polluted" condition of an industrial waterway, it will be obliged to estimate the cost of doing everything required to reclaim a water resource for wide ranging recreational use in an urban center. While the Authority, in response to political forces, will not consistently select the projects which seem the most beneficial in purely technocratic terms,

3. In short, we are here attempting to implement the persuasive argument advanced by Frank Michelman, who suggests that in the past we have relied far too heavily on courts and their use of constitutional criteria to determine the adequacy of governmental compensation practices (see Michelman, 1967, pp. 1245–59).
4. See Maass, 1951, for a full discussion and analysis. See also Tippy, 1968, for a discussion of the cost–benefit analyses which the Corps of Engineers submits to Congress and of the review process which occurs before these studies reach the political decision makers.

nevertheless one could expect that at least most of the time the Authority's recommended programs will yield substantial recreational opportunities. For it will be difficult for a Recreational Authority to survive in the political marketplace if its costly projects provide no more in the way of enhanced recreational opportunities than will the DRBC's DO control program.

Moreover, granting the possibility of some thoughtless planning resulting from ad hoc political pressures, it would be wrong to ignore the benefits that may sometimes accrue from legislative influence on the technocratic decision-making process. As we have seen, cost–benefit analysis, even when controlled by our hypothetical Review Board, is as much an art as a science. Although the discipline has advanced sufficiently to permit the analyst to eliminate clearly unmeritorious projects, the tools of the trade are insufficient to permit the decision maker to select mechanically "the best" project from a number of seemingly worthwhile proposals. Since the exercise of substantial discretion is inevitable, there is much to be said for a system in which the agency's discretion is guided to some extent by the political process through control over appropriations.

Similarly, before a final decision is made on any particular project, it would be appropriate to invite interested groups to give their own interpretations of the cost–benefit studies. Finally, and less obviously, it might be desirable to subject the Recreation Authority's decisions to judicial review, limited to the question of whether the Authority's decision bears a rational relationship to its cost–benefit analysis. The issues argued would be illuminated by the critical study the Review Board had undertaken as well as by the comments of interested parties at the agency hearing.

From this sketch of the Recreation Authority's functions, it appears that we may not here be dealing with an agency which, like the Poison Control Board, must operate on the national level to be most effective. Indeed, considering the insight into local conditions necessary for sensitive application of cost–benefit analysis, much can be said in favor of regional, state, or metropolitan political control over the operation of the technocratic agency. Moreover, unlike the poison problem, that of providing mass recreational opportunities for a heavily industrialized area generally does not have important nationwide effects. Coney Island's fate is of much greater concern to the residents of New York and its environs than to the citizens of Philadelphia, not to speak of those of San Francisco. Consequently, its future should be left largely to citizens of the metropolis immediately affected.

PROTECTING NATURE

Instead of attempting to "save" the fish in the "critical" region of the Delaware, it would be better to set up a Nature Preservation Trust, which would concentrate on protecting areas still relatively untouched but now threatened by urban industrialism. In addition, the Trust should seek to expand the geographic range in which a broad variety of nonhuman life forms could maintain a vital existence.

To a certain extent the Trust can fulfil its purposes through an expanded land purchase program that dedicates government property to the rights of animal and plant life to exist regardless of man's convenience. However, it will generally be necessary to go further than this and permit the Trust to impose especially stringent development controls on some "natural" areas remaining in private hands, since water and air pollution will often have a profoundly unsettling impact on life in the government preserves.

Needless to say, an aggressive Nature Trust would be subjected to powerful political opposition in discharging its functions. Since it will not impose a blanket "no development" policy everywhere, its decision to limit economic growth in some areas while permitting full scale industrial exploitation in other areas will inevitably be quite arbitrary. There is no fully satisfactory way to explain why a boundary line between nature and industrialized mankind should be drawn here rather than there. Consequently property owners who find their interests significantly impaired by the Trust's decisions will make strenuous efforts to induce the Trust to alter its boundary lines.

What is more, in many areas the Trust will be generally unpopular and under tremendous pressure to withdraw its development controls completely. It is precisely the relatively unexploited areas that are the poorest in the nation, and indeed, it is *because* these areas are undeveloped that their inhabitants are poor. Thus the antidevelopment policies of the Trust may often be seen by the residents of the proposed nature reserves as an effort by the rich urban centers to frustrate the efforts of their country cousins to develop an industrial base that will permit them to share more fully in the delights of twentieth century life.

It is true, of course, that residents in the "minimal development" Trust zones remain free to move nearer to urban centers if they wish to participate more fully in their particular pleasures. Nevertheless migration imposes severe costs in the form of cultural dislocation. To make matters worse, it is possible that in discharging its functions the Trust will sometimes limit not only industrial and commercial expansion but also block the development of those recreational facilities which may significantly endanger important nonhuman forms of life. Thus, on occasion, the Trust may sometimes find itself in the politically awkward position of advising the present inhabitants of a region to resist the temptations of prosperity and rejoice that the best things in life are free.

In response, the region's political representatives will often do all in their power to frustrate the Trust's activities, supported not only by business interests which stand to profit by further development but by the majority of the region's inhabitants as well. Designing an institutional framework that can fairly reconcile the interests of nature with those of the inhabitants of the "limited development" regions will thus be a task to tax the talents of the most gifted social engineer.

In seeking the kind of institution most likely to overcome local resistance, one would probably be led, in the end, to propose that a national administrative agency be put in charge of formulating Trust policy. This is the only way the Trust could obtain the support of those (primarily urban) groups willing to support a selective "limited development" policy despite its costs to the inhabitants of the regions selected by the Trust. Moreover, a national institution would be in the best position to develop a coherent nationwide plan in which the limited development areas would be located where they would do the greatest good for nature while causing the least harm to human interests. Nevertheless, despite the powerful reasons for relying on national initiative, it is undoubtedly true that a proposal, like the present one, which contemplates aggressive federal intervention in land use decisions, will be greeted with widespread suspicion, for this is a nation that has traditionally formulated such policies in an extremely fragmentary manner through countless local governments. Thus, despite the importance of creating an aggressive Nature Trust, it is here that a forceful national effort seems least likely unless the environmental movement clarifies its objectives and concentrates its political energies on its most important—and most difficult—tasks.[5]

THE ENVIRONMENTAL DEFENSE AGENCY

In proposing the construction of a set of specialized institutions, each dealing with a salient dimension of the environmental problem, we do not

5. For a brief canvass of current state and local efforts, see Ch. 2.

mean to suggest that these single-purpose agencies may be relied on to resolve every environmental issue. Problems will arise which the specialized institutions will ignore or which fall outside their limited jurisdictions entirely. It would be unsatisfactory, for example, if the DO problem on the Delaware were so completely ignored that the river each summer generated an omnipresent odor pervading the fabric of life in large areas of Philadelphia and Camden. Simply because the Delaware's DO problem is not entitled to high priority does not imply that conditions should be permitted to deteriorate indefinitely. Instead, some steps should be taken to assure that the unpleasant, but tolerable, condition prevailing in the "critical region" of the Delaware should be controlled even if not eliminated.

The problem can be put more broadly. While the Poison Control Board, Recreation Authority, and Nature Trust may be conceived as the fundamental components of our society's *affirmative* effort to *improve* the relationship between man and nature, another set of institutions is required to fulfill the *defensive* function of assuring that low-priority problems do not get completely out of hand. It is here, of course, where the institutions which have traditionally served as the principal source of environmental policy fit into a sophisticated scheme. Each of the states now possesses at least a rudimentary pollution control structure, which has often been recently rechristened as the Department of Environmental Protection. While these bodies may have changed their names, they typically do not have the legal powers, fiscal resources, or scientific capacity to perform any of the complex, specialized functions required by any of our three proposed institutions. Nevertheless, they do provide an institutional base for developing a cadre of generalists who can perform the innumerable regulatory tasks required to control low-priority problems in areas not marked for dramatic improvement. Moreover, in areas like the Delaware Estuary, where interstate cooperation is desirable, a Defense Agency may well be grounded in an interstate compact. Finally, there seems no reason why the federal government should not fulfill its normal functions in specifying minimal environmental goals and assuring that local and regional Defense Agencies are structured so as to promise a modestly effective operation.

The Delaware story serves as a caution, however, that the creation of an Environmental Defense Agency is a task worthy of special care. If EDA officials lose sight of the defensive aspect of their mission, they may seek to use the regulatory tools at their disposal to embark on an exceedingly expensive "battle against pollution" which will substantially benefit neither man nor beast. To assure that the EDA's activities will be kept within rightful bounds, it is first necessary to articulate the EDA's objective so that its "defensive" mission is clearly understood both by the decision makers within the agency and by the officials who will review its actions.

Two approaches to this task seem fruitful. Under the first aletrnative the EDA's founding statute would direct the agency "to take those regulatory actions and only those actions which are reasonably necessary to assure the preservation of the levels of environmental amenity prevailing at the time of the passage of this Act." This statutory sanctification of the status quo has all the advantages generally associated with this common legislative tactic. The standard is relatively easy to administer and once an environmental inventory is taken, the agency's objectives are defined with precision without use of any discretion by the EDA's policy makers. Moreover, the status quo objective seems to fulfill in a crude fashion the general "defensive" objective of the EDA. If the agency fulfills its statutory trust, we can be reasonably confident that environmental problems ignored by the three specialized agencies will not be permitted to get entirely out of hand as a result of neglect.

Unfortunately, this first, simplistic approach has the vices associated with its virtues, since on some occasions conditions now existing can be modified to the great benefit of a region's inhabitants. Sometimes a competent cost–benefit analysis will suggest that an environmental improvement ignored by the three specialized agencies is nonetheless well worth attempting. Similarly, analysis may clearly indicate that the costs of maintaining the environmental status quo far exceed the costs of permitting a degree of further degradation in some aspect of the area's environmental quality. While the simple "status quo" standard would blind the EDA to these obvious facts, under a second approach, the EDA would be authorized to transcend its general commitment to the status quo and fashion an objective "contemplating either environmental enhancement or environmental degradation when one or the other seems clearly indicated by a competent cost–benefit analysis."

While this second approach is obviously the more sophisticated one, it should not be adopted without a recognition of its dangers. As soon as a substantial quantum of discretion is confided to the EDA to tolerate deterioration or mandate improvement, much more stringent steps must be taken to assure that its trust will not be abused. When the EDA rules that the prevailing DO level on a given river will be permitted to decline considerably, we must have some confidence that the decision has been taken after a mature consideration of the costs and benefits involved and not simply in response to pressures by polluting cities and industries. Similarly, if a step is taken to improve existing water quality, there must be some reason to believe that the decision is consistent with the "defensive" mission of the institution. Otherwise, the simpler "status quo" rule, while more primitive, may in fact generate a set of more appropriate outcomes in the long run than will the sophisticated approach.

Fortunately, however, it should not prove impossible to design a set of controls to assure that the more sophisticated mandate will not be too often abused. First, steps must be taken to ensure employment of competent analysts by the EDA whenever it seriously considers departing from the status quo. Second, a body like the Review Board will play a role of fundamental importance in inducing analysts to resist the temptation to write reports which cater to their superiors' prejudices. Finally, judicial review—when informed by a record that includes the Review Board's critical appraisal—promises to serve as a moderately effective mechanism for assuring that the substance of the defensive statutory policy is respected.

UNANSWERED QUESTIONS

While our institutional design will doubtless seem overly elaborate to some, it is far from comprehensive. This is attributable in part to the nature of our case study. Thus, in proposing the four environmental agencies, we have been moved principally by the desire to design an institutional framework which would avoid the blunders being perpetrated on the Delaware and other major industrial rivers in the United States. It may well be that a serious student of air pollution or some other environmental problem, after articulating the basic policies which should govern society's effort in the area, will reasonably conclude that the design proposed for the management of water resources is inappropriate in one way or another. While we hope our general institutional proposals will prove suggestive in related fields, our discussion has been premised on the notion that it is a mistake to divorce institutional design from the problem of devising appropriate substantive policy. Instead of talking about institutional structure in the abstract, we have recommended our four agencies because they seem to promise best the fulfillment of the substantive policies we favor. Those who believe that a different set of outcomes are in the public interest will favor different kinds of institutions to develop them.

Our proposals are limited in a second, related respect. We have ignored entirely a range of institutional issues dealing with the environmental policies of agencies whose principal responsibilities lie in other areas. To what extent, for example, should the Federal Power Commission, when considering an application for a new power facility, employ its own staff to weigh the environmental consequences of a proposed site and design, and to what extent should it rely instead on the personnel of the four environmental agencies? When the environmental impacts have been analyzed, should the FPC be the sole judge of the relative importance of adverse environmental consequences when weighed against the nonenvironmental advantages of locating a particular plant at a particular site? Or should the environmental agencies play a role in this decision? If the latter, in what way should they participate? Should the Nature Preservation Trust, for example, be given the right to veto any power project it finds to be fundamentally inconsistent with its wildlife protection program? Should the Recreation Authority or Poison Control Board or EDA be granted similar veto rights? In the alternative, should any (or all) of these agencies be given the right to file a protest with the FPC, which would have the legal effect of requiring the power agency to demonstrate a compelling need for the project in the face of the environmental agency's finding that its goals will be significantly frustrated?[6]

The importance and difficulty of these and similar questions are obvious. We do not attempt to consider them here, however, since a sensible answer requires not only a deeper understanding of the detailed structure and probable functioning of our four proposed agencies but also a careful treatment of the alternative ways an agency regulating the power industry may be organized. Consequently, we can only note the existence of the vexing problems of institutional interrelationship in the hope that other students of the regulatory process will undertake the empirical and theoretical effort required even for tentative answers.

Finally, our institutional design is incomplete in that it fails to consider adequately the proper role of the judiciary in the development of environmental objectives. We have suggested at various points in the analysis that courts have a valuable role to play in reviewing the decisions of other

6. A more modest version of this procedure is already in effect. Under The Clean Air Act of 1970, 42 U.S.C.A. §1857 et seq. (Supp. 1973), the administrator of the EPA reviews and comments on any matter contained in any proposed federal legislation or agency action, if such matter relates to the duties and responsibilities of the EPA; *id.* §1857h-7. If the administrator decides that the proposed action is unsatisfactory from the standpoint of environmental quality or public health, he refers the matter to the Council on Environmental Quality, which petitions the President (*loc. cit.*).

agencies, especially if there exists a Review Board to help the lay judge pierce the veil of technical jargon so as to determine intelligently whether the challenged decision conforms to the fundamental policies established by the organic statute. We have, however, refrained from suggesting that the judiciary should transcend its reviewing function and become a front-line institution attempting to initiate policy as it now creates common law. Our failure to consider this option seriously is once again explained by the distinctive character of our case study. It seems obvious that a judge (or even a team of judges) would make utter hash out of a problem as complex and arcane as the DO problem on the Delaware, even if the judge (or the parties) had the wit to obtain relevant information about the magnitude of BOD loads, consumer surpluses, and costs associated with attaining each of a number of different environmental objectives. This is not to suggest that a traditional common-law judge may never appropriately serve as a front-line decision maker on environmental questions. The common-law concept of nuisance, however crude it may be, can doubtless be refined sufficiently to permit sophisticated judges to resolve rather simple problems, involving a relatively small number of parties in relatively straightforward ways. And if, for some reason, these localized problems escape the serious attention of any of the involved environmental agencies, a strong case can be made for judicial intervention—though even here there are certain counterarguments that may sometimes have weight. Once again, we shall leave the detailed analysis of these questions to others.[7] The only contribution that our case study can make is to dramatize the fact that even the most activist judge ought not be relied upon to serve as a front-line policymaker in more than a small fraction of the cases that raise important environmental issues. What our society requires most urgently is not a corps of judges earnestly striving to do what is "good"; what we require instead is to recognize that defining "the good" in an industrialized society is a complex task, and that an attempt to simplify may often induce costly blunders, thus not only curtailing accomplishment in terms of the environment but, in the end, also impairing public confidence that political power may be used in a reasonable way to improve the conditions of modern life.

7. For a sensitive discussion of these issues, see Michelman, 1971, pp. 675–83.

PART IV

Achieving the Objective: Regulation through Legal Orders and Some Alternatives

Three Models
of Regulation

THE BASIC ISSUES

The final part of this book considers the means by which policies, once
determined, can be implemented both efficiently and fairly to assure
prompt compliance. This issue is of fundamental importance because the
problems raised by the Delaware put distinctively modern strains on the
traditional regulatory system.

The problem lies deeper than the obvious difficulties posed by inducing
reluctant dischargers to move promptly to satisfy the agency's objectives.
While delay is a problem, at least we have a fairly clear notion about the
way it may be solved: if the price of delay is the imposition of heavy taxes,
fines, or even more stringent criminal sanctions, a more prompt performance may be expected. While there are, of course, important issues involved in fashioning a sanctioning scheme severe enough to induce prompt
compliance without undermining the requirements of procedural justice,
these issues are at least familiar, and centuries of thought have been devoted to their solution.

The same cannot be said of a second fundamental issue the DRBC confronted: to achieve its objective, it was required to allocate clean-up responsibilities among the estuary's hundred dischargers. To see the difficulty of this task consider the simple problem posed if there were only two polluters—X and Y—in the Filadelphia region, each discharging raw sewage equal to 100,000 pounds of FSUOD a day.[1] If the agency wished to reduce the 200,000-pound discharge to 80,000 pounds, a large number of cutback patterns can be imagined which would satisfy its water quality objective. At one extreme, X could be induced to eliminate all of its discharge while Y would be required only to cut back by 20,000 pounds; at the other extreme, the cutback responsibilities of X and Y could be reversed; and there are innumerable intermediate patterns which will also result in attaining the 80,000-pound limit.

The desirability of each of the innumerable cutback patterns may be judged by two different criteria. First, one configuration may be much more costly than another (the "efficiency" criterion); second, one may seem less fair than another (the "fairness" criterion). To see the potential conflict between fairness and efficiency, it is only necessary to elaborate our simple Filadelphia problem. Assume that cleaning up is far more expensive for X than for Y. To make the example concrete, imagine that the daily total cost of treating q hundred pounds of waste is $.125q^2$ for X while it is $.025q^2$ for Y. Thus the marginal cost of treatment rises steadily for both X and Y but rises five times faster for X than for Y. Given these facts, an agency seeking to achieve its DO goal in the cheapest way would induce Y to cease discharging completely (at a cost of $25,000) while X would be permitted to continue dumping 80,000 of its 100,000 pounds (at a cost of $5,000).[2] Any other outcome would increase total costs since it involves requiring X to treat a pound of waste when Y could do so at less cost.

Nevertheless, as this extreme outcome suggests, a cost-minimizing strategy may be condemned as unfair. To support a claim of inequity, it is only necessary to invoke the rather common principle of fairness, which requires two individuals who have *jointly* caused a harm in *equal* measure to make an *equal* effort to eliminate the harm. While the "equal effort"

1. For definitions of BOD, FSUOD, and SSUOD, see Ch. 3, pp. 18–22.
2. Total cost in this case is given by:

$$C = \tfrac{1}{2} \{.25(\alpha q)^2 + .05[(1 - \alpha)q]^2\}$$

where q is total load treated in hundreds of pounds ((q = 1200 in the text example) and α is the proportion treated by X. If $q \leq 1200$, this function is minimized with respect to α where $\alpha = \tfrac{1}{6}$ and total marginal cost is q/24. For q > 1200, $\alpha = 1$ and marginal cost = .25q.

criterion is frequently used in ordinary discourse, its meaning is in fact ambiguous. On the one hand, "equal effort" may be understood to require both X and Y to make the same *financial* sacrifice; on the other hand, it may require that each polluter treat the *same percentage* of his waste. If either of these fairness criteria appeals to the agency,[3] it must of course seek to reconcile its cost-minimizing goal with its fairness constraint.

It is possible to imagine a world in which this reconciliation would be a simple matter. The agency would follow a two-stage procedure. First, it would induce the polluters to cut back their wastes to minimize total costs—X would cut back 20,000 pounds at a cost of $5000 while Y would stop discharging, at a cost of $25,000. Second, if equal financial sacrifice were the fairness test, X would be induced to pay Y $10,000.[4] Unfortunately, this freedom to reconcile equity and efficiency objectives is not open to officials operating in real-world institutions. Basic regulatory structures control the extent to which cost minimization may be achieved and the way in which the clash between fairness and efficiency is perceived and resolved.

To see this, consider in general terms three different models of control. We shall call the first "regulation through legal orders." Under this traditional approach, the agency regulates conduct by issuing orders to each polluter specifying what he must do to escape sanctions. Thus, in our simple Filadelphia case, the ideal final product of an agency's effort to achieve cost minimization will be two legal commands: X is to remove 20,000 pounds (at a cost of $5000) and Y 100,000 (at a cost of $25,000). Under this model, however, the agency will confront two basic problems in achieving cost minimization and reconciling it with equity.

3. It is beyond the scope of this book to consider the fundamental philosophical issues involved in determining whether either version of the "equal effort" principle should be accepted as a measure of fairness in cases like the present one. It is enough here to recognize that "equal effort" criteria have an important role in the present legal system although their appropriate status is a subject of controversy among legal scholars (see Epstein, 1973; Posner, 1973; Fletcher, 1972; Coase, 1960, and Hart and Honore, 1959).

4. If, instead, the agency's fairness standard is equal percentage removal, fairness and efficiency might also be reconciled by using a two-stage procedure. First, the agency would calculate the costs of a uniform percentage treatment plan that would meet its water quality objective. Second, the agency could once again induce X and Y to cut back their wastes to minimize total costs, but would require monetary transfers to achieve a proportionate division of costs equivalent to that which a uniform treatment regime would produce. To continue with our Filadelphia example, uniform treatment requires that both X and Y remove 60 percent of their waste. The cost to X is $(\frac{1}{2})(.25)(600)^2 = \$45,000$ and to Y is $(\frac{1}{2})(.05)(600)^2 = \$9,000$. Thus Y pays one-sixth of the total cost of $54,000, with X paying the rest. In the least-cost solution, total costs are $30,000 with Y paying $25,000. Thus, to meet this form of the fairness criterion, X must pay Y $20,000.

First, it must design a fact-finding mechanism that will accurately determine the extent to which Y can treat less expensively than X. Second, if it does not like the fact that Y will be spending $25,000 while X spends only $5,000, it must in one way or another adjust its first set of legal orders to satisfy the "equal effort" criterion.[5]

In contrast, an agency adopting the "market" model of regulation conceives its task in a different spirit. Instead of specifying the precise quantity each polluter may legally discharge into the river, the agency establishes a price that dischargers must pay for each pound of waste emitted. Given a price, polluters will treat their wastes to the point where the marginal cost of further treatment equals the emission price established. Thus, if the price for Filadelphia were set at 50 cents a pound, X would treat 20,000 pounds and Y, 100,000, thereby fulfilling the agency's quality goal at least cost.

An agency proceeding under this model, then, confronts the efficiency and equity questions in somewhat different terms. To achieve an efficient solution, it becomes critically important to set the "right" price, and various kinds of market schemes[6] must be evaluated according to the ease with which they perform this function. Second, the distribution of burdens may once again violate fairness criteria,[7] and the agency must design a mechanism for transfering funds which does not distort market incentives.[8]

Finally, it is useful to introduce an "activist" approach as a third basic regulatory option. Here the central authority is not content with seeking to control the conduct of others either through the issuance of legal orders or the construction of market incentives. Instead, the agency undertakes to do a large portion of the treatment job itself by building and operating its own treatment plants and requiring or otherwise inducing dischargers to use the agency's facilities. The user fees charged to polluters obviously could be set on any of a number of different principles; the important distinction between "activism" and the two preceding models, however, does

5. Basically the agency has two choices. Either it can maintain cost minimization and issue a second set of legal orders requiring cash transfers between polluters or it can abandon strict cost minimization and issue a single set of orders that attempts to balance equity and efficiency criteria (see Ch. 16).
6. Alternative market approaches are discussed in Kneese and Bower, 1968, pp. 98–101, 109–79, 191–93; Rose-Ackerman, 1973; Bohm and Kneese, 1971; Baumol and Oates (forthcoming); Dales, *Pollution, Property and Prices,* 1968; Dales, *Land, Water and Ownership,* 1968; Trelease, 1965; Johnson, *Optimal State Water Law,* 1971; Milliman, 1959; Montgomery, 1971; Selig, 1971, pp. 36–43.
7. It should be recognized, however, that the distribution of burdens under a cost-minimizing effluent charge will be different from that prevailing under a cost-minimizing set of cutback orders. In Filadelphia, for example, the cost-minimizing effluent charge will mean that X's burden is heavier than Y's, while Y carries most of the burden under a legal orders approach.
8. As Ch. 18 will show, this is not a simple task.

not depend on the nature of the fee schedule but rather on the state's decision to intervene affirmatively in the treatment process. Here, the fundamental issues center on the way the agency should be structured to act fairly and efficiently and the principles it should use in dealing with various classes of dischargers.

Having outlined in the most general terms three basic options that confront an agency considering a cost-minimizing strategy, we are now in a position to present our basic thesis concerning the regulatory effort of the DRBC. In Chapters 16 and 17 we shall argue that the DRBC's decision to regulate polluter conduct almost entirely through legal orders fundamentally compromised its effort to achieve its objectives efficiently and justly. Chapter 18 argues that the agency's performance could have been significantly improved by a sophisticated incorporation of market elements into its regulatory framework and proceeds to sketch a particular market approach which, all things considered, seems to resolve the difficulties of using economic incentives in the most satisfactory fashion possible. Finally, Chapter 19 develops a series of Delaware case studies that suggest an important range of situations where an "activist" approach may well prove fruitful, and proceeds to sketch some basic principles to guide activist agency behavior.

The DRBC's Zoning Plan: The Fate of Innovation within the Traditional Model of Regulation

THE TRADITIONAL REGULATORY RESPONSE

Water pollution regulation in the United States has traditionally been based on a rather simplistic application of the "legal orders" model.[1] Generally speaking, all polluters have been ordered to remove a predetermined percentage of their FSUOD before discharge regardless of their treatment costs or the degree to which the waste of any particular polluter impaired alternative water uses. Thus, in the Filadelphia situation developed in Chapter 15, the pollution authority would order X and Y each to reduce its discharge by 60 percent, from 100,000 pounds to 40,000 pounds, and so satisfy the 80,000-pound Filadelphia limit.

Whatever the fairness of the "uniform percentage treatment" approach, its inefficiency should be plain. In contrast to the $30,000 price tag attached to the "cost-minimizing" pattern of regulation, under which X alone was permitted to continue an 80,000-pound discharge, the traditional

1. For a discussion of the traditional regulatory devices and a series of well directed criticisms, see Kneese and Bower, 1968; Kneese, 1971, pp. 35, 36; *Examination of Construction Program*, 1969; *Cost of Clean Water*, 1971, and Zwick and Benstock, 1971.

"uniform percentage treatment" approach would achieve the same DO goal at a cost of $54,000. The added cost is, of course, explained by the fact that the high-cost polluter, X, is being required to eliminate waste which Y could remove more cheaply.

To make matters worse, "uniform percentage treatment" seems even more inefficient when the position of a third polluter, Z, is considered. Like X and Y, Z also is discharging 100,000 pounds of FSUOD into the stream untreated; however, Z is located in the relatively unpolluted section of the river below Vilmington, where it is the sole pollution source. Assume, further, that after considering the potential uses of this section of the stream, the control agency decides that no more than 50,000 pounds of FSUOD can be tolerated. Under the "uniform percentage treatment" approach, the control agency, after deciding that 50,000 pounds is the appropriate limit, is faced with an unhappy dilemma. Since X and Y should be treating at 60 percent to solve Filadelphia's problem, it would seem that the uniform treatment standard requires that the Vilmington polluter also must treat at 60 percent. This means, of course, that the Vilmington plant will be required to engage in expensive overtreatment, since, by hypothesis, Z need only treat at 50 percent to meet the 50,000-pound limit set for Vilmington's waters. This problem of expensive and unnecessary treatment can of course be resolved if the agency is willing to establish a uniform 50 percent requirement for polluters X, Y and Z. While this strategy will lead to the desired result in the Vilmington area, it will of course be unsatisfactory in Filadelphia, where X and Y will each discharge 50,000 pounds and the 80,000-pound limit set for the area will not be respected. Thus, in one way or another, the requirement that Z eliminate the same percentage of its waste as X and Y will lead to an inefficient pursuit of the agency's water quality objectives.

Uniform percentage treatment, then, suffers from a two-pronged weakness from the efficiency point of view. When imposed on polluters whose marginal impact on water quality is similar (like X and Y), it fails to discriminate between high- and low-cost treatment possibilities. When imposed on polluters who have significantly different marginal impacts on water quality, all objectives can be achieved only at the cost of needless overtreatment.

THE DECS ANALYSIS AND THE DRBC RESPONSE

It is one thing to grasp the basic inefficiencies of uniform percentage treatment in the simplified world of Filadelphia and Vilmington; quite another to make it clear to public policy makers that the extra cost of the traditional approach is so substantial that an innovative strategy should be considered. And it is here that the DECS staff once again attempted to fill the gap between theory and practice. Using its BOD-DO model, together with data concerning each of the estuary's "44 major polluters,"[2] the DECS set out to quantify the cost of meeting each of its five DO programs under a uniform percentage treatment approach. It then estimated the costs of meeting each of these same objectives under a BOD cutback configuration which its analysis suggested was the cost-minimizing one. As Table 7 indicates, the difference between the two strategies was considerable indeed.

Table 7.[3] **Estimated Total Costs of Objective Sets**

	In Millions of Dollars	
Objective Set	Uniform Treatment	Cost Minimization
I	$490	$490
II	335	235
III	175	135
IV	145	100

We have said enough about the BOD-DO model and the DECS cost-estimating procedure to suggest that the precise figures should not be given any great weight. Nevertheless, the figures brought home the fact that millions could be saved by devising a regulatory approach more sophisticated than uniform percentage treatment.

Moreover, unlike DECS' other messages, this one was not transmitted through communication channels distorted by state and federal political and administrative interests. After the Governors and Interior Secretary made their decision in the spring of 1967, they naturally turned not to their own state and federal staffs but to the DRBC staff when it came to the task of framing a regulatory system for achieving Objective II. For it

2. See Ch. 6.
3. DECS, Table 16, p. 66. Costs are measured in 1964 dollars and are the sum of capital costs and operating costs discounted at 3 percent over 20 years. The table records only the costs of improving the river conditions over 1964 quality levels. The cost of maintaining current quality levels was estimated at $30 million in DECS, p. 66, but increased substantially in subsequent estimates (see Ch. 6). The cost of maintaining current conditions never seems to have been explicitly allocated among dischargers and does not vary with the method of allocation.

was only the DRBC that had the legal authority to frame a coordinated response to the problem of implementation. Moreover, the DECS critique of uniform treatment provided the single point of contact between the technocratic analysis tendered by the "thinking" agency and the needs of the "action" agency. The DRBC staff, under Executive Director Wright, was determined to make a mark for itself as an innovator and, up to that point, had had precious little opportunity to do so. Consequently, the DRBC staff eagerly accepted DECS' invitation to move beyond uniform treatment.

Unfortunately, however, the DRBC did not manifest a similar inclination to scrutinize the premises of the traditional regulatory approach but relied on the "legal orders" model, although the DECS had generated some tentative analyses indicating the potential of a market mode of regulation.[4] Instead, armed only with the tools provided by the legal orders approach, the DRBC staff began an ambitious effort to construct a viable regulatory structure more efficient and no less fair than the traditional one. While we shall shortly appraise the success of the DRBC's enterprise, our effort will be more fruitful if, for a moment, we return to the simpler world of Filadelphia and Vilmington and seek to assess the tensions that are generated by any effort to minimize costs through legal orders.

THE INHERENT LIMITATIONS OF REGULATION
BY LEGAL ORDERS

To strip matters to their essentials, we will first restrict our attention to Filadelphia's two polluters, X and Y, ignoring Vilmington's Z. Since it costs Y much less to treat its waste than X, we have seen that the ideal final product of a cost-minimizing legal orders agency is two commands, ordering X to reduce its waste load by 20,000 pounds and Y to eliminate its 100,000-pound discharge entirely. Unfortunately, however, in the real world it is almost never obvious that X's marginal treatment costs are higher than Y's. Thus, the agency will be obliged to conduct lengthy hearings at which the two polluters can be expected to argue strenuously that treatment is exceedingly expensive in their own particular cases. At the end of the presentations, the agency staff will be required to make informed guesses as to which arguments advanced by X and Y are meritorious and which are merely sophistical efforts to obtain the desired status of "most expensive polluter." Costly errors will, of course, often result.

4. See Johnson, 1967, pp. 291–305.

Added to the cost of holding elaborate hearings (borne both by the staff and private polluters), the costs of delay and of administrative error, there is a final factor that cannot be quantified but may well be of the first importance. We refer to the ease with which the "least cost" allocation process can be corrupted. Precisely because each polluter's marginal treatment costs are difficult to determine, the original staff decision will be difficult to review by agency supervisors. This means, in turn, that a corrupt official can engage in a lucrative business of selling large BOD quotas to the highest bidders—who may merely be the most unscrupulous polluters and not necessarily those who can remove their BOD at the highest cost.[5] In the alternative, generous BOD allocations may be assigned to polluters who are political favorites of the agency, with the real motive for the decision easily hidden in complex data constructed to suggest that the recipients of largesse are really X's, not Y's.

Even if the formidable administrative obstacles of a least-cost plan were somehow transcended, a legal orders agency must meet the fairness problems raised by a scheme which requires X to spend only $5000 to clean up 20,000 pounds while Y spends $25,000 to clean up 100,000 pounds.[6] In principle, a legal orders regime is flexible enough to resolve this violation of the equal effort principle. To satisfy a fairness criterion demanding equal financial sacrifice, for example, the agency need only issue a second legal order, this time commanding X to pay Y $10,000.[7] This "transfer payment" policy has the further advantage of easing the administrative burden of fact finding that afflicts the legal order agency's pursuit of cost minimization. If dischargers are informed that their share of the total costs of cleanup will not depend on their own marginal treatment costs, they will no longer have an incentive to attain the previously desirable status of most costly polluter, and will not attempt to distort their true cost situation. Unfortunately, however, a transfer payment system gives polluters little incentive to seek out and report the most efficient treatment methods, since each discharger's share of *total* costs will not in general be greatly affected by the efficiency of its own operation.[8] Nevertheless, this lack of incentive to provide the agency with data on the

5. A similar set of concerns is analyzed in Rose-Ackerman, 1975. It should be emphasized that we are dealing with a theoretical problem and that there is *no* evidence of corruption in the DRBC's actual regulatory processes.
6. For elaboration of these fairness problems, see Ch. 15.
7. Similarly, under an equal percentage treatment criteria of fairness, X pays Y $20,000 (see Ch. 15, n. 4).
8. However, if a single discharger, such as Philadelphia, is responsible for a large proportion of the area's waste production, this polluter will have some incentive to be efficient.

cheapest possible means of waste removal seems a far easier problem to solve than a system that creates perverse pressures for distorted reporting.[9]

Although the transfer payment system seems to provide a promising—if not perfect—means for the legal orders agency to attain equity, minimize administrative burdens, and retain a cost-minimizing set of cutback requirements, as far as we know it has never been implemented. Instead, the traditional agency does not follow its first series of orders stipulating treatment requirements with a second series requiring monetary transfers. As a consequence, it stands helpless before the fairness problem raised by the cost-minimizing approach and exacerbates further its administrative difficulties. It would seem, then, that an agency which relies exclusively on the traditional mode of regulation through legal orders will face almost insurmountable obstacles in its pursuit of a cost-minimizing solution to its problem of control.

REGULATION THROUGH LEGAL ORDERS: SOME MODEST STEPS TOWARD COST MINIMIZATION

In spite of these difficulties, it would be wrong to assume that when an agency is constrained by the traditional model of legal orders, it is never possible to take some modest steps in the direction of least cost. The possibility for cost saving can be appreciated when Vilmington's sole polluter, Z, is recalled. In our highly simplified world, we imagined the control agency had determined that 50,000 pounds of FSUOD could be tolerated in the Vilmington region while no more than 80,000 could be tolerated around Filadelphia. Since Z's 100,000-pound daily discharge was the only emission affecting Vilmington, it made sense to require Z to reduce its waste load by only 50 percent, although both X and Y would be required to reduce their waste loads by 60 percent if the Filadelphia objective were to be achieved.

In contrast to the situation we considered in the previous section, treating Z differently from X and Y does not raise either the administrative or fairness problems which hampered "legal order" attempts to minimize costs in the Filadelphia region alone. No elaborate hearings on comparative costs of removal would be required in order to treat Filadelphians differently from Vilmingtonians. Instead, the agency may justify its action

9. Dischargers could, for example, receive subsidies for engaging in research that seeks more efficient methods of pollution control or they could be awarded prizes for spending their own funds to develop particularly innovative methods of waste removal.

by invoking the fact that by virtue of its geographic position near Vilmington—which was obvious to all—Z could discharge 50,000 pounds of
FSUOD without impairing the agency's water quality objectives for the
region. Similarly, treating Z differently does not violate the "equal effort"
principle since Z's discharge is not causing as serious harm as X's or Y's.

It appears, then, that a consideration of the inherent limitations of the
traditional form of regulation by legal orders suggests that an agency seeking to pursue a cost-minimizing strategy would, at best, adopt an approach which may usefully be called a "zoned-uniform percentage treatment" scheme. In our example, the agency would divide the river into two
zones and declare that all those discharging into the Filadelphia zone must
treat at 60 percent while those in Vilmington can make do at 50 percent.
This approach seems even more attractive when it is recognized that
zoning in our simple world may be administered with only a small risk
of corruption or political favoritism, for, under a zonal approach, in order
to favor a particular polluter with a low percentage treatment requirement,
an agency must favor *all* of the other dischargers in the zone to the same
degree. Thus, any single polluter must spend a great deal in graft or political capital to gain a benefit that may redound principally to his honest
zone-mates. This is a situation far less propitious for favoritism than one
in which an individual polluter can appropriate all benefits of agency bias,
and hence is a less serious threat to the appearance of agency integrity.

Thus, it was with high hopes that the DRBC embarked upon a "zoned-
uniform percentage treatment" approach to regulation. Unfortunately,
however, even this effort to cut costs under a legal orders regime proved
vain in a world more complex than Filadelphia and Vilmington.

THE DRBC ZONING SCHEME

According to the 1966 DECS Report, the savings to be gained from a
seemingly feasible zoning scheme were substantial indeed. DECS predicted
that dividing the 86-mile estuary into four zones, for example, would mean
that achieving Objective II would cost $275 million, only $40 million more
than the "perfect" cost-minimizing scheme and $60 million less than the
uniform percentage treatment regime.[10]

Unfortunately, however, as the DECS cost estimates began their

10. DECS, Table 16, p. 66. The zonal designations used in this book are the same
ones used in the DECS Report. The DRBC, however, designated its four estuarine
zones II–V, reserving zone I for the nonestuarine section of the Delaware above
Trenton.

dramatic inflation during 1967 and 1968,[11] it became apparent that if the zonal pattern were to generate the substantial cost savings predicted, polluters in different zones would be required to treat their wastes to very different degrees. By early 1968,[12] when the DRBC was establishing its four-zone regulatory scheme, DECS calculations suggested that polluters in zones I and III should remove 95 percent of their FSUOD while polluters in zones II and IV would be permitted to eliminate only 85 percent of their waste load.[13] While ten percentage points may not seem terribly significant, in fact it represents the difference between installing a conventional secondary treatment plant and installing an extremely advanced tertiary facility at far greater cost.[14]

This ten-percentage-point differential stands in sharp contrast to the zonal requirements imposed by the final regulations issued in June 1968. Under the DRBC plan, the greatest disparity was only 3.25 percentage points between zone II (86.0 percent) and zone III (89.25 percent), with zones I (88.5 percent) and IV (87.5 percent) coming in between.[15] In short, when the unavoidable variability in the efficiency of treatment plants is taken into account, the DRBC four-zone scheme was nothing more than a public relations triumph, masking a traditional uniform treatment regime.

WHY COST MINIMIZATION FAILED

It is far too simple to attribute the DRBC's failure to implement a meaningful zonal plan to a lack of commitment to the efficiency ideal. Instead,

11. See Ch. 6.
12. In 1966 DECS reported that substantial cost savings could be achieved with considerably smaller interzonal disparities than those recorded in the text. Thus the original DECS Report indicates that a cost-minimizing zonal approach would require polluters in zones I, II, and IV to remove 85 percent of FSUOD while in zone III polluters would be required to remove 90 percent (DECS, Table 15, p. 65).
13. Letter from Ethan Smith to Professor Rose-Ackerman, June 28, 1971. The letter endorses the cost data provided in Smith and Morris, 1969.
14. See Kneese and Bower, 1968, p. 53.
15. DRBC files. Actually, the first zonal requirements issued by the DRBC in April 1968 contemplated even smaller disparities than the final set issued in June 1968.

Zone	Percentage Removal Required—April 1968
I	88.0
II	86.0
III	87.5
IV	86.0

After the April levels were set, a number of dischargers succeeded in having their estimated raw loads increased through informal negotiation (see Ch. 17). As a result, the zonal requirements were recalculated in June 1968, leading to the figures cited in the text.

the retreat represents a dramatic example of the difficulty of taking even modest steps toward cost minimization when constrained by the traditional version of the legal orders model. To see this clearly it is only necessary to consider the basic ways in which the simple Filadelphia-Vilmington problem must be complicated in order to depict the essential aspects of the regulatory problem confronted along the real Delaware estuary.

Interzonal Impact and the Necessity of Cost Comparisons

Our earlier, simple discussion of zoning treated Filadelphia and Vilmington dischargers as if they bordered on two entirely unrelated bodies of water; in order to achieve its 50,000-pound FSUOD limitation for Vilmington we assumed it was only necessary for the agency to worry about polluter Z. If, however, Filadelphia's effluent has an impact on water quality in Vilmington (as is the case along the estuary) it no longer seems so simple to make a regulatory distinction between X and Y, on the one hand, and Z, on the other.

Imagine, for example, that the control agency's BOD-DO model reports that a pound of BOD dumped in Filadelphia has the same impact on Vilmington's DO profile as a half pound dumped in Vilmington itself. This means that, before regulation is imposed, Vilmington is subjected to a daily discharge equivalent to 200,000 pounds a day: 100,000 from X and Y, as well as 100,000 directly from Z. Given this fact, it should be clear that to achieve its 50,000-pound Vilmington limit, the control agency can manipulate its zonal scheme in a large variety of ways. At one extreme, for example, the authority could require the polluters in the Filadelphia zone (X and Y) to remove *all* their waste, while permitting the Vilmingtonian (Z) to treat at 50 percent; at the other extreme, the zonal treatment requirements can be imposed in the opposite proportions. (And, of course, on an estuary, Vilmington dischargers will also affect Filadelphia water quality, complicating the problem still further.) To determine the set of zonal percentage treatment requirements which minimize cost, then, it is necessary to solve a complex programming problem which links the cost of treatment by one zone's polluters to the cost of treatment in the other zones.[16]

16. Assuming Z's marginal treatment costs are $.10q_z$, where q = hundreds of pounds of waste removed, the problem that must be solved, when X and Y affect Vilmington but Z does not affect water quality in Filadelphia, is to minimize:

$$(\tfrac{1}{2})[.25q_x{}^2 + .05q_y{}^2 + .10q_z{}^2]$$

subject to,

Solving this problem requires a serious data gathering effort. Once again, complex hearings are necessary to determine—this time on a zonal basis—the way marginal treatment costs for Filadelphians compare with those of Vilmingtonians. As soon as this is perceived, one source of the DRBC's reluctance to impose a cost-cutting zoning scheme can be readily discerned. The DECS data were not accurate enough to use as a basis on which some zones would be required to achieve tertiary treatment while other zones would be permitted to install only secondary facilities.[17] Similarly, the DRBC was unwilling to launch a new round of hearings which would both delay ultimate compliance and yield data of doubtful accuracy.

Nevertheless, while these factors render the DRBC retreat to uniformity understandable, they also suggest ways in which such a massive retreat could, perhaps, have been avoided. *Some* progress could have been made, for example, if the agency had based its regulatory scheme on the assumption that the marginal costs of removing wastes were identical for all dischargers. While this solution will not, of course, take into account interpolluter cost differences, it will at least conscientiously attempt to exploit the potential savings generated by the fact that pollution has a differential impact on water quality objectives, depending on the location of discharge.[18] Indeed, it may be possible to go a bit farther toward a cost-

---

$$q_X + q_Y \geq 1200$$
$$(\tfrac{1}{2})(q_X + q_Y) + q_Z \geq 1500$$

This is a conventional problem in nonlinear programming for which solution methods exist. In this particular case the solution is simple. The Filadelphia constraint can be met only by X and Y and thus the least-cost solution is for X to treat 20,000 pounds and Y, 100,000 pounds. This implies that 90,000 more pounds must be removed from the river near Vilmington. Given that the marginal cost of X's removing an extra pound at Vilmington is $2(.25)(200) = \$100$, Z is the least-cost discharger, for $0 \leq q_Z \leq 1000$, since Z's marginal costs equal $100 when $q_Z = \$1000$. Therefore, Z should treat the remaining 90,000 pounds itself. However if Z's treatment costs were more expensive, say $MC_Z = \$.25q_Z$, then Z should treat 40,000 pounds plus a proportion, α, of the remaining 50,000 pounds with α chosen to minimize:

$$f(\alpha) = \tfrac{1}{2} \{.25(\alpha 500)^2 + .25[(1 - \alpha)2(500)]^2\}$$
$$f'(\alpha) = 0 = .25(\alpha 250,000) - .25(1 - \alpha)500,000$$
$$\alpha = \tfrac{2}{3}$$

Thus $q_Z = 733$ and $q_X = 367$ and the least-cost solution in this second case would require the Filadelphia region to exceed the agency's cleanliness standard.

17. See Chs. 6 and 17 for discussions of the way the cost data were collected.
18. Such a simplified approach could, however, be more costly than uniform treatment if dischargers located in highly polluted regions had very high costs while outlying polluters had low costs. Consider the case of two polluters, each located in a different zone. In the figure below, q_1 and q_2 are the loads treated by dischargers 1 and 2 respectively. The C_i curves are iso-cost curves based on *actual* treatment

minimizing solution without the need for accurate polluter-by-polluter cost data: instead of assuming identical treatment cost curves, the agency might try to specify a series of "typical" cost functions for dischargers of various sorts. For example, sufficient data exist to permit at least a very crude approximation of the cost function confronting the "typical" municipality and some tentative work has been attempted for various industrial groupings.[19] If these early studies are developed further, it may in time be feasible for the agency to use "consensus" judgments of "typical" costs in

---

costs. Their shape indicates that 2 is the high-cost discharger. The lines T_1 and T_2 are the water quality standards in zones 1 and 2 expressed in terms of load removed. Any cutback configuration that is on or above both T_1 and T_2 will fulfill the quality goals. Point A is the true cost minimizing point. If, following the suggestion in the text, the authority assumes that 1 and 2 have equivalent cost functions and simplifies its task further by imputing a marginal cost function with a constant slope, the agency's estimated iso-cost lines will be circles, such as the one labelled EC, and point B will be chosen by the authority. This solution can be more or less costly than uniform treatment. For example, if 2's raw load is relatively high, uniform treatment is represented by $\dfrac{q_2}{q_1} = \dfrac{W_2^0}{W_1^0}$, where W_1^0 and W_2^0 are the raw loads of 1 and 2 respectively, which fulfills the water quality standards at point E and is more expensive than B. On the other hand, if $\dfrac{q_2}{q_1} = \dfrac{W_2^1}{W_1^1}$ holds, where raw loads are now W_2^1 and W_1^1, uniform treatment is cheaper than the approach suggested in the text.

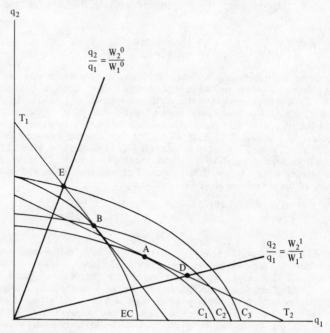

19. See Ch. 6, nn. 30, 31.

its zoning calculations.[20] Of course, even when this day arrives, each polluter will doubtless exclaim that his is not the "typical" facility. Moreover, most of these exclamations will, to some extent, be justified in fact. Nevertheless, as long as the general studies are solidly based, the agency could plausibly refuse to consider these appeals on the ground that only a rough justice is attainable[21] and that the greater accuracy (if any) of time-consuming, complex hearings is greatly outweighed by their costs.[22]

20. The 1972 Federal Water Quality Act requires the Administrator of the Environmental Protection Agency to embark upon an extremely ambitious effort to determine on an industry-wide basis the modes of treatment which represent the "best practicable control technology currently available." This in turn will require an assessment of the costs of achieving varying levels of treatment in the "typical" plants in each industry (see 33 U.S.C.A. §§11311[b][2]A; 11311[b][1][1973]). Given the present state of our knowledge, we have grave doubts as to the outcome of this statutorily mandated enterprise. For a more detailed discussion of the 1972 Act, see Ch. 20.
21. Such a firm stand can be further justified on the ground that no single polluter will bear the brunt of the inaccuracies in the cost data although low-cost dischargers within an industry are likely to benefit more than high-cost dischargers.
22. A final approach to the problem discussed in this section avoids the necessity of obtaining any individual polluter cost estimates. To understand this approach, it is necessary to recognize that the *true* cost-minimizing solution can be found by minimizing:

$$\sum_{i=1}^{n} C_i(q_i)$$

subject to,

$$\sum_{i=1}^{n} a_{ij}[W_i - q_i] \leq T_j, \qquad j = 1, ..., n$$

$$W_i \geq q_i \geq O, \; i = 1, ..., n$$

where:

C_i = aggregate total cost for dischargers in i;

T_j = maximum pounds of BOD permitted in water section j;

W_i = raw load produced by dischargers in i;

q_i = waste treated by dischargers in i;

a_{ij} = impact of a pound of waste dumped in i on water quality in j.

Under this final simplified approach, however, the agency assumes that *all* the zonal constraints must be met exactly; i.e.,

$$\sum_{i=1}^{n} a_{ij}[W_i - q_i] = T_j, \; j = 1, ..., n$$

Then we have n equations in n unknowns and, assuming the constraints $W_i \geq q_i \geq 0$

The Problem of Zonal Definition

Even if the problem of allocating clean-up responsibilities among different zones could be resolved in a plausible way, a second important factor—obscured from view in our simple treatment of Filadelphia and Vilmington—would hamper the implementation of a meaningful zoning scheme in the situation confronting the DRBC. Up to this point we have assumed that Filadelphians and Vilmingtonians were easily separated into two different geographic areas, so that the location of zonal boundaries did not raise an important issue. In fact, the reality is quite otherwise, as suggested by a map of the estuary indicating the location of 44 of the major dischargers (Figure 10).

It seems clear from an inspection of the map that neither the number nor location of the zones is unambiguously suggested by any clustering of dischargers into "natural" groups. Moreover, the failure of intuition to reveal a compelling pattern cannot be remedied by an appeal to theoretical reasoning. From an economic perspective, costs are minimized if *a single* polluter is the sole occupant of each zone, provided that each polluter's cost function is known with accuracy. But the problem involved in determining costs on an individual basis is precisely the reason zoning was adopted in the first place. Similarly, wherever the zonal lines are drawn, serious equity problems will arise. Given the fact that over a large section of the river polluters are within hailing distance of one another, there will inevitably be very strong resentment when polluter A finds he is in a zone required to treat at 95 percent, while neighbor B is only required to treat at 85 percent.

Since neither intuition nor theory could serve as a sound source for zonal definitions, the DRBC confronted a very serious problem in drawing

---

are satisfied, we can solve these equations for the q_i without any knowledge of costs. The solution is the point where T_1 and T_2 intersect in the figure in fn. 18. Treatment levels can be assigned to dischargers $k = 1, ..., m_i$ within zone i by reference to the formula:

$$q_k = W_k \, \frac{q_i}{W_i}$$

where

$$W_k = \text{raw load of } kth \text{ discharger in zone } i$$

$$q_k = \text{waste treated by } kth \text{ discharger in zone } i$$

Clearly, this simplified method will diverge substantially from least cost if treatment costs for dischargers within the same zone differ widely or if the least-cost solution requires that water quality goals be substantially exceeded in many zones.

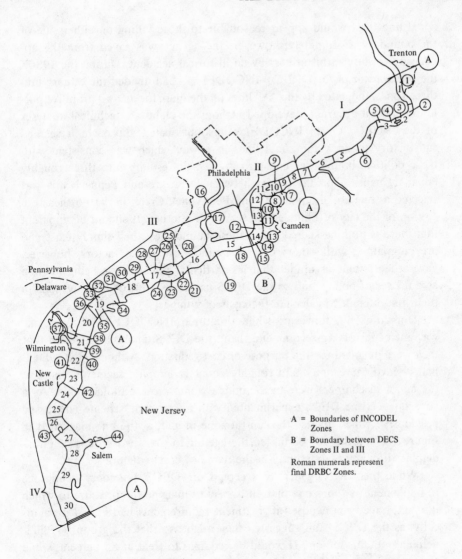

Figure 10

Map of Delaware Estuary with Locations of 44 Major Dischargers[23]
(From Glen W. Graves, Gordon B. Hatfield, and Andrew B. Whinston,
"Water Pollution Control Using By-pass Piping," Water Resources Re-
search, Vol. 5, Fig. 5, p. 27, No. 1, 1969. Copyright by American
Geophysical Union. Reprinted with permission of American Geophysical
Union, Water Resources Research, and the authors.)

zonal lines that would appear reasonable to those falling on either side of the boundary. Fortunately, however, the agency was saved from the appearance of utter arbitrariness by an historical accident. During the 1930's the predecessor of the DRBC—INCODEL[23]—had divided the estuary into three zones, indicated by the "A" lines on the map, for its own primitive pollution control program, developed without the elaborate technical analyses of the 1960's.[24] Given INCODEL's unsophisticated approach, it seemed satisfactory to draw the zonal lines in a way which was consistent with basic political boundaries and also divided the estuary into three roughly equal segments. Thus the border between Delaware and Pennsylvania was selected as one zonal boundary, and Pennypack Creek in the northeastern section of the city of Philadelphia served as another. It should be apparent that there is nothing sacred about these boundaries; they simply exist and are compatible with other sorts of boundaries. These factors, however, gave at least some assurance that no particular polluter was being favored as a matter of policy, and so the DECS used these INCODEL divisions in their first attempt to calculate the costs of zoning.

Unfortunately, however, while the three INCODEL zones had the warrant of history to recommend them, the DECS' analysis suggested that they were ill suited for the purpose of cost reduction. Although INCODEL had divided the estuary into roughly equal *geographic* segments, most of the major dischargers were in the middle zone, around Philadelphia. As a consequence, the DECS experimented with a four-zone scheme (discussed previously) which divided the central zone in half, at the line marked B in Figure 10, and thereby permitted the agency to treat two groups of Philadelphia dischargers differently in the name of cost reduction.[25]

While the DRBC generally accepted the DECS' boundary definitions to implement its four-zone plan, it is easy to imagine the pressure to which it would have been exposed if treatment requirements had varied dramatically, as the DECS staff suggested they might, so that the group of Philadelphia polluters in zone II would be required to treat at 85 percent, while the group in zone III would be told to meet a 95 percent standard. Since the zonal boundary had been arbitrarily defined, polluters in zone III would make strenuous attempts to redefine the zones so that they would be in a less stringent regulatory grouping.

Indeed, even under the DRBC's zoning program, which involved relatively small zonal differentials, it is possible to detect one instance in which

23. For a history of INCODEL's efforts see Martin, et al., 1960.
24. DECS, pp. 63, 64 (map).
25. *Loc. cit.*

zonal boundaries were altered to benefit a favored polluter. As we have seen, in drawing its boundary between zones III and IV, the DECS followed INCODEL tradition by drawing the zone line at the Pennsylvania-Delaware state line. This decision was of some consequence to a large Sunolin oil refinery, just north of the state border in zone III, since the treatment requirements were slightly more demanding in zone III than zone IV. When the final regulations were issued in June 1968, the line had been moved to place Sunolin on the other side. Since the company was the second-largest private discharger along the estuary, this transposition, although it benefited Sun by requiring it to treat to 87.5 percent instead of 89.25 percent, perceptibly increased the percentage treatment required of the dischargers in the enlarged zone IV—much to the bitterness of other downstream polluters, who expressed a great deal of discontent at being classed with Sunolin upstream.[26] If such pushing and shoving could take place when stakes were small, one can only imagine the free-for-all that would have been generated if the interzonal stakes had been considerable.

CONCLUSION

To sum up: a traditional legal orders agency that strives to be sensitive to cost-saving possibilities can accomplish part of its objective in very simple real-world cases which happen to resemble our earlier hypothetical discussion of Filadelphia and Vilmington. In the more common situation, however, where groups of polluters are not so clearly isolated from one another, fundamental forces compel the agency to undertake only the smallest steps beyond uniform percentage treatment. Aggressive cost-minimizing regulation through the traditional form of legal orders is deterred not only by formidable administrative and equity factors but also by the prospect that any polluter could well attempt to use political influence, or other means at his disposal, in an effort to have zonal boundaries drawn to his personal advantage.

26. See the "Technical Report on Getty Oil Company's Objection to the Proposed Waste Load Allocation for the Delaware Refinery, Delaware City, Delaware," Nov. 1968, which states at p. 3 that "examination of the individual load allocations for Zone 5 discloses that . . . 95 percent is granted to dischargers in the upper 10 miles (out of 30) of the zone where the oxygen deficit can be critical. It further appears that 25 percent of Zone 5's allocation has been granted a discharger physically located in Zone 4." (In this quotation, Getty is using the zonal identifications developed by the DRBC rather than those developed by DECS and used in this book [see n. 10]. Thus Gett'ys "Zone 5" is our zone IV, while its "Zone 4" is our Zone III.)

Administering a Legal Orders Regime

INTRODUCTION

Even after the DRBC had determined the basic shape of its regulatory scheme, there still remained the important task of transforming its zonal approach into individualized orders, specifying the treatment obligation of each discharger. Here, once again, the DRBC, aided by the DECS analysis, sought to transcend the traditional mode of regulatory control. Moreover, the innovative way in which the DRBC framed its legal orders was of far greater ultimate significance than any of the novel methods discussed in the preceding chapter. A consideration of the DRBC's manner of defining each polluter's clean-up obligation is not only important in itself, however, but also offers another perspective on the legal orders model, different from the one we developed in the preceding chapter. There we considered the extent to which a legal orders regime could achieve a cost-minimizing solution which was at the same time consistent with fairness. Here, we have a more humble, but equally important, objective in view. We wish to assess the extent to which the legal orders model *actually achieves* its goal of requiring dischargers within the same estuarine zone to treat their wastes to an equal degree. If the innovative DRBC system does not even possess the equity of treating like cases alike, then the argument for moving beyond the traditional legal orders model becomes compelling indeed. The inquiry seems even more relevant when it is recognized that the DRBC's regulatory mode is a prototype of the legal orders technique adopted on a nationwide basis under the 1972 amendments to the Federal Water Quality Act.[1]

BEYOND PERCENTAGE TREATMENT: THE ALLOCATION CONCEPT

The nature of the DRBC's regulatory breakthrough can be understood when the problem of industrial and population growth—previously ignored—is explicitly taken into account. Under the traditional "equal percentage treatment" approach, the legal order issued by the agency simply requires a polluter to remove a specified percentage of its raw waste load. Thus, if the required percentage removal were 85 percent, a growing firm whose waste load increased from 1,000 to 10,000 pounds per day of BOD would be permitted to increase its *legal* discharge from 150 to 1500 pounds. This means that if the valley is experiencing substantial growth, a "uniform percentage treatment" scheme—even assuming perfect compliance—contemplates a constant deterioration of water quality over time. Of course, the control agency is not powerless to offset the traditional scheme's tendency to degradation by acting at appropriate intervals to raise the percentage treatment required of dischargers in its jurisdiction. Nevertheless, the fact remains that a percentage treatment approach *places the burden of affirmative action* on the control agency on pain of countenancing degradation over time.

In contrast, the regulatory scheme selected by the DRBC allocated the burden of affirmative action in the opposite direction: once the agency's quality objectives had been achieved, they would be maintained over time (assuming perfect compliance) unless the agency made an affirmative decision to permit further deterioration. To achieve this objective, instead of ordering a hypothetical X, now discharging 100,000 pounds of BOD, to reduce its waste load by 85 percent, the DRBC framed its order to forbid X to discharge more than a *set amount* (15,000 pounds per day) into the river. In this way, if X grew so that its raw waste load equalled one million

1. The relevance of this and other aspects of the Delaware experience to prevailing policy under the 1972 Act will be discussed at greater length in Ch. 20.

pounds, it would still be confronted with the fact that, under the regulations, it was permitted only a 15,000-pound BOD allocation. Thus, instead of the river's bearing a substantial share of the costs of growth, all of these costs would be borne by the polluter in question—unless, of course, the agency chose to raise X's allocation and not to reduce correspondingly the poundage allocations of other dischargers.

Before examining the difficulties of the poundage allocation concept, it should be emphasized that its goal of shifting the burden of affirmative action seems fundamentally sound. Given the limited time of high level decision makers, it is unrealistic to expect that they will continually, or even regularly, monitor the goals of the Delaware program. This unhappy reality suggests that the quality goals that have been established should be respected until the agency leadership, responding either to the proddings of its staff or to external forces, opens the program to searching reassessment. Moreover, imposing the costs of growth on polluters rather than other river users will probably increase the likelihood of such reconsideration. The costs of growth visited on individual polluters by the poundage allocation scheme often will be substantial, prodding those who feel the shoe pinch to induce the agency to ask whether the added costs are worth the benefits; in contrast, the slow and constant degradation permitted by the percentage treatment regime will generally result in only a vague and relatively small sense of loss to a large group of potential river users. The large costs of organizing these users, as well as the relatively small benefit each will obtain from a stricter program, will mean that their agitation for a reappraisal of program policies will be rather infrequent.[2]

Consequently, our ensuing discussion should not be interpreted as an attack on the wisdom of shifting the burden of affirmative action in the way achieved by the poundage allocation plan. Instead, our inspection of the frailties of the DRBC system will prepare the way for consideration of whether the same objective might be accomplished more effectively by a different system, in which elements of the market model of regulation are introduced.

THE FAIRNESS OF THE ALLOCATION SCHEME: THE PROBLEM OF GROWTH

At the time a poundage allocation program is instituted, it can be designed so that its impact on individual dischargers does not differ from that of the

2. This difficulty is most cogently analyzed in Olsen, 1965.

traditional uniform percentage treatment alternative. If, for example, the control authority wishes to impose an 80,000 limit on Filadelphia's wasteload, it can either grant wasteload allocations of 40,000 pounds each to polluters X and Y or order both to remove 60 percent of their waste and achieve the Filadelphia objective consistently with the "equal effort" principle requiring dischargers making equal contributions to the pollution problem to cut back their waste loads equally. Over time, however, the allocation plan can be expected to violate more and more seriously this "equal effort" standard. Since dischargers will grow at disparate rates, an allocation scheme will generate a situation in which X will be required to treat a higher percentage of its waste than Y simply because X was a less significant pollution source at the time the allocation system was instituted—a fact that will seem increasingly insignificant with the years. Thus, a scheme that originally had the virtue of satisfying the equal effort criterion will increasingly be transformed into one in which dynamic cities and firms subsidize their stagnating fellows. While the importance of respecting the equal effort principle may itself be doubted,[3] the equity of an allocation plan that places a special burden on the young and vibrant is even less apparent. Surely there are far more efficient ways to aid distressed towns and industries than by this haphazard mechanism.[4] Thus, while the poundage allocation plan serves the important function of properly allocating the burden of affirmative agency action in the face of waste load growth, it does so in a way many will consider intrinsically unfair. Both X and Y may at present be discharging 100,000 pounds in Filadelphia, but X will be required to eliminate 80,000 pounds and Y, 40,000 pounds, simply because *ten years earlier* Y had already been polluting the stream as intensively as it does today, while X has only recently become a big polluter.

To cushion the inequities caused by growth, the agency can take recourse to ameliorative measures to lighten the cost burden on those most injured by their fixed allocations. Indeed, in anticipation of this problem, the DRBC set aside approximately 10 percent of each zone's permissible waste load in an "unallocated reserve" for the purpose of awarding addi-

3. See Ch. 15, n. 3.
4. It is possible that the relatively harsh impact of the poundage plan on growing polluters can to some extent be justified on efficiency grounds. Since growing polluters can be expected to take new technologies more fully into account in their capital planning, they will, *ceteris paribus,* treat their waste more cheaply than dischargers using older plant and control technologies. This point will not be developed, however, both because our present discussion is addressed only to the fairness problem and because we shall demonstrate subsequently that there are far more effective ways of approximating the cost-minimizing solution than one that relies so heavily on a crude distinction between stagnating and growing polluters (see Ch. 18).

tional quotas either to new towns and industries locating along the estuary or to present polluters whose waste loads were growing the fastest.[5] At the time of our study, however, it was too soon to assess the way this program would be administered, though—even at best—it could be used to cure only the most egregious departures from the "equal effort" principle.

FAIRNESS IN ADMINISTRATION: THE RAW WASTE LOAD CONCEPT

Even putting aside the growth problem, an agency adopting the DRBC's regulatory scheme confronts formidable administrative difficulties in doling out quotas fairly. A major problem involves the seemingly innocuous task of determining each polluter's raw waste load. If matters were as simple as they were in the case of Filadelphia, measuring each polluter's waste load would be relatively easy. In that hypothetical world, we assumed that X and Y—before the present regulatory effort—did not treat their waste *at all,* each discharging raw sewage with a BOD load of 100,000 pounds each day. Given this fact, it is a simple matter for the agency to conclude that both X and Y should be awarded allocations of 40,000 pounds if no more than 80,000 pounds of BOD are to be introduced into the Filadelphia region. In the real world, however, almost all of the estuary's hundred-odd dischargers had already subjected waste streams to one kind of treatment or another. Moreover, to ignore this and proceed as if current discharges measured *raw* loads would obviously result in fundamental unfairness. Whatever else may be said about equity, it seems clear that if X is currently eliminating 50 percent of his waste and Y is discharging raw sewage, the simple fact that each is *at present* discharging 100,000 pounds cannot provide a satisfactory basis for assigning each a 40,000-pound allocation. Instead, in order to avoid penalizing X for his earlier pollution control investments, he must be treated *as if he were dumping 200,000 pounds* of raw sewage into the stream. Thus X should be credited with a "raw waste load" of 200,000 pounds and so would obtain a poundage allocation twice the size of Y's, whose "raw waste load" was only 100,000 pounds. The use of the raw waste load concept, then, seems to permit the agency to remain faithful to the equal effort principle in a world in which polluters have made unequal clean-up efforts before the regulatory scheme

5. In addition, the DECS claimed to be using estimates of 1975–1980 raw loads to calculate polluter-by-polluter allocations. As Ch. 6 suggests, however, these growth projections were unreliable.

was institutionalized. It permits the agency to avoid penalizing the previously conscientious by allocating relative shares of the river's scarce BOD capacity on a principle that treats the conscientious as if they had done no more than the polluter who had done nothing to limit his discharge.

Problems in Administering the "Raw Waste Load" Concept: Theory

While the equity of using raw waste load as the basis for allocating quotas is clear in principle, its application in concrete cases allows serious opportunities for arbitrariness and abuse. Consider, for example, a problem raised by the typical oil refinery. After the crude oil is refined, waste products flow through an "oil skimmer" which removes crude oil components remaining in the waste stream that would otherwise considerably inflate the BOD the refinery discharges. Should the agency consider the skimmer a treatment device, inflating the refinery's "raw waste load" substantially and thereby increasing its poundage allocation?

The answer would seem to depend on the agency's assessment of might-have-beens. If the company installed the skimmers *because it was genuinely concerned with pollution control,* it would be altogether appropriate to measure the refinery's raw waste load by the BOD content in the waste stream *before* the skimmers skimmed. On the other hand, if skimming is a profitable investment, since it increases the quantity and hence the value of refined oil more than the cost of skimming, then it would be no more appropriate to consider the skimmer a pollution control device than any other investment intended to refine oil efficiently. Thus the question the agency must consider is: Would a profit-maximizing refinery have installed the skimmers even if it were not trying to clean up? Indeed, the correct question is even more difficult than this. It should be obvious that skimmers add to output to some degree; hence, the agency should attempt to estimate the *extent* to which skimming is profitable on ordinary business criteria and the extent to which it can be justified only on pollution control grounds, and inflate the refinery's "raw waste load" to reflect only the latter factor.

But even a close approximation of this process is an almost impossible task for administrators. Not only can refineries be counted on to argue that skimmers are indeed primarily treatment facilities, they may be expected to generate plausible figures "proving" that they would never have installed skimmers but for the firm's pollution control objective, since cost accounting is not a science but an art. Thus, the bemused fact finder will be required to guess the extent to which the costs and benefits the industry imputes to skimming accurately reflect industrial realities.[6] To make matters worse, the problem posed by skimmers is pervasive. Almost every production process can be designed in many ways, some more pollution-intensive than others. When a particular discharger argues that a particular process has been selected largely to lower pollution loads, the agency must either take evidence on might-have-beens or invoke rules of thumb which may be arbitrary indeed.[7]

Problems in Administering the "Raw Waste Load" Concept: The DRBC Procedures

Having sketched the awesome complexity of an accurate determination of "raw waste loads" required by equity, we may now profitably consider the way the DRBC dealt with this matter in practice. Since the DRBC's raw waste load calculations relied heavily on the DECS study, it is necessary to look back to 1964, when the federal project conducted its systematic monitoring of the estuary's major polluters.[8] In conducting this phase of its

6. The DRBC, following the estimates made by the DECS, assumed that skimmers were treatment devices and that they removed 35 percent of the refinery's FSUOD (Porges, transcript of the Scott Paper Co. hearings, Jan. 20, 1969, p. 180; letter from N.C. Vasuki, Director, Water Pollution Control Division, Water and Air Resources Commission, State of Delaware, to Ralph Porges, Sept. 20, 1967, p. 3; and DECS cost data). This level of treatment efficiency is the upper limit given in the U.S. Department of the Interior's *Cost of Clean Water,* which states that the efficiency of A.P. Separators (skimmers) ranges from 5 to 35 percent (Vol. III, Industrial Waste Profiles, Number 5—Petroleum Refining, Table 10).

7. Getty Oil, for example, initially provided the DRBC with no independent cost estimates and hence, like the other refiners along the estuary which provided no data, was credited with removing 35 percent of its raw load by skimming. At a later date Getty submitted data to support the claim that because of the efficiency of in-plant methods of waste removal, its level of treatment was much higher (letter to E.V. Geismar, Project Director, DECS, from R.W. Ladd, Senior Engineer, Getty Oil Company, March 28, 1967, and supporting documents on file at the Biddle Law Library, University of Pennsylvania). Many of these documents are also included in the record of Getty's hearing before the DRBC, Dec. 13, 1968. As a result, Getty was assigned a raw waste load based on a finding that 92 percent of its raw waste load had been removed (letter from E.V. Geismar to Richard W. Ladd, Sept. 27, 1967). In a public hearing before the DRBC on Dec. 13, 1968, Getty was able to increase its raw waste load estimate further, thereby obtaining an allocation equal to its current discharge (see n. 11).

8. Some of the procedures used by the DECS to estimate costs are reported by E.V. Geismar, Project Director of DECS, at public hearings held in late 1968 and early 1969 to consider the requests of dischargers for increased waste load allocations (see transcripts of hearings before the DRBC Special Hearing Board).

survey, the DECS attempted to obtain information from dischargers concerning both the present degree of treatment and the quantity of BOD being discharged. While the DECS did monitor the BOD discharged from the end of each polluter's sewer pipe, the discharger's claims as to its degree of treatment were accepted by the DECS, so long as the estimates conformed roughly to those of the staff's engineers. Thus, the question of which industrial processes should count as "treatment" processes was left to the ad hoc joint determination by DECS staffers and plant engineers. Moreover, the DECS staffers we spoke with could recall no occasion on which an industry estimate was seriously challenged.[9]

This ready acceptance of polluter estimates is easy to explain once it is recognized that throughout the study the staff had very considerable difficulty in obtaining any information at all from polluters. Indeed, lacking subpoena power, the staff was frequently required to plead with polluters for their voluntary cooperation, sometimes to no avail. Consequently, the staff was understandably reluctant to undermine cooperation from the more responsive polluters by impugning the data they did provide. Moreover, at the time the figures on raw waste loads were provided, their importance for subsequent regulation was not clearly perceived either by the DECS staffers or the polluters themselves; and so the issue seemed of minor significance when contrasted to the larger problems of estimating the costs and benefits of competing clean-up strategies. Thus, the "raw load" data submitted by DECS to DRBC were a combination of casual estimates provided by polluters and—when even this was absent—estimates generated by the DECS staff itself.[10]

Despite the obvious frailties of DECS raw waste load reports, the DRBC, eager to press forward with its regulatory scheme, refrained from conducting a series of lengthy hearings in which raw waste loads would be redetermined in a careful manner consistently with preannounced criteria. Instead, in April 1968, polluters were assigned tentative allocations on the basis of the DECS raw waste load estimates and were then given an opportunity to attempt to persuade the DRBC staff that the DECS estimates were incorrect in their particular cases. Moreover, if a polluter failed in this effort he was given the right to demand a hearing before a special board composed of a ranking member of the DRBC engineering staff, a representative of the state bureau in whose jurisdiction the polluter was located,

9. DECS, pp. 30, 31, 62. Interviews with Matthew Sobel and other members of the DECS staff.
10. Interview with Matthew Sobel.

and Mr. Albert H. Garretson, a law professor from New York University, who chaired all the hearings that were actually held.[11]

It should be apparent that this set of procedures was poorly adapted to assuring equality of treatment for all dischargers. If a polluter obtained an

11. Sixteen appeals from the April 1968 allocations were made and settled in private negotiations. Access to these documents was denied to us by the DRBC. After a revised set of allocations was issued in June 1968, 14 dischargers obtained public hearings, which were held in Dec. 1968 and Jan. and Feb. 1969. The identity of the dischargers, the hearing dates, and the resulting changes in allocations are listed below.

		Allocation	
Discharger	Date	*July 1968*	*Dec. 1969*
Industries			
Atlas Chemical	12/13/68	4,310	4,640
FMC	1/10/69	520	670
Getty Oil	12/13/68	2,500	3,750
Harshaw Chemical	12/11/68	28	260
National Sugar	2/17/69	490	1,800
Paterson Parchment	2/17/69	290	440
Publicker	2/17/69	180	180
Scott Paper	1/20/69	3,750	3,750
Tenneco Plastics	12/11/68	310	590
Texaco	12/10/68	650	692
U.S. Steel	1/10/69	2,110	2,500
Municipalities			
Central Delaware	12/16/68	2,640	2,640
Darby Creek	12/17/68	4,000	4,000
Philadelphia (3 plants)	12/16/68	131,500	131,500

Thus appeals were successful in raising the allocations of all of the firms except Publicker and Scott. None of the municipalities, however, obtained increased allocations.

A summary list of the arguments put forward by the various dischargers who requested load increases is given below.

1. Growth since 1964 – Tenneco, Atlas; future growth predicted: Phila., Darby, Central Delaware.

2. Operating in 1964 at fraction of capacity – FMC.

3. Waste stream missed – Texaco, FMC.

4. In-plant devices not counted as waste removal techniques by DRBC – Scott, Publicker.

5. Own study reveals larger raw load – Atlas, Harshaw, Paterson.

6. Little impact of waste on river – Getty.

7. Inconsistent standard used for similar firms – Getty, Scott.

8. Allocation should be based on BOD_5, which implies a higher FSUOD allocation if after-treatment ratio is used – Texaco.

9. Own study in progress; requests delay – U.S. Steel.

10. Critical of model – Philadelphia, Central Delaware.

11. Worried about ability to comply with allocation given variability in load – Atlas, U.S. Steel, Getty, FMC.

overly generous waste load calculation from the DECS staff, no one would be the wiser, since no mechanism was provided to review the decision in the absence of a complaint by *the polluter in question*. Similarly, when a polluter did seek to persuade the DRBC staff of the impropriety of the *DECS* raw waste load calculation, the *DRBC* staff was obliged to decide the question without a clear sense of the way in which *DECS* staffers resolved similar issues in their earlier canvass. Since most of the important issues were resolved either at DECS or DRBC staff levels, without the publicity of open hearings, it seems that once again the coherence of the Delaware program suffered as a result of the bifurcation of functions wrought by "cooperative federalism."[12]

TESTING THE FAIRNESS OF THE ALLOCATIONS

"Raw Waste Load" and the Petroleum Industry

Unfortunately, we have been unable to analyze exhaustively the accuracy of raw waste load determinations generated by the rather disorganized fact-finding procedures we have described. An attempt at definitive analysis was hampered gravely both by the refusal by the DRBC staff to provide the relevant files and by the fact that many of the estuary's firms employ such widely different industrial processes that it is impossible without the most refined consideration of engineering and cost factors to determine whether raw waste loads were defined by the agency sensitively and consistently.

Nevertheless, a fortuitous circumstance has permitted us some insight into this issue. The estuary, it happens, is the second largest center for oil refining in the country, with seven major refineries generating roughly similar end products. Since the capacity of each of the refineries, as well as their BOD allocations, is a matter of public record, and the respective refinery personnel were quite cooperative with our interviewers, it seems profitable to report in some detail the degree to which the DRBC's alloca-

12. Consider, for example, the way the DECS resolved the skimmer question for the oil industry and compare it to the way the DRBC dealt with a seemingly analogous problem in the paper manufacturing process. While the DRBC followed the DECS approach and assumed that skimmers "treat" 35 percent of an oil refinery's waste load, it refused to give comparable credit to Scott Paper's seemingly similar save-all apparatus. While there may be basic differences between skimmers and save-alls they are not apparent from a reading of the testimony at the Scott hearings on file at the DRBC. The only major difference noted by DRBC Water Quality Chief Ralph Porges was that skimmers removed floatable oils while save-alls removed settled material. Transcript of Scott Paper Co. hearing before DRBC Special Hearing Board, Jan. 20, 1969, p. 180.

tions to the refineries can be understood to be grounded in consistent policies.

If each of the seven refineries were manufacturing precisely the same end product, our test of the DRBC's consistency in applying the raw waste load concept would be very simple. Since the capacity of each of the refineries is well known, each allocation should bear a proportional relationship to the number of barrels of crude oil each refinery could process daily. It is true, of course, that in refining its oil, one refinery may have selected production processes more pollution-intensive than others; but this does not mean that such a refinery should be treated more leniently. Indeed, it is precisely the purpose of the raw waste load concept to deprive the "dirtier"

Table 8.[13]   Oil Refinery Attributes and DRBC Allocations

(1) Refinery	(2) Capacity (thousands of barrels/ day of crude oil)	(3) Heavy Oil Production	(4) Did Own Study of Raw Load	(5) DRBC Allocation (pounds of BOD/day)
Atlantic	160	Yes[1]	No	6,560
Sun	158	Yes	Yes	14,400
Mobil	90	Yes	No	4,250
Texaco	85	No	No[2]	692
Gulf	158	No	No	2,928
British Petroleum	100	No	Yes[3]	2,650
Getty	140	No	Yes	3,750

1. Since the assignment of DRBC allocations, Atlantic announced (*Wall Street Journal*, May 25, 1971) that it was discontinuing heavy oil production in Philadelphia.

2. Texaco did attempt a very minor independent study to measure the ratio between FSUOD and BOD_5 in raw load and treated waste and argued that their allocation should be based on BOD_5. This argument was rejected by the DRBC but evidence that waste from a tank farm had been omitted from the original calculations was used to increase their allocation slightly, from 650 pounds/day to 692 pounds. (Texaco Hearings, Dec. 10, 1968.) For a discussion of the distinction between FSUOD and BOD_5, see pp. 69, 70.

3. A telephone interview with a company pollution control specialist revealed that BP's initial allocation was 650 pounds but that after the company hired Roy Weston Associates to perform a survey of the plant's raw load, their allocation was raised to 2,650 pounds.

13. Columns (2) and (3) of Table 8 are from Moody's Industrials; column (4) was derived from interviews with company officials, and column (5) is from DRBC data.

refinery of the advantage it might have if poundage allocations were based simply on actual discharges.

Unfortunately, reality provided us with a more difficult problem in judging the extent to which the agency allocated waste load quotas in an equitable fashion, for the Delaware refineries do not generate precisely the same product mix. Three of the refineries not only produce regular fuel oils but also refine heavy oils (lubricants, waxes, and coke) which are more BOD-intensive. Thus, we should expect that these three refineries would be awarded substantially greater raw waste loads than the four "light fuel" facilities. This hypothesis can be verified in general terms by a simple inspection of Table 8.

Despite the rough correlation between product mix and allocation, substantial anomalies remain. Why does Sun have a raw load and hence an allocation more than twice Atlantic's? Why is BP's allocation over three and one-half times Texaco's? Part of the explanation can be found in column 4. Both BP and Sun complained that the DECS' estimates of raw load were too low and both hired their own consultants to calculate new estimates, which were adopted by the DRBC staff without going to a formal hearing. Similarly, Getty, whose refinery is the newest along the estuary, complained bitterly that it was being penalized because its more modern plant was less pollution-intensive than its competitors'.[14] After initiating its own study and pressing forward with a hearing, the staff "compromised" the dispute by giving Getty a raw waste load suggested in reports prepared by the firm's consultants. These facts suggest that, given the elusiveness of the raw waste load concept when applied on a case-by-case basis, the agency tended to be greatly influenced by a polluter who took the trouble to marshall his facts in an impressive way to demonstrate that his plant had taken all sorts of subtle steps to control BOD before it entered the treatment plant. To check this hypothesis in a somewhat rigorous way, we used linear regression techniques on the primitive data reproduced in the preceding table, and found that we could explain 80 percent of the variance between refinery allocations on the basis of two simple factors. First, it was estimated that the presence of a facility for producing heavy oils would increase a firm's allocation by 45 pounds for every 1,000 barrels of refinery capacity. Second, and more remarkable, if a firm performed its own waste load study its allocation increased by 26 pounds for every 1,000 barrels.[15]

14. See n. 7.

15. In the statistical estimate presented below, the dependent variable, $\frac{DRBC}{BBL}$, is a firm's DRBC waste load allocation in pounds/day divided by the capacity of the plant

Although these findings are highly suggestive, we do not mean to place undue weight on them. Even before we introduced our regression results, we had already pointed to important institutional factors which made it very likely that a poundage allocation scheme would be administered inequitably, even under the best of procedures, and would be especially defective under the fact-finding processes developed by the DECS-DRBC. Our statistical survey is intended simply to suggest that there is strong reason to believe that our fears have been realized.

Moreover, the statistical results also serve to highlight another inequitable characteristic of the poundage allocation scheme, which we have previously considered only abstractly. In our earlier discussion we emphasized the extent to which the allocation mechanism virtually guaranteed an inequitable result over time as polluters grew at greatly varying rates. The history of the oil industry in the Delaware Valley bears this out even in the short period between 1968, the year the allocations were assigned, and the present (1973). During that time, one of the three refineries, which (as the linear regression suggests) had been credited with a large raw waste load because of its heavy oil production, announced that its heavy oil facilities would be completely eliminated (Atlantic).[16] Furthermore, a second refinery (Sun) closed old and inefficient segments of its facility shortly after determining the size of its raw load.[17] In response to these announcements, the DRBC has done nothing to reduce the allocation of

---

in thousands of barrels of crude oil per day (BBL). Both of the independent variables are zero–one dummies; the t values are given in parentheses below the coefficients.

$$\frac{DRBC}{BBL} = 6.87 + 45.10\,LUB + 25.24\,OWN$$
$$(5.14)* \qquad (2.99)*$$

$$\overline{R}^2 = .80 \qquad F = 15.57$$

degrees of freedom $= 4$

$* =$ significant at a 95 percent level of confidence

$LUB = 1$ if heavy oils are produced

$\quad\quad\ = 0$ if not

$OWN = 1$ if firm did own waste load study

$\quad\quad\quad = 0$ otherwise

The results should be interpreted with care since the number of observations is small and both independent variables are dummies. Nevertheless, the $\overline{R}^2$ of .80 and the high significance levels (over 95 percent confidence) of both coefficients suggests that analysis has isolated two important determinants of the DRBC's waste load allocations.

16. *The Wall Street Journal,* May 25, 1971, p. 9, col. 3.
17. Telephone interview with Sunolin official, spring, 1971.

Atlantic (6560 pounds) and Sun (14,400 pounds). Nevertheless unless such steps are taken the major asset of the DRBC's allocation plan—its supposed conformity with the "equal effort" equity criterion—seems increasingly insubstantial.[18]

CONTROLLING THE MUNICIPALITIES

The DRBC's problem in defining a municipality's raw waste load was far less difficult than the one raised in the industrial context. Since the city simply treats the wastes produced by its residents, the difficult problems raised in distinguishing "production processes" from "treatment processes" do not arise; instead, its "raw waste load" may simply be measured by sampling the steady flow of human excrement and commercial and industrial discharge[19] that arrives at the municipal treatment facility.

While calculating raw waste load thus seems simple, the DRBC encountered problems of a different kind in regulating the estuary's towns and cities. When Trenton, the second largest city along the estuary, received its BOD allocation from the DRBC in 1968, its officials gave the matter no thought whatever. After the time had expired for appealing the allocation to the special DRBC hearing panel, it came to the Trentonians' attention that as a result of a mistaken set of DECS measurements, which greatly underestimated the city's raw waste load, Trenton's allocation required the city to treat in excess of 95 percent of its waste load, in contrast to the 87 percent generally required of polluters in Trenton's zone. Instead of requesting a belated hearing, at which the mistaken measurements could have been rectified, city officials pursued a more informal approach. Arguing that their relatively modern "secondary treatment" facility was already eliminating about 85 percent of the town's raw waste load, the city fathers proposed that the DRBC simply forget the entire business about the quota

18. We do not mean to suggest that if the DRBC had held supplementary hearings it would *necessarily* have been obliged to reduce the allocations awarded the two refineries. It was at least open to the firms to argue that their decision to close down facilities was motivated entirely by pollution control considerations, and that hence their shutdowns should be deemed a way of *treating* their enormous "raw waste load," and should not therefore be considered a reason for reducing the "raw waste load" with which they had been previously credited. Such an argument, of course, raises all the administrative problems considered previously (see 250–253). Moreover, if the dischargers' arguments were ultimately vindicated, the result would highlight the unfairness of determining allocations on the basis of a polluter's waste load at a single point in time.
19. Major American cities, like Philadelphia, typically treat a substantial part of the commercial-industrial waste generated within their borders (see DECS, pp. 20, 29).

and deem Trenton to be in virtual compliance. According to Trenton officials,[20] the DRBC informally agreed to this approach, and has not required the city to take any steps to improve treatment, despite the fact that Trenton may be currently discharging more than twice its daily BOD quota of 2,350 pounds.[21]

A similar—if not so egregious—story can be told of Philadelphia, by far the largest discharger in the DRBC's jurisdiction. After losing his battle for relatively unambitious quality objectives for the estuary, Philadelphia's Water Department head, Samuel Baxter, refused to submit a compliance program to the DRBC, and demanded a hearing on the city's allocation, during which the DECS' scientific model and accompanying analyses were subjected to renewed attack.[22] The DRBC stood firm and, indeed, began to move to the offensive, encouraging the Pennsylvania Sanitary Water Board to impose severe sanctions on Philadelphia's builders during 1969 and 1970 by refusing intermittently to issue sewer permits authorizing them to hook up with the city system. Stung by the board's sewer freeze, which obliged them to keep their new structures unoccupied, the builders urged Baxter to reach a compromise with the DRBC. By late 1970, Baxter submitted a compliance schedule to the agency under which the city promised to improve its three large treatment facilities by 1976. A number of city officials have reported to us, however, that the city will substantially exceed its allocation even when the plants are improved. Thus, in the Philadelphia case, the agency's poundage allocation seems the beginning, not the end, of a process by which the extent of the city's clean-up obligation will be defined.[23]

As for the other two major cities along the estuary, the DRBC had more success in inducing the city fathers to accept their quotas, at least in principle. Unfortunately, the city of Camden then proceeded to undertake a course of action (described in Chapter 19) which made compliance within the 1970's problematic. Thus it is only the city of Wilmington that promises to meet its allocation in a timely fashion; and the prompt and effective action forthcoming from this quarter is explained principally by the

20. The discussion in the text is based on interviews with Trenton officials conducted in the summer of 1970.
21. When we inquired of DRBC officials concerning Trenton, the essence of the story told by the city's officials was confirmed, although we were assured that, in some unspecified way, the problem would be resolved.
22. Hearings before DRBC Hearing Board, December 16, 1968.
23. This account is based on interviews with DRBC and state and city officials during 1970 and 1971. Once again, DRBC officials do not expressly deny the fact that the city may still not be in compliance after their construction program has been completed, promising to take further steps in 1976 if this is required.

fact that this city had, as early as 1964, been planning the construction of a modern treatment facility which—*mirabile dictu*—promised to meet the DRBC requirements imposed four years later.[24]

CONCLUSIONS

Despite the desire of the DRBC staff and political leadership to move far beyond traditional approaches, their unwillingness to abandon the traditional regulatory premises condemned the agency's innovations largely to futility. The much-heralded zoning approach so overtaxed the capacities of the legal orders model that the substance of zoning was almost completely compromised. Similarly, while the poundage allocation system contained real advantages over its uniform percentage treatment rival, it nevertheless proved impossible for the agency to administer in an equitable manner. Instead, after one takes into account the impact of widely differing growth rates, the imprecision of the raw waste load concept and the pushings and shovings by various municipalities, it would be surprising if the resulting set of allocations conformed over time even remotely to the "equal effort" principle of fairness. Constrained by the traditional version of the legal order regime, even an innovative agency like the DRBC could not devise a regulatory system that was either efficient or fair. The agency's experience suggests that a desire to innovate within the conventional regulatory structure is not enough; what is required is reconsideration of the basic premises of an effort to regulate conduct primarily through the issuance of legal orders.

24. Interviews with DRBC and Wilmington officials.

The Market Model:
Its Strengths
and Weaknesses

INTRODUCTION

When compared to the legal orders regime, a market approach seems, at
first glance, to provide a much simpler mechanism for attaining a cost-
minimizing cutback configuration. Indeed, two alternative market schemes
present themselves as promising regulatory tools. Under the first approach,
an "effluent charge" is levied on Filadelphia's polluters[1] at a rate of P
cents a day for each pound of FSUOD discharged, with P set so as to
induce X and Y to diminish their total discharge from 200,000 to 80,000
pounds each day. Thus, if a charge of 50 cents per pound per day is imposed, polluter X will find that its marginal treatment costs exceed the
charge after 20,000 pounds of BOD are removed and so will choose to
pay the charge for 80,000 pounds rather than embark upon more ambitious
treatment efforts. In contrast, Y will find that it can eliminate its entire
discharge at a marginal cost no greater than 50 cents a pound and will

1. See Ch. 15, n. 6, for references to the standard discussions of effluent charges and
some critiques.

do so rather than pay the effluent tax. In short, the effluent charge seems to provide a way for the authority to fulfill its water quality objective in the Filadelphia region at minimum total cost without the need for cumbersome individualized fact-finding proceedings. Furthermore, an effluent charge regime will generate more rapid compliance than the legal orders approach. Under the traditional mode of regulation, each polluter has a substantial incentive to delay action up to the point at which the agency is willing to back up its legal commands with credible sanctions. In contrast, an effluent charge imposes constant cost pressure on polluters to limit their discharge.

As we shall show, the analysis of an effluent charge is a good deal more complex in the real world of the Delaware Valley than is suggested in our simplified Filadelphia example. Indeed, in certain situations a market mode of control may not even be as efficient as the traditional "uniform percentage treatment" scheme considered previously. Our principal objective in this chapter, however, is not merely to enumerate some of the most important practical difficulties involved in implementing a charge scheme so as to achieve substantial cost savings, but to compare the effluent tax with an alternative market approach. Under this second strategy, the authority does not attempt to tax polluters for their discharges at a predetermined rate; instead, after setting a limit on the allowable discharge in the region, the authority auctions off pollution rights to polluters willing to bid the highest for them.[2] It should be apparent that in the simple Filadelphia problem the outcome prevailing under the "rights" system can be made identical to the one prevailing under the "charge" system: if the authority simply issues 80,000 rights, X will outbid Y for all of them just as X will find it more profitable to pay the 50-cent tax on 80,000 pounds of his waste than to engage in costlier treatment efforts. More generally, a rights market will generate an equilibrium price at the point where the capitalized value of the marginal cost of treating an extra pound of waste just equals the price of the right. This means that each polluter's marginal cost of treatment will equal that experienced by every other Filadelphia discharger, thereby assuring that the authority's water quality objective will be satisfied at minimum total cost.

While a rights system and a charge system thus generate identical cutback patterns in our simple world, we shall argue that a series of weighty practical considerations indicate that a rights scheme will generally produce results significantly superior to those generated by the charge approach.

2. See Ch. 15, n. 6, for references to earlier discussions of this idea.

EFFLUENT CHARGES VERSUS POLLUTION RIGHTS IN A SIMPLE WORLD

The Costs of Making a Mistake

Even when we probe the simple world of Filadelphia, some of the most important practical advantages of the pollution rights system over the charging approach become apparent. In discussing the charge scheme, we have assumed that the pollution control agency could readily establish a fee schedule which would induce Filadelphia's polluters to reduce their aggregate waste load just enough to meet its 80,000-pound limitation. In reality, however, the task of setting P at the "right" level is a difficult one. And if the charge is set at the wrong level, the agency will find that the costs of making a mistake can be substantial.

To compare the costs of error under the rights and charge systems, it is necessary to define our regulatory problem with more sophistication. Thus far we have failed to investigate the way our hypothetical agency went about selecting its 80,000-pound goal for Filadelphia. To determine the loss incurred when the agency sets the wrong charge, however, it is necessary to specify the way marginal costs and marginal benefits vary as water quality changes. To begin with a simple case, portrayed in Figure 11, we assume the agency values each extra pound of waste treated less than the previous one; thus the marginal benefit (MB) curve in Figure 11 is continuously declining. In contrast, the region's polluters find it more and more expensive to reach higher levels of treatment, and so their marginal cost (MC) curve increases continuously.[3]

Having defined our terms, we are able to portray graphically the consequences of erroneous information. Let us assume that the agency does not know the polluters' actual treatment costs (MC_1) but must rely on its own (erroneous) estimates (MC_0). Thus, instead of setting a charge of 50 cents, where $MC_1 = MB$, it imposes a fee of 25 cents, where $MC_0 = MB$.[4] As a result of the underestimation of costs, only q_1 of the FSUOD load in the Filadelphia region will be treated, not the q_0 the agency expected. Since costs have been underestimated, however, the optimal amount of pollution control is no longer q_0 but q_2, the point at which the true MC_1

3. A somewhat fuller discussion is presented in Kneese and Bower, pp. 98–101.
4. The discussion in the text considers only the more common case of underestimated costs. Costs could, of course, be overestimated, and although this case is not considered separately, it is a simple matter to extend the argument to cover this possibility. The analysis of charges presented in the text parallels Rose-Ackerman, 1973.

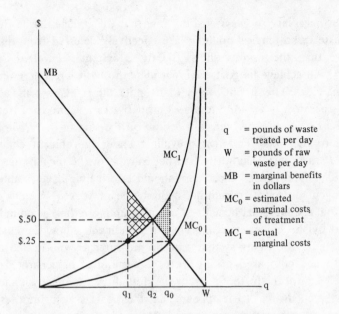

q = pounds of waste treated per day
W = pounds of raw waste per day
MB = marginal benefits in dollars
MC_0 = estimated marginal costs of treatment
MC_1 = actual marginal costs

Figure 11
The Costs of Making a Mistake—Effluent Charges vs. Pollution Rights

curve crosses the MB curve. It follows that as a result of selecting the "wrong" effluent charge, the agency will suffer a cost equal to the area of the crosshatched triangle in Figure 11, which shows the difference between the marginal benefits and marginal costs of eliminating q_2-q_1 pounds of FSUOD from Filadelphia. Of course, the agency may respond to this difficulty by raising its fee from 25 to 50 cents. Nevertheless it will incur costs of making a mistake during the extra time it takes to achieve the 80,000-pound objective indicated by the point where $MB = MC_1$.[5]

Having illustrated the costs of making a mistake under an effluent charge system, we can now assess the way a rights plan responds to the same difficulty. Again we assume that the authority believes, on the basis of erroneous information, that q_0 pounds of waste in Filadelphia should be treated; this time, however, it proceeds to auction off $(W - q_0)$ rights to the highest bidder, where W is the dischargers' total raw load. Thus, it is

5. The cost of making a mistake is experienced only *after* the mistake is discovered. Dischargers will take several years to complete the capital investments needed to comply with any charge. After this time has elapsed and the agency, noticing its mistake, sets a new fee, the costs of making a mistake outlined in the text are experienced while dischargers react to the new charge. These future costs, of course, should be discounted by an appropriate factor when considering their present value.

no longer necessary to *guess* at a tax rate that will induce the desired cut-back. Instead, so long as polluters are effectively deterred from discharging more than their rights allow, the rights system *guarantees* that the authority will achieve its goal *even if it underestimates prevailing marginal treatment costs*. This is not to say that, under the rights system, no costs will be generated by a failure to assess properly the magnitude of treatment expenses. The costs, however, will accrue on the side of *overtreatment* as opposed to the *undertreatment* prevailing under the effluent charge approach. If the control authority had been aware of the higher costs of attaining their Filadelphia objective, it should in principle have established a less stringent objective, permitting a discharge of $W - q_2$ pounds on the ground that the marginal benefits of cleaning up more than q_2 pounds were exceeded by the higher marginal costs of treatment. Thus, the costs of a mistake under the rights system may be measured by the dotted area in Figure 11 and compared readily with the costs of error generated by the "charges" approach. In the diagram the dotted area is much smaller than the crosshatched area, so it appears that the rights system imposes lower costs than the effluent charge system. But a conclusion on this point depends entirely on the shape of the marginal cost and marginal benefit curves the agency confronts.[6] In a world of pure theory, sometimes the

6. For example, if marginal benefits have a constant slope, $-b$, such that $MB(q) = a - bq$, and if both actual and estimated marginal costs have constant slopes, c_A and c_E, such that $MC_A(q) = c_A q$ and $MC_E(q) = c_E q$, then the costs of making a mistake are higher with a fee than a pollution rights system if $b > c_A$. This can be shown as follows. The annual cost of making a mistake with a fee is the difference between costs and benefits at the actual optimum, q_2 in Figure 11, and their difference at q_1 or:

$$(6.1) \quad TB(q_2) - TC_A(q_2) - TB(q_1) + TC_A(q_1) > 0$$

The analogous cost for rights plan is:

$$(6.2) \quad TB(q_2) - TC_A(q_2) - TB(q_0) + TC_A(q_0) > 0$$

Subtracting (6.2) from (6.1) we obtain:

$$(6.3) \quad TC_A(q_1) - TC_A(q_0) - TB(q_1) + TB(q_0) \gtrless 0$$

If this expression is > 0, the cost of making a mistake with a fee is greater than with a rights plan, and the converse if (6.3) is < 0. Substituting for $TC_A(q)$ and $TB(q)$, (6.3) becomes:

$$(6.4) \quad (\tfrac{1}{2})(c_A + b)(q_1{}^2 - q_0{}^2) - a(q_1 - q_0) \gtrless 0$$

$$\text{But } c_E q_0 = a - b q_0, \text{ or } q_0 = \frac{a}{c_E + b}$$

$$c_A q_1 = c_E q_0, \text{ or } q_1 = \frac{c_E a}{c_A(c_E + b)}$$

advantage runs in favor of one system, sometimes of the other. Further-more, disinvestment may be more difficult than investment, and so under a rights scheme the results of the error could persist for a considerably longer period.

Given our special concern with water pollution control, however, we cannot leave the analysis at this level of abstraction; our earlier discussion of the benefits of water pollution control permits a clearer choice between the two competing "market" techniques. As we explained, the benefits of cleanup do not, as the MB curve in Figure 11 assumes, increase con-tinuously at a steadily decreasing rate with increases in pollution control expenditure. These earlier discussions demonstrated that, so far as BOD and DO are concerned, the shape of the MB curve portrayed in Figure 11, while conventional in standard discussions of the subject, does not ac-curately describe reality. Instead of yielding benefits whose value con-tinuously increases at a decreasing rate, BOD removal generates a benefit schedule that exhibits important discontinuities. Thus if an investment in BOD removal induces oxygen levels in Filadelphia to rise from zero ppm DO to 1 ppm DO, so that river stink ceases to be a serious problem, river users will obtain very substantial benefits from control expenditures. In contrast, further investments—raising DO from 1 to 3 ppm, for instance—would generate little in the way of added benefits: river stink would already have been eliminated while the stream was still too oxygen-poor for fish. A second threshold is reached at 4 ppm, where some fish species can sur-vive, with others viable as oxygen levels rise to 5 ppm. Beyond this point marginal benefits fall once again, although they are still positive as the amount of aquatic life increases.[7]

To see the importance of the two thresholds—river stink and fish life—

Substituting for q_0 and q_1 in (6.4) gives:

$$(6.5) \quad \frac{a^2(c_E - c_A)^2(b - c_A)}{2c_A^2(c_E + b)^2} \gtrless 0$$

Since all the terms except $b - c_A$ are always positive, this implies the expression is

$$> 0 \text{ if } b > c_A$$
$$= 0 \text{ if } b = c_A \text{ or if } c_E = c_A$$
$$< 0 \text{ if } b < c_A$$

Thus, if marginal benefits fall quickly as treatment levels rise while actual marginal costs rise relatively slowly, then a fee will be more costly in terms of lost net benefits than will a rights plan. Note that although the size of the discrepancy between net benefits at q_2 and net benefits at q_1 or q_0 depends upon the discrepancy between actual and estimated costs, the sign of (6.5) is independent of this difference.

7. See Chs. 3 and 7 for a discussion of the benefit thresholds.

in the choice between charges and rights, imagine that the agency attempts to set a charge, P, such that Filadelphia's polluters will cut back to permit fish to live in the region under tolerable DO conditions of 4–5 ppm. Once again, however, P is set on the basis of a marginal cost curve that proves to be substantially underestimated. It follows from our previous analysis that underestimating costs leads to too little reduction in pollution levels. Say 100,000 pounds, rather than the anticipated 80,000, of BOD are being discharged. The consequences of this agency error are far more drastic than first appears, since the waste load permitted by a P charge may not permit *any* fish to live in Filadelphia. As a result of a relatively minor miscalculation of treatment costs, then, the effluent charge scheme may induce polluters to invest *much more than was required* to prevent river stink, but *too little* to prevent the fish from dying. In contrast, a rights scheme will guarantee that the fish will live, since regardless of the underestimate of costs, only 80,000 rights will have been distributed. To put the point in its clearest graphical form, consider Figure 12, which describes the *total* costs and *total* benefits of treating waste. The graph permits a more precise understanding of the scenario we have been discussing. At the time it initiates its program, the agency is provided with a cost curve representing its best estimate of costs—TC_0. Given this information, a tax of $\$P_0$ is announced, equal to the slope of TC_0 at the point q_0, which maximizes the

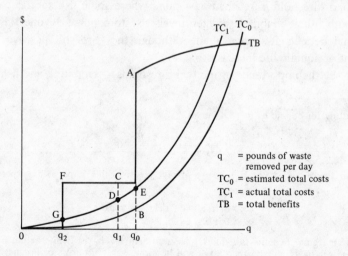

Figure 12
The Costs of Making a Mistake, Given Discontinuous Total Benefits

difference between total benefits and costs, represented by the line AB in Figure 12. In response to this tax, it is expected that q_0 pounds of waste will be removed, a treatment level that we assume implies DO levels of 4 ppm. However, after a four-year lag, the firms' real pollution control costs are revealed to be TC_1, greater than the previous estimate (TC_0). Consequently the polluting firms treat to q_1, where $P_0 = MC$, and a DO level of somewhat less than 4 ppm is obtained; the fish die, and the difference between the program's costs and benefits is only CD.[8]

In contrast, the rights program requires the firms to treat q_0 of their BOD loads, thereby permiting the fish to breathe successfully. Since the treatment costs are higher than those initially estimated (TC_0), the social gain involved in the program is no longer AB but AE; nevertheless, over a wide range of cases AE will be the maximum net benefit, given TC_1, since it is greater than FG, which is the net benefit at the "stench threshold." In this common case, then, an effluent rights system will permit a mistake to be made at *no* cost, whereas the damages will be considerable under an effluent charge system.[9]

Let us turn from the graphs and try to put the matter in words as simply as possible. Imagine that the control agency believes the benefits of having fish in Filadelphia would substantially exceed any plausible set of costs that would be incurred in cleaning up the Delaware to the necessary DO level; imagine further that the agency, relying on a relatively accurate mathematical BOD-DO model of Filadelphia, has reason to believe that reducing BOD levels to 80,000 pounds will permit the fish to breathe. Should it not then move directly to limit discharge to 80,000 pounds, instead of setting an effluent charge and taking the chance that, if its fee has been set too low, polluters will cut back by only 100,000 pounds to the severe detriment of the fish? Why accept the costs entailed in further postponing the day when the fish can again live in the river?

Information Costs

Up to this point we have considered only one important aspect of the regulatory problem that arises when information is imperfect. In the present section, we shall show that when other facets of the problem are con-

8. It should be apparent that, under the circumstances illustrated in Fig. 12, it would be better to simply remove river stink with an investment of G than to require an investment more than enough to prevent noxious odors yet too little to permit a plentiful fish life.
9. However, if q_2, the "stench threshold," were the actual optimum, then the costs of making a mistake under the rights plan could be large if estimated costs erroneously indicated that q_0, the "fish threshold," should be chosen.

sidered, the rights scheme seems even more attractive. This is true when the interests of both the polluters and the agency are considered.

Since many forms of pollution control are long-lasting, polluters will have a legitimate interest in knowing the way fee levels will vary over the 20- or 30-year life of their treatment plant. Otherwise they will find it difficult to determine which clean-up method minimizes total costs.[10] Unfortunately, however, an agency relying on an effluent charge will be reluctant to provide dischargers with such information, not only because it is unwilling to commit future decision makers to any one pollution policy but also because limiting its discretion to change the tax will increase the costs of making a mistake if the original fee was set on the basis of an erroneous understanding of marginal treatment costs.

Under a rights plan, however, the authority may, if it wishes, deal with the dischargers' need for information in a more sophisticated way. When issuing its 80,000 BOD rights for the Filadelphia area, the authority is free to issue pollution rights with varying maturities; thus 40,000 of Filadelphia's rights might carry 20-year maturities, while the others might expire after only five years. In this way, dischargers to whom future uncertainty is relatively costly can purchase the long-term rights at a premium which would reflect the fact of added certainty. Similarly, staggering maturities permits the present generation of pollution controllers to limit future agency actions to some degree, though not entirely. Of course, the proper trade-off between the information needs of present dischargers and the flexibility needs of future policymakers remains a question of judgment,[11] not susceptible of a single easy answer. Nevertheless, the rights scheme permits the question to be defined in a way which exposes its complexity and permits some of the polluters' most important long-term informational requirements to be satisfied.[12]

10. Of course, this problem is not unique to the effluent charge. It is a common problem for all firms operating in private markets facing uncertain future prices of both inputs and outputs. One way for dischargers to react to the uncertainty created by an agency's refusal to fix fees for many years into the future is to adopt a wait-and-see attitude, investing as little as possible until they are relatively sure that the agency is not planning any massive changes in fee levels.

11. Of course, rights could be retired prematurely if the authority wished to purchase them at the market price then prevailing. This would be difficult to arrange, however, if—as will be suggested in a subsequent discussion—a large portion of the revenue generated from the original rights sales is appropriated by the cities instead of the pollution control agency itself.

12. The effluent charge could also be adapted so that large fee changes are avoided. The agency could, for instance, promise not to raise or lower the fee more than a small, defined percentage each year. Such a policy would reduce uncertainty but could entail high costs of making a mistake if the total benefit curve exhibits substantial discontinuities.

At the same time, the rights plan makes the information-gathering job somewhat easier for the agency. The agency's own guesses of the costs of meeting its quality objective can be checked against the trend of rights prices over time, since firms and cities may be expected to enter the market for speculative purposes so that they may resell the rights at a profit to new entrants when they arrive in Filadelphia and wish to begin polluting. This means that decision makers will have a richer set of data on basic cost issues than they would have under the charge regime, where the agency must wait until dischargers actually invest before the impact of agency market incentives can be assessed. Thus, a rights plan will permit both a more rapid change in policy if early auction prices suggest that treatment costs have been badly misestimated, and a more sophisticated understanding of economic variables whenever basic pollution policy is subjected to reconsideration.[13]

Controlling Growth

As time passes and pollution loads grow, it will generally be increasingly expensive to maintain a given level of water quality,[14] since more sophisticated and expensive treatment will be required to keep effluent levels constant. Thus, unless the tax rate is regularly increased, an effluent charge system will permit the gradual deterioration of water quality over time. This slow decline takes on special importance once the threshold problem is recalled. If, for example, a DO objective of 4–5 ppm is set for Filadelphia to assure a viable fish population, a rather modest erosion of water quality tolerated by a fixed effluent charge in a growing economy can have a profound impact.[15] Of course there is nothing to prevent an aggressive authority from raising the charge whenever this is appropriate. Nevertheless, like the traditional "percentage treatment" regime discussed in Chapter 16,[16] an effluent fee system will place *the burden of affirmative action* to maintain the agency's original environmental objectives *on nonpolluting*

13. This is not to say that the central agency ought not to make any independent cost estimates under the rights scheme; otherwise, dischargers might collude to make bids for the purpose of misleading the agency. This point is developed further at n. 34.
14. However, technical change could conceivably occur at a fast enough rate so that costs might fall over time.
15. In response to this problem, the agency could set a fee that it knows is "too high" under current conditions, but which would maximize the net social benefits of pollution control over the entire period during which the fee will remain unchanged. The utility of such a strategy, however, is limited by the difficulty of predicting both growth and future pollution control costs (see Ch. 6).
16. See pp. 228, 229.

river users. In contrast, under the effluent rights system, the maximum permissible discharge is fixed at the time of the original decision, and the costs of growth will be borne only by polluters who will bid the price of the rights up over time.[17] Thus, the rights system places the *burden of affirmative action on the polluters* to convince the agency that the increasing marginal compliance costs so outweigh the marginal environmental benefits of the status quo that some degradation below current levels should be permitted and additional rights issued.[18]

As suggested previously, it seems far wiser to allocate the task of undertaking political initiatives to a rather small, easily organized group, like polluters, each of whom individually has a great deal at stake in the standards issue, than to impose it upon a diffuse group of river users whose individual interest in the matter is relatively small. Moreover, it seems appropriate to require that once a quality objective is set, it should not be eroded without a second considered decision by the relevant policy makers. It seems, then, that an effluent rights system assures the integrity of the decision-making process and its subsequent responsiveness to changed conditions far more effectively than does its effluent charge competitor.

Municipalities and Perverse Revenue Flows

In any urbanized river system, a substantial proportion of the total waste load—sometimes more than 50 percent[19]—is discharged by municipal treatment facilities. The city plants do not typically restrict themselves to the treatment of human excrement but process much commercial and industrial waste as well. Consequently, any market approach must be carefully scrutinized to determine whether an incentive structure designed principally with private firms in mind generates unanticipated consequences when governmental entities play an important role.

When viewed from this perspective, the effluent charge approach seems once again to contain significant weaknesses when compared to the rights system. If cities are treated no differently from firms, an effluent charge

17. Even if rights have long terms, the adjustments described in the text would occur since rights can be traded back and forth between dischargers.
18. The agency might be concerned that issuing additional rights would reduce the value of all existing rights, inflicting windfall losses on dischargers. This does not seem to be a particularly weighty problem since, in pressuring for increased rights, dischargers would presumably take the over-all fall in rights prices into account. Nevertheless, if the agency were concerned about these losses, it could make one-time payments to existing rights holders to compensate them for the lost value.
19. In the Delaware Estuary, municipal wastes constituted 65 percent of the 1964 point-source waste load discharged into the estuary measured in pounds of carbonaceous oxygen demand/day (DECS, p. 22).

scheme will produce a flow of revenue away from the localities to higher levels of public authority. Consequently it is likely that if an effluent tax were levied upon municipalities, ways would be found to reduce the financial burden of the tax through a subsidy program.[20]

Such subsidies, however, run the risk of distorting the town's clean-up incentives: if the city fathers know, for example, that 50 cents of every treatment dollar will be returned to them in subsidy, they will have an incentive to treat up to the point where the true marginal cost is twice the fee. This means that, when a uniform fee is imposed on both towns and firms, the municipalities will treat more (and the firms less) than they would under a cost-minimizing approach. To resolve this difficulty, one of two subsidy approaches must be considered. First, the subsidy can be a lump-sum transfer, designed to be independent of the locality's spending on pollution control. Thus if a general revenue sharing program assures a town of a million dollars regardless of its treatment expenditure, it will not have an incentive to consider each treatment dollar as if it were 50 cents. While general revenue sharing has a clear efficiency advantage, it may seem inequitable to some precisely because it subsidizes towns independently of their differing clean-up efforts.[21] If these doubts are given weight, however, a much more complex alternative to lump-sum transfers must be considered. Under the second approach, towns are offered a subsidy which covers a percentage of total treatment costs, but the perverse incentive effects are counteracted by devising a two-tiered effluent charge.[22] Thus, even though towns consider a treatment dollar to cost them only 50 cents, this will be of no concern if the effluent charge that towns face is one half

20. In fact, under present water pollution legislation, municipalities generally receive substantial subsidies from both state and federal sources (see Ch. 19, nn. 39, 47).
21. For a discussion of the "equal effort" principle involved here see Ch. 15. We wish to emphasize, however, that in speaking of the "equal effort" principle here or elsewhere, we are not indicating that we ourselves are convinced of its relevance, but only that many consider "equal effort" principles of fairness applicable for reasons which cannot be considered within the confines of this book (see Ch. 15, n. 3).
22. More formally, let the total cost to a municipality of treating q pounds be $C(q)$. Thus, marginal cost is $C'(q)$. Let W equal the municipality's raw load, and let q_0 be the level of treatment where $C'(q)$ equals marginal benefits. Given any subsidy rate, $(1 - s)$, we can find the effluent charge p such that $p = s\,C'(q_0)$. In particular, the agency might wish to set s and p so that the cost under this scheme equals the cost of a legal orders plan in which the city is allocated $(W - q_0)$ pounds. In this case:

$$C(q_0) = sC(q_0) + p(W - q_0)$$

$$C(q_0) = s[C(q_0) + C'(q_0)(W - q_0)]$$

$$s = \frac{C(q_0)}{C(q_0) + C'(q_0)(W - q_0)}.$$

that of the firms.[23] Of course, this two-tiered approach not only requires good cost data, but will also create an incentive for firms to enter municipal systems even when the firms could in fact have treated at lower social cost if they had acted independently.[24] In response to these difficulties, drastically truncated versions of the charge strategy are often the ones offered for serious public consideration. In the effluent charge bill proposed by Senator Proxmire, for example, municipalities are not required to pay a tax on any waste generated in the course of ordinary domestic living, although commercial and industrial effluent is subject to the proposed tax.[25] This bill has the advantage of removing any incentive for a firm to enter a municipal system, but its effort to regulate domestic waste through legal orders has most of the disadvantages we have associated with this mode of control.

In contrast, it is a rather straightforward matter to design a pollution rights system which will avoid the difficulty presented by perverse revenue flows. So long as the pollution agency determines the number of rights permissible for the region (80,000 in our Filadelphia problem), X will outbid Y for the 80,000 rights *no matter who receives the proceeds of the auction.* Even if the pollution control agency declares that Y will receive the auction revenue, Y will choose to sell the 80,000 rights to X at 50 cents apiece since X's marginal cost does not exceed 50 cents even if it treats its entire waste load. This means that the problem of perverse revenue flows may be solved through the simple expedient of initially assigning BOD rights in an equitable fashion to the cities bordering the estuary[26] and authorizing them to sell off as many rights as they believe

23. In reality, the problem of designing a two-tiered system is complicated by the existence of subsidies for firms in the form of special tax treatment for pollution control equipment (Int. Rev. Code of 1954, §169; Treas. Reg. §§1.169-1 to 1.169-3, 602.1 to 602.10 [1973]). The 48 percent corporate tax rate also implies that every dollar of pollution control expenditure "costs" only 52 cents. However, since effluent fees would also be considered tax deductible expenses, this will have no incentive effects.
24. Finally, a third approach would exempt municipalities from the charge and instead pay them a bounty for each pound treated. See Baumol and Oates 1974, Ch. 12, for a detailed discussion of this case. Since opportunity costs are not distorted, it appears that although firms will wish to join municipal systems, cities will not accept them unless the marginal cost of treating any firm's waste is less than the bounty paid per pound treated. Firms, however, would be willing to pay municipalities bonuses (or bribes) for being permitted to use municipal systems since municipal treatment, under a bounty plan, will generally be much cheaper for the firm than the sum of individual treatment and fee costs imposed upon it if it chooses to treat independently of the system.
25. See Senate Bill 3181, 91st Cong., 1st Sess. (1969), §4(a) and §5(a).
26. We have assumed in the text that the reader considers the cities the most worthy beneficiaries of all the revenues generated by the auction. It is arguable, however, that at least some portion of the revenue should be reserved to the pollution authority itself, thereby guaranteeing it the requisite finanical support for long-range

proper at an auction to be held under the authority's auspices. At such an auction private firms will, of course, bid varying sums for varying quantities of BOD rights, leaving it up to the representatives of the municipalities to determine the extent to which it will minimize their costs to sell the rights at the bid prices and treat their wastes instead. At the end of the auction both the public and private polluters will have redistributed the BOD rights in the way *they believe* will generate the cheapest pattern of cleanup, given the pollution authority's quality objective. If at a later time one of the polluters finds it has misjudged costs, it remains free to buy or sell some rights at the regular markets the control authority will hold for this purpose.[27] Thus the rights system, properly structured, may generate both a solution to the pollution problem which moves in the cost-minimizing direction and a new source of income for the revenue-starved cities.

CHARGES AND RIGHTS IN A COMPLEX—BUT REALISTIC—WORLD

The four factors which favored the rights mechanism in our simplified Filadelphia problem are supplemented by additional considerations when more realistic contexts, like the Delaware River, are examined. The essential complexity to be considered here is the fact that Delaware polluters affect water quality differentially, depending on their location, their proximity to other important polluters, and the nature of the agency's quality objectives for individual sections of the stream. As a consequence it will no longer be possible for the control agency to attain its quality objectives simply by setting a *single* tax rate P, however difficult this itself may be. A "perfect" charge scheme would require the agency to take into account each polluter's relative costs of treatment and the relative impact of his wastes on quality up and down the stream. Thus, to determine the proper

---

research and planning for the river's future. If this were the preferred outcome, it could of course be achieved simply by reserving a certain number of rights for sale by the pollution authority while the remainder were assigned to the municipalities for use or resale as the localities thought best.

27. This system may also seem to incorporate the same perverse incentives for joint municipal-industrial treatment that limited the usefulness of two-tiered effluent charges or bounty-fee schemes. Once again municipalities are in a favored position that firms would like to share by paying bonuses or bribes to persuade the municipality to treat their waste. However, when a municipality accepts a firm's wastes for treatment, the firm ceases to purchase rights and the municipality must retain more rights for its own use. Thus, the maximum payment the firm will make is the sum of foregone treatment costs plus the cost of rights, while the payment demanded by the municipality is the sum of lost rights revenues plus additional treatment costs. Therefore, only if it is actually cheaper for the municipality to treat the firm's waste will joint treatment occur.

tax on a polluter X at location A, the authority must have an accurate under-standing of the extent to which other polluters up and down the river will react to the imposition of various effluent taxes on *their* wastes. Similarly, when determining the proper tax for polluter Z, the authority must know how X will react to various levies. While solving a set of simultaneous equations will determine the set of tax rates that minimizes total com-pliance costs,[28] it should be apparent that such a calculation assumes the agency understands each discharger's treatment cost curve to a degree which is altogether unrealistic. Moreover, any effort to discriminate between dischargers' costs in the way required would generate the familiar difficul-ties canvassed in Chapter 16 resulting from an institutional effort to deter-mine complex facts accurately.

As a consequence, it seems most likely that an agency implementing a charge strategy would be driven to divide the river into a number of geo-graphical zones and levy an *identical* charge on the wastes of all polluters located in the same general river area. The adoption of a zoning scheme will, of course, generate significant inefficiencies since, thanks to their differing locations, each polluter's waste will impose different marginal costs on the river but will be subjected nonetheless to the same zonal effluent charge. Far worse than this, however, will be a second tendency whose importance we emphasized in an earlier discussion of the fate of the DRBC's actual zoning plan. As shown in Chapter 17, since the DRBC's zonal boundary lines were defined in a necessarily arbitrary fashion, the agency had a difficult time justifying the imposition of very different re-quirements on dischargers who had the misfortune of falling on the "wrong" side of the boundary. Instead, the DRBC was under substantial pressure to impose only very modest inequalities in interzonal treatment requirements to avoid the appearance of arbitrariness and conscious favorit-ism. Similarly, under an effluent charge strategy, the control authority will be exceedingly reluctant to levy a 10-cent/pound tax on polluter X and a 50-cent/pound tax on nearby polluter Z simply because they fall on differ-ent sides of a boundary line. This tendency toward uniformity in rates, while thoroughly understandable, will nevertheless often generate very sub-stantial inefficiencies. Indeed a uniform effluent charge may be even less efficient than a "legal orders" regime which requires each polluter to treat a uniform percentage of its waste.[29]

While these pressures toward uniformity will be felt under the rights regime as well, there is reason to believe they can be controlled more readily in this regulatory context. Imagine, for example, that the authority

28. See Rose-Ackerman, 1973.
29. For a demonstration of this proposition see Rose-Ackerman, 1973.

divides the river into several zones and allocates a fixed number of rights to each. If zonal prices vary considerably, polluters can be given the freedom to pipe their wastes to low-cost zones and purchase discharge rights there. Thus, a polluter near a zonal frontier has little cause for complaint since he can cheaply transfer his waste to a neighboring zone. This flexibility in piping, however, cannot be reasonably accorded polluters under an effluent charge approach. The critical problem, once again, is posed by the existence of water quality thresholds. If, for example, the authority establishes a set of effluent charges in the hope of preserving aquatic life throughout the river, clearly this expectation will be disappointed if waste dischargers respond to the zonal variation in fees by concentrating their wastes in a few low-fee zones. Instead, before piping can be permitted, the authority must determine the extent to which these interzonal transfers are inconsistent with the agency's water quality goals and alter effluent fees accordingly. Not only does this task require accurate data and economic sophistication, but it will expose the agency to further risks of corruption, political favoritism, and arbitrariness. In contrast, interzonal transfers do not endanger the agency's water quality objectives since the number of rights in each zone remains fixed and prices adjust automatically in response to polluters' decisions.[30]

FAILINGS OF THE POLLUTION RIGHTS SCHEME

Despite the formidable practical advantages of the pollution rights proposal, a mature appraisal must of course consider its disadvantages not only in relation to the effluent charge but with respect to other, nonmarket

30. If the agency had accurate data on piping costs as well as treatment costs, it could design either a zonal effluent charge or a zonal rights plan that took the possibility of piping into account. If a fee scheme were used, a discharger would treat until the marginal cost of treatment equalled the fee in its own zone and would divide the untreated portion between its own and a neighboring zone so that the marginal cost of piping plus the fee in the bordering zone equalled the fee per pound in the discharger's own zone. In analogous fashion, under a rights scheme, dischargers would divide their rights purchases between rights in their own zone and rights in neighboring zones in such a way that the price of rights in their own zone equalled the marginal cost of piping plus the price of rights in the neighboring zone.

Rights will be superior to fees, however, when zonal water quality standards are set at threshold benefit levels and piping costs are not known accurately. Thus, as our Filadelphia problem is complicated to approximate real world conditions, another potentially costly element of uncertainty is built into an effluent charge scheme. Even if treatment costs are known accurately, dischargers' piping could seriously affect the benefits received for pollution control by causing standards in some zones to be overfulfilled, while thresholds in others are violated. In contrast, with a rights plan, water quality will not be affected by piping. Prices will simply adjust to reflect the higher demand for rights in some zones and the lower demand for rights in others. Once again the rights plan has the advantage of providing the agency with information about dischargers' costs without any diminution in water quality.

modes of regulation. In the present section, we shall take up the first task, deferring to Chapter 19 the question whether the market model itself contains important limitations which require that it be supplemented by regulatory tools based on either the "legal orders" or the "activist" models of control.

Ideological Objections: The "Right" to Pollute

Market models of regulation, whether of the charge or rights variety, generally receive a suspicious reception among committed environmentalists. The most disturbing thing about the effluent charge to these groups is the implication that a firm or city may discharge its obligation to the environment not by cleaning up its waste completely but by continuing to emit waste simply by paying a fee.[31] Thus the use of the effluent charge device carries with it the symbolic implication that public authorities do not consider all pollution an unambiguous evil, but instead believe that the costs of totally eliminating man-made pollution everywhere exceeds the benefits generated by a return to an (urbanized) State of Nature. While this of course is one of the implications of charge schemes (at least where the fee is not set at astronomic levels), it is not clear how this fact alone sets the effluent charge apart from *any* method of control (be it by "legal orders" or "activism") which does not contemplate the *immediate* cessation of pollution in all its forms. Nonetheless, after numerous unsystematic conversations with environmentalists, we can attest to the fact that there is something specially offensive about the charge. To some it is the fact that discharge privileges are obtained in return *for money* which taints the charge technique. Why this is worse than obtaining the opportunity to pollute for *free,* as is the case under the legal orders model, remains inexplicable to us.

Others, however, adopt a more sophisticated line of argument. They suggests that at least under a legal orders approach which requires all polluters to clean up as much as the "best available technology" permits,[32] public policy has assumed a position of great symbolic importance: while the verbal formula demanding the "best available technology" recognizes that *some* "pollution" is tolerable in the short run, it suggests that the long-

31. It should be noted, however, that conservationist opposition to market approaches seems to be moderating. For example, the Coalition to Tax Pollution is a recent outgrowth of the environmental movement which advocates an effluent charge strategy.

32. As Ch. 20 indicates, this is the approach taken by the 1972 Federal Water Quality Act.

run goal remains complete elimination. In contrast, an effluent charge of P cents a pound does not imply a similar long-term abolitionist objective. And if it is assumed (as is plausible) that such symbolic points have an impact on the future course of public opinion, opposition to the effluent charge makes sense to those who embrace the abolitionist goal with a fervor which justifies the substantial costs of the "legal order" model in the here-and-now.

Of course, as has been made clear, the authors are not abolitionists either in the long or in the short run. Nonetheless, it is at this point that a candid discussion of the regulatory means of achieving objectives merges into the larger question about the nature of the objectives themselves. And if the discussion in the first three parts of the book has not convinced the reader that a simplistic "no pollution anywhere" goal should be rejected, we have little more to say.

Assuming, however, that at least some conservationist opposition to the effluent charge device may be anticipated, the political opposition may be expected to swell to far greater proportions if the rights scheme were seriously proposed as a primary mechanism for regulating the environmental problem. As we have seen, it is an essential part of the market approach favored here that the state auction off "rights to pollute" the environment. Thus, in adopting the rights strategy, the state is explicitly recognizing that "pollution" in certain amounts in certain places is a legitimate activity, given the society's finite resources and the existence of other pressing social and private goals. Once again, we cannot with candor deny that the adoption of the rights scheme has such a symbolic implication, and one which is even more emphatic than the decision simply to tax all discharges. All this means to us is that a very considerable effort at education is required before our society can begin to frame a rationally defensible environmental policy. Nevertheless, we can understand that less hardy souls will reject—on grounds of political expediency alone—a rights approach simply because it emphasizes that cleanliness should not always be next to godliness in the American hierarchy of values.

We can, however, urge upon such pragmatists two factors which should be considered soberly before the charge scheme is preferred over the rights approach on the grounds of political expediency. First, we have attempted to demonstrate in the immediately preceding section that a rights approach has in fact many operational advantages over the effluent tax scheme. Second, in earlier chapters we have charted out the unfortunate policy consequences generated when technocrats, bureaucrats, and politicians choose a symbolic, politically expedient stand against "pollution" instead of making an effort to think soberly about the relationship between man and nature in an industrialized society. And if even those who have the time and training to understand the issues at stake shape their policy proposals with an overly anxious concern for short-run political expediency, the quality of discussion and policy a decade hence will be little more sophisticated than at present.

The Possibilities of Collusion

There is a second, far more technical, argument which may be raised by those who favor a charge scheme over the rights approach. Under a rights regime, it may be suggested, bidders will have powerful incentives to enter into collusive arrangements in order to keep the price of rights down, thereby diminishing the total amount of revenue raised at the auction. In contrast, it appears—on the surface—that a charge scheme permits the dischargers far less room for collusive behavior: whatever cartels they attempt to form among themselves, the fact remains that each will be obliged to pay P cents a pound for as much waste as each chooses to discharge.

Let us, for a moment, assume that this distinction between the two plans is valid, and proceed to assess its importance. However paradoxical it may appear on first glance, even if a cartel were to succeed in depressing the price of the rights, it seems likely that the program would achieve most, if not all, of its objectives so long as it is the pollution control authority which is selling the rights. Collusion will not affect water quality, since the number of pollution rights in each zone has already been fixed. Nor is it likely that collusion will alter the allocation of rights among polluters that would prevail under competition. Once the cartel has obtained the effluent rights, it will itself be obliged to allocate them among its members—and those polluters whose marginal treatment costs are high can be expected to bribe or otherwise induce low-cost polluters to transfer rights until the marginal costs of treatment are equal throughout the cartel. Moreover, any polluter dissatisfied with the share of rights promised him by the cartel can always break away and bid independently at the auction. Since the tendency to break away will increase as the cost savings to be derived from independent action increase, this will induce cartel members to allocate along marginal cost lines in order to assure the solidarity of the illegal monopoly. Thus, while collusion will reduce the amount of revenue at the auction, it will not greatly undermine the program's pollution control objectives: some of the money which otherwise would be devoted to public purposes will simply be diverted to the monopolists' pockets.

Collusion does seem a greater threat to the program's pollution control objectives, however, under a rights approach in which it is the cities, rather than the authority, that garner the revenues from the rights sale. For in this case, the supply of rights is not fixed to the cartel but depends positively on the price they are willing to pay; and it can be easily shown that if the marginal cost of treatment for municipalities rises with an increase in treatment levels, then the cartel will buy too few rights and treat to too high a level while municipalities will undertreat.[33] Thus under the

33. The figure below measures the marginal treatment costs of all firms, $C_1'(q_1)$, on the left-hand vertical axis and the marginal costs of municipalities as a group, $C_0'(q_0)$, on the right-hand axis. W_0 is the raw load of municipalities and W_1 is the raw load of firms. W_0 and W_1 are separated by a distance α equal to the number of rights issued. Thus the length of the horizontal axis is $(W_0 + W_1 - \alpha)$ or the total quantity of waste that must be treated. Clearly the optimal distribution of rights is achieved at q_1^* where $C_1'(q_1^*) = C_0'(W_1 + W_0 - \alpha - q_1^*)$, i.e., where the marginal costs of treatment in the two sectors are equal. This minimizes $C_1(q_1) + C_0(W_1 + W_0 - \alpha - q_1)$. If the firms form a cartel, they will try to minimize $C_1(q_1) + p(W_1 - q_1)$ where $p = C_0'(W_1 + W_2 - \alpha - q_1)$, the price that will induce the municipalities to sell exactly $W_1 - q_1$ rights. This expression is minimized with respect to q_1 at $C_1'(\hat{q}_1) = C_0''(W_1 + W_0 - \alpha - \hat{q}_1)[W_1 - \hat{q}_1] + C_0'(W_1 + W_0 - \alpha - \hat{q}_1$. Since $(W_1 - q_1) > 0$, if $C_0'' > 0$, i.e., if marginal cost is rising, then $C_1'(\hat{q}_1) > C_0'(\hat{q}_0)$ and the cartel treats to a higher level and buys fewer rights than is optimal. The shaded area in the diagram indicates the cartel's costs at $\hat{q}_1$.

If municipalities form a cartel and firms do not, then the results are reversed. The municipalities wish to maximize: $C_1'(q_1)(W_1 - q_1) - C_0(q_0)$ or: $C_1'(W_0 + W_1 - \alpha - q_0)(q_0 + \alpha - W_0) - C_0(q_0)$. This expression is maximized with respect to q_0 at: $C_0'(q_0) = C_1'(q_1) - C_1''(q_1)(W_1 - q_1)$. If $C_1'' > 0$, then $C_0'(q_0) > C_1'(q_1)$ and municipalities treat to a higher level and sell *more* rights than is optimal. Firms, of course, treat to too low a level.

If both sides of the market cartelize, the problem is one of bilateral monopoly with the outcome depending upon the bargaining strength of the two sides of the market.

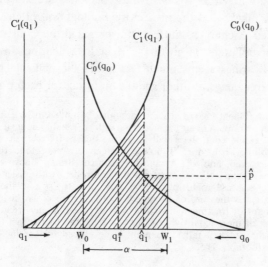

variant of the rights scheme which seems to us most desirable, collusive behavior may to some extent undermine efficiency objectives.

The seriousness of this point, however, depends upon the likelihood of cartelization; and, all things considered, we think the risk to be quite small. Cartels are, of course, illegal under both state and federal antitrust laws. Moreover, on an industrialized river like the Delaware, where there are many polluters, the costs of maintaining and policing the illegal conspiracy will be great indeed. Finally, the recipient of the revenues generated at the auction (whether it be the pollution authority or the riparian cities) will be exceedingly suspicious when the sums received are far less than expected. Thus, even if a cartel of industrial dischargers alone could distort the allocation of rights in the case when municipalities are rights sellers, we judge the likelihood of a successful cartel sufficiently small to discount its importance as a problem.[34]

Enforcement Costs

There is a final factor to be considered which weighs in favor of the charge system, but which seems insufficient to outweigh the countervailing factors. We refer to the costs of policing the two schemes. Under either approach, the agency must recruit a staff of inspectors to undertake a regular series of unannounced site visits to each pollution source. Under the rights approach, however, the policing task will be more complex. It will be necessary for the agency not only to determine the amount of various effluents discharged, but also to levy penalties for each pound of waste emitted beyond the quantity authorized by rights. If these penalties are substantial, as they should be, it is likely that the inspector's findings will often be challenged by the penalized discharger, and both fairness and the Constitution require that protesting polluters be given the right to a hearing. In contrast, the likelihood of hearings seems much less under the effluent charge system, where a discharger pays a rather small sum in tax for each pound, no mat-

---

34. Moreover, an effluent charge scheme may also be undercut by collusive behavior over a longer time frame. Given the agency's lack of reliable data, it is only reasonable to expect that the controllers will judge the optimality of their charge schedule by observing polluter behavior: if polluters clean up more than they expect, the charge will be lowered, and vice versa. This control strategy, however, may be exploited by polluters who collude to present the controllers with misleading behavioral responses. It makes sense to form a cartel and agree to treat to the level of water quality that minimizes the sum of treatment costs plus fee costs. Instead of choosing the optimal amount of treatment, the cartel will choose a *higher* treatment level since the marginal cost of more extensive treatment is balanced by the fact that the fee paid on *all* units discharged will fall. This point is developed further in Rose-Ackerman, 1973, especially footnote 18.

ter how much he chooses to emit. Nevertheless, this added cost of enforcing the rights scheme will not as a rule offset the many advantages we have canvassed.

CONCLUSIONS

While Chapters 16 and 17 detailed a wide range of weaknesses in the "legal orders" approach, it should be clear that the design of a viable market mode of regulation will not be as simple a task as some of its proponents have suggested. Moreover, it is particularly unfortunate that the market technique which seems most promising—the rights auction—has received relatively little attention in the public debate on the direction of environmental policy. Nevertheless, given the failures of the traditional mode of control, it could well be that the introduction of even inferior market control mechanisms—like the effluent charge system—would constitute a considerable improvement over present practices. It is important, however, to keep firm control over an understandable yearning to transcend the inadequacies of the prevailing legal orders regime by embracing uncritically a market mode (like the effluent charge) which, however wondrously it may operate in the simple cases of Filadelphia and Vilmington, contains serious difficulties in the real world.[35] Indeed, at the present stage in the discussion, even the superior variants of the market model have been presented in far too favorable a light. As the next chapter will show, an urbanized industrial society generates a distinctive set of environmental problems whose complexity often makes even the best type of market regulation an inadequate policy making tool.

---

35. A line of argument complementary to our own is developed by Baumol and Oates 1974, Ch. 11. They recommend legal orders as a supplement to effluent taxes since an agency using orders is better able to respond to sudden emergencies. Legal orders can be issued which have a direct and rapid impact, while lag times involved in the use of taxes are too long to produce action certain to lead to the rectification of an urgent problem.

The Limits of
Passive Regulation

INTRODUCTION

Having described and criticized some of the basic elements of the DRBC's regulatory effort, we are now in a position to probe more deeply and identify a fundamental contradiction between the agency's regulatory premises and the nature of the problem it was confronting on many important segments of the estuary. In doing so, we shall not only explore the limitations of the DRBC's legal orders approach but also recognize that market modes of control, whatever their advantages, are inadequate in fundamental respects in dealing with some of today's complex environmental problems.

Legal Orders and the Problem of Coordination

To see the problem, it is first necessary to recognize that the DRBC's regulatory strategy was grounded on fundamentally individualistic premises. Each polluter, upon receipt of its quota, was instructed to prepare a "compliance schedule" which not only stipulated the date by which its new controls would be in actual operation, but also contained a set of interim targets indicating the various dates on which pollution planning was to be completed, construction contracts let, and building actually begun. Thus, while the commission asserted the right to approve both the compliance schedules and the pollution plans themselves, control over the shape of compliance plans was—at least in the first instance—delegated to each discharger on an individual basis.

It soon became apparent to the agency, however, that in a number of cases it would be better for all concerned if neighboring dischargers cooperated to build large joint treatment facilities than if each polluter attempted to meet its quota in an individualistic way. Constructing a small number of "regional" treatment plants would make it easier both for the commission to police compliance and for the polluters to attract skilled employees, thereby assuring a higher level of performance. Even more important, regionalization promised dramatic reductions in the overall cost of compliance, since there are substantial economies of scale in the construction and operation of large plants. In order to cut costs in this way however, complex planning is necessary. Since pumping and piping are expensive, there comes a point where the savings a polluter gains by using a larger regional plant are outweighed by the expense it incurs in piping the waste over distance. Moreover, in the case of industrial wastes, polluters must determine whether their effluents react chemically with one another in a way that makes combined treatment more expensive than separate treatment. Finally, a satisfactory formula for apportioning the cost of the project amongst the polluters must be devised. All this means that regionalization planning is a time-consuming process.

Moreover, the DRBC's decision to give each polluter the right to shape its own plans can be expected to complicate further joint treatment negotiations. First, the environmental engineers of one or another polluter may be ill accustomed to thinking in regional terms and so press on with individual treatment despite its inappropriateness. If one or two crucial dischargers happen to be controlled by provincial managers, an otherwise promising regional action could easily be aborted. Second, individual polluters will be tempted to manipulate a regionalization proposal to buy time during which no substantial control costs are incurred. Indeed, each polluter may be trying to outwit not only the control authority but also other participants in the joint treatment scheme. A regional plant may be designed in any number of ways at any number of places; it may be financed by any number of formulas. This range of indeterminacy can be expected to arouse the hard bargaining instincts in any self-respecting businessman. It would seem, then, that the DRBC's individualistic, decentralized system promises the agency the worst of both worlds. On the one hand, regional plans will be scuttled when they should be pursued; on the other, regional enterprises (both worth while and not) will be subjected to interminable discussion and negotiation.

Market Models and the Problem of Coordination

To make matters worse, a simple shift from the legal orders model to a market mode of control will not satisfactorily resolve the problems of joint treatment. Just as with the DRBC's allocation plan, a market scheme may not deter a critical polluter controlled by officials ill accustomed to cooperative endeavors from refusing to cooperate with a promising regional proposal. In the case of cities and towns especially, fears of loss of political power and influence may outweigh cost considerations where water and sewer departments are a major source of patronage. Furthermore, firms and cities will still be tempted to obtain the best possible deal for themselves by bargaining endlessly about the location of the plant and the fairest formula for cost apportionment.[1] And if the pollution agency attempts to force the polluters to come to a decision by requiring that they pay effluent charges or purchase effluent rights by a date certain, the result may well be that negotiations will reach an impasse—with each polluter holding out for the lion's share of the savings to be generated by cooperative activity—and that one or more of the participants will choose to embark upon an individual treatment project to minimize short-term costs, thereby scuttling the entire program.[2] Even more important, the prospect of regionalization will play havoc with the authority's original decisions establishing a market model program. An agency may reasonably decide to issue 50,000 pounds of BOD rights in a given river zone if the distribution of the discharges within the zone remains roughly as it has been in the past. If, however, the zone's dischargers channel their waste to a single point for

1. See Williamson, 1971, pp. 112–123, for an analogous discussion of high bargaining costs in the context of industrial organization. Just as Williamson sees vertical integration of industry as the institutional solution to the bargaining cost problem, so here the "activist" agency may be the proper response to the regulatory problems posed by extreme decentralization. Marc Roberts also notes that fees "provide neither the incentive nor the organizational basis for important river basin planning or for use of basinwide treatment techniques." (Roberts, 1970, p. 1554).
2. For a discussion of how such "strategic moves" can lead to non-Pareto optimal outcomes, see Schelling, 1960, especially Chs. 6 and 8. The possibility is also mentioned by Marc Roberts, 1971, pp. 105, 125.

regional treatment, and then proceed to discharge all 50,000 pounds a day, the impact of the waste discharged on the zone's water quality configuration will be far different than originally anticipated. Given this fact, the control agency may well wish to increase or decrease the number of rights initially allocated to the zone. Yet such a decision cannot be made before it is clear that regionalization will in fact occur. And if it is made after the zone's polluters have come to a tentative agreement, the polluters themselves may find a different set of treatment projects is then in their interest.

Moreover, the agency will often be interested in the precise location of the regional plant in the zone. If the plant is placed at one site, the concentrated waste stream may destroy another zone's recreational uses, while if it is located at another site the desirable recreational area will be greatly enhanced. Nevertheless, so long as the number of zoned BOD rights is fixed in advance, the dischargers will have no financial incentive to locate at the point within the zone where they will do relatively little damage. To make the problem even more complex, the cost-conscious agency will not always insist that the regional plant be placed at the point where the *least* damage is done to water quality—for it may be that the added costs of piping wastes to this location are higher than the marginal damage caused by placing the regional facility in a more central location. Thus both in determining a regional plant's optimal location and optimal level of discharge, an agency will have to intervene far more actively in the planning process than contemplated by the market models considered in the preceding chapter.[3] Needless to say, the case for active intervention is even stronger when an intelligent regionalization strategy would require either that polluters in *different* river zones treat their waste in a central location or that several regional plants be built in different sections of the river.

Agency Activism and the Problem of Coordination

Given the inadequacies of both legal orders and market models, it seems wise to consider seriously the merits of a more activist approach to regulation than either of these strategies contemplates. Under this new approach, the agency first must take a major share in planning potential regional facilities so as to assure that important regional opportunities will not be overlooked, that the complex planning process will not be used for dilatory purposes, that plans will be competently executed, and that issues of re-

3. See Rose-Ackerman, 1973.

gional importance will be fully developed.[4] Second, the agency must be willing and able (a) to compel polluters engaging in endless dilatory negotiation to join the treatment system and (b) to impose a cost allocation formula upon the participants. Third, if it seems appropriate, the authority must be willing and able to build and operate joint facilities on its own initiative, forcing the region's dischargers to enter the system when it is completed.

It is true, of course, that the activist mode of intervention suggested here has dangers of its own. If the regional authority is to invoke such substantial powers, steps must be taken to assure their responsible use. Moreover, since we have thus far lacked the wit to devise mechanisms to assure responsibility in public works planning (witness the Army Corps of Engineers and New York Port Authority) it may be suggested that whatever the defects involved in an overly decentralized scheme, the possibilities of abuse are even greater if an agency sets out to "solve" the pollution problem through an activist approach. Furthermore, in order to choose the most efficient number of regional plants and their location, the agency must have reasonably accurate cost data as well as information about the compatibility of different types of wastes. In principle, it ought to have cost estimates of regional treatment, piping and individual treatment in order to strike an efficient balance between individual and joint treatment. Of course, the difficulty of obtaining accurate data, especially for individual treatment, is a major constraint on centralized action.

At the present stage in our understanding of institutional engineering, we think it impossible to make any firm judgments as to the possibilities of the coherent use of activism by pollution control agencies and its relative merit compared to passive regulatory techniques. The purpose of the present chapter, at any rate, is far more modest than this. First, we shall detail some of the DRBC's experiences in inducing cooperative activity among polluters in the State of New Jersey[5] so as to reveal the dramatic consequences of the agency's selection of a decentralized, passive approach to regulation. Second, we shall isolate some of the structural weaknesses which help account for the failure both to plan coherently and to carry

4. Using the cost data generated by DECS, one group of researchers has attempted to estimate the optimal location of regional treatment plants and the list of dischargers that ought to be induced to join each one (see Graves, et al., 1970). The problem was a complex programming exercise, but its practical applicability is questionable both because of the weakness of the cost data and the fact that all wastes were assumed to be compatible.
5. We have also collected similar data on the regionalization process in Pennsylvania. It would, however, inordinately lengthen the presentation to analyze it here.

through joint projects efficiently, as well as sketch some general lessons to be learned from the DRBC's activist efforts.

CAMDEN COUNTY—REGIONAL INACTION, STATE PLANNING, AND LOCAL POLITICS

Introduction

Efforts at regionalization in New Jersey began in 1965, long before the DRBC set water quality standards, when the state enacted legislation which directed its health department to encourage regional plants through planning grants[6] and construction subsidies.[7] Pursuant to the Act, the department's water quality division made a grant to the Camden County Board of Freeholders to undertake a regionalization study, which was soon begun by a Camden engineering firm, John Reutter Associates. The firm moved promptly, and by December 6, 1967 a lengthy report[8] was submitted to the Freeholders proposing that nearly all of the county's 37 municipalities should consolidate their sewage treatment operations into a single large plant in the city of Camden. The Reutter report was then published and made available to the municipalities on December 29, 1967; as we shall see, they did not greet it warmly. Before considering the fate of the proposal, however, it is wise to consider the nature of Camden's pollution problems and the interests which the state, the county, and the county's consulting firm might have in advancing regionalization as a cure.

The Pollution Problem in Camden County

Camden County's 37 municipalities[9] may be usefully subdivided for our proposes into two subregions. Along the riverfront the cities of Camden and Gloucester have been declining in population and economic vitality over the past generation.[10] The stagnating city of Camden has the worst

6. N.J. STAT. ANN. §26:2E-4 (1965).
7. N.J. STAT. ANN. §26:2E-8 (1965).
8. *Camden Study*, 1967.
9. Among these are 2 cities, 27 boroughs, and 8 townships. For definitions of these terms see N.J. STAT. ANN. §40:86 et seq.
10. Camden's population has declined steadily from a peak of 124,555 in 1950 to 117,159 in 1960 and 102,557 in 1970. At present the city contains 14,000 fewer inhabitants than it did 50 years ago, in 1920, when the number reached 116,309. Like Camden, Gloucester City reached a plateau in 1920 when the population grew to 12,162. By 1960 the total had edged upward to 15,511, but the 1970 census revealed a loss of 804 inhabitants, leaving a population of 14,707 (1 *Census of Population*, 32-5—32-14, 1960; *Census of Population*, VPC (VI)-32, New Jersey, 4-5, 1970).

treatment plant in the county, eliminating only 30 to 40 percent of its FSUOD. When it was built in 1955 it was planned to be the first stage of a secondary facility which would have reduced FSUOD by 85 to 90 percent. The secondary plant, however, has remained on the drawing boards.[11] While Gloucester does possess a secondary treatment plant, its efficiency is low and it removes, at best, only about 80 percent of the FSUOD in its influent.[12] Thus the state's regulatory problem along the county's shore was simply to force these declining cities, with deteriorating tax bases, to issue bonds to construct modern facilities and to obtain sufficient revenue to maintain high standards in their operation.

An examination of the second subregion, however, makes the state's regulatory problem seem more complex. The inland section of the county is experiencing substantial growth, with the population of the dominant township of Cherry Hill doubling to 60,000 between 1960 and 1970,[13] and each of the county's important streams suffers significant pollution problems. Odors are not uncommon, turbidity and coliform levels are high, and algae often coat the banks with green slime.[14] Moreover these conditions cannot be attributed to grossly inadequate treatment facilities. Almost all of the Camden towns have secondary sewage treatment plants,[15] and most are justly proud of them. While some rapidly expanding communities are seriously troubled by overloaded facilities, the situation is in general not nearly so pressing as in neighboring New Jersey counties (and various other areas throughout the United States).

The fundamental problem is that even modern secondary treatment facilities will probably not eliminate the odor, fish kills, and algae bloom.

11. The history of Camden's pollution control effort is recounted in the *Camden Study,* pp. 191–94.

12. The Gloucester City Sewerage Authority reported that its plant reduced FSUOD by 80 percent. State analyses of samples collected at the plant in 1970 show effluent FSUOD of 37 ppm on February 18, 36 ppm on April 14, and 36 ppm on June 2 (*Department of Environmental Protection State of New Jersey v. Borough of Audubon,* Superior Court, Camden County, Docket No. C-1178-70, Brief for Plaintiff, at Exhibit E). Since official state records contained no data on BOD influent, state officials advise us that it is most plausible to assume an average influent of 250 ppm. On this basis, the state analyses translate to 85 percent, 64 percent, and 86 percent removal, or an average of 78 percent.

13. Cherry Hill's 1970 population was 64,395 (*Census of Population,* 1970, Advance Report, Final Population Counts, VPC (VI)-32 New Jersey 4, December 1970). Formerly known as Delaware Township, its population grew from 5,811 in 1940 to 10,358 in 1950 and 31,522 in 1960 (1 *Census of Population,* 32–13, 1960).

14. See *Camden Study,* pp. 164–166. Sampling data for all streams in Camden County are contained in the same study, pp. 236–258.

15. *Camden Study,* pp. 139–40, 161–62, 178, 190–91. Two negligible exceptions are the modest 0.32 mgd plant of Woodlynne Borough which has an Imhoff-type primary treatment plant (*Camden Study,* p. 190), and the somewhat smaller Imhoff primary treatment plant operated by the Borough of Brooklawn (*ibid.,* p. 140).

For the BOD, nitrates, and phosphates that remain after secondary treatment will still overtax the moderate flows to be found, especially during the summer, in the county's streams.[16] Given the inadequacies of secondary treatment, the state bureaucracy was obliged to choose among three moderately unsatisfactory strategies. First, it could try to force the inland communities to build sophisticated tertiary treatment facilities which, given the present state of the art, are far more expensive than secondary plants. Second, it could force the towns to cease discharging into the streams altogether and, instead, pipe their wastes to a regional plant on the Delaware River whose dilution capacity far transcends that of the smaller tributaries.[17] Third, it could conclude that the costs of either regionalization or tertiary treatment were so excessive that it was wisest to permit the tributaries to remain in their present condition.

Unfortunately, the state health department's approach to the problem did not permit it to confront this policy trichotomy with any clarity. Instead of fashioning regulations that took the distinctive nature of Camden's problem into account, the department promulgated regulations on a statewide basis, which, while mandating water quality improvement, provided little explicit guidance to the Reutter firm, selected by the Freeholders, on the question whether a regional solution was to be preferred to individual tertiary treatment.[18]

Private Planning in the Public Interest?

Consequently, this choice was delegated to a private enterprise, controlled informally by pressures from the state health department, and Camden County's Freeholders. Before assessing the text of Reutter's report it is best to consider the nature of these bureaucratic and political pressures. From the state agency's point of view, regionalization had several important

16. The *Camden Study* indicates that in 1965–66 the Cooper River experienced low summer flows varying from 1.2 cfs to 8 cfs (*ibid.*, p. 165). Since the total sewage treatment plant effluent above the measuring station averages 2.5 mgd or 3.8 cfs (*loc. cit.*), there is good reason to believe that on the worst days of the year the river is almost completely composed of treated effluent. Even when average conditions are considered, *Camden Study* indicates that the dilution ratio is a very low 4.2 parts of fresh water to one part sewage (*ibid.*, p. 89).
17. The Delaware River has an average flow of 11,680 cfs at Trenton, and a recorded seven-day low of 1309 cfs. Moreover, its volume increases dramatically as the river flows downstream.
18. New Jersey State Department of Health, Regulations Concerning Treatment of Waste Waters, Domestic and Industrial, Separately or in Combination, Discharged into the Waters of the Delaware River Basin, Being Waters of the State of New Jersey (filed with Secretary of State, Oct. 17, 1967, to be effective Nov. 17, 1967); N.J. STAT. ANN. §58:12, §I.

advantages over tertiary treatment. First, it assured the cleanup of the county's tributaries by piping the effluent to a single facility on the estuary. Of course this meant an increased BOD load upon the Delaware. However, state officials discounted this factor substantially, since the estuary's pollution problems were principally the responsibility of the DRBC. In contrast, the results of a tertiary treatment program on the county tributaries were uncertain. Second, the construction of a single large facility, instead of 45 small ones,[19] promised to simplify significantly the state's task of enforcing effluent standards. Similarly, from the Freeholders' point of view, regionalization had its attractions. Not only would a countywide sewer authority provide a source of patronage, it also promised the chance to award a number of lucrative construction contracts. Finally, the consulting firm's self-interest could be promoted by coming out for regionalization. If the firm fulfilled the expectations of its state and local benefactors, it could expect the more lucrative engineering contract to follow a well received regionalization study. In contrast, if it opted for tertiary treatment, it would have to convince each of many localities to award it their smaller assignments, instead of giving them to competing engineering firms with which they often had preexisting relationships.

Thus, on beginning a study of the Reutter report, one should not have high hopes that the choice between regionalization and tertiary treatment will be thoroughly and impartially canvassed. The report fulfills these low expectations. While Reutter argues that tertiary treatment is neither technologically nor economically desirable, its analysis is simplistic and flawed by obvious errors.[20] Indeed, even the report's favored proposal, contemplating a countywide system centering on Camden's treatment plant, is sketched in an exceedingly vague form.

In characterizing the report in this way, we do not mean to suggest that a careful analysis would not vindicate regionalization. Our point here is simply that the Reutter firm itself, the state agency that made the study grant, and the county that hired the firm, all had substantial incentives to press forward with regionalization, and it is the dynamic of these pressures which explains the Reutter position better than anything in the report.

There was, however, at least one agency whose bureaucratic interests should have led it to monitor the Reutter effort with care. That agency was

19. Of the County's 48 existing sewage treatment plants, *Camden Study,* pp. 100–107, (but see p. 224 where the figure of 42 is used), all but three would be abandoned or converted into pumping stations under the regionalization plan. (see *ibid.,* pp. 141, 169, 206, Map 4 following 207).
20. A detailed analysis of the *Camden Study* is available upon request from the authors. See also, the discussion at pp. 292, 293, *infra.*

the Delaware River Basin Commission. To implement its Delaware River objectives over a reasonably short period of time, it was necessary to force the stagnating riverfront cities to invest significant sums in pollution control. The difficulty of this task would be compounded by a plan requiring not only Camden City and Gloucester City to upgrade treatment but also forcing all the inland localities to enter into a regional confederation. Nevertheless, despite the obvious inadequacies of the Reutter analysis, despite the fact that countywide regionalization promised to delay the DRBC program substantially, the agency and its staff did not take any interest in the problem during the time Reutter was developing its proposal. In noting the DRBC's passivity, we do not mean to suggest that a more aggressive agency would have opposed regionalization in Camden County. It seems clear, however, that from the very beginning such an agency would have taken steps both to assure that the proposal was well conceived and to guarantee rapid compliance through the use of legal sanctions.

Planning and Local Politics

Instead the DRBC stood idly by as the Reutter report was offered on December 6, 1967 to an eager County Board of Chosen Freeholders and an angry group of local officials. The Freeholders were eager to act because their time in office had been rudely cut short by a statewide Republican landslide on November 7, 1967, which led to the defeat of three of Camden County's Democratic Freeholders.[21] Until the first of the year, however, the Democrats remained in control by a five to two margin. And on December 6, the lameduck Freeholders seized control over Camden County's sewerage system. Despite the protests of the two Republican Freeholders,[22] the board adopted one of the report's principal recommendations by creating a Camden County Sewerage Authority (CCSA), which would administer the proposed regional system, and on December 28 named a five-man slate to the authority that was dominated by Democrats.[23]

The partisan triumph was short-lived. On January 1, 1968, the new Republican Freeholders assumed office, denounced the Democratic CCSA, and even refused it permission to continue meeting in the county's offices.[24]

21. *The New York Times*, Nov. 8, 1967, p. 1, col. 6.
22. Freeholders Peter Del Grande and Thomas Schuster tried to postpone the vote until after Jan. 1, 1968 (Camden *Courier-Post*, Dec. 6, 1967, p. 1, col. 7), and vainly sought to enjoin the appointments (*ibid.*, Dec. 22, 1967, p. 21, col. 1).
23. Camden *Courier-Post*, Dec. 23, 1967, p. 5, col. 4.
24. See Camden *Courier-Post*, Dec. 30, 1967, p. 11, col. 7; Jan. 5, 1968, p. 2, col. 3; April 26, 1968, p. 10, col. 1; Feb. 25, 1969, p. 8, col. 1.

To make matters worse for the CCSA, New Jersey law permits each locality to withdraw from a countywide sewer authority within 60 days of its
creation.[25] Even before the Christmas holiday, secessionist rumblings were
audible from the largely Republican towns.[26] In addition to the partisan
politics surrounding the genesis of the embryonic CCSA, several additional
factors further undermined the chances of successfully stemming a stam-
pede away from the authority. The Reutter report failed to provide CCSA
Chairman David Epstein with credible cost estimates for the regional proposal.[27] Moreover, it failed to make clear whether the new county authority
would compensate the towns for their treatment facilities which would no
longer be needed.[28] Finally, the CCSA was not greatly helped by the
assistance it received from the state bureaucracy, its godfather. Shortly before the Reutter report was published, the health department issued orders
to 22 of Camden's 37 municipalities requiring them to build improved
facilities by 1971.[29] These orders were part of a statewide enforcement
effort intended to dramatize the dawning of a new era of pollution control
throughout the state.[30] Nevertheless, they had an unhappy impact upon the
town fathers of Camden localities. While the language of the orders was
ambiguous, the city fathers assumed they were being ordered to build
facilities individually.[31] This seemed highly arbitrary since the state would
neither grant the necessary permits for new sewer construction nor approve
any application for state or federal subsidies on that basis.[32] Moreover, as
they became aware of the Reutter report, they could see that much more

25. N.J. STAT. ANN. §40:14A-4(g) (1967).
26. Haddon Township had already voted to leave the authority and the Boroughs of
Runnemede and Barrington had voiced objections to the high, and relatively vague, cost
estimates (Camden *Courier-Post,* Dec. 22, 1967, p. 21, col. 1).
27. While the *Camden Study* did provide some crude cost estimates (pp. 218–20),
our interviews indicate that they were widely disbelieved.
28. The report left this question open, noting that a $12.3 million bond issue would
be required if no compensation were to be paid, while otherwise a $25 million bond
issue would be needed (*ibid.,* pp. 217–218).
29. Department of Environmental Protection v. Borough of Audubon, Brief for
Plaintiff at 5 and at Exhibit E.
30. Interviews with state officials who prefer to remain anonymous.
31. The ambiguity arose from a final section reading:

"6. The work performance scheduled herein shall be in conformity with the
master engineering plan for sewerage services in the County of Camden as
approved by the New Jersey State Department of Health."

Since the *Camden Study* had not yet been published at the time the orders were
received, the rather inconspicuous reference to a "master engineering plan" for the
county merely created doubt as to what the precise requirements would be.
32. The state's power to regulate arises under N.J. STAT. ANN. §40:62–67 (1967).
The department's authority to approve applications for federal subsidies arises under
N.J. STAT. ANN. §26:2E-8(c-d) (1967) and 33 U.S.C.A. §1158(b) (1970).

work had to be done before it could serve as the basis of an agreement for a regional plant. Most importantly, while the Reutter report estimated the capital cost of the new regional facility to be $53 million, the firm's subsequent public statements indicated that the final cost could range between $55 million and $80 million.[33] Much hard bargaining as well as technical study would be required before firm cost figures, as well as a cost apportionment formula, could be hammered out.

Resentful of the state's premature summary orders, fearful of the costs of the new proposal, and angered by the politically motivated way in which the CCSA had come upon the scene, the towns of Camden County were in a rebellious mood. While it is, of course, impossible to know whether the DRBC could have intervened at this late date to save the Reutter proposal or to maintain a semblance of peace until an alternative could be devised, the fact of the matter is that at no point during the critical weeks did the Commission or its staff attempt to do so.

The Dominance of Local Politics

Instead, another local force moved into the power vacuum. Angelo Errichetti, now mayor of Camden and chairman of the city's Democratic Party, was city Director of Public Works during that period. Errichetti saw in the impasse a chance to build an alternative countywide sewerage authority under his own chairmanship. While at the time he could proffer no engineering plans, his overtures to the outlying towns[34] seemed more attractive than those contained in the Reutter report. Unlike the CCSA, Errichetti proposed a "home rule" plan which, instead of phasing out local facilities completely, simply required each town to pump its waste to the Camden city plant for a second round of treatment.

"Home rule" had two advantages. First, debt on a number of plants remained outstanding. Under the bonds' terms, the bondholders' consent was required in order to close some of these plants.[35] And, of course, the bondholders could be expected to demand a higher interest rate—more in line with high 1968 rates—if their security was disturbed. Second, under

33. Camden *Courier-Post*, Dec. 6, 1967, p. 1, col. 7; May 1, 1968, p. 13, col. 1.
34. The details of the plan were presented orally to the various municipality leaders at various times without precise refinement. The rough description of the plan which follows is based on our interviews with some of these leaders during the summer of 1970.
35. This problem came up often in our interviews, although—as in some other matters of financial detail—we are unable to report precise data. It is clear, however, that under N.J. STAT. ANN. §40:14B-30 (1957) such provisions may be included in municipal sewerage authority bond resolutions, and bondholders may be given a veto or similar power.

"home rule," each municipality would retain its own sewerage mini-bureaucracy, while under the CCSA plan the towns would lose this right. Similarly, Errichetti permitted each community to parcel out the construction and maintenance contracts for the segments of the system within its geographic boundary, while CCSA proposed to select the contractors itself.

In addition to promising the towns at least a portion of their old autonomy, Errichetti had yet another bargaining chip provided by the chaotic structure of present federal subsidy programs. While the principal subsidy effort was then administered by the Federal Water Quality Administration,[36] an independent program was also operated by the Economic Development Administration in the Department of Commerce.[37] The EDA program is reserved for "economically distressed" areas,[38] including the stagnating city of Camden. Thus, if the city played a leading role in the project, a more liberal subsidy might be forthcoming from the EDA than would otherwise be available from the FWQA. Indeed, it was possible that subsidies could be obtained from both the federal agencies.[39] Promising "home rule" and lower costs, Errichetti obtained a favorable hearing with the township and borough councils of the neighboring localities alienated by the strong-arm tactics of county and state. The critical negotiations were between the city of Camden and the township of Cherry Hill, a bedroom community which, by virtue of its size and critical location, would determine the position of many of the smaller communities.[40] Shortly before January 1, 1968, Cherry Hill exercised its statutory right to secede from CCSA, and was followed quickly by *all* of the remaining communities within the county.[41] It was plain that unless the state or the DRBC intervened in a forceful manner, the municipalities were in no mood to give further consideration to the CCSA, at least until the city of Camden's plans were developed and their implications made clear.

The next move was up to the state, and Chairman Epstein warned that the state would coerce the localities into the CCSA, since it was only in that way that the health department's clean-up orders could be effectu-

---

36. 33 U.S.C.A. §§1152–1175 (1970).
37. 42 U.S.C.A. §§3131–3136 (1970).
38. See 42 U.S.C.A. §3161 (1970).
39. The EDA is willing "to augment basic grants received . . . under other Federal grant-in-aid programs, provided the total Federal financial assistance for any project does not exceed 80 percent of the aggregate project cost." 13 C.F.R. §301.10 (1972).
40. Cherry Hill is the second largest municipality in Camden County, with a population of 64,000 (see n. 13).
41. Conversations with Edward Gramigna, Chairman of the CCSA during 1972.

ated.[42] In response to the threat of enforcement proceedings, a group of localities led by the Borough of Collingswood seized the initiative by instituting its own action in the Superior Court, petitioning for an injunction against the health department pending further development and refinement of the regional plan. The matter came up for hearing on February 21, 1968[43] and placed the state health department in an awkward position. First, the department had not yet lost hope that through voluntary negotiations a mutually satisfactory solution could be reached. To embark upon an adversary lawsuit seemed certain to polarize the parties further. Second, in order to defend the suit, the state government had to associate itself publicly with the lameduck Democrats on the CCSA who had been unable to command significant community support. Third, even if the state were successful in obtaining injunctive relief, the judgment could be appealed, thus considerably delaying any actual steps toward compliance. Finally, it was not at all clear that the court would uphold the regionalization aspect of the state's orders. While the statutes permit the health department to obtain an injunction "to restrain the [pollution] violation and *for such other and further relief in the premises as said court shall deem proper,*"[44] it seemed possible that a court would deem it "improper" to order the towns to join an authority which they ordinarily, under state law, had the right to abandon. For all these reasons, the state health department chose not to defend its orders in the Collingswood suit. Instead, it agreed to defer all enforcement efforts until the regionalization issue had been clarified. In return, the plaintiffs agreed to dismiss their lawsuit without seeking a judicial determination of the validity of the department's orders.[45] By failing to stand behind its orders, the state severely undermined its effectiveness in resolving the ongoing dispute. After all its tough talk of court action, the health department turned out to be a paper tiger.

At this point, it already had become clear that unless the DRBC attempted to induce relatively rapid action by invoking its own enforcement

42. Camden *Courier-Post,* Feb 8, 1968, p. 1, col. 3.
43. *Ibid.,* Feb. 22, 1968, p. 1, col. 3. The localities based their actions on N.J. STAT. ANN. §58:12-2 (1953). While we have been unable to obtain any official records of this action, it is summarized in the Plaintiff's Brief in Department of Environmental Protection v. Borough of Audubon, p. 3.
44. N.J. STAT. ANN. §58:10-8 (1953), emphasis supplied.
45. Each of the localities agreed simply to maintain its existing facilities in good condition and to "maintain frequent communication with the Division of Clean Air and Water in relation to further developments in the endeavors of the Borough to collaborate with the development and the construction of adequate regional sewerage facilities. . . ." Department of Environmental Protection v. Borough of Audubon, Brief for Plaintiff, at Exhibit F.

powers[46] no action would be forthcoming on the local level until Errichetti was given time to develop Camden's alternative "regional" proposal. Even after Errichetti's plan had been formulated, many months or years would elapse while each of the towns decided whether to join either the CCSA or to cooperate with the city. Nevertheless, throughout the period, the Commission remained quiescent.

Events began to move to a climax when, on December 12, 1968, the Mayor of Camden announced that Cherry Hill and neighboring municipalities would be invited to begin formal negotiations looking toward membership in the Camden Municipal Utilities Authority (CMUA). The CCSA, after denouncing the city's move, responded by brandishing a new weapon in its struggle. The nature of Chairman Epstein's weapon will be understood when it is recognized that federal law requires *state* approval of a project before the Federal Water Quality Administration will even consider the proposal for federal subsidy—which may amount to 55 percent of total cost.[47] Moreover, the State of New Jersey stood ready to subsidize on its own up to 30 percent of the cost of projects it approved.[48] Thus state approval of the CMUA would permit the localities involved to obtain the right to deflect a great deal of their cost onto higher levels of government. As a result, the Errichetti faction was greatly chagrined when the water quality division made it known that the state would not approve for subsidy any new facility in Camden County which had not been previously approved by its rival, the CCSA. When Epstein indicated unequivocally that he would refuse to approve any independent effort[49] Cherry Hill once again began negotiations with the CCSA.

In undertaking these negotiations, the city fathers were in part attempting to forestall the state's imposition of a sewer freeze which would halt further development in their fast-growing township. The state's water quality division had already filed suit against Cherry Hill's large southern neighbor, Gloucester Township, and obtained a consent order limiting the number of new sewer connections to be made in the township until regionalization became a reality.[50] Reportedly at the instigation of builders in Gloucester Township who were angered by the imposition of this consent

46. See DELAWARE RIVER BASIN COMPACT, 75 Stat. 688, §5.4, 1961. The DRBC has power to adopt rules and regulations for prevention and abatement of pollution and may issue orders compelling compliance with such rules. The Commission can bring court action to have such orders enforced.
47. See Hines, 1967, pp. 842, 43, for a discussion of the principles regulating federal construction grants under the Clean Water Restoration Act of 1966.
48. N.J. STAT. ANN. §26:2E-8(b) (1967).
49. Camden *Courier-Post*, Feb. 19, 1969, p. 4, col. 1.
50. New Jersey Dep't of Environmental Protection files.

decree[51] two private citizens in Cherry Hill brought a taxpayers' suit against their own municipality early in 1970, and obtained an order to show cause why the township should continue issuing construction permits and certificates of occupancy, since its sewerage treatment plants were allegedly "overworked."[52]

By the time the taxpayers' suit was instituted, however, Cherry Hill's lengthy negotiations with the CCSA had succeeded in warding off a sewer freeze long enough to allow Camden's consultants to complete a study in support of Errichetti's program. The report[53] was a meager document, which contented itself with extremely vague cost estimates and sketchy engineering proposals. Nevertheless, it was a *report,* and Errichetti, having it in hand, set out to reverse the state's earlier decision giving the CCSA a veto power over state and FWQA subsidy. At this time it became necessary for Errichetti to reckon with the DRBC, at least in passing. Even if the state were to approve the CMUA and authorize the subsidy, the Commission nevertheless retained the ultimate power to veto under the Compact.[54] Consequently, before negotiating with the state authorities, Errichetti got in touch with important DRBC staffers and was told informally that if the State of New Jersey found his plan acceptable, the commission's staff would raise no fundamental objections.[55]

Contenting himself with this informal inquiry, Errichetti concentrated on reversing the state bureaucracy's position on the subsidy question. This would be no easy matter. The water quality division held Errichetti responsible for subverting the Reutter report, which it had funded, and could be expected to fight for the CCSA to the last. Consequently, Errichetti decided to use his political influence at higher levels of the New Jersey executive. Despite the fact the administration in Trenton was Republican, as was the legislature, Democrat Errichetti found that he had sufficient political influence to induce Richard J. Sullivan, director of the clean air and water division,[56] to overrule his staff.[57] It would be a mistake, however, to believe that Sullivan simply buckled under pressure. At least

51. Interviews with anonymous state and local officials, summer 1970.
52. Camden *Courier-Post,* March 20, 1970, p. 23, col. 7.
53. *Development of Regional Plan,* 1970.
54. See DELAWARE RIVER BASIN COMPACT, 75 Stat. 688, §5.4, 1961, and n. 46.
55. Interviews with anonymous local, state, and DRBC staff officials.
56. Sullivan, a Democrat not active in politics, had been appointed to this position by Governor Hughes (also a Democrat) in February 1967. He continued to serve the State in this capacity even after Governor Cahill (a Republican) was inaugurated in 1968. In 1970, Cahill appointed Sullivan Commissioner of a new State Dep't of Environmental Protection. (Interview with reporters for the Trenton *Times,* May 1971).
57. Camden *Courier-Post,* April 10, 1970, p. 1, col. 4.

the city of Camden seemed eager to move ahead, thereby permitting the hope that the 18-month impasse could be resolved. Moreover, neither the CCSA plan nor the CMUA plan was precise enough to permit a confident judgment as to their relative merits.

Sullivan's announcement, however, did not inaugurate a new era of good feeling in Camden County. The CMUA planned to centralize treatment only in the more heavily populated sector of Camden County along the Cooper River; the less densely populated area along Big Timber Creek was ignored, regionalization in this sub-watershed being left to the CCSA. This division of the county in two "spheres of influence," however, meant that a number of localities along the dividing line could choose to join either the CCSA or CMUA. Thus, the two authorities began to compete for the allegiance of the border towns, while the towns themselves delayed their decisions in an effort to extract the most out of their favorable bargaining position. Even more important, the towns along the Cooper River found that CMUA's proposed regionalization terms were less attractive than they had initially appeared. Errichetti's CMUA proposed to assume the substantial indebtedness that remained outstanding on the city of Camden's large primary treatment plants[58] but refused to assume the indebtedness on the outlying facilities owned by the townships.[59] Moreover, the city's sewer system served substantial industrial polluters, and the share of the cost to be borne by industry had yet to be determined.[60] Finally, the estimated cost of the project had escalated from $20 million to $40 million.[61]

To make matters worse, other towns, noting the success of the city of Camden and Cherry Hill in maneuvering to further their own interests, began to play the same game. During 1969, the city of Gloucester began developing its own "regional alternative" to the CCSA. This incipient rebellion was very neatly nipped in the bud in the fall of 1970, when the new head of the CCSA, Edward Gramigna, secretly negotiated an option for a choice waterfront property on the city's main street, and then blandly informed the city fathers that if they refused to join the CCSA the au-

---

58. See *Service Contract*, schedule B.
59. Cherry Hill's existing bonded indebtedness allocable to sewerage facilities, for example, has been estimated by John H. Osler, the Township Engineer, at about $2.1 million (Camden *Courier-Post*, April 15, 1970, p. 25, col. 1).
60. Interviews with anonymous local and state officials, summer 1970.
61. Interview with Bruce Campbell, President, Middle Atlantic States Engineering Inc., Newtown, Pennsylvania, Sept. 1970. By January 28, 1971, CMUA estimated the total cost of its construction program at $49.7 million "less federal, state and EDA [sic] grants of $36.2 million" (or 73 percent of the total).

thority would in retaliation exercise its option on the city site and build a sewer plant in Gloucester City for the adjoining communities. This maneuver, if carried out, would not only deprive the city of a prime taxable property but also would deafen the city's quiet main street with months of construction noise. When faced with this prospect, the city fathers privately admitted they had been outmaneuvered and would probably join the CCSA in order to get the authority to build somewhere else.[62] However, the officials continued to keep up appearances by initiating a court action to restrain the CCSA from purchasing the choice property[63] and in January, 1971, the mayor of Gloucester City called a public meeting to protest the CCSA's secret maneuvering and generally "to cry 'foul' ".[64]

Judicial Intervention

While all this was taking place, the DRBC staff remained aloof from the political battle; the state's water quality division, however, despite its defeat at Errichetti's hands in March 1970, was unwilling to permit the situation to collapse into utter disorder. Pressures began once more to build, this time for legal action to coerce a countywide solution.

According to the state's 1967 orders to 22 of the county's municipalities, each was obliged to comply by February 1, 1971. Accordingly, on December 23, 1970, the newly created department of environmental protection filed suit in the Superior Court of Camden County against the municipalities, requesting the court to require each town to join either the CCSA or CMUA within 60 days, and to impose an immediate freeze on building permits and sewer connections to be administered by the department.[65]

As we have already suggested[66] the state's action appears to have been something of a desperate gamble. The legal issues involved had not changed significantly from the day in 1968 when the department of health refused to argue the merits of its regionalization plan in court. The state's practical position was strengthened, however, by increasing public (and judicial) consciousness of the pollution problem, and by judicial notice that no real

62. Interviews with anonymous county and local officials, Oct. 1970.
63. A temporary injuction restraining the CCSA from closing its deal on the Armstrong Cork property was obtained from Judge John B. Wick in Dec. 1970 (Woodbury *Daily Times,* Dec. 30, 1970).
64. Camden *Courier-Post,* Jan. 15, 1971, p. 1, col. 3.
65. Department of Environmental Protection *vs* Borough of Audubon, complaint sections a–k following 28th count.
66. See pp. 294, 295, this chapter.

progress had been made in three years' time.[67] And it was these practical considerations which exclusively occupied the mind of Judge Wick of the Superior Court when the matter came up for hearing on January 29, 1971. The Judge announced his decision orally immediately at the close of argument. The state statute's grant of a right of secession was ignored with the statement that:

Now by reason of the passage of the act [apparently N.J.S.A. 58112-2] by the Legislature of the State of New Jersey, it is now our policy to regionalize sewer disposition. You and I can't do a thing about it except accept it. . . .[68]

The problem posed by the vague nature of the CCSA and CMUA proposals was similarly dismissed:

Don't tell me that by reason of the fact that a period of three years have gone by that any of you gentlemen interested as far as your respective municipalities are concerned, that you could not have found out what it's all about as far as everything that these—that the Camden County Sewerage Authority had as far as information is concerned. They were ready, willing and hopeful of meeting with everybody who showed an interest. And they did go many times to discuss these problems. But I have a very distinct feeling that in many instances, because it was a county telling the small municipalities what to do, or because it was Democrats telling the Republicans what to, or because that particular municipality was not represented on the Board, they didn't want to hear it.[69]

In short, the legal solution for Judge Wick was simple:

Each and every one of you have until April the 1st to approve these ordinances [joining CCSA or CMUA] that are required [before the authorities are able] to agree to these contracts.

67. Department of Environmental Protection *vs* Borough of Audubon, pp. 4, 5, unpublished transcript of oral opinion. Indeed, the judicial concern with the passage of time was manifested in an extraordinary manner. On Jan. 12, 1971 Judge John B. Wick was publicly accused of prejudice by a Gloucester City businessman as a result of remarks made by the Judge on Jan. 7, after he dissolved the temporary restraining order requested by Gloucester City officials. According to the Camden *Courier-Post,* Judge Wick said, "I am sick and tired of politicians from both parties dragging their feet on the antipollution laws. And if they are looking for someone to get them off the hook, I'm going to be that man. I intend, on the 29th of this month, to rule that all municipalities involved will be prohibited from issuing any permits for new construction until such time as they join either authority." (Camden *Courier-Post,* Jan. 9, 1971, p. 1, col. 3; *ibid.,* Jan. 12, 1971, p. 13, col. 3) While Judge Wick was subjected to some criticism for announcing his order before hearing the arguments, the Camden *Courier-Post* came to his defense in an editorial on Feb. 3, 1971, praising him for his propollution-control decision despite the premature way in which it was announced (*ibid.,* Feb. 3, 1971, p. 18, col. 1).
68. Dep't of Environmental Protection *vs* Borough of Audubon, p. 6.
69. *Ibid.,* pp. 6, 7.

But after April the 1st if you have not agreed, don't issue any permits for any construction of any nature, type, or even any subdivisions.

Gentlemen, it's just as simple as that. If you do not agree to this regionalization, don't issue any building permits or don't issue any approval of land subdivision.

Thank you.[70]

Despite Judge Wick's sweeping order, many of the municipalities failed to join one or the other system.[71] The state bureaucracy, despairing of any progress, given the continuing competition of two authorities for membership, decided finally to desert its godchild, the CCSA, and press for the establishment of a single new authority to begin planning afresh. This new state initiative gained powerful support from the federal EPA, which announced that it would refuse to subsidize two "regional" systems on the ground that needless expense and duplication of effort would result.[72] In response to state and federal pressure, the CCSA and CMUA were dissolved and a new Camden County Municipal Utilities Authority, containing much of the old CMUA staff, was organized.[73] By the summer of 1973, this new organization was about to begin a new round of engineering studies, and optimistically[74] hoped that countywide system would be in operation by 1977—a decade after the Board of Freeholders first considered the Reutter report.

GLOUCESTER COUNTY AND DEEPWATER: COMMISSION vs STATE

It is tempting to move immediately from the Camden case study to an analysis of the legal and bureaucratic structures which made such chaos

70. *Ibid.,* p. 5.
71. Interview with Samuel Supnick, Solicitor to the Camden County Municipal Utilities Authority, July 1973; telephone conversation with Lawrence Stanley, Deputy Attorney General, State of New Jersey, July, 1973.
72. Interview with Samuel Supnick, July 1973; telephone conversations with Lawrence Stanley, and Peter Devine, Gen'l Counsel, Environmental Protection Agency (Region Two), and Charles Pike, Dir. of Div. of Water Resources of the State of New Jersey, July 1973.
73. The dissolution of the two previous authorities was opposed by a number of municipalities and bond counsel unless the new authority would accept responsibility for all the bonded indebtedness previously assumed by the CCSA and CMUA. Just before this law suit was heard by Judge Bishoff of the Camden County Superior Court, the DRBC threatened to intervene directly in the dispute. On July 16, 1973 the DRBC announced that it would consider imposing penalties on the municipalities unless they moved promptly on the new regionalization proposal (DRBC press release, July 16, 1973). After Judge Bishoff announced his approval of the new authority on July 21, however, the DRBC indicated that it would not move forcefully into the issue for the time being (*Philadelphia Inquirer,* July 28, 1973, p. 9, col. 1).
74. Interview with Samuel Supnick, July 1973.

possible. Camden, however, is an extreme case in the pathology of decentralized decision making. Before attempting even a tentative analysis, we should consider a situation in which decentralized decision making performed relatively well under the same legal structures. By comparing the two cases, we will obtain at least an impressionistic sense of the strengths and weaknesses of decentralization. Now it happens that Camden County's rapidly growing neighbor to the south,[75] Gloucester, fulfills our methodological requirements. It should be apparent, however, that two county histories can only be the beginning of a systematic study of the limitations and strengths of decentralized decision making. Nevertheless, it permits a somewhat richer appreciation of the problem before us.

A Tale of Two Counties: Why Gloucester Succeeded

At least in its early stages, the planning process in Gloucester resembled the one we have just discussed. Regionalization planning was initiated by a state grant in 1967; the Reutter firm was hired here as well; once again, it issued a report late in 1967, which recommended the establishment of a regional plant to serve the relatively densely populated area near the Delaware River.[76] In making this proposal, however, the Reutter firm confronted a situation fundamentally different from the one it faced in Camden. First, there was no discontinuity in political control at the local level which could undermine support for the plan.[77] Second, Gloucester contains no substantial city like Camden whose bureaucracy could seize the opportunity to aggrandize its own power by offering an alternative regionalization proposal. Third, as a result of rapid population growth, the townships had invested relatively small amounts in existing sewerage facilities, and so were less likely to balk at the expense of a new system. Fourth, because sewerage facilities were so primitive, regionalization was generally seen as an alternative to the construction of facilities by each locality, rather than (as in Camden County) an alternative to facilities already constructed. Fifth, regionalization appeared a desirable solution to the pollution prob-

75. While Camden County's population increased from 392,035 to 456,291 between 1960 and 1970, that of Gloucester County was rising from 134,840 to 172,681. Thus, the population of Camden County increased by only 16.4 percent while that of Gloucester County increased 28.1 percent. The State of New Jersey as a whole grew 18.2 percent during the 1960's (1 *Census of Population,* 32–5—32–14, 1960; *Census of Population,* Advance Report, Final Population Counts VPC (VI)-32 New Jersey, 4–5, 1970).

76. *Gloucester Study,* 1967.

77. Woodbury *Daily Times,* Jan. 2, 1968, p. 1, col. 1. As of Jan. 1, 1968, the County Freeholders were all Republicans. Party affiliation data on file at Woodbury *Daily Times,* Woodbury, New Jersey.

lems of several of the county's municipalities because a regional scheme could obtain state and federal aid. Finally, housing developers were complaining as local inspectors delayed the issuance of vital building permits on the ground that treatment facilities were inadequate.[78]

Thus, the chances for fruitful regionalization negotiations seemed high when, in response to the Reutter GCSA report, the Republican Board of Chosen Freeholders appointed a panel of five members to the newly created Gloucester County Sewerage Authority in February 1968. From what we can determine, all five were Republicans; each was a local politician serving on the GCSA at a salary of $1,000 a year both because it was in the "public interest" to do so and because it would, to some extent, permit visibility in county political circles. Jack Sheppard, for example, chairman of the GCSA, is a successful businessman in Philadelphia and Mayor of the small borough of Wenonah with somewhat larger political ambitions. Consequently, Sheppard explained to us that he was quite happy to address "countless" groups to emphasize the need for speedy regionalization if the county were to escape the constant threat of the "sewer freeze," on the one hand, and the death of fish and fowl on the other. Sheppard was successful in his effort to obtain general assent to the Reutter plan, and although he was obliged to undertake long and difficult negotiations with each of the 13 towns in the system, the omnipresent threat of the sewer freeze permitted the project to move forward slowly but steadily. Thus, in April 1973, five years after Reutter published its plan, a modern regional plant went into operation at Paulsboro, New Jersey.

How Gloucester Failed: The Breakdown of Negotiations

A study of Gloucester County is, however, useful not only for purposes of understanding the reasons why Gloucester succeeded slowly to organize a regional enterprise where Camden failed under the same legal structure; it also indicates the limits of the crude structure of authority even under favorable conditions. For Sheppard was capable of inducing only the area's municipalities to join forces under the GCSA banner. The story of his efforts to coordinate his activities with those of the industrial giants along the riverfront came to a far less happy—if equally enlightening—conclusion.

While suburbanites were discovering Gloucester County only in the

78. For typical problems see Woodbury *Daily Times,* May 16, 1969; *ibid.,* Sept. 11, 1969.

past decade, major oil and chemical companies had more foresight. Attracted by access to the Delaware River and low land prices, firms such as Mobil Oil, Texaco, and DuPont had already located major plants in Gloucester County.[79] Thus, when Reutter undertook its survey in 1967 it attempted to assess possibilities of municipal-industrial collaboration. The river industries, however, were uncooperative. The DRBC had not yet presented each firm with its wasteload allocation; and until BOD quotas were distributed, neither the Commission nor the state was placing any pressure upon the firms to reduce their pollution loadings. Consequently, the firms provided Reutter with only primitive data and the Reutter report gave industrial problems scant attention.

With the DRBC's final allocation of BOD quotas to individual polluters in June of 1968, however, the state health department made it clear that the firms would be required to comply promptly on an individual basis by 1971. In contrast to its policy for municipalities, the department manifested no great concern for the fact that regionalization might be cheaper for the companies than individual compliance. So long as shareholders, workers, and consumers, rather than local tax payers, were bearing the cost, the department preferred the relatively rapid compliance that only individual construction promised.

Given the stern state enforcement policy, the firms came to look upon the GCSA in a different light. Cooperation with the GCSA promised four principal advantages: first, the complex negotiations required would delay the date of capital expenditure by several years beyond 1971; second, industry's share of the cost of a regional facility might be less than that required for individual compliance, given the economies of a large plant; third, the share would probably be diminished further if the combined industry-municipal project qualified for federal and state subsidy, as then seemed likely; fourth, if the regional plant failed to operate properly, enraged conservationists would no longer demonstrate their wrath at the company's front door (or back sewer pipe) but would direct their anger at the GCSA, a governmental institution.[80]

Thus, during the early fall of 1968, representatives of the firms and GCSA held two exploratory meetings. This tentative courtship was cut short, however, in November 1968 by a sudden announcement from the

79. Other firms included Shell Chemical, Paulsboro Chemical, Hercules, Monsanto, and the Houdry Process & Chemical Company (*Gloucester Study*, p. 8). B.F. Goodrich also now has a major plant along this section of the Delaware (*Deepwater Study*, 1970, IV-25).

80. Conversations with industrial and local officials who prefer to remain anonymous, summer 1970.

DRBC. With much fanfare, the regional authority proposed the construction of an ambitious 30-mile pipeline linking the plants in the GCSA area with the enormous plants owned by the DuPont Company south of Gloucester in Salem County at Deepwater, New Jersey.[81] Under the Deepwater plan, the pipeline would conduct all the river industry waste to a single giant treatment plant for advanced treatment.

The announcement caught the GCSA by surprise. Its bitterness increased when the DRBC Executive Director James F. Wright justified the agency's proposal by noting that the Reutter report of 1967 did not envision river industry participation and thus had left a vacuum which the DRBC considered itself obliged to fill.[82] The authority resented the Commission's public charge of incompetence, especially when it was moving to remedy this failing, which was initially caused by the firms' refusal to cooperate meaningfully with Reutter.

Similarly, the DRBC initiative met with a cool reception among the officials in the state bureaucracy. To them, Deepwater meant a greatly protracted period of planning and negotiation which could ultimately lead to no final agreement whatsoever. Nevertheless, the state staff could not move aggressively against the DRBC project during the time of its development. Not only would this step antagonize the major industrial interests flocking to the Deepwater banner but it would also appear "unenlightened." For the Deepwater proposal, by crossing county lines, demonstrated the limitations of the state's planning process and seemed to break new ground in encouraging the solution of industrial waste problems in an economically efficient manner. Thus, all the state bureaucrats could do was hope for the best and order the firms to prepare plans for individual treatment if Deepwater failed.[83]

Industry reaction was naturally quite different. While "good faith" negotiations with the GCSA might induce the state to defer its demand for rapid individual compliance, participation in a DRBC-sponsored project was certain to do so. Second, the introduction of the enormous pipeline and the large southern plants was certain to expand enormously the time that would be required before the system became operational. Third, cooperation with the DRBC was far more congenial to the corporate executives than negotiations with the part-time politicians of the GCSA. In con-

81. *Deepwater Study,* Figure XI-1; DRBC press release, July 2, 1969. Monsanto had also built a large plant in this area, and B.F. Goodrich was completing construction of a new facility scheduled to begin production in 1970.
82. Conversations with local officials who prefer to remain anonymous.
83. Our understanding of the state strategy is based on interviews with state and industrial officials, summer 1970.

trast to the nonengineers on the county level, the regional agency was equipped with a staff of trained professionals who could "speak the same language" as the industry's executives. Fourth, the project seemed sufficiently precedent-making as to be worthy of a governmental "demonstration grant" despite the fact that the facility's principal beneficiaries were some of America's largest corporations.[84] Fifth, regardless of the subsidy, the large size of the treatment plant suggested the possibility of major cost savings over plant-by-plant compliance.

These facts not only help explain why industry greeted Deepwater so warmly but why the DRBC intervened so aggressively in the first place. After all, the deteriorating Camden situation represented a far greater threat to the timely achievement of the DRBC's objectives. Nevertheless, the DRBC remained severely aloof from this problem, which neither the state nor localities had handled well, and instead plunged into an area where its assistance was not nearly so important. The fundamental difference between the two situations is, of course, that in Gloucester, industry was interested in obtaining DRBC intervention, while in Camden none of the parties had an interest in inviting DRBC aid. The hypothesis that the DRBC intervened in Deepwater at the behest of industry is given further support by events occurring after the formal agency announcement of the regional proposal. The DuPont Corporation, which had by far the most to gain from the DRBC proposal,[85] exerted its leadership in a forceful manner. First it offered to contribute *gratis* land at Deepwater near its Chambers facility in Salem County, to serve as a site for the pilot plant to test the feasibility of the proposal. Second, it eagerly proffered the lion's share of the cost of embarking on the necessary engineering studies.[86] Given this considerable DuPont assistance after the announcement of the project, it seems reasonable to believe the company played an important role in its formulation from the beginning.[87]

84. The Clean Water Restoration Act of 1966 specifically authorized grants for demonstration projects dealing with the treatment of industrial wastes (see 33 U.S.C.A. §1156(b) [1970]). The 1972 Amendments, however, do not include such explicit authorization (see 33 U.S.C.A. §§1255(a), 1255(b) [Supp. 1973]).

85. DuPont's Chambers Works facility in Salem County was by far the largest polluter embraced by the DRBC regional treatment plan, discharging 100 million gallons a day in 1969. DuPont also owned the second largest plant, at Repanno, which discharged 70 mgd. The largest non-DuPont plant was operated by Mobil Oil, and discharged 30 mgd (see *Deepwater Study* Table V-1, p. V-3).

86. DuPont contributed $496,583 toward the cost of the feasibility study. The total cost of the study was $995,650, plus the value of staff time contributed by the Commission (DRBC press release, July 2, 1969, p. 1).

87. Interview with DuPont officials, summer, 1970; DRBC press release, July 2, 1969, p. 2. It also should be recognized that by focussing interest on the Deepwater site, DuPont would be in a highly favorable bargaining position in negotiating its

In contrast to the Camden case, the DRBC then proceeded to obtain a "demonstration grant" of $646,700 from the FWQA to support the Deepwater study; in addition, the agency contributed substantial amounts of its own professional staff time (valued at $150,000) to the planning effort. Despite this million-dollar effort, however, Deepwater was not to be.

How the DRBC Failed

As planning proceeded, a critical issue emerged upon which the project ultimately foundered. Both the firms and the Commission were obliged to consider the extent to which the project should be built to accommodate the rapid growth in waste loads projected for the region. From the agency staff's view, one of Deepwater's principal attractions was that it would create a structure to handle future pollution sources. Consequently, the plans developed envisioned a treatment plant big enough for 1990 waste loads and a piping system big enough for 2020.[88] In contrast, the firms were unwilling to finance a plant too large for their present purposes if they were required to bear the risk that the future polluters the DRBC anticipated would not arrive to buy into the project. The matter became critical in their eyes when their cost calculations suggested that individual treatment might be cheaper than the Commission's enormous regional alternative.

Given the conflict of interest between Commission and polluters, the DRBC had only two options if it hoped to make Deepwater a reality. First, it could use its abundant legal power to compel the existing polluters to build an oversized plant sufficient for the long run. Second, it could agree to bear the costs of building an oversized plant, levying on existing polluters only that share of the capital and maintenance which was justified by their own discharges. This second solution seemed the fairer one, since there seems little justification for a small number of firms to bear the principal burden of assuring that the Commission's policies would maintain their integrity over time.

The problem with this second strategy was obvious enough: If the existing polluters were not to bear the costs of future entrants, who was? The problem was particularly acute since the Commission had no inde-

---

"fair share" of the cost of the project, since the bulk of the considerable piping expense would then be incurred to transport Gloucester industrial waste to the Deepwater plant, while if the treatment plant were located in Gloucester much of the piping expense would be incurred to transport DuPont waste to Gloucester.

88. See *Deepwater Study: Interim,* pp. XI-1, 2.

pendent source of revenues to finance the project. As it began its search for funds, the agency soon encountered the unhappy fact that none of the complex subsidy programs in existence was designed for its problem. The agency's need for subsidy was really very limited. In order to finance the system's "excess capacity" (EC) it did not require a flat cash grant of the entire EC cost. Instead, as new firms entered the valley, it would be possible to recoup much or all of the original EC cost (plus interest) by imposing an appropriate lump sum charge on new entrants to the system. Thus, all that was required was a program in which the subsidizing authority would tide the DRBC over the early years of the project, expecting repayment of its grant as the anticipated polluters arrived on the scene.

Unfortunately, the primary federal program provides grants, not loans, and is designed to ease the burden of municipalities. The only source of funds for financing EC costs seemed to be the all-purpose "demonstration grant" provision of the Federal statutes, a catch-all which authorizes the FWQA to subsidize innovative treatment projects of whatever type so as to demonstrate their feasibility. The demonstration program, however, contemplates the provision of flat grants—not loans—to recipients.[89] It was on this aspect of the transaction that the FWQA and DRBC ultimately reached an impasse. As the environmental movement blossomed during 1970 and 1971, federal officials became unwilling to grant flat cash subsidies to a project which, however innovative, would almost exclusively assist the nation's largest industries in meeting their clean-up responsibilities. Consequently, despite early encouragement from the federal government, it became increasingly clear that "demonstration" assistance would not be forthcoming.

By the middle of 1971, then, the DRBC was obliged to return to the Deepwater firms with the news that the project would require them to bear the EC burden themselves. Moreover, the Commissioners rejected the idea of using their legal power to compel the industrial giants to join the system and so were content to see four years of work on a project go down the

---

89. The original 1948 Water Pollution Control Act contained provisions for loans to state, municipal, or interstate agencies for construction of treatment works (see 62 Stat. 1155, §5, §7 [1968]). The loan provisions were deleted by the 1956 amendments, which substituted grants as the sole source of federal funding (see 70 Stat. 498, §4[a][2] [1956]). S.2947, 89th Cong., 2d Sess., §8(h)(1) (1966) would have reinstated a loan program, but this provision was deleted in conference. The Clean Water Restoration Act of 1966, as finally enacted, provided only for grants, but explicitly allowed grants of up to one million dollars for demonstration projects dealing with industrial wastes (see 33 U.S.C.A. §§1156[b], 1156[d][1] [1970]). However, substantial discretionary power was retained to deny applications on rather broad, vague grounds (see 33 U.S.C.A. §1156[d][3] [1970]), allowing the political climate a direct entry into the decision-making process.

drain despite Deepwater's promise of creating a structure for accommodating growth in an orderly manner. Thus in 1972 the Deepwater industries had not advanced perceptibly beyond the day in 1968 when they received their BOD quotas from the DRBC. It should be apparent, moreover, that until these major dischargers actually conform to the DRBC plan, Gloucester County's success in organizing a regional *municipal* treatment system will have little perceptible impact on the Delaware's water quality, since the firms account for the greater part of the discharge from the Jersey shore.

ANALYSIS: PRINCIPLES OF AN ACTIVIST STRATEGY

We now are in a position to assess the structural and legal features which help explain the failures we have recounted. We shall first consider the distinctive problems involved in inducing municipalities to cooperate, then deal with industrial cooperation, and finally delineate the basic tensions that will afflict agency activist efforts.

Sources of Failure: Municipal Planning Resources

Our case studies emphasize the risks involved in relying on even moderately large local governments to undertake the planning necessary for coordination. In the absence of sufficient staff, it was inevitable that the counties of Camden and Gloucester should call on private firms to undertake the analytical work. Moreover, the fact that the local governments did not possess a staff capable of evaluating the work gave the firm selected little incentive to generate a technically competent analysis. To make matters worse, no other governmental body subjected the reports to careful scrutiny, nor were steps taken to assure that the same low level of performance was not repeated in subsequent engagements.

The poor quality of analysis created a situation in which the supervising state authorities were ultimately willing to approve any project so long as it promised relatively prompt action. Thus neither the DRBC nor the State of New Jersey ever systematically considered whether regional configurations other than the ones actually proposed promised greater cost savings. Moreover, Gloucester County was permitted to push ahead with its regional operation, despite the likelihood that the merger of the county and Deepwater facilities would save costs all around, and the fact that the county cleanup would have no significant impact on the river without a parallel industry effort. Finally, the state authorities were for a long time willing to accept two regional systems in Camden largely because Errichetti seemed eager to push ahead.

Sources of Failure: Legal Sanctions and Municipal Cooperation

The state's willingness to approve almost any regional program for municipalities, however, is explained not only by poor planning resources but also by the inadequacy of its traditional legal controls. While New Jersey's statutes—like those of almost all states—grant the department of environmental protection wide powers to *deny* municipalities permission to construct sewerage facilities, the sanctions available to the department to *induce* towns to take part in regional planning are much less satisfactory. Of course, the state may seek an injunction in state court, but this will prove to be an exceedingly time-consuming affair. Moreover, many judges, unlike Judge Wick, will be reluctant to order towns to embark upon a regionalization plan formulated by a private consulting firm, which has not been subjected to any expert administrative review, and which is vague as to the fundamental question of cost. Courts are ill equipped to undertake the task of reviewing the validity of a regionalization report requiring the consideration of complex engineering questions. Accordingly, it seems likely that while courts will be quite willing to order compliance on an individual basis, they may be unwilling to coerce compliance with Reutter-type studies.

Injunctive relief, however, is not the only sanction available to the New Jersey bureaucracy and similar agencies throughout the county. The statutes permit the state to deny municipalities the right to connect and provide sewer services to new construction,[90] and imposing a sewer freeze has the effect of mobilizing a powerful real estate lobby to apply pressure on each town to come to an agreement. The freeze, however, is too powerful a sanction to invoke lightly. It is doubtful that the state bureaucracy could withstand the pressures generated if it imposed the freeze on a very broad basis. Moreover, aside from politics, the state is understandably reluctant to injure an area's economy unless the pollution problem is extremely serious. Finally, the sewer freeze is more effective in areas experiencing a substantial amount of new construction, like Gloucester County, and has limited value in the economically depressed regions of Camden County. For all these reasons, the water quality division reserves the use of the freeze for especially severe cases in which rapidly growing municipalities show no inclination to take steps to meet the problem. If,

90. N.J. STAT. ANN. §58:11-25 (1954).

as in Cherry Hill Township, the town fathers engage in a show of good faith bargaining, a sewer freeze is unlikely to follow.

In addition to an injunction or sewer freeze, the health department may use the criminal law against polluting municipalities.[91] If it is necessary to go to court, however, department officials much prefer to request "forward looking" injunctive relief rather than generate the recriminations involved in a criminal action. Even the sewer freeze seems more symbolically appropriate than the criminal process, since the freeze prevents further environmental degradation. Of course, if a consistent policy were pursued under which polluting municipalities were fined, localities would have a substantial economic incentive to come to terms on regionalization. The symbolic inappropriateness of resolving intragovernmental conflicts by the use of the criminal law, however, generally overshadows the "economic incentive" argument in the eyes of state officials.

Finally, the state may induce regionalization by using the carrot of state and federal subsidy, rather than the stick of coercion. Bureaucrats may warn that if a regionalization agreement is not forthcoming, state funds will be exhausted by the grant of subsidies to other projects. As long as the localities are required to bear a substantial share of the cost, however, the federal and state subsidies can only sweeten the bitter pill.

Each of the sanctions in the state's current arsenal, then, has substantial limitations: an injunction is time consuming and places a significant strain on the capacity of judges; a sewer freeze has such a devastating effect that it can only be used in the worst cases; criminal actions are symbolically inappropriate; the threat to deny subsidy does not disguise the fact that the facility must be paid for in part by local revenues. Because of these defects even a relatively aggressive agency—like the one in New Jersey—is much more apt to *threaten* to use its sanctions than *actually* to invoke them. Threats will not be sufficient, however, when political tensions reinforce each town's reluctance to embark upon a costly project which does not substantially serve its parochial interests in any direct way. In order to forestall endless "negotiations" in a fractionalized political context, the state must follow through on its threats with action—and at that point the inherent limitations of the weapons at the state's command become manifest.

Activism and Municipalities

Our analysis suggests, then, the need for a full-blown "activist" agency if municipalities are to be induced to embark on cooperative treatment

91. N.J. STAT. ANN. §58:10 (1954); §23:5–28 (1950); §23:9–18, 32, 52 (1968).

schemes. The activist agency must not only be equipped with ample planning resources, it must also be given the right to build its own plants and
order towns and cities to enter its facilities. It is only if the agency can
credibly threaten to act on its own that the localities will have an incentive
to retain some measure of autonomy by promptly reaching a regional
agreement. As we made plain earlier, we do not view an "activist" agency
as a panacea. There is no guarantee that the activist agency will not make
serious errors; nor can one expect that review by a Review Board or a
court—if this were thought justified—will eliminate all serious blunders.
Nevertheless, activism seems a sound strategy at least where the economies
of scale from regionalization are large.

Industrial Coordination

The case for full-blown agency activism in situations involving large-scale
industrial collaboration like Deepwater, however, seems far less persuasive.
Firms like DuPont have more engineering sophistication than even a well
staffed agency. If the activist agency assumes leadership in such a project,
its staff may all too easily be overwhelmed by the superior resources of
its industrial "collaborators" and find itself adopting positions which a
more impartial body would perceive as detrimental to important public
interests.

While the risks of an overly activist intervention are considerable, the
risks of simple passivity are, unfortunately, even greater. Once industry
seems embarked upon the serious consideration of a regional endeavor,
the agency cannot afford to adopt a simple passive mode of regulation
through legal orders or market incentives. Whenever exclusive control over
planning is retained by the polluters themselves, issues of public importance
run the risk of being slighted. The location of the regional plant, its capacity to accommodate future growth, and the pollutants it will treat are all
matters of great importance to the ultimate water quality configuration.
Nevertheless, if these issues are left to the polluters themselves, they can be
expected to decide them on the basis of bargains grounded in their own
self-interest, presenting the pollution authority with a *fait accompli* which
can be rejected only at the cost of more painful delay. Similarly, when
polluters are in sole control of the planning process they will be tempted to
delay matters up to the very point at which the authority will seriously
consider imposing severe sanctions for continuing inaction.

All this means that the agency must intervene at the planning stage, but
in a different spirit than it employs to coordinate local governmental

projects. Instead of serving as the primary planning vehicle, the agency should seek to maintain an arm's-length relationship. Instead of seeking to develop the substance of the plan, the staff should attempt to define the important public interests at stake and articulate the constraints within which the firms should be permitted room to maneuver.

Even with an agency staff prodding the firms ahead, profit-maximizing firms will have overpowering incentives to delay the day of heavy capital investment. Consequently, it is essential that the agency maintain an alternative system of passive regulation which assures that the polluters will be obliged to treat on an individual basis if they delay excessively on a cooperative project. Under a legal orders model, the agency should announce from the outset that while firms may consider joint treatment possibilities, all those who are found to be violating their individual cutback orders by a predetermined future date will be subject to a stiff "delay" tax on each pound of waste discharged over their legal limit.[92] A similar approach should be followed under the market model. While dischargers should (perhaps)[93] be given a period of time to consider their treatment options without cost, the time at which the original market scheme will go into effect should be announced in advance.[94]

---

92. Vermont's well publicized "effluent charge" law is essentially just such a "delay" tax (see Selig, 1971, pp. 16–21).

93. The disadvantage of the proposal for a grace period is, of course, that it reduces the cost of delaying construction below what would obtain if the fee were charged immediately on all waste dumped.

94. Indeed, even when the dischargers reach an agreement on a joint facility, the agency's mode of passive regulation cannot be entirely abandoned, although it may be modified in the light of the developing situation. Thus, under a legal orders model of the DRBC type, the new regional facility must be assigned a waste load allocation which it may not legally exceed without incurring financial penalties. Moreover, the allocation assigned the regional facility may well be either larger or smaller than the sum total of the allocations previously granted the members of the consortium on an individual basis, since the concentrated discharge emitted by the single large plant may have a different impact on water quality objectives than the more diffuse discharges which would prevail in the case of treatment on an individual basis. Indeed, during a properly structured planning process, one of the most important issues for arm's-length negotiation between the agency and the firms will be precisely the question of the amount regional facilities at various locations will be permitted to discharge. Similarly, under a market approach, the regional facility will be required to pay an effluent fee or purchase discharge rights, although the level of the fee or quantity of rights may well be altered depending on the location of the plant and the impact of a concentrated discharge on agency objectives (see Rose-Ackerman, 1973).

If, however, the public authority chooses to operate the plant directly, it will transcend the problems raised in the preceding paragraph only to confront a new set when it seeks to establish a fee schedule for the use of its facility. The important point here is that in general the authority will be forced to compromise between the competing goals of (a) generating sufficient revenue to cover the costs of the plant and (b) setting a fee that induces only those firms for which individual treatment is relatively expensive to join the combined system. As Kneese and Bower, 1968,

The regulatory task for an agency in the industrial context is, then, of extraordinary complexity. Neither purely passive nor purely active, the agency would be intervening substantially in the planning process, manipulating a complex enforcement strategy, all the while attempting to remain at arm's length from the firms so as to avoid the real risk of cooptation.

Nevertheless, even this summary oversimplifies the agency's managerial problem. As Deepwater shows, the agency's active role must be enlarged further if the regional project is located in an area in which substantial growth is anticipated during the lifetime of the project. For in this rather common case, the control authority should itself finance that portion of the facility fairly allocated to future growth. Thus, an effective agency must, even in industrial projects, not only take an active role in planning and constructing the facility but must also serve as part owner of the operation in its early stages if the costs justly belonging to future entrants are not to be imposed upon existing dischargers.

Joint Municipal-Industrial Cooperation

While we have discussed the problems of industrial and municipal coordination separately, the typical project will generally require the collaboration of both cities and firms in a single endeavor. It should be apparent that in this common case the differing varieties of agency activism come in conflict with one another. On the one hand, the agency may, as in a purely municipal project, take the primary planning role. If it takes this approach, the agency runs the clear risk of being overwhelmed by the technical staff of the industrial firms with which it is "collaborating." On the other hand, if the agency attempts to maintain an arm's-length relationship with the participants—as in the purely industrial project—it runs the risk that the municipalities will fail to fulfill the responsibilities thrust on their shoulders.

It is perhaps possible in theory to avoid both horns of this dilemma and chart an agency course responsive to the mixed industrial-municipal character of the problem at hand. Under this approach, the agency would only serve as the primary planner for the towns while remaining at arm's length from the firms. Nevertheless, it seems doubtful to us that an agency can maintain this studied schizoid behavior coherently. Instead, if activism

---

p. 192, point out, and as Boyd (in an appendix to Kneese and Bower, 1968, pp. 199–212) proves, a single fee schedule will not accomplish both these objectives unless the marginal cost of regional treatment is a constant and all pollution in the water originates with identifiable point-source polluters. Otherwise a fee set where the marginal costs of point-source polluters equal marginal costs for the regional authority will bear no necessary relationship to the regional authority's total costs.

is to be embraced, either one or the other form should be adopted despite the obvious disadvantages of either in the most common mixed municipal-industrial context.

CONCLUSIONS: THE FAILURE OF COOPERATIVE FEDERALISM

Having sketched the policy options suggested by the New Jersey experience, we are in a position to appreciate the extent to which the DRBC's strategy was poorly conceived. First, the agency failed to state well in advance the date on which it would impose heavy sanctions on dischargers who failed to cut back their wastes either individually or jointly, thereby encouraging polluters to engage in interminable "good faith" bargaining on joint treatment in an effort to defer timely compliance. Second, in cases involving countywide municipal treatment—in which the need for activist planning and enforcement measures was most compelling—the DRBC retired from the field. Third, in the case involving industrial polluters almost exclusively, the agency acted with alacrity, moving far beyond the limits of the arm's-length activism we have recommended in this context. Instead of maintaining distance from the firms, the DRBC deferred state demands for quick compliance, contributed substantial amounts of staff time to the project, and led an ultimately fruitless search for large federal subsidies. It would be difficult to devise a strategy which seems less appropriate to the problems at hand.

Taking an institutional perspective, the agency's failure to develop sounder activist policies may be attributed once again to its larger failure to become more than a weak confederacy of jealous state and federal agencies. While on issues of the first importance, the Governors and the Secretary of the Interior *personally* cast their ballots, the DRBC's monthly meetings are attended by a group of alternate Commissioners who are generally high-level state environmental officials.[95] Each of these officials is anxious to preserve the autonomy of the state bureaucracy, with which he is in far closer contact. Consequently, all are unwilling to permit the regional agency to intervene actively even in another state, knowing full well

95. In the cases of Pennsylvania, New Jersey, and Delaware, the three states most concerned, the alternate's position has usually been filled by the state cabinet officer charged with environmental matters. Similarly, the New York alternate occupies an important place in the state bureaucracy. The two federal alternates who have served in the Commission's 13-year history have, however, been far removed from the center of bureaucratic influence in the federal structure.

that, once a precedent is established, theirs may well be the next ox gored. Thus, so far as the alternate Commissioners were concerned,[96] it remained to the State of New Jersey to put teeth into a regionalization approach, except in a case like Deepwater where the State had no clear policy whatever and the riverfront industries were exceedingly happy to cooperate with any agency initiative which promised a delay in compliance.

It seems, then, that *if* activist regulation is required for an important interstate river, one should not rely upon an interstate agency of the DRBC type to compensate for the failures of state control. Instead, either an adequate activist structure should be developed on the state level[97] or, if this is not politically feasible, the federal government should attempt to construct federal river basin agencies with sufficient bureaucratic power to fashion an activist strategy that will not be frustrated by deference to state officialdom.

Unfortunately our study of the Delaware does not permit us to move to a sophisticated discussion of the important matters concerning the way in which the activist agency should be structured to best discharge its planning and coordinating functions. Since the DRBC failed even to attempt a sophisticated activist effort, its experience cannot illuminate these issues of institutional design. While only a beginning has been made in thinking about the problem,[98] the DRBC experience emphasizes the importance of this line of research. It further suggests that unless the states or the federal government creates coherent activist structures, a "regional" agency will prove to be incapable of generating a coherent strategy when activism appears to be the wisest course.

---

96. Interviews with alternates, see Appendix D.
97. So far it appears that only Maryland has fully embraced the activist approach. ANN. CODE OF MARYLAND Art. 33B (1971) established an environmental service both to create waste treatment regions and to construct and operate treatment facilities (§5f). Any existing works are to be purchased and run by the service (§5h), and no person may discharge waste "onto" the ground or water except through a service-owned treatment facility (§5k, §5d). The full costs of such facilities, including operating costs, are paid for by charges on the municipalities and private dischargers in the region (§7).
98. See Roberts, 1970, pp. 1527–56 and Roberts, 1971, pp. 75–141.

The Fate of the
Environmental Revolution

INTRODUCTION

This book has had both an empirical and a normative purpose. It has not only described the dynamics of a paradigmatic example of public policy making of the 1960's but has attempted to use the case study as a basis for charting the directions in which the environmental policy of the 1970's ought to develop. Our recommendations can be most usefully divided into three broad categories. First, on the level of substantive environmental policy, we have argued for the recognition that "pollution" is a label concealing a broad range of phenomena of widely varying importance. Thus, there must be a far more self-conscious effort to set priorities and concentrate social attention upon the most important issues that arise from the necessarily uneasy relationship between industrialized man and nature. While we have developed a set of priorities that represent our own effort to integrate technocratic with unquantifiable concerns,[1] the validity of our program is far less important than the recognition that there must *be* a

1. See Ch. 9.

program, that it is not enough to make war on "pollution." Second, on the level of institutional reconstruction, we have sketched two fundamental areas for primary concern. On the one hand, the Delaware experience suggests the importance of control for the coherent development and evaluation of technocratic intelligence. On the other hand, it demonstrates the dangers of giving a single agency a blank check to define and resolve any "pollution problem" it deems worthy of concern, instead of designing institutional structures in the light of a set of substantive policies defined in advance. Once again, while we have proposed institutional structures to better fulfill the institutional needs we have identified,[2] we emphasize that our Review Board, Recreation Authority, Poison Board, Nature Trust, and Environmental Defense Agency have been sketched to give a sense of direction for future development rather than serve as definitive blueprints. Finally, on the level of policy implementation, we have explored the limitations of innovation within the traditional model of regulation through legal orders, and proposed a discriminating incorporation of market and activist models of control.

Having defined the principles which should guide environmental policy during the 1970's, we can only view with the deepest regret the shape of policy as it is in fact evolving. On all three levels of analysis—substantive policy, institutional reconstruction, policy implementation—the 1970's have witnessed retrogression even from the standards set by the DRBC's earlier performance. This is not to deny that some good will come from the revolutionary concern for environmental values characteristic of recent legislation. After all, when projected expenditures are measured in the hundreds of billions[3] of dollars, it will be difficult to waste every million. Nevertheless, a consideration of the broad outlines of the governmental effort suggests that rarely have such good sentiments been translated into such bad policy.

2. See Chs. 10 and 14.
3. The total projected pollution control expenditure for 1971–1980 is $297.1 billion (Council on Environmental Quality, *Annual Report*, 1972, p. 276). Of this total, $87.3 billion is slated for water pollution control, $106.5 billion for controlling air pollution, and $86.1 billion for solid waste control (*loc. cit.*). Conversations with officials in the CEQ in August, 1973 indicate that by far the greatest part of the water pollution funds will be devoted to the construction of "secondary treatment" facilities of the sort presently planned for the Delaware. It should be noted, moreover, that enormous expenditures will be required between 1980 and 1983 to meet the 1972 Act's demand for "the best available treatment" by 1983. Thus it seems safe to believe that by 1984 a sum considerably in excess of $100 billion will have been spent on water pollution control alone. It should be noted further that this sum does not include the enormous expenditures required to "solve" the problem of combined sewers, deal with general sediment control, or reclaim areas previously ravaged (*loc. cit.*).

SUBSTANTIVE POLICY: THE ROMANTIC IDEAL
AND INDUSTRIALIZED REALITY

In 1972 Congress passed the most ambitious piece of environmental legislation in the nation's history, which not only will set the course of water
pollution policy for the next generation, but is characteristic of the prevailing response to other important environmental problems.[4] Without
entering into an exhaustive discussion of the 89 pages of the Federal Water
Pollution Control Act Amendments of 1972, it is still important to confront the issues of basic principle they raise.

On the level of substantive policy, the Act's fundamental mistake rests
in its refusal to take a sophisticated view of "pollution." Rather than
recognize that this label covers a multitude of problems—some far more
serious than others—the Act strikes a romantic pose with its declaration
that "it is the national goal that the discharge of pollutants into the
navigable waters be eliminated by 1985."[5] A thorough reading of the Act,
however, makes it apparent that the legislators were unwilling to accept
the enormous social costs which this position, if taken seriously, would
entail.[6] As a result, the stated goal is merely a politically attractive mask
for a policy that is similar to the one pursued on the Delaware.

As an interim measure, the EPA is to require all industrial dischargers
to install the "best practicable control technology currently available by
1977."[7] Although "practicable" is not self-defining, and the agency is given
considerable discretion in formulating precise requirements,[8] all knowledgeable observers we have heard from believe that industry will in general be
required to construct facilities which, like those currently being installed
along the Delaware, will remove FSUOD by 87 to 93 percent.[9]

4. See, for example, Clean Air Act Amendments of 1970, 42 U.S.C.A. §1857 et seq.
(Supp. 1973). For a good discussion of the amendments and the problems they
present see Anonymous Student Author, "Clean Air Act Amendments of 1970: A
Congressional Cosmetic," 1972. For a good detailed discussion of the 1972 Water
Pollution Act, see Zener, 1973.
5. 33 U.S.C.A. §1251(a)(1) (Supp. 1973).
6. See for example H. Rep. No. 92–911, 92d Cong., 2d Sess.
7. 33 U.S.C.A. §1311(b)(1)(A).
8. *Id.* See also §§1314(b), (c).
9. As of July, 1973 the EPA has not defined "best practicable control technology"
for any industry. The agency is currently working on a report for 20 or 30 industries
which they hope to have completed by Sept. or Oct. 1973 (telephone conversation
with Alan Cywin's office, EPA, July 16, 1973). Our suspicion that "best practicable
treatment" will be construed to require secondary treatment would seem to find some
basis in the explicit statutory directive that towns and municipalities install secondary
treatment by the same deadline. (33 U.S.C.A. §1311[b][1][B] [Supp. 1973]).

By 1983, Congress demands that industrial dischargers must have installed the "best available technology."[10] While this formula seems relatively unambiguous, the statute muddies the waters by indicating that only the "best available technology" which is "economically achievable" need be required.[11] This caveat must be read in light of legislative history which recognizes that treatment costs increase dramatically as requirements become more demanding and that the cost of complete elimination of discharges may well be unreasonable.[12] Thus, even though the 1983 limitations will be somewhat more stringent than those currently imposed by the DRBC, one cannot be sure how much greater severity the EPA will demand in 1983. Moreover, even if the 1983 limitations are quite stringent, it is not at all clear that the 1983 cutbacks will in fact generate water quality levels in the Delaware much better than those contemplated by DECS Objective II. As we have seen, the waste load to be treated along the Delaware will increase substantially with the growth of existing dischargers and the entry of new ones.[13] Thus increasing cutbacks will be required simply to hold the line. In short, a generation of expensive effort will culminate in 1983 with a river whose improved DO levels will generate only the trivial benefits we have enumerated.

Fortunately, the draftsmen of the statute have foreseen this unhappy possibility and have provided that "where water quality in a specific portion of the navigable waters [does not] assure . . . the protection and propagation of a balanced population of shellfish, fish, and wildlife and allow recreational activities in and on the water," treatment facilities even better than "the best available" are to be imposed.[14] Having driven their commitment to cleanliness at any price to the point of semantic absurdity, the

---

10. 33 U.S.C.A. §1311(b)(2)(A) (Supp. 1973). In contrast, municipalities are only required to install the "best practicable treatment facilities" then available (*Id.*, §§1311[b][2] & 1201[g][2][A]). Thus, for rivers like the Delaware, where municipal plants contribute two thirds of the point-source BOD load, the impact of the 1983 standards on water quality will be even less substantial than is suggested in the text that follows.

11. 33 U.S.C.A. §1311(b)(2)(A) (Supp. 1973).

12. Some of the clearest signs of this can be found at S.Rep. No. 92-414, 92d Cong., 1st Sess., pp. 11, 52; H.Rep. No. 92-911, 92d Cong., 2d Sess., p. 103; Conf. Rep. No. 92-1236, 92d Cong., 2d Sess., p. 121.

13. See Ch. 6, pp. 87–96. For new sources, regardless of the date of their installation, the Act requires "the best available demonstrated control technology . . . including where practicable, a standard permitting no discharge of pollutants"; from 33 U.S.C.A. §1316(a)(1) (Supp. 1973). The difference between the "best available demonstrated technology" and "best available technology" is unclear (see Zener, 1973, pp. 28–29). For a discussion of EPA's notion of what will suffice under the name of "best available demonstrated technology," see 3 BNA (Current Developments) *Environment Law Reporter* 1552 (1973).

14. 33 U.S.C.A. §1312(a) (Supp. 1973).

draftsmen pause to permit the EPA to consider whether better than the best must be imposed in every single case. Upon finding that the "best available" will not do, the EPA must hold a hearing "to determine the relationship of the economic and social costs of achieving any such greater limitation . . . to the social and economic benefits to be obtained . . ."[15] If any individual discharger can show that there is "*no* reasonable relationship,"[16] the EPA will permit the "best available" technology to suffice in his particular case. The scientific and economic arguments we have presented suggest that the dischargers of oxygen-demanding wastes along the "most polluted" regions of the Delaware and similar rivers should have little difficulty in making out a case even under this demanding "no relationship" test.

By 1984, then, polluters may free themselves from the Orwellian requirement that treatment better than the "best available" be attained. Unfortunately, the larger social failure cannot be evaded by invoking newspeak. Billions will have been wasted in a spurious war on pollution in the Delaware and elsewhere that could have been devoted to constructing a sounder relationship between industrialized society and the natural environment.[17]

To sharpen the contrast, compare the multibillion dollar effort to con-

15. *Id.* §1312(b)(1).
16. *Id.* §1312(b)(2) (emphasis supplied).
17. In addition to the programs considered in the text the Act provides the EPA with the tools required to limit stringently the discharge of hazardous substances (*id.* §§1317, 1321). The operative standards are, however, rather vague. For example, in regulating poisons the EPA is instructed to "take into account the toxicity of the pollutant, its persistence, degradability, the usual or potential presence of the affected organisms in any waters, the importance of the affected organisms and the nature and extent of the toxic pollutant on such organisms. . . ." (*id.* §1317[a][2]). Moreover, it is told that "Any effluent standard . . . shall . . . [provide] an ample margin of safety" (*id.* §1317[a][v]), though the agency is not told how much risk can be tolerated consistently with a commitment to "safety" or whether the discharge must be "safe" only for humans or for other beings as well. As suggested, we are in favor of a vigorous program to control hazardous substances of all sorts. We only fear that this effort will not be forthcoming precisely because the Act's other commands will divert a large portion of the energy and resources which can be plausibly allocated to environmental issues. This fear is partially borne out by the fact that—at the same time a massive effort is being made to improve the DO profile throughout the nation—a Public Health Service study reports that the quality of drinking water in a large number of areas leaves much to be desired (see *Community Water Supply,* 1970). Much could be done to improve the situation by introducing new methods of water treatment which, though costly, would be far less expensive than the present misguided effort to clean up oxygen demanding discharges. Current legislation's focus on the control of discharges, however, may have just the opposite effect. *The New York Times* recently reported that water and sewer departments throughout the nation, faced with the enormous expense of improving effluent treatment, have been cutting back their treatment of drinking water (*The New York Times,* May 18, 1973, p. 12, col. 3).

struct conventional secondary treatment facilities by 1977 with the degree of concern devoted to other, far more pressing, environmental priorities. First, existing legal machinery to control discharges posing a real and present hazard to health is exceedingly primitive. Only in 1973 did the Congress first seriously consider establishing minimum standards for drinking water.[18] Indeed, we have yet to establish a sophisticated nationwide monitoring system that would provide adequate information on the location, quantity, and impact of potentially harmful discharges.[19]

As for controlling the poisonous discharges themselves, the Act of 1972 again responds in a simplistic manner. While the EPA is given ample power to limit, or ban entirely, harmful pollutants,[20] it is not given authority to subsidize firms particularly hard hit by stringent controls, or otherwise to ameliorate the dislocations caused by plant shutdowns. Consider a paradigmatic case that has received a great deal of publicity. Recently, the EPA discovered that discharges of asbestos by the Reserve Mining Company posed a threat to the water supply of the inhabitants of Duluth, Minnesota. The agency is now considering whether to impose controls on Reserve which may lead to closing down 20 percent of the nation's taconite production, unemployment of 3,200 persons, and the economic devastation of the one-industry town of Silver Bay, Minnesota (population 3,272)—or so, at least, the company claims. If such choices between ecology and economy must be made, it is likely that the EPA will often (if not always) water down limitations on poisonous discharges in the interest of saving jobs. If, however, a partial subsidy were a possibility, or if the agency were empowered to assist in economically sound relocation of the unemployed, it could act aggressively in behalf of Duluth without utterly destroying Silver Bay.[21] Of course, subsidies will sometimes be mis-

18. S. 433, 93d Cong., 1st Sess. (1973). This proposed legislation would require the Administrator of EPA to prescribe standards which establish

> the maximum permissible levels for any contaminants which may exist in any public water system in the United States which may cause or transmit disease, chemical poisoning, or other impairments to man, allowing adequate margins of safety. . . .

Id. §4(b)(1)(A). This relatively unambiguous mandate, which gains further specificity from a definition of "contaminant" elsewhere in the bill (*id.* §3[4]), promises better results than the provisions of the Pollution Act of 1972 (See n. 17).
19. There are no immediate plans even to begin establishing such a national monitoring system, despite the clear mandate of the act in 33 U.S.C.A. §1254(a)(5) (Supp. 1973) (Telephone conversation with staff members of the EPA, July 1973). Reliance is placed on state monitoring under §1314(h). See also 38 Fed. Reg. 13570 (1973), where proposed rule §131.300 details the monitoring required of state programs.
20. Recall, however, the caveats contained in n. 17.
21. For a more extensive discussion of this problem see Ch. 14 and Michelman, 1967, pp. 1214–1256.

used as companies or communities make false claims of "dire need." Nevertheless, if one seriously wishes to embark on a stringent poison control strategy, it would seem this is a risk worth taking, so long as institutional steps are taken to minimize cheating. By failing to address the subsidy question seriously, we fear that the Act of 1972 once again promises far more than it will deliver.[22]

Controlling poisons, however, is not the only high priority item that may well be slighted by the environmental revolution. Existing programs to protect and expand wilderness areas in the United States also remain relatively undeveloped. While a Wild and Scenic Rivers Preservation Act is on the books, the program is underfunded,[23] as are other federal wilderness programs.[24] More generally, national lands management leaves much

22. Indeed, this failure to cushion the severe impact imposed on discrete groups by general policies is characteristic of much American legislation. As a result of this defect the severely damaged interest can be expected to lobby intensively, and often successfully, to frustrate programs which, like pollution control, redound to the advantage of much more numerous and diffuse groups. For another example of the phenomenon, consider the protectionist response of industries injured by foreign competition who nevertheless have been denied subsidies by the Tariff Commission (see Manley, 1965; Fulda, 1972; Weinberg, 1970, and Hoy, 1970). While there does exist a general program that concentrates on the economic development of areas suffering from high unemployment (see the Public Works and Economic Development Act of 1965, 42 U.S.C.A. §3121 et seq. [1970]), its operation has not been one of the high points of the War on Poverty (see Pressman and Wildavsky, 1973).

23. Only $17,000,000 was authorized for acquisitions under the 1968 Act, and when that is used up, a new authorization act will be needed, 16 U.S.C.A. §1287. The program is administered jointly by the Secretaries of Agriculture and the Interior, id. §1274, the Secretary of Agriculture being involved primarily through his stewardship of the National Forests (16 U.S.C.A. §471 [1970]). It is difficult to determine how much money has been appropriated in fact, as lands acquired by the Department of the Interior become part of either the National Park or National Wildlife Refuge Systems (16 U.S.C.A. §1281[c] [Supp. 1973]), and are funded by Interior either out of the appropriation for National Park acquisitions, which amounted to $76,871,000 in 1973 (86 Stat. 508 512 [1972]), the appropriation for land acquisition by the Bureau of Sport Fisheries and Wildlife, amounting to $4,602,000 in 1973, id., or the $1,829,000 made available for the same purpose to the Bureau of Land Management, id. For a detailed breakdown see S. Rep. No. 92-921, 92d Cong., 2d Sess. 9, 10 (1972). The Department of Agriculture could acquire land in the program through the $29,655,000 appropriated for Forest Service acquisitions (86 Stat. 508 [1972]). Finally, the Secretary of Agriculture received $7,648,000 in fiscal 1973 not classified under any budget category, which is presumably available for this program (86 Stat. 591 [1972]). The Forest Service was slated to receive $1,816,000 for "National Wild and Scenic Rivers," but this was eliminated in committee (S. Rep. No. 92-921, 92d Cong., 2d Sess. 9 [1972]). The total federal land acquisition budget for 1973 was $98,257,000 although appropriations totalled $112,957,000 (id.; 86 Stat. 508,512 [1973]).

24. The National Wilderness Preservation System gets no funds, since lands brought into the System remain under the ownership and management of their donors (16 U.S.C.A. §1131 [b] [Supp. 1973]). Although in 1972 some 1,300,000 acres of existing federal lands were proposed for inclusion in the wilderness network (Council on Environmental Quality, Annual Report, 1972, p. 141), the significance of this potential addition to the 10,400,000 acres already classified as wilderness must be assessed in light of the federal government's ownership of more than 750,000,000 acres of the

to be desired from a naturalist's point of view, and it is far from clear that recent efforts to rethink policy in this area are improving the situation.[25]

Finally, planning for the expansion of meaningful recreational opportunities for the urban masses remains confused and fragmentary. On the national level, there has been only a slow development of significant projects, such as the proposal to develop a national seashore in New York City.[26] Nor has there been a substantial development of the national park program.[27] While events on local and state levels are more difficult to trace,

---

nation's land (Nation's Land, 1970, p. 22). While this represents one third of the land in the United States (id., p. x), it should be noted that 95 percent of Alaska is federally owned, and this makes up almost half the federal holdings (id., 22). The Forest Service received $539,000 in 1973 for "wilderness and primitive areas" (S. Rep. No. 92-921, 92d Cong., 2d Sess. 9 [1972]). The Bureau of Sport Fisheries and Wildlife received $100,000 for "wilderness" (id., 10). An additional $1,650,000 was budgeted for wilderness protection and acquisition, but this was eliminated by the House Appropriations Committee (H.R. Rep. No. 92-1119, 92d Cong., 2d Sess. 15–16 [1972]).

25. The basic study in this area is Nation's Land, 1970, a report by the Public Land Law Review Commission. The report analyzes policy for the use of federal lands at a truly Olympian level of generality, advocating planning of land uses "to obtain the greatest net public benefit" (ibid., p. 45). The Commission seems blithely to accept the current "multiple-use" statutory structure (ibid., pp. 41–66), although it has been cogently argued that the multiple-use system itself does not provide a sound basis for federal land management (see Anonymous Student Author, "Managing Federal Lands," 1973).

As might be expected, since the federal government has not developed a coherent substantive policy for the use of its own lands, Congress has declined to establish such a policy for privately-owned lands. A bill recently passed by the Senate, S.268, 93d Cong., 1st Sess., speaks directly to land use policy. This bill would require states to generate comprehensive land use plans and establish permanent planning agencies, financed by federal grants of up to 90 percent of the cost (§606[a]). As the Senate Report indicates, this is only the second national land use policy bill ever to be considered (S. Rep. 93-197, 3d Cong., 1st Sess. [1973], p. 37). The bill, however, mandates no coherent national policy but simply provides funds to permit local initiative within state guidelines, Ibid., pp. 40–49. This same attitude and structure is also characteristic of the Coastal Zone Management Act of 1970, 16 U.S.C.A. §1451 et seq. (Supp. 1973).

26. See Council on Environmental Quality, Annual Report 1972 p. 139. The Gateway National Recreation Area was finally established in Oct. 1972, 16 U.S.C.A. §§460cc to 460cc-4 (Supp. 1973); a similar area was established near San Francisco at the same time, id. §§460bb to 460bb-5. There are, in all, perhaps several dozen national seashore and recreation areas, each created by a separate Act of Congress and each subject to different sets of uses and conditions negotiated at the time of acquisition. There is no apparent comprehensive national plan for the development of these areas. Instead, each project is lobbied through Congress in an ad hoc fashion and the rate at which each area is developed is dependent upon Congress' annual appropriation.

27. Fourteen National Parks and National Historical Parks have been authorized by individual Acts since 1960, 16 U.S.C.A. §79(a) et seq. (Supp. 1973). Of the four authorized since 1970, two were merely changes in the name of a previously existing National Park; Council on Environmental Quality, Annual Report, 1972, p. 317. Congressional authorization does not suffice, in and of itself, to bring a park into

it is our impression that a massive expansion of recreational opportunities is not a high priority item on local agenda.[28]

In short, the nation's environmental program of the 1970's is based on the same confused notion of the relationship between urbanized man and nature that afflicted the DRBC's efforts in the 1960's.

INSTITUTIONAL RECONSTRUCTION:
THE FAILURE OF FEDERAL INTERVENTION

A recurring theme throughout this book has been the failure of interstate cooperation, even with federal assistance, to be equal to the challenge of

---

existence. At least two, and perhaps as many as seven of the parks which have been authorized since 1960, had not been established as of Aug. 1972. *Loc. cit.*

Nine National Recreation Areas have been authorized since 1970, 16 U.S.C.A. §460(n) et seq. (Supp. 1973). Vacation cabins and other permanent signs of civilization are permitted in such areas unless the specific authorizing act of Congress prohibits them, see n. 26. Again, the bare fact of authorization does not mean that such areas have actually been established. Specific appropriations must be made and the land actually acquired before the area is truly "established," see n. 26.

This distinction between authorization and establishment is significant. For example, the Act establishing Redwood National Park authorized $92 million to be appropriated for land acquisition, 16 U.S.C.A. §79(j) (Supp. 1973). However, the entire National Park Service appropriation for land acquisition in fiscal 1973 was only $76,871,000; Pub. L. No. 92-369 (August 10, 1972), and this represented an increase over past years, S. Rep. No. 92-921, 92d Cong, 2d Sess., 1972, p. 9.

28. See Weinberg, 1971, for a good discussion centered on New York State. More generally, see Sax, 1970; Howard, 1972; Vaughn, 1964; *New York Times,* March 19, 1973, p. 1, col. 5.

This is not to deny that some substantial activity is taking place. The National Recreation and Parks Associations estimated that states spent $384.1 million on state parks, $71.7 million of which went for acquisition of new lands; Council on Environmental Quality, Annual Report, 1972, p. 189. These outlays were doubtlessly enhanced in many cases by matching federal funds under the Department of Interior's Land and Water Conservation Fund program; *Ibid.,* p. 138. Nevertheless, this $71.7 million expenditure seems dwarfed by the multibillion dollar annual effort to reduce oxygen demanding wastes. Moreover, planning at the state level is often chaotic or nonexistent at the present time, see S. Rep. 93-197, 93d Cong., 1st Sess., p. 44–47, 72–83. As suggested in nn. 25, 27, the proposed federal legislation S.268, 93d Cong., 1st Sess., will do little to help. A good example of the lack of cooperative planning at the interstate level involves the Delaware Bay Wetlands. Delaware had a relatively strong Coastal Zone Act meant to preserve the wetlands, 7 DEL. CODE ANN. §7001 et seq. (Supp. 1972), and recently amended it to make it more comprehensive, Sen. Amendment No. 2 to Sen. Substitute No. 1 to Sen. Bill No. 218, 127th General Assembly, 1st Sess. 1973, see also the recently passed Sen. Bill No. 217, 127th General Assembly, 1st Sess., 1973. However, the corresponding New Jersey laws and regulations are far less stringent, N.J. STAT. ANN. §13-9A-1 et seq. (Supp. 1973), *State of New Jersey Department of Environmental Protection: Proposed Wetlands Order* (1972). Thus, unless the two states collaborate on a joint use plan, with the assistance of the DRBC, the wetlands can be slowly ravished from the New Jersey side despite Delaware's efforts.

region-wide pollution problems. "Cooperative federalism" has been an attractive label concealing spasmodic research, parochial political decision making, and unsatisfactory policy implementation. Thus, in placing many primary decision-making responsibilities on the federal level, the draftsmen of the 1972 Act had an exceptional opportunity to build a sounder institutional base for policy formulation. Unfortunately, careful examination of the Act suggests that we have traded an overly fractionalized system for an overly centralized one.

From an institutional point of view, a sound federal response to the pollution problem need not attempt to remedy the ills of cooperative federalism by imposing a single set of emission standards uniformly on all parts of the nation. Instead, we have seen that government must carefully mark out certain water resources for specially intensive control if it is successfully to develop new recreational opportunities for its citizens or to fulfil its obligation to provide nonhuman life forms a congenial existence. Indeed, even in those areas—like poison control—in which uniform national objectives are desireable, much of the detailed work involved in framing discharge limitations can best be undertaken on the regional level. In short, a prime institutional task is the construction of a system of federal river basin agencies capable of framing regional policies in the light of a national strategy which includes a commitment to poison control, conservation, recreational opportunity and environmental defense.[29]

Instead of making even a tentative effort along these lines, however, the Act imposes nationwide standards without any regard to distinctively regional needs and priorities. In imposing effluent limitations on dischargers throughout the country, the federal EPA is forbidden, for example, to take into account even the obvious fact that factories will have different impacts on the environment depending on where they are located—along the near-virgin shores of Lake Superior, for instance, or the "polluted" region of the Delaware. Instead, all across the nation polluters are to march in lockstep to satisfy demands that they install "the best practicable treatment" by 1977, and "the best available" by 1983, without anyone in the federal government asking whether these requirements make sense in a particular regional context.[30] No effort is made to base judgments on a set of policies grounded in the sophisticated use of technocratic and non-

---

29. See Chs. 10 and 14. In devising appropriate regional institutions, it will of course be necessary to confront the institutional problems raised in the control of technocratic intelligence, considered in Ch. 10.

30. Recall, however, that if the Administrator requires better treatment than the "best available," the parties affected have the right to a public hearing before such treatment levels take effect. 33 U.S.C.A. §1312(b) (Supp. 1973).

technocratic criteria. A decision-making approach closely tied to individual problems is avoided by the simple faith that there is a final solution to the "pollution" problem which can be achieved by fiat from Washington, D.C.

To make matters worse, the Act does not confront the fact that different aspects of the environmental problem require different decision-making structures if satisfactory policy is to be made. Thus, problems as diverse as BOD control and poison control are consigned by the statute to "the Administrator" of the EPA, giving this godlike figure discretion [31] as to whether he should create a Poison Control Board or an Environmental Defense sub-agency,[32] or whether he should deal with all water pollution problems in the same fashion.[33] Moreover, in a curious way, the authors of the statute confided more discretion over substantive policy to the Administrator than at first appears. While it is true that the Act is replete with demands for a quick and total victory over pollution, these statutory formulae are generally hedged with a number of concessions to reality which make their application far from clear.[34] Equally important, the Act places so many demands on the EPA that the Administrator will almost inevitably find that he commands far too few resources to accomplish them all.[35] Thus the Administrator will find that he must make judgments as to the relative merits of his many programs without much guidance from the Act—for a statute which implies that *everything* is important offers no help when it comes to setting priorities. It seems, then, that the Administrator is faced with the unhappy task of defining policy without the aid of strong statute-based institutional structures to provide a basic sense of direction.

31. See 33 U.S.C.A. §1313(a) (b) (Supp. 1973), general control; *Id.* §1317(a)(1), toxic pollutants (defined in §1362(13)); *Id.* §1321(b)(2), hazardous substances.
32. See Ch. 14, pp. 209, 210.
33. There are glimmers of hope, however; 33 U.S.C.A. §1363 establishes an Advisory Board to make recommendations to the Administrator on the policy and functioning of the agency. One uncodified part of the Act mandates an investigation of the feasibility of establishing an environmental court, Pub. L. No. 92-500 §9 (Oct. 1972), but this does not seem to help the Administrator in making initial decisions.

A promising development is, moreover, contained in S.433, 93d Cong., 1st Sess. §7 (1973), the "Safe Drinking Water Act of 1973." The bill would establish a national drinking water council composed of 15 "scientifically qualified members... from a list of individuals recommended ... by the National Academy of Sciences" with other appropriate limitations on membership to assure impartiality, §7(a). "Such Council shall advise, consult with, and make recommendations to the Administrator.... Such Council shall, upon request of the Administrator, review any proposed action of the Administrator and shall report its views and reasons therefor in writing....", §7(c).
34. See pp. 319, 320.
35. It should be remembered that the Administrator is also in charge of the federal air pollution programs, see 42 U.S.C.A. §1857 (Supp. 1973) and n. 4.

There is a final institutional failure worth noting. While EPA is given wide statutory authority over water quality, it is given virtually no direct control over related land use decisions, although such decisions are at the heart of any adequate program either (a) to preserve nonhuman life forms or (b) to expand recreational opportunities for the urbanized masses. Instead, insofar as the federal government is concerned with these matters, responsibility is diffused among a number of federal bureaucratic suzerain- ties,[36] and the EPA will have a very difficult time coordinating policy among them, as well as among the innumerable state and local agencies with independent powers.[37] While this organizational failure is unfortunate for mass recreation, it is perhaps tolerable, since it is plausible that state and regional agencies should have much primary responsibility in this area.[38] On the other hand, the failure to develop a more integrated conser- vation policy-making structure may well lead to deplorable consequences, for we have seen that the federal government must play a central role in assuring that industrialized society discharges its obligations to nature.[39]

POLICY IMPLEMENTATION: THE UNCRITICAL ACCEPTANCE OF THE LEGAL ORDERS MODEL

Finally, in seeking to achieve its ambitious nationwide objectives, the EPA will rely almost exclusively on a "legal orders" regulatory system similar in most respects to the one adopted by the DRBC. Each of the nation's more than 300,000 dischargers is slated to receive a permit specifying the

36. For example, the Wild and Scenic Rivers program is administered by the Secre- taries of Agriculture and Interior, 16 U.S.C.A. §1271 (Supp. 1973); the Army Corps of Engineers is responsible for parks and recreational facilities at water resource de- velopment projects, 16 U.S.C.A. §460(d) (Supp. 1973); the National Park Service is under the Secretary of the Interior, 16 U.S.C.A. §1 et seq. (1960); the National Wilderness Preservation System is under the Secretary of Agriculture, 16 U.S.C.A. §1131 (Supp. 1973); and the Open Space Act is administered by the Secretary of Housing and Urban Development, 42 U.S.C.A. §1500 et seq. (Supp. 1973). The Fish and Wildlife Coordination Act, 16 U.S.C.A. §§661-666(c) (1960) attempts some unification of water resource development by requiring the agency responsible for a project to consult with the Fish and Wildlife Service. Id., §662(a). However the Fish and Wildlife Service can only advise and recommend; since it has no veto or modification power, the numerous bureaucratic enclaves remain secure.
37. The most recent federal effort to deal with land use problems is S.268, 93d Cong., 1st Sess. (1973). But, as seen in n. 25, the committee report specifically disavows any attempt to create a unified federal substantive policy for land use, S. Rep. 93-197, 93d Cong., 1st Sess., pp. 40–49, 61–62. In addition the bill's only sanction to ensure state compliance is the termination of funds granted under the bill itself, Ibid., pp. 40–41, 104–109.
38. See Ch. 14.
39. See Ch. 14.

quantity of waste[40] it will be permitted to discharge, taking into account the statutory requirement of "best practicable" or "best available" treatment. There is every reason to expect that this nationwide effort—to be administered directly by EPA in any case where a state does not comply with federal guidelines[41]—will be no more successful in achieving fairness than was the similar effort of the DRBC.[42] Indeed, when certain peculiarities of the EPA system are considered it seems likely that, in action, the nationwide system will seem far less fair than its Delaware predecessor. In granting its poundage allocations, the DRBC tried to require the polluters in each zone to make an equal effort by removing the same percentage of their raw waste load.[43] In contrast, the EPA's allocation scheme simply requires that *all plants of the same type throughout the nation* make an equal effort.[44] Thus neighboring polluters on the same river will find themselves confronted with different clean-up requirements—a result difficult to reconcile with common sense principles of fairness.[45] Moreover, the 1972 Act permits any polluter to apply for the right to increase his discharge, on the ground that the treatment level required is not "economically feasible" in his particular case.[46] The chances that arbitrariness, error, and corruption will infect this ad hoc process are very real indeed.[47]

In its single-minded commitment to the legal orders model, the Act not only entirely ignores the large cost savings possible through the development of a feasible market approach—like the effluent rights scheme[48]—but seems to ban any state effort to enforce the Act through a market model program.[49] Finally, the statute deals in an exceedingly primitive fashion with the difficult problem of inducing nearby polluters to cooperate with one another in a prompt and efficient manner. While the statute gives the governor of each state the right to designate an area for regional treat-

40. 40 C.F.R. §124-43 (1973). This is an advance over previous regulatory controls, which merely required polluters to eliminate a predetermined percentage of their waste load, for reasons discussed in Ch. 17, pp. 245, 246. The 300,000 figure is from Council on Environmental Quality, *Annual Report,* 1972, p. 32.
41. See 33 U.S.C.A. §§1313(b)(1), (e)(3) (Supp. 1973) on rules, and *Id.* §1341(a)(1) on permits.
42. See Ch. 17.
43. For a discussion of the failings of this attempt see Ch. 17.
44. 33 U.S.C.A. §§1314(b)(1), (b)(2) (Supp. 1973); *Id.* §1316(b)(2). See also S. Rep. 92-414, 92d Cong., 1st Sess. (1971), p. 50, and *Cong. Rec.* Daily Ed., October 4, 1972, p. H9128.
45. See Ch. 15, pp. 224, 225.
46. 33 U.S.C.A. §1311(b)(2)(A), §1311(c) (Supp. 1973).
47. See Ch. 17, pp. 246–257.
48. See Ch. 18.
49. We ground this judgment on the basic structure of the permit system and the guidelines for state programs. See 33 U.S.C.A. §§1313(b)(1), (e)(3) (Supp. 1973); *Id.* §1341(a)(1) and 37 Fed. Reg. 28396 (1972).

ment,[50] it does not give the EPA the power to intervene directly if the state fails to create the legal framework necessary for coherent activism.[51] Moreover, the statute shows no appreciation of the complex problems that will arise if, as is contemplated, both municipalities and industries participate in the same planning structure.[52]

THE UNCERTAIN SEARCH FOR ENVIRONMENTAL QUALITY

In itself, the DRBC's effort to reconcile Technocracy with Democracy, Policy with Law, is cause neither for disappointment nor alarm. The gap between the Real and the Ideal is always large and, as we have seen, it is not easy to define practical ways to achieve even a tentative and partial integration of our basic values. What is disappointing, even alarming, is the prospect of government, frustrated by the difficulty of structuring a coherent response, embarking on an urgent quest to achieve a poorly defined goal without institutions present to raise the right questions, and without the regulatory tools to achieve objectives either efficiently or fairly. The environmental revolution of the 1970's suggests that we have yet to learn the lessons of the 1960's. After all these lessons have been mastered, however, we shall only have taken the first step toward a system of government that will permit modern men to live in harmony with themselves and nature.

50. 33 U.S.C.A. §1288(a) (Supp. 1973).
51. Moreover, the fact that an agency has been designated as qualified for a regional planning grant does not assure that the state framework could support a coherent activist approach. See 33 U.S.C.A. §1288(f)(1) (Supp. 1973).
52. 33 U.S.C.A. §1284(b)(1)(B), §1288(b)(2)(A) (Supp. 1973), and see Ch. 19, pp. 303–307 and 314, 315.

APPENDIX A

The DECS BOD-DO Model: A Technical Analysis

MODEL FORMULATION

The DECS mathematical model is based on a materials balance analysis of a hypothetical segment of the river. Repeating the same analysis for a large number of sections of the river results in a set of simultaneous differential equations.[1]

Since the concentration of DO is directly related to BOD, it is necessary to model, for each section of the river, both DO concentration and BOD concentration. Thus there are twice as many differential equations as there are sections. In the DECS' model of the Delaware River 30 sections were used, requiring 60 differential equations. In writing the differential equations, it is necessary to include all "sources" and "sinks" (*i.e.*, withdrawals) of BOD and DO. For example, BOD and DO "sources" and "sinks" in section i of the river are as follows:

Sources of BOD to Section i	Sinks of BOD from Section i
1. Current flowing downstream (and upstream, since we are dealing with an estuary).	1. Current flowing downstream (and upstream, since we are dealing with an estuary).
2. A contiguous section having a higher BOD concentration.	2. A contiguous section having a lower BOD concentration.
3. Municipal and industrial sewage outfalls in the section (including material from combined storm sewers).	3. Consumption by microorganisms.
4. Suspended solids resulting from either scouring action of the river bottom by high flows, stirring up of worms living in the sludge, or Corps of Engineers dredging activity. (Not included in DECS model.)	
5. Tributaries.	

Sources of DO to Section i	Sinks of DO from Section i
1. Current flowing downstream (and upstream).	1. Current flowing downstream (and upstream).
2. A contiguous section having a higher DO concentration.	2. A contiguous section having a lower DO concentration.

1. This technique is solidly rooted in the general theory of transport phenomena. For a clear presentation of a number of applications of the method, see Franks, 1967, pp. 228–58.

Sources of DO to Section i	Sinks of DO from Section i
3. Reaeration (this is the major source of DO to the section).	3. Consumption by microorganisms in consuming BOD.
4. Photosynthetic activity in the river. (Not included in DECS model.)	4. Consumption by benthic demand.
5. Tributaries and plant outfalls.	5. Consumption by chemical oxygen demand.
	6. Industrial water intake streams. (Not included in DECS model.)

From the enumeration above, the equations for section i are as follows:[2]

(1) For BOD:

$$V_i \frac{dL_i}{dt} = Q_{i-1,i}[e_{i-1,i}L_{i-1} + (1 - e_{i-1,i})L_i]$$
$$- Q_{i,i+1}[e_{i,i+1}L_i + (1 - e_{i,i+1})L_{i+1}]$$
$$+ E_{i-1,i}(L_{i-1} - L_i) + E_{i,i+1}(L_{i+1} - L_i) - d_iL_iV_i + f_i$$

(2) For DO:

$$V_i \frac{dc_i}{dt} = Q_{i-1,i}[e_{i-1,i}c_{i-1} + (1 - e_{i-1,i})c_i]$$
$$- Q_{i,i+1}[e_{i,i+1}c_i + (1 - e_{i,i+1})c_{i+1}]$$
$$+ E_{i-1,i}(c_{i-1} - c_i) + E_{i,i+1}(c_{i+1} - c_i) + V_ir_i(c_i{}^s - c_i)$$
$$- d_iL_iV_i + P_i.$$

Where:

V_i represents volume, liters,

Q represents net flow, liters/day,

L_i represents BOD level in the section, mg./liter,

e represents tidal mixing parameter, dimensionless,

E represents eddy exchange coefficient, liters/day,

d_i represents decay rate, day^{-1},

f_i represents BOD discharged to the section, mg./day,

c_i represents dissolved oxygen level in the section, mg./liter,

r_i represents reaeration rate, day^{-1},

$c_i{}^s$ represents saturation level of DO, mg./liter,

P_i represents other sources or sinks of DO action on the section, mg./day·

EXPLANATION OF TERMS

1. The terms

$$Q_{i-1,i}[e_{i-1,i}L_{i-1} + (1 - e_{i-1,i})L_i]$$
$$Q_{i,i+1}[e_{i,i+1}L_i + (1 - e_{i,i+1})L_{i+1}]$$

2. Thomann, 1963, p. 9.

and the corresponding terms in the DO equation, deal with the rate at which material (item 1 in the sources and sinks tables above) enters and leaves the section because of net dispersive flow into or out of the section. This is termed dispersive transfer and e is termed the dispersive coefficient. The dispersive coefficient is merely a proportionality constant used to express the effective concentration at the boundary between the sections.[3]

2. The terms

$$E_{i-1,i}(L_{i-1} - L_i) + E_{i,i+1}(L_{i+1} - L_i)$$

and the corresponding terms in the DO equation deal with the rate at which material (item 2 in the sources and sinks tables above) enters and leaves the section because of diffusion between sections, *i.e.*, they represent material transported between sections due to the driving force of concentration differences.

3. The term

$$d_i L_i V_i$$

which occurs in both the BOD and DO equations represents the rate at which BOD leaves the section by oxidation, *i.e.*, by aerobic biochemical reaction. It occurs in both the equations because the rate at which BOD is consumed must equal (by definition) the rate at which oxygen is consumed during the oxidation of the BOD.

4. The term f_i represents the rate at which BOD enters the section from external sources.

5. The term P_i represents other sources and sinks of DO acting on the section. There are two types, the first being benthic oxygen demand and the second being chemical oxygen demand.

6. The term $V_i r_i(c_i^s - c_i)$ represents the rate at which DO enters the section by reaeration.

7. The terms $V_i \dfrac{dL_i}{dt}$ and $V_i \dfrac{dc_i}{dt}$ represent, respectively, the rate of change in the amount of BOD in section i and the rate of change in the amount of DO in section i.

THE PROBLEMS RESULTING FROM SMALL ERRORS IN THE PARAMETERS

Consider a highly simplified situation for purposes of illustrating the difficulties involved. Suppose we consider a section i that has the same level of

3. For a detailed discussion, see Bunce and Hetling, 1967.

DO and BOD as sections $i - 1$ and $i + 1$. Moreover, suppose that $e_{i-1,i}$ and $e_{i,\,i+1}$ are equal, that the flow rate $Q_{i-1,i} = Q_{i,i+1}$ and $E_{i,i-1} = E_{i+1,i}$. Moreover, assume a steady state condition. Equations (1) and (2) reduce, under these conditions, to

$$(3) \qquad V_i \frac{dL_i}{dt} = 0 = -d_i L_i V_i + f_i$$

$$(4) \qquad 0 = V_i r_i (c_i^s - c_i) - d_i L_i V_i + P_i$$

It follows that:

$$(5) \qquad c_i = c_i^s + \frac{1}{V_i r_i}(P_i - f_i)$$

This equation, while admittedly a rough approximation, allows us to think about the significance of some of the terms more easily than if we try to grapple with equations (1) and (2).

First of all, note that P_i is usually negative, that is, P_i represents an oxygen demand on the system, either from benthic demand or from chemical oxygen demand. Let P_i' represent oxygen demand, that is, $P_i' = -P_i$. Then

$$(6) \qquad c_i = c_i^s - \frac{1}{V_i r_i}(P_i' + f_i)$$

This simple equation asserts that the equilibrium concentration of DO (c_i) is linearly related to the total load on the section.

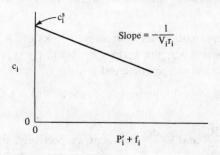

It is clear that the assurance with which we can predict DO is directly related to the confidence that can be placed in the values of r_i, P_i', and f_i (the value of V_i is known quite accurately).

Consider equation (6). Under Plan II devised by the DECS, we would like c_i to be 4.0 ppm and c_i^s is about 8 ppm. Evidently

$$\frac{1}{V_i r_i}(P_i' + f_i) \sim 8.0 - 4.0 = 4.0$$

Since the values of P_i', f_i, and r_i are all open to much question, the problem we address here is how much of an error in the parameters would make a significant difference in the results. Suppose V_i and r_i are exactly as estimated, but the sum of P_i' and f_i is 10 percent higher or 10 percent lower than anticipated. In the former case c_i will be 3.6 ppm, in the latter 4.4 ppm. Now suppose f_i and P_i' are exactly as anticipated but the value of r_i is either 10 percent higher or 10 percent lower than anticipated. If 10 percent higher, the level of DO will be about 4.4 ppm, if 10 percent lower, the level of DO will be about 3.6 ppm.

From the arguments in the main text, it would be unusual if the errors involved were of the order of a mere 10 percent. This simple illustration, then, demonstrates the hazards of (a) not determining both probable values of all parameters and probable values of their errors, and (b) not running sensitivity analyses on the model, utilizing the probability distribution data on the parameters, to determine what level of certitude is being proffered to the decision maker by the model.

APPENDIX B

Deriving Clean-up Cost Estimates for Individual Polluters along the Estuary

The DECS staff estimated the cost functions of each of the estuary's 44 major dischargers to determine the costs of a variety of plausible clean-up proposals. The staff, however, maintained a policy of confidentiality which was intended to make it impossible to associate individual cost estimates with particular polluters. Thus when researchers asked for data from DECS, cost figures were provided which did not identify each of the 44 dischargers by name, but only by an arbitrarily selected number. Nevertheless, a complex set of inferences from the documents that were made available to us made it possible to identify each of the 44 polluters' cost data with precision. Since a number of the statements we have made are based on these inferences we elaborate them here, along with the various sets of cost data made available by the DECS. In keeping with the DECS policy, however, we have not identified polluters by name.

To understand the following table, it is necessary to recognize that the DECS staff have at various times provided their cost data on individual polluters to researchers. Grant Schaumberg obtained data in 1966, Glenn Graves and his coworkers in 1967, and the present authors in 1970. Grant Schaumberg kindly provided us with his data set, and Graves' data is available in an article authored by Graves, Whinston, and Hatfield.[1]

In each data set dischargers are identified by number, and the marginal cost of removing waste over specified ranges is reported in dollars per pound per day. Both Schaumberg's data and that provided by the DECS separate capital and operating costs. Schaumberg's information also includes data indicating the state in which each polluter is located, its river section, and whether it is a municipality or a firm. Graves' data report the level of discharge in 1964. Graves, Hatfield, and Whinston also present a map of the estuary showing the location of each polluter along the river.[2] The polluters are numbered differently in each set of information, but the basic ranking is from upstream to downstream.

From the DRBC we know the identity of the largest dischargers and their locations along the river. We also know each polluter's estimated 1964 raw load as recorded by the DRBC, and the waste load allocations each has received. Combining all of this information made it possible to identify each of the 44 polluters by name, reconcile the disparate numbering systems so that changes in the data could be analyzed, and determine what levels of waste removal were indicated by the data points. Once this had been done it was a simple matter to calculate the polluter-by-polluter costs of reaching the DRBC allocations, or any other allocation pattern

1. Graves et al., 1969.
2. *Ibid.*, pp. 13, 27. This map is reproduced in Chapter 17.

that specified either percentage or tonnage removal in advance. The accompanying table summarizes this information. It is important to remember that the cost figures given here are not the total costs of treating all wastes, but only the costs of reducing 1964 discharges. The cost of reaching the DRBC allocation is $289 million with Schaumberg's data, $301 million with Graves', and $267 million with the DECS staff's 1970 list. These estimates are close to, but consistently higher than, the $225 million cost reported in *Where Man and Water Meet*. Thus there may be minor misspecifications included in the current estimates.

Table B.1.   Polluter-by-Polluter Cost and Waste Load Data

Costs (Millions of 1964 Dollars)[6]

No.[1]	Type[2]	State[3]	Section[4]	Data Source[5]	K_1	O_1 & M_1	Annual Tot$_1$	L_1	K_2
1	M	NJ	1	S,G,D	3.20	.605	12.20	2,040	
2(3)	M	NJ	2	S,G,D	1.12	.212	4.30	1,133	
3(2)	I	P	2	S,G,D	1.18	.223	4.50	1,833	
4	I	NJ	3	S,G	.25	.032	.73	396	.64
				D		OUT OF BUSINESS			
5	M	P	3	S,G	.96	.181	3.66	2,093	
				D	2.70	.064	3.64	1,888	
6	M	NJ	4	S,G,D	.09	.003	.13	1,333	.56
7(8)	I	NJ	10	S,G,D	.21	.008	.33	5,808	.32
8(7)	M	NJ	10	S,G	.10	.005	.17	892	.64
				D	.10	.005	.17	1,095	.65
9	M	P	10	S,G,D	.66	.066	1.64	50,100	2.91
10	M	NJ	13	S	2.50	.020	2.80	46,332	3.60
				G,D	2.50	.020	2.80	42,507	.70
11	I	NJ	13	S,G,D	.70	.050	1.44	9,712	.72
12	M	P	14	S	17.30	.591	26.10	130,854	2.26
				G	—	—	26.00	130,854	—
				D	17.30	.591	26.00	94,450	2.26
13	I	NJ	14	S,G,D	.10	.005	.17	12,238	.32
14	I	NJ	14	S	1.30	.101	2.80	1,780	.64
				G	—	—	3.30	1,780	—
				D	.0036	.099	1.45	1,780	0
15	M	NJ	14	S,G	0	.015	.22	880	.64
				D	0	.015	.22	1,077	.64
16	I	P	15	S,G,D	2.50	.175	5.12	20,673[13]	
17(18)	I	P	15	S,G,D	2.10	.031	2.56	9,923	1.78
18(17)	I	NJ	15	S,G,D	1.07	.054	1.87	3,346	.32
19	M	NJ	15	S,G	.12	.006	.21	1,552	.40
				D	.12	.006	.21	2,420	.40
20	M	P	16	S,G,D	18.50	.585	27.20	117,150	2.30
21	M	NJ	16	S	.09	.005	.16	1,455	.13
				G	—	—	.16	1,335	—
				D	.09	.005	.16	1,180	.13
22	I	NJ	16	S,G,D	1.20	.140	3.28	9,471	2.80
23(24)	I	NJ	17	S,G,D	.80	.007	.90	5,091	.35
24(26)	I	NJ	17	S	.94	.140	3.03	22,073	.90
				G,D	1.90	.232	5.37	27,160	1.90
25(23)	M	P	17	S	1.52	.363	6.90	2,107	
				G	—	—	7.30	2,107	
				D	1.92	.364	7.30	3,720	

1. The numbering system is that used for the Graves *et al.* data and for the 1970 data obtained from the DECS. In cases where Schaumberg's data are numbered differently his numbers are given in parentheses.

2. M = Municipality
   I = Industry

3. P = Pennsylvania
   NJ = New Jersey
   D = Delaware

4. Section of river. The DECS divided the estuary from Trenton to Liston point into 30 sections; see frontispiece map.

Table B.1.

Costs (Millions of 1964 Dollars)[6]

Annual O_2 & M_2	Tot_2	L_2	K_3	Annual O_3 & M_3	Tot_3	L_3	1964[7] Discharge	1964[8] % removal	DRBC[9] Allocation
							3,060	85	2,350
							1,700[10]	85	1,540
							2,750	85	2,110
.121	2.44	228					990[11]	66	NONE
							3,140	85	2,410
.158	2.14	445					2,000	55	510
.061	1.22	1,161					7,550	35	1,620
.121	2.44	892					2,230	75	1,530
.121	2.44	1,090					2,730	75	
.256	6.75	35,070					129,000[12]	74	69,300
.005	3.67	11,953					59,510	30	11,900
.008	.77	8,501							
.141	2.82	1,942					12,625	35	2,720
.189	5.20	18,319					170,110	45	33,200
—	5.20	94,450							
.189	5.20	16,590					130,000		
.060	1.22	2,448					15,910	35	3,430
.121	2.45	356							
—	.31	214					3,560	0	500
.021	.31	214							
.121	2.44	587					1,760	70	1,000
.180	2.43	715					2,150	70	
							21,925[14]	65	6,560
.336	6.76	1,985					12,900[15]	35	2,910
.106	1.90	305					3,955	35	6,692
.075	1.50	345					2,070	38	570
.168	2.90	533					3,320		
.202	5.31	18,223					165,000[16]	39	29,000
.024	.49	187					1,870	30	255
—	.49	267							
.024	.49	236					1,650	30	
.214	6.00	8,287	6.40	.430	12.72	1,973	25,650	35	4,250
.007	.45	1,389	.35	.007	.45	1,389	8,100	65	2,480
.080	2.09	5,255	4.80	.410	10.92	5,781	34,160	35	9,800
.170	4.43	4,000	2.90	.240	6.45	2,000			
							3,160	85	4,000
							5,580	85	

5. S = Schaumberg
    G = Graves, Whinston & Hatfield
    D = Data supplied to authors by the DECS staff in 1970

6. K_i = Total additional capital costs to remove L_i
    Annual
    O_i & M_i = Annual operating and maintenance costs of removing L_i
    Tot_i = K_i plus (O_i & M_i) discounted at 3% for 20 years [(O_i & M_i) × 14.9]
    L_i = Additional load removed over and above other lower numbered data points
         and 1964 treatment level.

7. Pounds of oxygen demanding waste (FSUOD) per day. Where 2 figures for 1964
    discharge are given the first is the discharge reported in the Graves data and the

Table B.1.　(*Continued*)

Costs (Millions of 1964 Dollars)[6]

No.[1]	Type[2]	State[3]	Sec-tion[4]	Data Source[5]	K_1	Annual O_1 & M_1	Tot_1	L_1	K_2
26(25)	M	P	17	S,G	.64	.121	2.44	717	
				D	.64	.121	2.44	1,287	
27	M	P	17	S,G	.10	.005	.17	1,350	.26
				D	.08	.005	.18	174	.26
28	M	P	17	S	2.40	.032	2.88	5,962	2.24
				G	—	—	1.87	5,365	
				D	.91	.056	.95	12,310	1.11
29(30)	I	P	18	S	1.60	.141	3.70	5,164	2.00
				G,D	1.60	.141	3.70	3,745	2.00
30(29)	M	P	18	S,G	1.30	.030	1.83	7,275	1.60
				D	1.37	.030	1.83	13,115	1.60
31	I	P	18	S,G,D	.23	.006	.32	1,219	.31
32	I	P	18	S	.16	.061	1.07	1,694	.02
				G,D	.23	.077	1.39	2,855	
33(34)	M	P	19	S,G	.08	.005	.15	1,400	.24
				D	.08	.005	.15	1,167	.24
34(33)	I	NJ	19	S	2.55	.170	5.08	19,590	.60
				G,D	1.96	.130	3.88	19,590	.60
53	I	P	19	S,G,D	1.60	.100	3.08	8,044	6.40
36	I	D	19	S,G,D	.67	.033	1.16	1,445	.55
37	M	D	21	S	2.80	.006	2.89	21,493	4.00
				G,D	6.75	.162	9.20	53,732	1.10
38(42)	M	NJ	23	S	.08	.005	.15	975	.19
				G	—	—	.15	1,073	—
				D	.08	.005	.15	855	.19
39(38)	I	NJ	21	S	1.90	.437	7.40	2,544	2.00
				G,D	1.90	.382	7.60	2,500	3.40
40(39)	I	NJ	22	S	12.00	.733	22.90	54,154	16.00
				G	—	—	34.60	7,400	—
				D	11.80	.885	25.00	55,000	11.90
41(40)	I	D	22	S	.61	.007	.70	1,689	.32
				G,D	.93	.067	1.93	5,066	
42(43)	M	NJ	23	S	.08	.005	.15	975	.19
				G	—	—	.15	1,402	—
				D	.08	.005	.15	1,111	.19
43(41)	I	D	26	S,G,D	.36	.035	.88	1,923	1.60
44	M	NJ	28	S,G,D	.08	.005	.15	1,298	.19

second is a revised figure used by the DRBC. When only 1 load is given, the 2 sources agree except as noted. In general the cost figures provided to us by the DECS staff are consistent with the revised DRBC discharge data because where the discharge has been changed the loadings have also changed, generally so as to keep the *percent removals* unchanged. One interesting aspect of these changes is that when the load is increased or decreased, the total cost of reaching that level of percent removal remains unchanged. Consider for example the polluters numbered 8, 12, 15, 19, 21, 25, 26 and 30. Except for dischargers 9 and 20, Graves' data are used where only 1 set of cost estimates exists and the 2 discharge estimates differ, since these data seemed more consistent with the cost data. For numbers 9 and 20 the differences in reported discharges were small, and the DRBC data appeared more consistent with the cost estimates.

8. Pounds of oxygen demanding waste removed as percentage of total pounds produced per day. DRBC data.

Table B.1.

Costs (Millions of 1964 Dollars)[6]

Annual O_2 & M_2	Tot_2	L_2	K_3	Annual O_3 & M_3	Tot_3	L_3	1964[7] Dis- charge	1964[8] % re- moval	DRBC[9] Alloca- tion
							1,075	85	1,380
							1,930	85	
.048	.98	270					1,890	85	310
.048	.97	48							
.424	8.59	1,192					7,750	35	2,640
.039	4.26	2,460					16,000		
.175	4.60	1,290	2.75	.585	11.45	1,033	7,745[17]	64	3,750
.176	4.60	2,000	2.60	.183	5.30	1,400			
.303	6.10	1,455					10,185	35	2,830
.301	6.14	2,650					17,095		
.054	1.11	1,273	.59	.123	2.42	831	3,600[18]	35	2,650
.006	.11	483	.05	.011	.21	678	3,145	35	520
.045	.92	280					1,820	35	255
.044	.92	235					1,520		
.038	1.17	2,857	1.10	.101	2.60	3,265	32,650	20	4,390
.038	1.17	2,857	1.10	.101	2.60	3,265			
.498	13.80	16,089	4.00	.403	10.00	3,448	28,730	75	14,400
.103	2.07	289					2,890	57	845
.005	4.07	32,239	1.10	.008	1.11	8,059	85,970	20	13,400
.120	2.90	8,059							
.036	.73	217					1,430	40	230
—	.73	238							
.035	.73	190					1,110		
1.140	19.00	2,714					8,480	0	1,060
.700	13.90	2,750							
1.200	33.90	50,769					110,000	35	21,110
—	21.00	30,500					91,000		
.600	21.00	30,500					91,000		
.067	1.32	3,377					6,755	80	4,310
.036	.73	217					1,870	40	350
—	.73	312							
.036	.73	246					1,480		
.302	6.10	385					2,500	92	2,500
.036	.73	288					1,730[19]	40	395

9. Pounds of oxygen demanding waste (FSUOD) per day. Delaware River Basin Commission—Final Allocations, Delaware River Estuary, June 1968.

10. Graves' data, revised figure is 1810.

11. Graves' data, firm is now out of business.

12. DRBC data, Graves reports 125,250.

13. Actually, Schaumberg reports 2 data points, the first removing 6,264 pounds and the second 14,409.

14. Revised to 21,350 by Commonwealth of Pennsylvania, 21,925 on DRBC list.

15. Revised to 17,615 by Pennsylvania, 12,900 on DRBC list.

16. DRBC data, Graves reports 156,200.

17. Graves' data and figure on DRBC list, revised by Pennsylvania to 12,565.

18. Graves' data. DRBC reports 4,700, revised by Pennsylvania to 16,000.

19. Graves' data, DRBC reports 1890.

APPENDIX C

The Mystery of the DECS Benefit Estimates: Of Picnicking and Pollution Control

According to the DECS, the only quantifiable recreation benefits are to be attributed to enhanced possibilities for swimming, fishing, and boating. As one important property of scientific results is that they should be reproducible, we set out to repeat the DECS' effort to estimate benefits. This attempt led us to examine more closely the study performed by the Institute for Environmental Studies (IES) at the University of Pennsylvania upon which the DECS' benefits estimates are based. We applied the DECS staff's discounting procedure to the net benefits which the IES asserted would arise in 1976 from enhanced swimming, fishing, and boating opportunities generated by each of the proposed water improvement programs— above and beyond those associated with Objective V (maintaining current conditions). The results are shown in the two columns of Table C.1, labeled "Net Benefits IES SFB." The net benefits estimates from the DECS are reproduced for comparison. The discrepancy is striking. Comparing the maximum estimates, we find that the IES estimates range from 12 percent of the DECS estimate for Objective IV to 30 percent of the DECS estimate for Objective I. What accounts for this divergence?

Because neither DECS nor our interviews with the DECS staff suggest that the IES swimming, fishing, or boating estimates were revised dramati-

Table C.1.[1]

Source of Estimate Objective Set	Net Benefits DECS Preliminary Report		Net Benefits IES SFB[2]		Net Benefits IES SFBP[3]	
	Max.	Min.	Max.	Min.	Max.	Min.
I	355	155	107	64	307	182
II	320	135	66	40	224	145
III	310	125	62	36	219	141
IV	280	115	34	24	103	70

1. Data obtained from *DECS*, p. 80, and IES Study, Phase II, p. 54.
2. Institute for Environmental Studies—swimming, fishing, and boating benefit estimates.
3. Institute for Environmental Studies—swimming, fishing, boating, and picnicking benefit estimates.

cally, it seemed plausible to suspect that—despite DECS' contrary statement—some other kind of recreational benefit was taken into account in the figures provided to the DRBC. This hypothesis gained credibility from our inspection of the IES Study upon which the DECS work was based. The Study attempts to value the impact pollution control will have on a fourth activity, picnicking, which is not mentioned in DECS. By adding picnicking to the other three activities, calculating net benefits over those of Objective V, and applying the DECS' discounting procedure, we arrive at the results presented in the two columns labeled "Net Benefits IES SFBP" in Table C.1. Comparing these estimates with the others in the table reveals two important facts. First, when picnicking benefits are included, the discounted IES estimates are much closer to those presented in DECS, although a considerable discrepancy remains. Comparing the maximum estimates, we find that the discounted IES estimates range from 37 percent of the DECS estimates for Objective IV to 86 percent of the DECS estimates for Objective I. Second, the IES estimates including picknicking are, in general, about three times the IES estimates excluding picknicking. Given the possible importance of picknicking in the DECS estimates, we will consider the extent to which the economist would consider it significant.

The impact of cleaner water on picnicking can be divided into two component parts. First, although picnicking need not take place near sparkling, odor-free water, some people may enjoy it more if it does. Thus pollution control may increase the value of the "pure picnicking" experience. Second, some may find it more valuable to picnic at a place where they can also swim, boat, or fish. Thus pollution control may redound to the benefit of those who engage in "picnicking plus."

Having defined the relevant activities with sufficient precision, we can now consider how the economist would evaluate them. As to "pure picnicking," it is easy to see that the effect of pollution control will be negligible. The argument is essentially the same one we made when discussing "pure" boating. The odor of the river is not a significant problem now, and the appearance of the river is not likely to be changed much by pollution control. Neither will it alter the urban character of the Trenton and Philadelphia-to-Wilmington areas. Thus in the area where Delaware-type "pure" picnicking could take place, the quality of the experience of picnicking by the Delaware will be virtually unaltered by pollution control. Of course, more parks would improve the opportunities for Delaware-type picnicking, but this observation suggests a cost–benefit analysis of parks, not of pollution control.

Similarly, the impact of improved water quality on "picnicking plus" will be but a small fraction of the "picnicking benefits" calculated in the IES Study. In applying the "sacrifice test" to "picnicking plus" the analyst should ask: "How much extra will consumers sacrifice so that they can picnic and fish (and/or boat and/or swim) *at the same place* instead of picnicking and fishing (and/or . . .) *in different places*?" The question is framed in this way because earlier in the analysis, we have *already* estimated the value consumers would place on "pure" picnicking, swimming, fishing, and boating *when each activity is considered separately*. Consequently, to avoid double-counting at this stage, we must only consider the *extra* value people would place on participating in more than one of these activities at the same place. As soon as this is recognized, we think it apparent that the DECS' claim that picnicking benefits are twice the benefits accruing from boating, fishing, and swimming combined is greatly overstated. For surely it is implausible to assume that if a consumer will sacrifice only $1 for the opportunity to swim, boat, and fish in the Delaware, he will suddenly sacrifice $3 simply because he can also picnic in a park close by. This is not to say that the consumer may not sacrifice something for this extra amenity. But surely this something will be only a fraction of the amount sacrificed for the new boating, fishing, and swimming opportunities, since picnicking opportunities are available at a large number of parks within easy reach of the river by car and bus.

Once again, then, we are driven to consider the way in which the IES could have generated such enormous benefit figures for picnicking activities. The result was achieved by applying a procedure similar to the one we have presented and criticized in Ch. 8. The same artificially restricted study area was canvassed for picnicking sites. These sites were found to be inadequate to meet 1976 "demand" since they would not satisfy "typically recommended standards for recreation land per 1,000 persons." In this case, the IES did not utilize 1976 "demand" estimates based on the ORRRC studies as it had done for the other recreation activities. Satisfied that existing facilities were decidedly substandard, the IES then assumed that all newly "available" parks would be used to "capacity." A park site was assumed to be "available" if *water-contact recreation* could take place in the estuary at that point under a given pollution control program. Given the standards which the DECS used to determine whether or not an area was suitable for water contact recreation, this criterion for "availability" implies that all four of the recreational activities we have considered must be possible under the DECS water quality predictions if a park is to be considered "available." Thus for each pollution control program the total "capacity" in activity-days of the parks "available" under that program was multiplied by the assigned value of an activity-day of picnicking, to obtain picnicking benefits for that pollution control program.

Since we are familiar with the shortcomings of the IES-DECS approach from our earlier discussion, we would expect the benefits from picnicking to be inflated, but even so, the absolute size of the assigned picnicking benefits calls for further scrutiny. The explanation seems to lie in the IES method of calculation. After estimating the number of acres of "available" parkland, IES assumed that 500 people or, given the relative age distribution at the time of the study, 390 people over twelve years of age, could "be served" by an acre of park land. They then took a participation rate for people over twelve for picnicking from an ORRRC study—3.21 activity-days per person per year for 1976—and multiplied it by 390 to get their estimate of the number of activity-days which could be undertaken on each acre per year: 1251.9 activity-days per acre per year. If, however, the IES had applied their 1251.9 number to their own estimate of 24,000 acres of *already existing parkland* in the study area, they would have found a "capacity" of 30 million activity-days, which would more than accomodate 1976 demand (only 16 million activity-days) as estimated elsewhere in the IES Study using an ORRRC report. It thus appears that the IES estimates of picnicking benefits are grossly overstated, even given the study's methodological premises.

APPENDIX D

Interview Data

During the summer of 1970, a group of six law students, under the supervision of the authors, conducted a set of face-to-face interviews with approximately 80 of the estuary's 95 significant municipal and industrial polluters. Using the information obtained from this first wave of interviews, we proceeded to select the actors who, on the basis of polluter perceptions, seemed to be playing important roles. Our list was then supplemented by scrutinizing documents which indicated which persons participated actively at various formal stages of the decision-making process, and during the two years following the summer of 1970, we tried to conduct personal interviews with those whose roles seemed most important. Many interviews were conducted in the summer of 1972 by Professor Bruce Ackerman, with the able assistance of Mr. Bruce Ludwig, then serving as a research assistant. We shall list here only the 40 interviews conducted in the second phase of the investigation. Except where otherwise indicated the persons interviewed were kind enough to give us from one to three hours of their time. We wish to thank them all.

From the DRBC – The Hon. Richard J. Hughes, former Governor of New Jersey; The Hon. Raymond Shafer, former Governor of Pennsylvania; The Hon. Stewart Udall, former Secretary of the Interior.

Alternate members of the DRBC – H. M. Adams (former alternate), New Jersey; Maurice Goddard, Pennsylvania; Harold Jacobs, Delaware; Dr. Mason Lawrence, New York; Vernon Northrup, former federal alternate; Paul M. Van Wegen, federal alternate.

Advisors to the DRBC – Samuel Baxter, former Commissioner of the Philadelphia Water Department and Advisor to the Pennsylvania representative to the DRBC.

Staff of the DRBC – Herbert Howlett, Chief Engineer; William Miller, counsel to the DRBC; Ralph Porges, Chief, Water Quality Division; A. Brinton Whitall, Secretary of the DRBC; James F. Wright, Executive Director, DRBC.

Federal, state, and local governmental information sources:

Federal – Correspondence with Henry P. Caulfield, former aide to Secretary Udall on environmental matters; James Quigley, former Commissioner of the Federal Water Pollution Control Administration.

Delaware – The Hon. John Barbiaz, Sr., former Mayor of Wilmington, Delaware.

New Jersey – Alfred A. Fletcher, former Director of New Jersey's Division of Environmental Health; telephone conversation with The Hon. Alfred R. Pierce, former Mayor of Camden.

Pennsylvania – Telephone conversation with Robert J. Bielo, former Executive Director of the Pennsylvania Fish Commission and member of the Pennsylvania Sanitary Water Board (PSWB); telephone conversation with Dr. H. B. Chormburg, former Secretary of the Pennsylvania Department of Mines and Mineral Industry and member of PSWB; Dr. Thomas W. Georges, former Secretary of Health and Chairman of the PSWB; Walter Lyon, Director of the former Department of Sanitary Engineering and staff advisor to the PSWB; correspondence with James H. Pierce, of Pierce Engineering Associates and a former member of the PSWB; telephone conversation with Jack C. Sheffler, former member of the PSWB.

Delaware Estuary Comprehensive Study (DECS):

Staff – Edward Geismar, former Project Director of DECS; Everett MacLeman, former Project Director of DECS; Ethan Smith, staff; George D. Pence, Jr., staff; Alvin Morris, staff.

Water Use Advisory Committee (WUAC) – Frank Dressler, Executive Director of the Water Resources Association/Delaware River Basin, (WRA/DRB) and former chairman of the General Public subcommittee; Paul Felton, former director of the WRA/DRB and chairman of the General Public subcommittee; Carmen F. Guarino, Commissioner, Philadelphia Water Department, and former chairman of the Local Governments and Planning Agencies subcommittee; William B. Halladay, Supervisor of Pollution Control, the Atlantic Richfield Co., and former chairman of the Industry subcommittee; Edmund Harvey, President of the Delaware Wildland, Inc. and former chairman of the Recreation, Conservation, Fish, and Wildlife subcommittee.

Business – R. R. Balmer of the Engineering Department of E. I. Dupont de Nemours & Company and a former member of the Industry subcommittee at WUAC; Charles Day, former Assistant Executive Director of the Greater Philadelphia Chamber of Commerce; Harold Elkin, Coordinator, Environmental Conservation of Sun Oil Company and former member of the Industry subcommittee of WUAC; Dr. Lloyd Falk, of the Engineering Department of E. I. Dupont de Nemours and Company, and former member of the Technical Advisory Committee of DECS; Loren U. Forman, Chairman of the Pollution Control Committee of the Greater Philadelphia Chamber of Commerce and Vice-President of Scott Paper Co.; Dr. Nicholas J. Lardieri, Assistant to the Vice-President, Scott Paper Company; W. H. Roach, of the N. J. State Chamber of Commerce and Chief Chemist, Texaco, Inc., in Philadelphia.

APPENDIX E

Members of the DECS' Water Use Advisory Committee

Chapter 12 describes and analyzes the ambitious effort undertaken by the DECS to fashion a distinctively regional consensus around one of the pollution policies it had analyzed technocratically. Central to this attempt was the DECS' Water Use Advisory Committee, whose entire membership is enumerated below:

SUBCOMMITTEE MEMBERSHIP

1. Recreation, Conservation, Fish and Wildlife

A. Shellfish Industry
B. Audubon Society
C. Pennsylvania Pleasure Boat Association
D. Delaware River Yachtsmen League (Corinthian Yacht Club)
E. Pennsylvania Federation of Sportsmen's Clubs
F. New Jersey Federation of Sportsmen's Clubs
G. Delaware Wildlife Federation
H. Izaac Walton League
I. Philadelphia Conservationists
J. Outdoor Writers' Association of America
K. Marine Resources Committee
L. Delmarva Ornithological Society
M. Brandywine Valley Association
N. Wilmington Garden Club
O. Delaware Federation of Garden Clubs
P. Citizen's Committee for Parks

2. General Public

A. WRA/DRB
B. League of Women Voters
C. Federation of Women's Clubs
D. Delaware Valley Council
E. Joint Council of Pennsylvania Farm Organizations
F. New Jersey Farm Bureau Federation
G. New Jersey State Grange
H. American Water Works Association
I. Delaware State Grange
J. Water Pollution Control Federation
K. Delaware River Watersheds Assoc.

L. Pennsylvania State Chamber of Commerce
M. New Jersey State Chamber of Commerce
N. Delaware State Chamber of Commerce
O. Greater Philadelphia Chamber of Commerce
P. Pennsylvania Economy League
Q. Forward Lands, Inc.
R. American Society of Civil Engineers
S. Greater Philadelphia Movement
T. Philadelphia Suburban Research Co.
U. Bucks County Health Department
V. Philadelphia Water Department
W. Neshaminy Watersheds Assoc.
X. Gloucester County Citizen's Assoc.

3. Industry

A. N. J. Manufacturers' Assoc.
B. Pa. Manufacturers' Assoc.

Petroleum

A. Texaco, Inc.
B. Gulf Oil Corp.
C. The Atlantic Refining Co.
D. Mobil Oil Co.
E. Sinclair Refining Co.
F. Sun Oil Co.
G. Tidewater Oil Co.

Steel

A. U. S. Steel Corp.
B. The Colorado Fuel and Iron Corp.
C. H. K. Porter Co., Inc.

Electric Utilities

A. Public Service Electric and Gas Co.
B. Philadelphia Electric Co.
C. Atlantic City Electric Co.
D. Delaware Power & Light Co.

Paper

A. Paterson Parchment Paper Co.
B. Bestwell Gypsum Co.
C. MacAndrews & Forbes Co.
D. Scott Paper Co.

Food

A. Kind & Knox Gelatin Co.
B. National Sugar Refining Co.
C. Campbell Soup Co.
D. National Dairy Co.
E. Pepsi-Cola Co.

Chemical

A. Hercules Powder Co.
B. Cary Chemical Co.
C. Rohm & Haas Co.
D. Allied Chemical Corp.
E. Harshaw Chemical Co.
F. E. I. DuPont de Nemours & Co.
G. Shell Chemical Co.
H. Pa. Industrial Chemical Corp.
I. The Monsanto Co.
J. Atlas Chemical Ind., Inc.
K. N. J. Zinc Co.
L. FMC Corporation

Miscellaneous

A. Eastern Gas & Fuel Assoc.
B. Radio Corp. of America
C. Westinghouse Electric Co.
D. Linde Co.
E. Stokely Van Camp Co.
F. California Packing Co.
G. Ruberoid Co.

Distillers

A. Publicker Industries, Inc.

4. Local Governments and Planning Agencies

A. City of Burlington
B. City of Bristol
C. City of Camden
D. City of Chester
E. City of Dover
F. City of Philadelphia
G. City of Trenton

H. City of Wilmington
I. Regional Conference of Elected Officials
J. Delaware State Planning Commission
K. Delaware River Port Authority
L. N. J. League of Municipalities
M. N. J. Bureau of State & Regional Planning
N. Penn-Jersey Transportation Study
O. Pa. State Planning Branch
P. Pa. State Assoc. of Boroughs
Q. Pa. League of Cities
R. Pa. State Township Supervisors Assoc.
S. Pa. Municipal Authorities Association
T. Lower Bucks County Municipal Authority

BIBLIOGRAPHY

Most citations in the text are keyed to a work's author. When a study is written by an institution whose name is lengthy, however, the work is cited in the text by reference to its short title. To facilitate use of this bibliography, we have therefore divided it into two parts—the first listing references by author; the second, by short title.

I. References, by Author

Anonymous student author, "Clean Air Act Amendments of 1970: A Congressional Cosmetic." 61 *Georgetown Law Journal* 153, 1972.

—— "Health Regulation of Naturally Hazardous Foods: The FDA Ban on Swordfish." 85 *Harvard Law Review* 1025, 1972.

—— "Managing Federal Lands: Replacing the Multiple Use System." 82 *Yale Law Journal* 787, 1973.

—— "The Regulation of Nuclear Power After the National Environmental Protection Act of 1969." 24 *Rutgers Law Review* 753, 1970.

Bain, Joe S., Richard Caves, and Julius Margolis, *Northern California's Water Industry*. Baltimore: Johns Hopkins Press, 1966.

Barsby, Steve L., *Cost–Benefit Analysis and Manpower Programs*. Lexington, Massachusetts: Lexington Books, 1972.

Barth, E.F., M. Mulbarger, B.V. Salotto, and M.B. Ettinger, "Removal of Nitrogen by Municipal Wastewater Treatment Plants." 38 *Journal of the Water Pollution Control Federation* 1208, 1966.

Baumol, William J., "On the Discount Rate for Public Projects," in Robert Haveman and Julius Margolis, ed., *Public Expenditure and Policy Analysis*. Chicago: Markham, 1970.

Baumol, William J. and Wallace Oates, *The Theory of Environmental Policy: Externalities, Public Outlays and the Quality of Life*. Englewood Cliffs: Prentice-Hall, 1974.

Berglund, B. and C. Berlin, "Human Risk Evaluation for Various Populations in Sweden Due to Methyl-mercury in Fish," in Morton W. Miller and George G. Berg, eds., *Chemical Fallout: Current Research in Persistent Pesticides*. Springfield, Illinois: Thomas, 1969.

Bernstein, Marver H., *The Job of the Federal Executive*. Washington, D.C.: Brookings Institution, 1958.

Bohm, Peter J. and Allen Kneese, eds., *The Economics of the Environment: Papers From Four Nations*. New York: Macmillan, 1971.

Boyer, Barry, "Alternative Trial-Type Hearings for Resolving Complex Scientific, Economic and Social Issues." 71 *Michigan Law Review* 111, 1972.

Break, George F., *Intergovernmental Fiscal Relations in the United States*. Washington, D.C.: Brookings Institution, 1967.

Brown, John T. and Wallace L. Duncan, "Legal Aspects of a Federal Water Quality Surveillance System." 68 *Michigan Law Review* 1131, 1970.

352

Bunce, Ronald and Leo J. Hetling, "A Steady State Segmented Estuary Model." U.S. Dep't of the Interior Fed. Water Pollution Control Adm., Tech. Paper 11, Washington, D.C., 1967.

Burton, Weldon, *Interstate Compacts in the Political Process*. Chapel Hill: University of North Carolina Press, 1965.

Camp, Thomas R., *Water and Its Impurities*. New York: Reinhold, 1963.

Carroll, Bruce, "Intergovernmental Administrative Relations," in Daniel Elazar, ed., *Cooperation and Conflict: Readings in American Federalism*. Itasca, Illinois: F.E. Peacock, 1969.

Caves, Richard, *Air Transport and Its Regulators*. Cambridge: Harvard University Press, 1962.

Chase, Samuel B., ed., *Problems in Public Expenditure Analysis*. Washington, D.C.: Brookings Institution, 1968.

Churchill, M.A., H.L. Elmore, and R.A. Buckingham, "The Prediction of Stream Reaeration Rates." 88 *Proceedings of the American Society of Civil Engineers, Sanitary Engineering Division* 1 (SA4), 1962.

Churchman, C. W., "The Use of Science in Public Affairs," in Stephen Sweeney and James Charlesworth, eds., *Governing Urban Society: New Scientific Approaches*. Philadelphia: American Academy of Political and Social Science, 1967.

Cicchetti, Charles, "A Review of the Empirical Analyses that have been Based Upon the National Recreation Surveys." 4 *Journal of Leisure Research* 90, 1972.

Cicchetti, Charles J., and others, *Benefits or Costs*. Baltimore: Johns Hopkins, 1972.

Coase, Ronald Harry, "The Problem of Social Cost." 3 *Journal of Law and Economics* 1, 1960.

Cooley, Richard A., *Politics and Conservation: The Decline of the Alaska Salmon*. New York: Harper and Row, 1963.

Council on Environmental Quality, *Annual Report*, Washington, D.C., 1971 and 1972.

Cox, Geraldine V., "The Role of *Limnodrilus spp.* (Oligochaeta) with Regard to Sedimentary Degradation and Secondary Pollution in the Delaware Estuary." Unpublished M.S. thesis, Drexel University Library, Philadelphia, 1969.

Crenson, Matthew, *The Un-politics of Air Pollution: A Study of Non-decisionmaking in the Cities*. Baltimore: Johns Hopkins Press, 1971.

Currie, David P., "Motor Vehicle Air Pollution: State Authority and Federal Preemption." 68 *Michigan Law Review* 1083, 1970.

Dahl, Robert, *After the Revolution: Authority in a Good Society*. New Haven: Yale University Press, 1970.

Dales, John H., "Land and Water Ownership," 34 *Canadian Journal of Economics and Political Science* 1203, 1968.

—— *Pollution, Property and Prices*. Toronto: University of Toronto Press, 1968.

Davidson, Paul, F. Gerard Adams, and Joseph Seneca, "The Social Value of Water Recreational Facilities Resulting from an Improvement in Water Quality in the Delaware Estuary," in Allen Kneese and Stephen Smith, eds., *Water Research*. Baltimore: Johns Hopkins Press, 1966.

Davies, J. Clarence, *The Politics of Pollution*. New York: Pegasus, 1970.

Davis, Kenneth Culp, *Administrative Law Text*. St. Paul, Minnesota: West, 1972.

Davis, Otto A. and Andrew B. Whinston, "Piecemeal Policy in the Theory of Second Best." 34 *Review of Economic Studies*, 323, 1967.

—— "Welfare Economics and Theory of Second Best." 32 *Review of Economic Studies* 1, 1965.

Davis, Robert, *The Range of Choices in Water Management; A Study of Dissolved Oxygen in the Potomac Estuary*. Baltimore: Johns Hopkins Press, 1968.

Delaware Estuary Comprehensive Study, Water Use Advisory Committee, *Minutes of Meetings, 1964–66*. On file in Professor Ackerman's office, Yale Law School.

Delaware River Basin Commission, *Annual Report*. Trenton, N.J., 1967, 1969.

Delaware River Basin Commission, *Minutes of Meetings*, July 27, 1966; March 2, 1967; March 18, 1969; Oct. 2, 1969, and April 16, 1969. Unpublished; available from DRBC Headquarters, Trenton, New Jersey.

Division of Sanitary Engineering, "Report to the Sanitary Water Board (Pennsylvania) on Proposed Water Quality Standards for Interstate Streams (Delaware River Estuary)." Undated; available from Bureau of Water Quality Mgt., Pennsylvania Dep't of Environmental Resources, Harrisburg, Pennsylvania.

Dorfman, Robert, ed., *Measuring Benefits of Government Investments*. Washington, D.C.: Brookings Institution, 1965.

Dorfman, Robert, Henry D. Jacoby, and Harold A. Thomas, Jr., eds., *Models for Managing Regional Water Quality*. Cambridge, Massachusetts: Harvard University Press, 1973.

Downs, Anthony, *Inside Bureaucracy*. Boston: Little, Brown, 1967.

Dressler, Frank, Statement before the Air and Water Pollution Subcommittee of the Committee on Public Works of the U.S. Senate, at Philadelphia, June 3, 1965. Unpublished.

Edwards and Kelcey, Inc., *New Jersey Comprehensive Outdoor Recreation Plan*, 1970.

Elazar, Daniel, *The American Partnership*. Chicago: Chicago University Press, 1962.

—— "Federal-State Collaboration in the Nineteenth Century United States." 79 *Political Science Quarterly* 248, 1964.

Englebert, Ernest A., "Federalism and Water Quality Resources." 22 *Law and Contemporary Problems* 325, 1957.

Epstein, Richard, "A Theory of Strict Liability." 2 *Journal of Legal Studies* 151, 1973.

Esposito, John C., *Vanishing Air: The Ralph Nader Study Group Report on Air Pollution*. New York: Grossman Publishers, 1970.

Falk, Lloyd, *Memorandum*, DECS Technical Advisory Committee, Minutes of Technical Advisory Committee Meeting, Exhibit B, Sept. 8, 1965.

Fishlow, Albert and Paul A. David, "Optimal Resource Allocation in an Imperfect Market Setting." 69 *Journal of Political Economy* 529, 1961.

Fletcher, George P., "Fairness and Utility in Tort Theory." 85 *Harvard Law Review* 537, 1972.

Franks, Roger D., *Mathematical Modeling in Chemical Engineering*. New York: John Wiley & Sons, 1967.

Freedman, James O., "Review Boards in the Administrative Process." 117 *University of Pennsylvania Law Review* 546, 1968.

Fulda, Carl H., "Adjustment to Hardship Caused By Imports: The New Decisions of the Tariff Commission and the Need for Legislative Clarification." 70 *Michigan Law Review* 791, 1972.

Godlovitch, Rosaline, Stanley Godlovitch, and John Harris, eds., *Animals, Men and Morals*. New York: Taplinger, 1972.

Goldstein, Paul and Robert Ford, "The Management of Air Quality: Legal Structures and Official Behavior." 21 *Buffalo Law Review* 1, 1971.

Goodman, Brian L., *Manual for Activated Sludge Sewage Treatment*. Westport, Connecticut: Technomic, 1971.

Grad, Frank P., "Federal-State Compact: A New Experiment in Co-operative Federalism." 63 *Columbia Law Review* 825, 1963.

Graves, Glenn W., Andrew B. Whinston, and Gordon B. Hatfield, *Mathematical Programming for Regional Water Quality Management*, Water Pollution Control Research Series, 16110 FPX 08/70, U.S. Environmental Protection Agency, Washington, D.C., 1970.

Green, Harold P., "Safety Determinations in Nuclear Power Licensing: A Critical View." 43 *Notre Dame Law Review* 633, 1968.

Gronau, Reuben, *The Value of Time in Passenger Transportation: The Demand for Air Travel*. New York: Columbia University Press, 1970.

Grubb, Herbert W. and James T. Goodwin, *Economic Evaluation of Water Oriented Recreation in the Preliminary Texas Water Plan*, Reports 84 and 28, 1968.

Haefele, Edwin, "A Utility Theory of Representative Government." 61 *American Economic Review* 350, 1971.

Harberger, Arnold C., "On Measuring the Social Opportunity Cost of Public Funds" in *The Discount Rate in Public Investment Evaluation*, Conference Proceedings of the Committee on the Economics of Water Resources Development, Western Agr. Economics Research Council, Report 17, Denver, Dec. 17–18, 1968.

———— "Three Basic Postulates for Applied Welfare Economics: An Interpretive Essay." 9 *Journal of Economic Literature*, 785, 1971.

Hart, Herbert L.A. and Anthony M. Honore, *Causation in the Law*. Oxford: Clarendon, 1959.

Haskins, Robert L., "Towards Better Administration of Water Quality Control." 49 *Oregon Law Review* 373, 1970.

Haveman, Robert, "Common Property, Congestion and Environmental Pollution." 87 *Quarterly Journal of Economics* 278, 1973.

———— *The Economic Performance of Public Investment: An Ex-Post Evaluation of Water Resources Investments*. Baltimore: Johns Hopkins Press, 1972.

Haveman, Robert and Julius Margolis, eds., *Public Expenditures and Policy Analysis*. Chicago: Markham, 1970.

Hetling, Leo J., *The Potomac Estuary Mathematical Model*, Tech. Report 7, Chesapeake Tech. Support Lab., Middle Atlantic Region, FWPCA, March 1969.

———— *Simulation: Simulation of Chloride Concentrations in the Potomac Estuary*, U.S. Dep't of the Interior, Fed. Water Pollution Control Adm., CBSRBP Tech. Paper 12, Washington, D.C., 1968.

———— "Water Quality Models of the Estuary" in Robert Davis, ed., *The Range of Choice in Water Management: A Study of Dissolved Oxygen in the Potomac Estuary*. Baltimore: Johns Hopkins Press, 1968.

Hines, N. William, "Nor Any Drop to Drink: Public Regulation of Water Quality, Part III: The Federal Effort." 52 *Iowa Law Review* 799, 1967.

Hirshleifer, Jack, James DeHaven, and Jerome Milliman, *Water Supply: Economics, Technology and Policy*. Chicago: University of Chicago Press, 1960.

Hirshleifer, Jack and David L. Shapiro, "The Treatment of Risk and Uncertainty," in Robert Haveman and Julius Margolis, eds., *Public Expenditures and Policy Analysis*. Chicago: Markham, 1970.

Hoel, Paul Gerhard, *Introduction to Mathematical Statistics*. New York: John Wiley & Sons, 1962.

Hogarty, R., "The Delaware Water Emergency." Unpublished ms., Biddle Law Library, University of Pennsylvania, 1966.

Howard, A.E. Dick, "State Constitutions and the Environment." 58 *Virginia Law Review* 193, 1972.

Hoy, William, "Adjustment Assistance Under the Trade Expansion Act: A Critique of Recent Tariff Commission Decisions." 6 *Texas International Law Forum* 67, 1970.

Hull, C.M.J., "Polysynthetic Oxygenation of a Polluted Estuary," in E. Pearson, ed., 3 *Advances in Water Pollution Research: Proceedings of the (First) International Conference Held in London September 1962*, 374, 1964.

Jacoby, Henry D. and John D. Steinbruner, "Salvaging the Federal Attempt to Control Auto Pollution." 21 *Public Policy* 1, 1973.

Jaffe, Louis L., *Judicial Control of Administrative Action*. Boston: Little, Brown, 1965.

Johnson, Dudley D., "An Optimal State Water Law: Fixed Water Rights and Flexible Market Prices." 57 *Virginia Law Review* 345, 1971.

Johnson, Edwin L., "A Study in the Economics of Water Quality Management." 3 *Water Resources Research* 291, 1971.

Juliano, David W., "Reaeration Measurements in an Estuary." 95 *Proceedings of the American Society of Civil Engineers, Sanitary Engineering Division* 1165, 1969.

Kneese, Allen, "The Political Economy of Water Quality Management" in Joe S. Bain and W.F. Ilchman, eds., *The Political Economy of Environmental Control*. Berkeley: University of California Press, 1971.

Kneese, Allen and Blair Bower, *Managing Water Quality: Economics, Technology, Institutions*. Baltimore: Johns Hopkins Press, 1968.

Kneese, Allen and Stephen Smith, eds., *Water Research*. Baltimore: Johns Hopkins Press, 1966.

Knetsch, Jack L. and Marion Clawson, *Economics of Outdoor Recreation*. Baltimore: Johns Hopkins Press, 1966.

Knetsch, Jack L. and Robert K. Davis, "Comparison of Methods for Recreation Evaluation," in Allen Kneese and Stephen Smith, eds., *Water Research*. Baltimore: Johns Hopkins Press, 1966.

Krenkel, Peter A., "Turbulent Diffusion and the Kinetics of Oxygen Absorption." Unpublished thesis, University of California at Berkeley, 1961.

Krenkel, Peter A. and Gerald T. Orlob, "Turbulent Diffusion and the Reaeration Coefficient." 88 *Proceedings of the American Society of Civil Engineers, Sanitary Engineering Division* 53 (SA-2), 1962.

Krier, James E., "Environmental Watchdogs: Some Lessons From a 'Study' Council." 23 *Stanford Law Review* 623, 1972.

Krutilla, John V., *The Columbia River Treaty: Economics of an International River Basin Development*. Baltimore: Johns Hopkins Press, 1967.

——— "Welfare Aspects of Benefit–Cost Analysis." 69 *Journal of Political Economy* 226, 1961.

Krutilla, John V. and Otto Eckstein, *Multiple Purpose River Development*. Baltimore: Johns Hopkins Press, 1958.

Kuhn, Thomas S., *The Structure of Scientific Revolutions*. Chicago: University of Chicago Press, 1970.

Kurth, James, "A Widening Gyre: The Logic of American Weapons Procurement." 19 *Public Policy* 373, 1971.

Kusler, Jon A., "Carrying Capacity Controls for Recreation Water Uses." 1973 *Wisconsin Law Review* 1, 1973.

Leach, Richard, *American Federalism*. New York: W.W. Norton, 1970.

Leach, Richard H. and Redding S. Sugg, Jr., *The Administration of Interstate Compacts*. Baton Rouge: Louisiana State University Press, 1959.

Leavitt, Emily Stewart, *Animals and Their Legal Rights*. New York: Animal Welfare Institute, 1968.

Levine, Lester, "Federal Grants-in-Aid: Administration and Politics," in Daniel Elazar, ed., *Co-operation and Conflict: Readings in American Federalism*. Itasca, Illinois: F.E. Peacock, 1969.

Lindblom, Charles, *The Intelligence of Democracy*. New York: The Free Press, 1965.

Lipsey, R.G. and Kelvin Lancaster, "The General Theory of Second Best." 24 *Review of Economic Studies* 11, 1956.

Little, Ian, *A Critique of Welfare Economics*. Oxford: Clarendon, 1956.

Löf, George and Allen Kneese, *The Economics of Water Utilization in the Sugar Beet Industry*. Baltimore: Johns Hopkins Press, 1968.

Lowi, Theodore, *The End of Liberalism: Ideology, Policy and the Crisis of Public Authority*. New York: W.W. Norton, 1969.

Maass, Arthur, ed., *Area and Power*. Glencoe, Illinois: Free Press, 1959.

Maass, Arthur, "Benefit–Cost Analysis: Its Relevance to Public Investment Decisions." 80 *Quarterly Journal of Economics* 208, 1966.

—— *Muddy Waters: The Army Engineers and the Nation's Rivers*. Cambridge, Massachusetts: Harvard University Press, 1951.

Maass, Arthur, and others, *Design of Water Resource Systems*, Cambridge, Massachusetts: Harvard University Press, 1962.

MacEwen, Peter and Richard Tortoriello, "Forecasting of Water Quality Data in the Delaware River Estuary," in J. Kerrigan, ed., *Proceedings of the National Symposium on Data and Instrumentation for Water Quality Management* 99, 1970.

McKinley, Charles, "The Management of Water Resources Under the American Federalist System," in Arthur MacMahon, ed., *Federalism: Mature and Emergent*. Garden City, New York: Doubleday, 1965.

McManus, M., "Comments on the General Theory of Second Best." 26 *Review of Economic Studies* 209, 1958–59.

Maga, R., "Air Quality Criteria and Standards." *Proceedings of the Third National Conference on Air Pollution* 469, Public Health Service Pub. No. 1669, 1967.

Mamelak, Joseph S. and Joseph V. Radziul, "Time-Varying Dissolved-Oxygen Model, Discussion." 95 *Proceedings of the American Society of Civil Engineers, Sanitary Engineering Division* 365, 1969.

Manley, Jeffrey A., "Adjustment Assistance: Experience Under the Automotive Products Trade Act of 1965." 10 *Harvard International Law Review* 294, 1969.

March, James G. and Herbert A. Simon, *Organizations*. New York: John Wiley & Sons, 1958.

Marglin, Stephen, *Public Investment Criteria*. Cambridge, Massachusetts: M.I.T. Press, 1967.

Margolis, Julius, "Secondary Benefits, External Economies, and the Justifications of Public Investment," in Kenneth A. Arrow and Tibor Scitovsky, eds., *American Economic Association Readings in Welfare Economics*. Homewood, Illinois: R.D. Irwin, Inc., 1969.

Martin, Roscoe, and others, *River Basin Administration and the Delaware*. Syracuse, New York: Syracuse University Press, 1960.

May, Ronald, "Decision-making and Stability in Federal Systems." 3 *Canadian Journal of Political Science* 73, 1970.

Meade, James Edward, *The Balance of Payments*. London: Oxford University Press, 1951.

Merewitz, Leonard and Stephen H. Sosnick, *The Budget's New Clothes*. Chicago: Markham, 1971.

Michelman, Frank, "Pollution as a Tort: A Non-Accidental Perspective on Calabresi's Costs." 80 *Yale Law Journal* 647, 1971.

––––––– "Property, Utility and Fairness: Comments on the Ethical Foundations of 'Just Compensation' Law." 80 *Harvard Law Review* 1165, 1967.

Michelman, Frank and Terrance Sandalow, *Materials on Government in Urban Areas*. St. Paul, Minnesota: West, 1970.

Milliman, Jerome, "Water Law and Private Decisionmaking: A Critique." 2 *Journal of Law and Economics* 41, 1959.

Mishan, Edward J., *Cost–Benefit Analysis: An Introduction*. New York: Praeger, 1971.

––––––– "Pareto Optimality and the Law." 19 *Oxford Economic Papers* 255, 1967.

Montgomery, David P., *Market Systems for the Control of Air Pollution*. Unpublished Ph.D. thesis, Dep't of Economics, Harvard University, 1971.

Morris, Alvin and George D. Pence, Jr., "Quantitative Estimation of Migratory Fish Survival Under Alternative Water Quality Control Programs. Unpublished ms. under imprint of Fed. Water Pollution Control Adm., U.S. Dep't of the Interior, Edison, New Jersey. Undated.

Morris, Clarence, "The Rights and Duties of Beasts and Trees: A Law Teacher's Essay for Landscape Architects." 17 *Journal of Legal Education* 185, 1964.

Murphy, Patrick E., "Environmental Law: New Legal Concepts in the Antipollution Fight." 36 *Missouri Law Review* 78, 1971.

Musgrave, Richard A., "Cost–Benefit Analysis and the Theory of Public Finance." 7 *Journal of Economic Literature* 797, 1969.

Musgrave, Richard A., ed., *Essays in Fiscal Federalism*. Washington, D.C.: Brookings Institution, 1955.

Nelkin, Dorothy, *The Politics of Housing Innovation: The Fate of the Civilian Industrial Technology Program*. Ithaca: Cornell University Press, 1971.

—— *The University and Military Research: Moral Politics at M.I.T.* Ithaca: Cornell University Press, 1972.

Nelson, James, "The Value of Travel Time," in Samuel B. Chase, ed., *Problems in Public Expenditure Analysis*. Washington, D.C.: Brookings Institution, 1968.

Niskanen, William A., *Bureaucracy and Representative Government*. Chicago: Aldine–Atherton, 1971.

O'Connor, Donald G., "Oxygen Balance of an Estuary." 86 *Proceedings of the American Society of Civil Engineers, Sanitary Engineering Division*, 35 (SA 3), 1960.

O'Connor, Donald G., "Water Quality Analysis of the Delaware River Estuary." Unpublished report to Industrial Subcommittee of the Tech. Advisory Committee, Delaware Estuary Comprehensive Study; Biddle Law Library, University of Pennsylvania, 1966.

O'Connor, Donald G., John P. St. John, and Dominic M. DiToro, "Water Quality Analysis of the Delaware River Estuary." 94 *Proceedings of the American Society of Civil Engineers, Sanitary Engineering Division* 1225, 1968.

Olsen, Mancur, *The Logic of Collective Action*. Cambridge, Massachusetts: Harvard University Press, 1965.

Patinkin, Don, "Demand Curves and Consumer's Surplus," in Carl Christ, ed., *Measurement in Economics: Studies in Mathematical Economics and Econometrics in Memory of Yehuda Grunfeld*. Stanford: Stanford University Press, 1963.

Paulson, Richard W., "Dispersion Coefficient in the Delaware River Estuary as a Function of Fresh Water." 6 *Water Resources Research* 516, 1970.

—— "The Longitudinal Coefficient in the Delaware River Estuary as Determined from a Steady-State Model." 5 *Water Resources Research* 59, 1969.

Pears, David Francis, *Ludwig Wittgenstein*. New York: Viking, 1970.

Peck, Merton and Frederick Scherer, *The Weapons Acquisition Process: An Economic Analysis*. Boston: Division of Research, Harvard Business School, 1962.

Peltzman, Sam and Nicolaus T. Tideman, "Local versus National Pollution Control: Note." 62 *American Economic Review* 959, 1972.

Pence, George D., Jr., John M. Jeglic, and Robert V. Thomann, "Time-Varying Dissolved-Oxygen Model." 94 *Proceedings of the American Society of Civil Engineering, Sanitary Engineering Division* 393, 1968.

—— "Time-Varying Dissolved-Oxygen Model: Closure," 96 *Proceedings of the American Society of Civil Engineers, Sanitary Engineering Division* 179, 1970.

Porges, Ralph and Seymour D. Seltzer, "Allocation of Stream Capacity in the Delaware River Estuary." *Proceedings of the Second Mid-Atlantic Industrial Waste Conference* 71, 1968.

Posner, Richard, "Strict Liability: A Comment." 2 *Journal of Legal Studies* 205, 1973.

Pressman, Jeffery and Aaron Wildavsky, *Implementation*. Berkeley: University of California Press, 1973.

Prest, A.R. and R. Turvey, "Cost–Benefit Analysis: A Survey," 75 *Economic Journal* 683, 1965.

Price, Don, *Government and Science: Their Dynamic Relation in American Democracy*. New York: New York University Press, 1954.

—— *The Scientific Estate*, Cambridge, Massachusetts: Harvard University Press, Belknap, 1965.

Quirk, Lawler and Matuskey, Engineers, *Hudson River Water Quality and Waste Assimilative Capacity Study*. Report for the Div. of Pure Waters, New York Dep't of Environmental Conservation, New York, 1970.

Rawls, John, *A Theory of Justice*. Cambridge, Massachusetts: Harvard University Press, 1971.

Ridgeway, Marian, *Interstate Compacts: A Question of Federalism*. Carbondale, Illinois: Southern Illinois University Press, 1971.

Rivlin, Alice, *Systematic Thinking for Social Action*. Washington, D.C.: Brookings Institution, 1971.

Roberts, Marc, "Organizing Water Pollution Control: The Scope and Structure of River Basin Authorities." 19 *Public Policy* 75, 1971.

—— "River Basin Authorities: A National Solution to Water Pollution." 83 *Harvard Law Review* 1554, 1970.

Rose-Ackerman, Susan, "The Economics of Corruption." 4 *Journal of Public Economics*, 1975.

—— "Effluent Charges: A Critique." 6 *Canadian Journal of Economics* 512, 1973.

Russell, Clifford S., *Residuals Management in Industry: A Case Study of Petroleum Refining*. Baltimore: Johns Hopkins Press, 1973.

Sax, Joseph, "The Public Trust Doctrine in Natural Resource Law: Effective Judicial Intervention." 68 *Michigan Law Review* 473, 1970.

Sayre, Wallace and Herbert Kaufman, *Governing New York City*. New York: Russell Sage Foundation, 1960.

Schaumberg, Grant, "Water Pollution Control in the Delaware Estuary." Unpublished thesis, Harvard College, 1967.

Schelling, Thomas, *The Strategy of Conflict*. Cambridge, Massachusetts: Harvard University Press, 1960.

Schultze, Charles, *The Politics and Economics of Public Spending*. Washington, D.C.: Brookings Institution, 1968.

Selig, Edward, *Effluent Charges on Air and Water Pollution: A Conference Report, October 15 and 16, 1971*. Environmental Law Institute, 1973.

Selznick, Philip, *TVA and the Grass Roots: A Study in the Sociology of Formal Organization*. Berkeley: University of California Press, 1949.

Shafer, Raymond, "Chairman's Address" in DRBC Minutes, March 2, 1967; available at DRBC Headquarters, Trenton, New Jersey.

Smith, Ethan T. and Alvin Morris, "Systems Analysis for Optimal Water Quality Management." 41 *Journal of the Water Pollution Control Foundation* 1640, 1969.

Smith, Robert and Richard G. Eilers, *Cost to the Consumer for Collection and Treatment of Wastewater*. U.S. Environmental Protection Agency, Water Pollution Control Research Series, Report 17090-07/70, 1972.

Smolensky, Eugene and Douglas Gomery, *Efficiency and Equity Effects in the Benefits from the Federal Housing Program in 1965*. Reprinted from *Benefit–Cost Analyses of Federal Programs*, U.S. 92nd Cong., 2d Sess., Jan. 2, 1973, Reprint 88. Madison, Wisconsin: Institute for Research on Poverty of the University of Wisconsin, 1973.

Starr, Roger and James Carlson, "Pollution and Poverty: The Strategy of Cross-Commitment." 10 *Public Interest* 108, 1968.

Stone, Christopher, "Should Trees Have Standing?—Toward Legal Rights for Natural Objects." 45 *Southern California Law Review* 450, 1972.

Streeter, Harold W. and E. Phelps, *A Study of the Pollution and Natural Purification of the Ohio River: Three Factors Concerned in the Phenomena of Oxidation and Reaeration*. Public Health Service Bull. No. 146, Washington, D.C., 1925.

Tarzwell, Clarence M., "Water Criteria for Aquatic Life." Unpublished paper, 1957. (Reptd. in part in Thomas R. Camp, *Water and Its Impurities*. New York: Reinhold, 1963.)

Thomann, Robert, "Mathematical Model for Dissolved Oxygen." 89 *Proceedings of the American Society of Civil Engineers, Sanitary Engineering Division* 1, 1963.

—— *Reactions*. Unpublished ms., on file in Biddle Law Library, University of Pennsylvania, 1970.

—— Teaching Materials, 1970. On file in Biddle Law Library, University of Pennsylvania.

—— "Time Series Analyses of Water Quality Data." 93 *Proceedings of the American Society of Civil Engineers, Sanitary Engineering Division* 223, 1967.

—— "The Use of Systems Analysis to Describe the Time Variations of Dissolved Oxygen in a Tidal Stream," Unpublished Ph.D. thesis, New York University, 1963.

Tinbergen, J., "Four Alternative Policies to Restore Balance of Payments Equilibrium." 20 *Econometrica* 372,.1952.

Tippy, Roger, "Preservation Values in River Basin Planning." 8 *Natural Resources Journal* 259, 1968.

Trelease, F.J., "Policies for Water Law: Property Rights, Economic Forces and Public Regulation." 5 *Natural Resources Journal* 1, 1965.

Tribe, Laurence, *Channeling Technology Through Law*. Chicago: Bracton, 1973.

—— "Policy Science: Analysis or Ideology." 2 *Philosophy and Public Affairs* 66, 1972.

—— "Technology Assessment and the Fourth Discontinuity: The Limits of Instrumental Rationality." 46 *Southern California Law Review* 617, 1973.

—— "Trial By Mathematics: Precision and Ritual in the Legal Process." 84 *Harvard Law Review* 1329, 1971.

Tullock, Gordon, *The Politics of Bureaucracy.* Washington, D.C.: Public Affairs Press, 1965.

Turvey, R., "The Second-Best Case for Marginal Cost Pricing" in Julius Margolis and Henri Guitton, eds., *Public Economics.* New York: St. Martin's, 1966.

Vaughn, Gerald, "In Search of Standards for Preserving Open Space." 24 *Public Administration Review* 254, 1964.

Water Resources Division, U.S. Dep't of the Interior, Geological Survey. Unpublished data, Biddle Law Library, University of Pennsylvania.

Weidner, Edward W., "Decisionmaking in a Federal System," in Daniel Elazar, ed., *Cooperation and Conflict: Readings in American Federalism.* Itasca, Illinois: F.E. Peacock, 1969.

Weinberg, Philip, "Regional Land-Use Control: Prerequisite for Rational Planning." 46 *New York University Law Review* 786, 1971.

Weinberg, Steven K., "Adjustment Assistance: A New Proposal for Eligibility." 55 *Cornell Law Review* 1049, 1970.

Whinston, Andrew B., Glenn W. Graves, and Gordon B. Hatfield, "Water Pollution Control Using By-Pass Piping." 5 *Water Resources Research* 27, 1969.

White, James Bernard, *Design of Sewers and Sewage Treatment.* London: Edward Arnold, 1970.

Wildavsky, Aaron, "The Analysis of Issue-Contexts in the Study of Decision-Making," 24 *Journal of Politics* 717, 1962.

—— "The Political Economy of Efficiency: Cost–Benefit Analysis, Systems Analysis and Program Budgeting." 26 *Public Administration Review* 292, 1966.

Williamson, Oliver, "The Vertical Integration of Production: Market Failure Considerations." 61 *American Economic Review Papers and Proceedings* 112, 1971.

Wright, Deil, *Federal Grants-in-aid: Perspectives and Alternatives.* Washington, D.C.: American Enterprise Institute for Public Policy Research, 1968.

Wright, James F., "Evaluation of Estuary Report." Statement to DRBC Water Quality Conference, Philadelphia, July 27, 1966.

—— "Statement for DRBC Hearings," Confidential Administrative Paper of DRBC staff, February 11, 1967. On file in Prof. Ackerman's office, Yale Law School.

Zener, Robert, "The Federal Law of Water Pollution Control," in *Federal Environmental Law*. Washington, D.C.: Environmental Law Institute, 1973.

Zimmerman, Frederick and Mitchell Wendell, "New Horizons on the Delaware." 36 *State Government* 157, 1963.

Zwick, David and Marcy Benstock, *Water Wasteland*. Washington, D.C.: Center for the Study of Responsive Law, 1971.

II. References, by Short Title

1965 Survey—U.S. Dep't of the Interior, Bureau of Outdoor Recreation: *1965 Survey of Outdoor Recreation Activities*, Washington, D.C., 1967.

1985 Estimates—Wilmington Commission on Zoning and Planning: *1985 Estimates of Land Use, Population, and Employment Within Wilmington*, Wilmington, Delaware, 1966.

1985 Regional Projections—Delaware Valley Regional Planning Commission: *Report No. 1: 1985 Regional Projections for the Delaware Valley—Supplement*, Philadelphia, undated.

Camden Study—John G. Reutter Associates: *Regional Sewerage Feasibility Study*, prepared for Camden County Board of Chosen Freeholders, Camden, New Jersey, 1967.

Census of Manufacturers—U.S. Bureau of the Census: *Census of Manufacturers, 1967*, Vol. III of *Area Statistics*, Washington, D.C., 1967.

Census of Population—U.S. Bureau of the Census: *U.S. Census of Population, 1970*, Vol. 1, *Number of Inhabitants*, Parts 9, 32, 40, Washington, D.C., 1972.

Chesapeake Bay Study—U.S. Dep't of the Interior, Bureau of Outdoor Recreation: *Chesapeake Bay Study, Recreation Element, Planning Aid Report No. 1*, Vol. III, 131, Washington, D.C., undated.

Community Water Supply—U.S. Public Health Service: *Community Water Supply*, Washington, D.C., 1970.

Cost of Clean Water—U.S. Dep't of the Interior, Fed. Water Pollution Control Adm.: *The Cost of Clean Water and Its Economic Impact*, Washington, D.C., 1968.

DECS—U.S. Dep't of the Interior, Fed. Water Pollution Control Adm.: *Delaware Estuary Comprehensive Study: Preliminary Report and Findings*, Edison, New Jersey, 1966.

DECS Final Report—U.S. Environmental Protection Agency, Fed. Water Quality Adm.: *Delaware Estuary Comprehensive Study Final Report*, unpublished preliminary draft, Edison, New Jersey, undated.

DECS Report No. BDZ—U.S. Dep't of the Interior, Fed. Water Pollution Control Adm.: *DECS Report No. BDZ*, basic stream quality data sheets nos. 27 and 28, (available in File no. 4639, Trenton, New Jersey), undated.

Deepwater Study—Engineering-Science, Inc.: *Deepwater Regional Sewerage System Preliminary Engineering and Feasibility Study: Final Report*, prepared for the Delaware River Basin Commission, Washington, D.C., 1970.

Deepwater Study Interim—Engineering–Science, Inc.: *Deepwater Regional Sewerage System Preliminary Engineering and Feasibility Study: Interim Report*, prepared for the Delaware River Basin Commission, Washington, D.C., 1970.

Delaware Hearings—Delaware Water and Air Resources Commission: *Water Quality Standards for the Delaware River and Bay*, Dover, Delaware, undated.

Development of Regional Plan—Camden Municipal Utilities Authority: *Development of Regional Plan for Water Supply and Solid Waste Disposal Systems, 1970*, unpublished, on file in Biddle Law Library, University of Pennsylvania.

DRAFP Annual Report—Delaware River Anadromous Fish Project: *Annual Progress Report of the Delaware Anadromous Fish Project*, 1970, 1972. Available from Delaware River Anadromous Fish Project, U.S. Bureau of Sport Fisheries and Wildlife, Rosemont, New Jersey.

Economics of Clean Water—U.S. Dep't of the Interior, Fed. Water Pollution Control Adm.: *The Economics of Clean Water*, Vol. III, Washington, D.C., 1970.

Employment and Earnings—U.S. Dep't of Labor, Bureau of Labor Statistics: *Employment and Earnings: States and Areas, 1939–1970*, Washington, D.C., 1971.

Environment Hearings—U.S. Congress, Senate, Committee on Commerce, Subcommittee on Energy, Natural Resources, and the Environment: *Hearings on the Effects of Mercury on Man and the Environment*, 91st Cong., 2d Sess., 1970.

Evaluation Standards—U.S. Congress, Senate: *Evaluation Standards for Primary Outdoor Recreation Benefits*, Supplement No. 1, Senate Doc. No. 97, 87th Congress, 2d Session, Washington, D.C., 1964.

Examination of Construction Program—U.S. Comptroller General: *Examination into the Effectiveness of the Constructive Program for Abating, Controlling and Preventing Water Pollution*, General Accounting Office, Washington, D.C., Nov. 3, 1969.

Feasibility Report—U.S. Dep't of the Interior, Bureau of Outdoor Recreation: *A Feasibility Report on the Recreational Aspects of the Proposed English Ridge Unit Eel River Division North Cost Project, Mendacino and Lake Counties California*, Washington, D.C., 1968.

Final Population Projections—Delaware State Planning Office: *Advance Report: Final Population Projections—Delaware Counties, 1970–2000*, Dover, Delaware, 1972.

Gloucester Study—John G. Reutter Associates: *Gloucester County Regional Sewage Treatment Feasibility Study*, prepared for Gloucester County Board of Freeholders, Gloucester, New Jersey, 1967.

Hazards of Mercury—U.S. Dep't of Health, Education and Welfare: *Hazards of Mercury*, special report to the Secretary's Pesticide Advisory Committee, 4 *Environmental Research* 1, 1971.

IES Study—Institute for Environmental Studies, University of Pennsylvania: *Water Oriented Recreational Benefits Derivable from Various Levels of Water Quality of the Delaware River*, Philadelphia, 1966.

Impact of Highway Construction—Delaware Valley Regional Planning Commission: *The Impact of Highway Construction on the Economy*, Tech. Record No. 6, March 1972.

Man and Water—Delaware Estuary Comprehensive Study: *Where Man and Water Meet—A Report to the Public—Findings of the Delaware Estuary Comprehensive Study, Preliminary Draft*, Trenton, New Jersey, undated.

Nation's Land—U.S. Public Land Law Review Commission: *One Third of the Nation's Land: A Report to the President and to the Congress*, Washington, D.C., 1970.

New Jersey Population Projections—New Jersey Dep't of Labor and Industry, Office of Business Economics, Div. of Planning and Research: *New Jersey Population Projections: Preliminary*, Trenton, New Jersey, 1971.

New Jersey, 1964—U.S. Dep't of the Interior, Geological Survey, Water Resources Div.: *Surface Water Records of New Jersey* 88, Washington, D.C., 1964.

New Jersey, 1968—U.S. Dep't of the Interior, Geological Survey, Water Resources Div.: *Water Resources Data for New Jersey: Part 1, Surface Water Records* 99, Washington, D.C., 1968.

Outdoor Recreation Resources—U.S. Outdoor Recreation Resources Review Commission: *Outdoor Recreation Resources Review Commission Reports Nos. 19, 20, 26*, Washington, D.C., 1962.

Pennsylvania, 1964—U.S. Dep't of the Interior, Geological Survey, Water Resources Div.: *Surface Water Records of Pennsylvania* 41, Washington, D.C., 1964.

Pennsylvania, 1965—U.S. Dep't of the Interior, Geological Survey, Water Resources Div.: *Water Resources Data for Pennsylvania: Part 1, Surface Water Records* 42, Washington, D.C., 1965.

Pennsylvania, 1966—U.S. Dep't of the Interior, Geological Survey, Water Resources Div.: *Water Resources Data for Pennsylvania: Part 1, Surface Water Records* 47, Washington, D.C., 1966.

Pennsylvania, 1967—U.S. Dep't of the Interior, Geological Survey, Water Resources Div.: *Water Resources Data for Pennsylvania: Part 1, Surface Water Records* 47, Washington, D.C., 1967.

Preliminary Population Projections—New Jersey Dep't of Labor and Industry, Office of Business Economics, Div. of Planning and Research: *Preliminary Population Projections*, Trenton, New Jersey, 1971.

Pure Waters Program Report—State of New York Dep't of Health: *Pure Waters Program Report*, Albany, New York, 1969.

Report to PSWB—Pennsylvania Dep't of Environmental Resources, Bureau of Water Quality Mgt.: *Report* [to Pennsylvania Sanitary Water Board] *on Proposed Water Quality Standards for Interstate Streams* (*Delaware River Estuary*), Harrisburg, Pennsylvania, undated.

Service Contract—*1971 Service Contract between Cherry Hill and the CMUA*, on file in office of the Township Manager, 820 Mercer Street, Cherry Hill, New Jersey.

Summary—"Summary of and Comments on Relevant Testimony Presented at Philadelphia Water Quality Hearings," undated. Available from Bureau of Water Quality Mgt. of Pennsylvania Dep't of Environmental Resources, Harrisburg, Pennsylvania.

Technology Assessment—National Academy of Sciences, Panel of Technology Assessment: *Technology: Processes of Assessment and Choice*, Washington, D.C., 1969.

Thames Report—Her Majesty's Dep't of Scientific and Industrial Research: *Effect of Polluting Discharges on the Thames Estuary*, London, 1964.

U.S. Army Engineer Report—U.S. Corps of Engineers, Army Engineer District, Philadelphia: *Report of the Comprehensive Survey of the Delaware River Basin: Appendix C*, H.R. Doc. No. 522, 87th Congr., 2d Sess., 1962. Prepared by HEW, 1960.

U.S. Budget—(1) U.S. Bureau of the Budget: *The Budget of the United States Government for the Fiscal Year[s] 1966, 1968, and 1970;* (2) U.S. Office of Management and Budget: *The Budget of the United States Government for Fiscal Year 1974*, Washington, D.C.

Views and Comments on the AEC—U.S. Congress, Joint Committee on Atomic Energy: *Views and Comments on Improving the AEC Regulatory Process*, 87th Congr., 1st Sess., Joint Committee Print, 1961.

Water Quality Criteria—National Tech. Advisory Committee to the U.S. Secretary of the Interior, Fed. Water Pollution Control Adm.: *Water Quality Criteria*, Washington, D.C., 1968.

Water Quality Model—Water Resource Engineers, Inc.: *A Water Quality Model of the Sacramento–San Joaquin Delta*, report to the U.S. Public Health Service, Div. of Water Supply and Pollution Control, Region E, 1965.

Water Quality—Pennsylvania, 1964—U.S. Dep't of the Interior, Geological Survey, Water Resources Div.: *Water Quality Records in Pennsylvania* 24, Washington, D.C., 1964.

Water Quality—Pennsylvania, 1966—U.S. Dep't of the Interior, Geological Survey, Water Resources Div.: *Water Resources Data for Pennsylvania: Part 2, Water Quality Records* 27, Washington, D.C., 1966.

WUAC Minutes—Water Use Advisory Committee of the DECS, *Minutes of Meetings*. On file in Professor Ackerman's office, Yale Law School.

Index

INDEX

Access to Delaware Estuary, 28, 118 *n*.
Activist regulation:
 allowing for growth and, 307–308, 314
 definition of, 226
 and efficiency, 226–227
 and fairness, 226–227
 and problem of coordination, 285–287
 limitations of state sanctions for prompting municipal cooperation, 310–311
 role of activist agency in insuring industrial cooperation, 312–315
 shortage of municipal planning resources and, 309–310
 role of activist agency in insuring municipal cooperation, 311–312, 315
 role of activist agency in insuring municipal and industrial cooperation, 314–315
 and state officials' desires to preserve autonomy, 315–316
 see also Camden County; Gloucester County
Army Corps of Engineers, 4, 12, 26 *n.*, 112, 152, 212, 286, 328 *n*.

145, 174, 186, 197–198, 211, 213, 216, 232 *n.*, 242, 258, 303, 343

Baxter, Samuel, former Commissioner of the Philadelphia Water Department and adviser to the Pennsylvania representative to the DRBC, 25 *n.*, 173–175, 181–182, 198, 258

Philadelphia Water Department, 25 *n.*, 173–174, 258

Tate, Hon. James, former Mayor of Philadelphia, 174 *n.*

see also Pennsylvania

Philosophy: *see* Nature

Piping of waste, 282–316

Poisons: *see* Environmental policy; Institutional design; Water quality

Policy: *see* Environmental policy; Institutional design; Policy implementation

Policy analysis, 1–3

Policy implementation:

current

cooperative treatment efforts under, 329–330

pollution rights and effluent changes under, 329

reliance on legal orders under, 328–330

version of equal effort principle under, 329

recommendations, 311–316, 318

see also Activist regulation; Effluent charges; Legal orders regulation; Pollution rights

Political decision making: and technocratic analysis, 165–220

Pollution: *see* Oil slicks; Water quality

Pollution rights:

and problem of coordination, 284–285

versus effluent charges in a more realistic world

collusion possibilities, 278–280

and differential impact of dischargers on water quality depending upon location, 273–275

enforcement costs, 280–281

idealogical objection to "right" to pollute, 276–278

versus effluent charges in a simple world

costs of making a mistake in estimating treatment costs, 262–267

and growth in waste loads, 269–270

as information generating device for firms and the pollution control agency, 267–269

and municipal treatment incentives, 270–273

see also Effluent charges

Pollution tax: *see* Effluent charges

Porges, Ralph: *see* Delaware River Basin Commission

Proxmire, Senator William, 272